Risks & Rights

IN PUBLISHING, TELEVISION, RADIO, MOTION PICTURES, ADVERTISING, AND THE THEATER

Second Edition, Revised

Risks & Rights

IN

PUBLISHING
TELEVISION
RADIO
MOTION PICTURES
ADVERTISING
AND
THE THEATER

Second Edition, Revised

By SAMUEL SPRING

W · W · NORTON & COMPANY · INC · *New York*

Second Edition, Revised

Library of Congress Catalog Card No. 56–10092

PRINTED IN THE UNITED STATES OF AMERICA
FOR THE PUBLISHERS BY THE VAIL-BALLOU PRESS

TO
IMOGENE
Astra Mea

Contents

PART TWO   Defamation

PART THREE   Copyright

PART FOUR   Unfair Competition

XX. EXPANDING PROTECTION AGAINST UNFAIR
COMPETITION   231

PART FIVE Television,
Ideas, and Censorship

Preface

In bringing out a revised and new edition of *Risks and Rights*, wherein are set forth all the new decisions and the current, important amendments to the copyright statute, one must stress the many constructive advances in entertainment law. Of these, the most notable is adherence of the United States to the Universal Copyright Convention. After many years of isolation the United States is now in copyright accord with almost all other civilized sovereignties. Those responsible for this advance, Hon. Luther H. Evans, Director-General of UNESCO, Hon. Arthur Fisher, the able and ever considerate Register of Copyrights, and the Committee of Lawyers who aided them, well merit the thanks of Bench, Bar and all active in entertainment.

It is with profound sorrow I note the passing on of Judge Harold M. Stephens. His death is a great loss to both Bar and Bench—and to his friends. His high achievements as judge and lawyer will long endure but the sorrow of those who were privileged to know him as a friend is not assuaged thereby.

SAMUEL SPRING

New York
August, 1956

Preface
to the First Edition

Risks and Rights was decided on while I was preparing a law text on "Personality Rights"; it seemed to me that a book for laymen, dealing with the various rights involved, might be desirable. I was encouraged in that thought by my partner, Mr. Lee V. Eastman. I am indebted to him and to Mr. Lawrence B. Simons, who read the manuscript and made many helpful suggestions. Also to Mr. Heywood Shelley, formerly Associate in Law, Columbia University School of Law, whose assistance in the collection of authorities and in the criticism of the text has invariably been of the greatest aid and discernment. I am markedly indebted to Mrs. Margaret Owens for her patient aid, particularly in preparing the index.

Judge Harold M. Stephens was kind enough, out of old friendship, to read the manuscript and make helpful suggestions for which I am indebted, as well as for his valuable Foreword.

SAMUEL SPRING

New York
February, 1952

xvi

Foreword

By HAROLD M. STEPHENS *

Risks and Rights is written for, not to mention all: publishers of books, newspapers and music; theatrical and motion-picture producers; operators of broadcasting and television stations; advertising and literary agencies; authors; speakers; editors; reporters; columnists; artists; poets; composers of music; song writers; musicians; band leaders; censors. The book has a common interest for this diversity of persons because all of them, except censors, are engaged in the expression and merchandising of ideas, and censors in an adjustment of the demand for freedom of expression of ideas and the demand for its limitation in the interest of decency. The topics discussed are: privacy as a new and developing right, and thereunder the dangerous borderland between entertainment and news; defamation, including new problems created by radio and television; copyrights —statutory, common-law and international; recent enlargement of unfair competition in entertainment; finally, a topic dealing with a number of problems, including those which concern ideas as property, monopoly restraints upon organized artists, and obscenity and censorship. This book finds unity and coherence in this variety of topics because they, again, all relate to the expression and vending of ideas, and also because the law relating thereto is tending to integrate itself within these subjects. Inventive advance in recent years in the media of communication makes the book timely.

Risks and Rights is a law book for laymen, but not a home-remedy manual. Doubtless bearing in mind that he who is his own lawyer has a fool for a client, the author seeks only to tell those

* Chief Judge, United States Court of Appeals, Washington, D.C.

for whom the book is written what risks and rights are involved in their affairs and what legal means are available for the avoiding of the one and the securing of the other.

The treatment of the topics is simple. Technical terms are eliminated so far as may be without undue loss of precision. Legal principles, rules, standards, and concepts are explained in terms of judicial decisions applying them. There is a review of statutes with pertinent portions printed in the text. Leading cases are stated and their consequences explained.

Although *Risks and Rights* is primarily for laymen, it will be useful also to lawyers, judges, and legislators. It tells what the law was, what it is, and what, in the author's view, it ought to be. Cases referred to in the text are listed in an appendix under chapter headings, with citations. There is an appendix reprinting Chapters 1 to 3 of the Copyright Title (17) of the United States Code.

The author has had broad and responsible professional experience, and is of recognized expertness in the field of practice concerning which he writes. *Risks and Rights* is interestingly and dependably written. I recommend it to the reader.

Washington, D.C.
November 23, 1951

Risks & Rights

IN PUBLISHING, TELEVISION, RADIO, MOTION
PICTURES, ADVERTISING, AND THE THEATER

Second Edition, Revised

I

Modern Publishing and Entertainment Risks and Rights

TODAY's new and varied media have multiplied markedly the risks and rights of those engaged in publishing and entertainment. Television, motion pictures, the radio, and graphic color reproduction not only consume vast quantities of literary and personality and musical material; they also have added new risks and rights to old ones. Dangers of privacy invasion, of unfair competition, of unfair idea appropriation, and new hazards of defamation have been added to older copyright problems. All are interrelated and all are insistently at the elbow of everyone engaged in the dissemination of ideas and amusement.

Book, newspaper, magazine, and music publishers, television and broadcasting stations, motion picture and theatrical producers, advertising and literary agencies, authors, playwrights, artists, actors, and models, all are confronted daily both by new and unexpected dangers and also by wider and novel opportunities to profit from unsuspected property rights. These modern opportunities and hazards arise from new legal theories in recent court decisions as well as from far-flung invention.

Thus copyright, though more important than ever, no longer forms the bulk of rights and risks in modern entertainment. A new right of privacy in news and fiction personality portrayal is creating increasing numbers of costly lawsuits. Unfortunate is the publisher, or television or motion-picture executive, who gets himself caught in a costly privacy lawsuit through his innocent unawareness of the rights of others to the privacy of personality. Though he may have portrayed a personality in the most laudable colors and committed no defamation, yet he still may be mulcted for heavy damages.

The risks concerning defamation have become more exacting and insistent than ever, raising greater and more numerous dangers for those who deal in either factual or fictional material. Also, the law of unfair competition, though still obscure, is now rapidly expanding; even when no copyright or privacy violation is involved it must be guarded against. The value of novel ideas and the exclusive right to profit therefrom also have markedly expanded. For ideas, though not copyrightable, create insistent new hazards for those who use the idea-property of others. And original ideas, for those who know how to protect their creations, can be surprisingly profitable. Obscenity and censorship problems are ever with us. And antitrust risks in entertainment enterprise and protection have come to the fore.

Where litigation is a probability or a serious risk, professional legal guidance, of course, is essential. But those engaged in entertainment and publication need more than legal aid; they require sufficient understanding of the risks and rights involved to know when they are on dangerous ground. Ignorance is no defense. Warning signs of danger are seldom evident when the fatal step is taken. Only by knowledge and caution exercised in time can the sorrows of lawsuits be avoided.

A workable understanding of today's rights and risks in entertainment thus requires more than a summation of copyright statutes; it requires also some acquaintance with the law of the newer phases of entertainment rights and risks. Suggestions gathered from professional experience and practical observation as to how these risks can be avoided, and how the skilled act where these differing rights and risks are involved, can be helpful. A review of the relation of each of the five aspects of entertainment rights, one in relation to the other, also will clarify the interplay of the several segments that must be considered, and thus can create an informative picture of the entire orbit of modern entertainment risks and rights.

Part One of this book, accordingly, sets forth the elements of the new right of privacy. Part Two is concerned with defamation, including new problems created by television and radio. Next, in

Part Three, is an explanation of the three forms of copyright: (a) common law; (b) statutory copyright under the United States Copyright Act of 1909; and (c) international copyrights. Part Four takes up the very recent enlargement of theories of unfair competition in entertainment. Part Five deals with varied problems: with those of obscenity, which unhappily still constantly creates censorship problems; with rights in ideas; and with the new monopoly restraints upon organized artists; all are set forth from realistic angles.

Viewed as a whole, or in detail, the entire subject of publishing and entertainment risks and rights need not seem either obscure or difficult. The examination of it, as a survey of modern creative conflict and change, can even prove interesting.

PART ONE

Privacy

II

Privacy as a New Legal Right

1. THE RIGHT TO BE LET ALONE

A NEW and important aspect of the protection of individual rights in the United States is called the right of privacy. This new right "appears only in a comparatively highly developed state of society".[1] * Its boundary limits are still evolving, thus requiring the prudent who portray or deal in personalities to inform themselves of the dangers involved and of the protective countermeasures available.

This modern legal right of privacy can be briefly defined as the right of an individual "to be let alone",[2] to be free from undeserved and undesired publicity. An individual has the unquestioned right "to be let alone" so far as injury to his body and threats to his physical safety are concerned. For centuries he also has had the right not to be caused mental anguish by having his reputation destroyed by defamation, i.e. by false statements subjecting him to "hatred, ridicule or contempt". Privacy, however, is a more modern right, wider than the right against defamation. It may be violated even though the person wronged has not been defamed but has been highly praised. Truth is no defense. For privacy involves a theory entirely distinct from defamation.

In defamation, truth is a complete defense. In privacy invasion, the greater the truth the greater the wrong. For where entertainment, advertising, and publishing are involved, as distinct from news reporting, an individual's right to be let alone includes a right not

* Notes used in the text refer to citations of cases and authorities, grouped in Appendix A, chapter by chapter. Each note refers to the authority given in the Appendix under the corresponding note number.

to have his name, picture, or character portrait used for advertising, for trade, or for entertainment without consent granted. In fact, whatever publicity and popular attraction an actor, model, performer, or professional athlete enjoys is akin to a property right and cannot be used without his consent, except in news reporting.

The importance of this aspect of privacy in television's portrayal of such personalities is later discussed in Chapter XXV, Section 192.

2. A RECENT EXAMPLE

A prominent novelist lately published a fictional narrative about life in Florida which hit the literary jackpot. Over 150,000 copies of *Cross Creek*, by Marjorie Kinnan Rawlings, were sold. The book was a Book-of-the-Month Club selection as was the author's preceding novel, *The Yearling*.

But Miss Zelma Cason of Island Grove, Florida, sued Miss Rawlings for $100,000, alleging that her right of privacy had been invaded by the similarities between Miss Cason and one of Miss Rawlings' characters in *Cross Creek*.[3] The litigation dragged on for four and a half years, not unlike the legal battles in Dickens' novels. Forty witnesses were cross-quizzed at the trial. Appeals went up to Florida's highest court twice until that court wearily wrote: " * * * it is the desire of the court to bring an end to the litigation at the earliest possible date." Therefore an odd decision was handed down by the Florida Supreme Court. Miss Cason's legal claim against Miss Rawlings for the invasion of privacy was upheld, but the court directed that Miss Cason be awarded no damages because Miss Cason had suffered no mental anguish that injured her health. This vacillation as to damages constitutes one of the obscurities in the evolving right of privacy. Other courts have imposed heavy damages.

Miss Rawlings wasn't sued for libel, nor for plagiarism. She was sued solely on the ground that in portraying an admirable character in *Cross Creek* she had intentionally portrayed the plaintiff Miss Zelma Cason and that the public so had concluded.

Miss Rawlings' character portrayal of Miss Cason was highly favorable. The author, said the court, had evidenced "a real admiration for Miss Cason as a fine, rugged character,—a highly intelligent and efficient person with a kind and sympathetic heart and a keen sense of humor." The fiction character, to be sure, was depicted as given to a touch or two of profanity. Yet the court concluded that there was nothing defamatory or malicious in the portrait. But the court held that since Florida recognizes the legal right of privacy, therefore Miss Cason's right to be free from publicity had been invaded when she was used as a model of a fictional character.

Since writers often use persons they know in drawing characters, this lawsuit warns authors of fiction and their publishers, and those who portray characters by television, the radio, and motion pictures, that they must add a new turn to their techniques of characterization to avoid the hazards of personality identification.

3. PRIVACY AND NEWS REPORTING

A somewhat similar recent privacy suit illustrates how personalities can safely be used where news reporting is involved.

Soon after the *Cross Creek* drama ended, the Supreme Court of Alabama had before it another conflict over privacy.[4] The Alabama court accepted the decision of the Florida court, held that the law of privacy also prevailed in Alabama, but that it had not been violated in any way by a radio story.

Here a chatty radio program called *Tuscaloosa Town Talks* made a daily business of broadcasting human-interest stories. One broadcast told the strange but actual story of John Lundgren. Farmer Lundgren had hitched his horses to his wagon, lovingly kissed his wife and two children good-bye, and driven off—forever. A neighbor was accused of murdering him. But after five months in jail without a trial, the neighbor was released. Then, twenty-five years later, a resident of California died, leaving a will bequeathing his property to his two children in Tuscaloosa. From the will it appeared that the prosperous Californian, now known under another name, was John Lundgren.

As Lundgren's body reached home, *Tuscaloosa Town Talks* broadcast his story. Lundgren's son and daughter sued the radio station, claiming that the broadcast of their father's disappearance after it had been forgotten for so long caused them mental anguish. The court held that they had no cause to object. Privacy was not violated, the court held, because John Lundgren had become a public character. A charge of murdering him had been brought against his neighbor, after his disappearance. The broadcast, even though twenty-five years had elapsed, was still a news item and the public interest in news permitted the radio station freely to use John Lundgren's personality. The court did not rest its decision upon the ground that privacy ends with death. That point will be outlined later (Section 12).

The distinction the court stressed was that Miss Rawlings was portraying a private individual as a character in fiction, while the radio station was broadcasting news about a public personage. Yet the Tuscaloosa broadcast was put on for semientertainment purposes and involved a news event that had occurred years before. This line of distinction, between the dissemination of news and of entertainment by fiction (aside from advertising, where the law now is crystal clear), constitutes today the pith of when and when not privacy may be invaded.

The same ruling as in Alabama about John Lundgren was reached in New York when a biography of Dr. Serge Koussevitzky, the noted conductor of Boston's Symphony Orchestra, was published against Dr. Koussevitzky's objections. The ruling was [5] that Dr. Koussevitzky's achievements as a musician made him a public figure, and anyone could freely write a biography about him and his career. But, the court added, a novelized portrayal of Dr. Koussevitzky would have been an invasion of privacy.

4. ORIGIN OF PRIVACY

The legal right of privacy is closely linked with the name of one of our ablest Supreme Court justices, the late Louis D. Brandeis. At the start of his legal career, in 1890, he published with Samuel D. Warren a law-review article [6] which first argued for this new personal right of property. This youthful essay has been quoted probably more often than any other law-review article. It may survive as the best known of Justice Brandeis' many legal contributions.

The young authors wrote their article in a decade when "yellow journalism" was emerging. Their aim was to place restraints upon the license of undeserved publicity abuses by an overaggressive press. They had few legal precedents to support their view. The only decision they could urge was an English ruling involving

Queen Victoria's right of privacy, as an individual, to keep her own and her husband's amateur etchings private.[7] A London printer got hold of a few of the tries at etching by the royal couple and published them. The Prince Consort sued, since the Queen couldn't very well be a litigant in her own courts, and the court enjoined further publication. The British courts did so on the theory of the Queen's right of control by virtue of a common-law copyright in her etchings.

From this ruling, Brandeis and Warren argued that, just as an author or artist, or letter writer, holding a common-law copyright in his manuscript or letter or etching, has the right not to have these made public, so every individual should have an analogous right not to have his personality publicized. This common-law copyright in unpublished manuscripts and letters and paintings has long been recognized. It is fully discussed in a later section dealing with copyright. (See Chapter VI, Section 39.)

The young authors also argued that, since the Roman law granted damages for mental suffering when an individual's honor was wrongfully assailed, so the law in the United States should grant damages for mental suffering arising from undesired and unwarranted publicity, as it does grant damages in the case of defamation.

5. NEW YORK'S FIRST STEPS

Five years after publication of the Brandeis article, the right of privacy was inferentially upheld by New York's highest court.[8] The decision arose from a feminine battle involving woman's suffrage. A group of militant suffragettes decided to erect statues of two famous deceased women at the World's Columbian Exposition: Susan Anthony and Mrs. Schuyler, a New York philanthropist. Mrs. Schuyler's surviving relatives objected, since neither Mrs. Schuyler nor they believed in woman suffrage.

The court refused an injunction forbidding the erection of Mrs. Schuyler's statue. It ruled that Mrs. Schuyler was dead and that personal rights such as privacy do not survive the grave. But the court, though it wavered, implied that relief might have been granted to Mrs. Schuyler had she been living, and suggested that rights of privacy were recognized in New York.

6. THE START OF MODELING

But soon the same New York court rejected its implication in the Schuyler decision.[9] A miller took a pretty girl's picture, without her consent, and plastered it widely about the state on a poster advertising the miller's brand of flour. The court denied the girl any relief, saying that if the law upheld this new right of privacy, the courts would be flooded with "litigation bordering upon the absurd."

The legislature thought otherwise. The next year (1903) the New York legislature enacted a statute [10] that now establishes the right of privacy in New York. This statute has had a wide influence in other states.

Thus the modeling profession was given legal impetus and reality. Without the statute, a pretty girl would not have an exclusive right in the public use of her face or figure. It is clear law now that pictures or names of individuals may not be used in advertisements without the consent (written consent is required in New York) of the person whose picture or name is so used. But wider issues other than those arising from advertisements remain. Since then, the supreme courts of twenty-one states have held that the law of privacy applies within their states. Only in two states has a contrary ruling been handed down.

7. THE NEW YORK PRIVACY STATUTE

The provisions of this New York statute are so important, and also so influential in setting the pattern for the right of privacy in other states, that they must be noted. In this statute appears the "great divide" between rights of privacy which are protected and those which are not protected. Use of personality "for advertising purposes" and for "purposes of trade", as distinct from the use thereof in the dissemination of news, constitutes the dividing line. Newspapers, magazines, television and radio stations, obviously, are operated for profit, i.e. for "purposes of trade". But since they disseminate news, generally their use of personalities in news is not deemed for "purposes of trade", and is not subject to the restraints of privacy.

Sometimes news reporting goes pretty far in the pursuit of trade as circulation. The bulk of the law of privacy involves the drawing of the line between the use of personalities in news and the use of personalities in fiction, i.e. as to distinctions between news reporting and varied forms of use in entertainment. The burdens of privacy restrictions unfortunately are now imposed largely upon the writers of meritorious imaginative fiction. The struggle also goes on to limit abuse in the reporting of news about persons other than public figures. Suits over the portrayal of actual persons in fiction, as a consequence, are increasingly common.

The New York Privacy Statute provides: [10]

Sec. 50. Right of Privacy. A person, firm or corporation that uses for advertising purposes, or for the purposes of trade, the name, portrait or picture of any living person without having first obtained the written consent of such person, or if a minor of his or her parent or guardian, is guilty of misdemeanor.

Sec. 51. Action of Injunction and for Damages. Any person whose name, portrait or picture is used within this state for advertising purposes or for the purposes of trade without the written consent first obtained as above provided may maintain an equitable action in the supreme court of this state against the person, firm or corporation so using his name, portrait or picture, to prevent and restrain the use thereof; and may also sue and recover damages for any injuries sustained by reason of such use and if the defendant shall have knowingly used such person's name, portrait or picture in such manner as is forbidden or declared to be unlawful by the last section, the jury, in its discretion, may award exemplary damages. * * *

Utah and Virginia (Utah Code 4–89; Virginia Code 8–650) have privacy statutes modeled after the New York Statute. The Utah Statute grants the right to sue to heirs of one whose privacy is invaded; Virginia to heirs also, but only if they are Virginia residents. (See Donahue v. Warner Bros. 272 P. 2d 177). Such rights in heirs are rare and unrealistic.

III

Distinctions between Entertainment
and News

8. EVOLVING CONFLICTS

DESPITE the enactment of New York's privacy statute, the courts of that state, adhering to their earlier ruling that there is no common law, i.e. no basic right, of privacy in New York, have tended to construe the legislative statute narrowly. The largest number of privacy cases originate in New York and in California, our two chief centers of entertainment creation. The California courts have held that a common-law right of privacy exists in California, under state constitutional language, without specific statutory enactment; [6] also the rulings of the California courts and of other states have been more favorable to privacy than has been the tendency in New York.

Since publishing and television and radio broadcasting carried on in New York may extend the publication involved into many other states, the narrower view of the New York courts is not complete protection to the publisher or producer. Consideration constantly must be given to the chance of more liberal rulings in other states if suits can be brought there.

Brandeis and Warren wrote in their law-review [1] article, as to abuses in disseminating news:

The press is overstepping in every direction the obvious bounds of propriety and of decency. Gossip is no longer the resource of the idle and of the vicious, but has become a trade, which is pursued with industry as well as effrontery. To satisfy a prurient taste the details of sexual relations are spread broadcast in the columns of the daily papers. To occupy the indolent, column upon column is filled with idle gossip,

16

which can only be procured by intrusion upon the domestic circle. The intensity and complexity of life, attendant upon advancing civilization, have rendered necessary some retreat from the world, and man, under the refining influence of culture, has become more sensitive to publicity, so that solitude and privacy have become more essential to the individual. * * *

This was the pith of their argument for a new right of privacy. Thus an important aspect of privacy today involves abuses of publicity in direct and factual news reporting, particularly about private events and little people, as well as in fiction.

9. FICTION CHARACTERS

Fiction writers often take ideas, events, and colorful characters from current news. Chekhov was an assiduous reader of newspapers in search of novel events and personality suggestions. Dickens, it is said, took his odd names from the London directory. Henry James published elaborate notes setting down the persons and events that set his imagination rolling. These tendencies are still common today among writers of fiction, though one shudders to think of what would happen today to a modern writer as candid as was Henry James about his character source material.

Four important New York cases, involving borderline cases of fictional and news characters, indicate the wavering retreat of the New York courts.

The earliest important New York case, specifying what fiction writers may not do in personality use under the privacy statute, arose in 1911 from publicity about the first use of wireless telegraphy to summon aid for a ship sinking at sea.[2] The plaintiff, Binns, a radio operator, saved hundreds of lives by sending out SOS signals from his ship. Overnight he became a newspaper hero. The Vitagraph Company, without Binns' consent, made a silent motion picture (a serial) out of the episode, using an actor to impersonate Binns; Binns' name was used in the titles. The court awarded Binns $12,500 damages. It concluded that under the New York statute a serial motion picture was "for purposes of trade" and was not privileged as a news report.

This case illustrates the three chief items involved in privacy: (1) name; (2) photograph; (3) personality portrayal. Here Binns' name and personality were used; not his photograph. A personality, of course, can be portrayed in fiction without using name or photograph. Clearly now none of the three can be used in advertising. Under the Binns case it was held that the interdiction applied to motion-picture fiction.

10. FACTUAL NEWS STORIES

After the Binns decision, a New York Federal Court dealt with two sketches published in 1937 in *The New Yorker* about prodigies.[3] The factual accounts included the sad history of a youthful prodigy named Sidis. A mathematical genius as a child, Sidis had lectured to professors at Harvard before graduating at sixteen. But he ended up a dismal failure, living in a hall bedroom. One *New Yorker* article was published with the subtitle "April Fool" because April 1 was Sidis' birthday. Both articles, the court found, were merciless detailings of Sidis' humiliating failure. But the court held that under the New York privacy statute Sidis had no right of recovery since the articles were factual news stories even though the news was no longer current.

In a recent ruling,[4] the New York court extended the result in the Sidis case, thus drastically limiting its Binns ruling. Here Molony, a much publicized Coast Guard hero when a bombing plane in 1945 spectacularly crashed into New York's Empire State Building, found himself, six months later, the hero of a "true story" account in a boys' comic magazine. Pictures of Molony were not used. But he was portrayed in five pages of drawings. The news event was stale; the magazine sought to entertain its readers of fiction by retelling the story. The court held that Molony could not recover for violation of privacy, saying of comic scripts "that this article is not to be classed as fictional merely because it is presented pictorially"; also that "a factual presentation need not be educational" even if "it does not pertain strictly to current news". The court added that though the incident was "described in a magazine containing other articles presented through the same medium that are of a fictional nature, an invasion of privacy did not result". Finally that though "all newspapers and magazines are published for profit, that is not the criterion of the uses of trade. * * *"

The result is that the comic magazine could profit from Molony's heroism without paying him the fee they would have to pay for material bought from an author, or for the value to the magazine of Molony's favorable publicity used, which in reality was Molony's property.

A case [5] decided in New York involved a magazine section of a newspaper containing the usual sensational and lurid articles. It published a married woman's picture "tenderly cupping in her hands a rose." The tale embroidered freely the "true story" of her unknown lover, a turret gunner killed in action. The lady had only known the turret gunner casually; she had never suspected his love. But just before his death in an air battle, the soldier had willed his slender estate for the purpose of sending the surprised lady one rose each day in remembrance of his unspoken love. The magazine story indulged in the usual spectrum coloring of the romantic bequest, and the recipient of the rose and of the lurid publicity, now married and a mother, objected since the episode was no longer current and the publicity served no public purpose. Three New York appellate judges left it to a jury to decide if the story was news reporting and thus allowed under the privacy statute, or if the story was entertainment and thus a violation. Two able judges, dissenting, argued that the elaborated romance was clearly news and the lady entitled to no relief whatsoever.

In Gautier v. Pro Football (1952) [5a] New York's highest court harmonized earlier cases. An animal trainer performed between halves of a pro football game and was televised although his contract specified no televising. The lower Appellate Court held that a professional actor lost all right of privacy. This ruling (criticized in an earlier edition hereof) was rejected by the higher Appellate Court. But the Court held that although an actor had a right of privacy, on performing voluntarily he waived that right. The Court implied if he had sued for breach of his contract clause prohibiting televising he might have recovered. Of a spectator at a public event, this Court said: "If a mere spectator, he may be taken (i.e. televised) as part of the general audience, but he may not be picked out of a crowd alone, thrust upon the screen and unduly featured for public view" (p. 360), thus warning all as to a spectator's rights.

A high New York Federal Court has reaffirmed the privacy right of performers.[5b] A ball player granted a gum advertiser the use of his photograph, and the right granted was enforced as a "right of publicity" valid though perhaps different from privacy because actors want publicity. No injury to "feelings bruised through public exposure of their likenesses" was involved. In Michigan a similar ruling allowed a jury to bring in damages against a cosmetic advertiser using the picture of a show girl and model, who had posed for a commercial photographer, as a show girl, unless it found she had intended to cast aside her right of privacy.[5c] In Illinois a blind girl was allowed to recover from a dog-food advertiser using her picture without her consent, plus a plea to buy her a "seeing eye dog".[5d]

Utah's Supreme Court reached a tortured construction of the Utah Statute (see Section 7) granting privacy. Warner Brothers Pictures made a picture using the comedian Jack Donahue, deceased, as a character. The Utah Statute permits heirs to sue therefor. The Utah Court refused recovery, holding that "a semi-fictional portrayal" of Jack Donahue was not for "purposes of trade" and not forbidden by the statute.[5e]

An interesting group of California cases involved suits by a man and his wife operating a concession in a farmers' market and photographed by a professional photographer without their license in an amorous pose. The picture was sold to *Harpers Bazaar* and then to the *Ladies Home Journal* who used it in an article depicting types of love. The plaintiffs recovered against the *Ladies Home Journal* [5f] but not against *Harpers Bazaar* where the statute of limitations had run, the Court holding that only photographing and selling a picture was not a violation of privacy.[5g]

Currently a reformed, paroled murderer's career was permitted to be televised under a *fictitious name*. Reform and time, the Court held, did not give the once public character privacy.[5h]

A comparison of these New York rulings with a ruling in California in the *Red Kimono* case [6] indicates the persistent attitude of the New York courts favoring the newspaper or other popular medium invading privacy. In the *Red Kimono* case, the plaintiff, a prostitute, had been tried for murder and acquitted. She reformed and lived an exemplary life. Seven years after her murder trial, the defendants made a motion picture entitled *The Red Kimono* and advertised the picture as being based on the plaintiff's life. The

California court held that the plaintiff could recover since her right of privacy was violated and that the defense of news reporting and use of a public personage was no defense.

It is to be noted that Molony the Coast Guard hero, Sidis the prodigy, and the lady of the rose, unlike the heroine in the *Red Kimono* case, had done nothing censorable. Yet their rights of privacy were protected far less than in the *Red Kimono* case. This illustrates the hesitant attitude of the New York courts when it comes to privacy. Surely newspapers should not be deemed to have a greater right to invade privacy than have motion pictures if a story a newspaper publishes is not in fact news reporting but is in reality for purposes of entertainment.

11. ABUSES IN NEWS REPORTING

The courts outside of New York are setting limits upon news reporting about little people. In a Georgia case,[7] plaintiff's child was born with its heart on the outside of its body. A weekly newspaper published a picture of the body of the dead child, and it was held that the parents of the child had a right to recover for the violation of the right of privacy and for their mental suffering. Here the right of privacy survived the child's death and was held to exist for the parents, an unusual but sensible ruling as to privacy.

Also a Kentucky court allowed the parents of dead Siamese twins to recover damages from those who had photographed the dead twins and published the picture.[8]

Where a patient in a hospital was suffering from a rare disease impelling her constantly to eat, she was allowed to recover damages from *Time* magazine for publishing her picture, taken while she was in the hospital, without her consent.[9]

Where a radio station broadcast a dramatization of a holdup, using the victim's name without his consent, the victim was allowed by a California court to recover for the violation of his privacy.[10] But where a woman committed suicide by leaping from an office window, the California court refused to allow her husband to recover from the newspaper for publishing her picture in its news account.[11] The distinction seems a sound one between current news and a radio dramatization.

The Saturday Evening Post published a picture of a feminine taxi driver in an article dealing humorously with taxicab drivers in Washington, D.C. The taxicab driver was allowed to recover damages for the violation of her right of privacy.[12] But in Texas, an All-American football player whose picture, tossing a football, had been used without his consent on a football calendar advertising beer, was denied relief because he was a public character, though a prohibitionist.[13] Here the use had been consented to by the publicity department of the player's college. (For more material as to photos, see Chapter VI, Section 44.)

Minor uses of one's name do not constitute a violation of privacy. Where Edna Ferber mentioned plaintiff's name once in her novel *Show Boat*, relief was denied.[14] Also where the name of an attorney accidentally was used as the name of a minor character in a murder-mystery novel, relief also was refused.[15] But when President Eliot of Harvard University, the editor of the *Harvard Classics*, found his name used in a rival publication called without his consent *Dr. Eliot's Five-Foot Shelf*, he was allowed relief, but on the grounds of unfair competition.[16] (See Section 161.) Vassar College, since it is a corporation and not an individual, was not allowed relief against the manufacturer of "Vassar Chocolates" using Vassar's name and a replica of a feminine college student on the cover of the candy box.[17] Privacy is a right enjoyed only by living *individuals*.

The New York courts are not sympathetic to individuals where news reporting abuses invade privacy. An early New York ruling enjoined a motion-picture company by a preliminary injunction from distributing its newsreel portraying a plaintiff carrying on her calling of selling bread and rolls on the sidewalk of the East Side. The Court of Appeals affirmed the preliminary injunction but postponed a final ruling.[18] But in another case at about the same time, a newsreel was allowed to publish against the plaintiff's objections pictures of a group of fat women, including the plaintiff, exercising to reduce weight, in a private gymnasium.[19]

And a New York court decided in favor of a magazine called *True Detective Mysteries*[20] when it published a story about an actual murder trial, using the picture of the murdered woman's mother in its dramatic account. It pictured the mother, not a participant in the crime, saying when a witness took the stand, "I could kill that man with my own hands." The state's appellate division held she had no right to complain. Such decisions permit harsh latitude to sensational news reporting.

Where a New York tabloid newspaper published a factual article about the Hindu rope magic trick, using the picture of the plaintiff, a well-known Hindu magician, without his consent, merely for Indian atmosphere and without other relevance to the investigation of magic, relief was denied.[21]

The *New York Herald*, in 1913, published a lurid story of explorers on the verge of being eaten by savages, written in the first person, and naming the plaintiff as the author. The plaintiff, who had not written the story, sued for the violation of privacy in the use of his name and for libel. The New York court denied relief for privacy invasion but allowed the case to go to the jury as to libel.[22]

12. PRIVACY SUGGESTIONS FOR AUTHORS

Privacy rights, like defamation wrongs, do not survive death, except in Utah and Virginia where statutes grant heirs the right to sue (see Section 7). In defamation children generally cannot sue for defamation of a parent except as to inheritable disease. In New York, when a newspaper account falsely described a deceased parent as having committed murder, and named the children in the account, they could not recover for defamation.[23]

Therefore, in privacy invasion, no concern need arise if the personality used be dead. The rulings before noted granting privacy damages to the parents of malformed children seem an exception and are based upon the unusual circumstances involved. But to suggest that fiction writers limit themselves to dead persons for character material is hardly enlightening.

In portraying characters drawn from actual personalities today, prudent fiction writers must avail themselves of defter techniques of alteration. They must be discreet. If they derive character ideas by observing living persons, they dare not be as frank as was Henry James.

One of the great concerns of authors and their publishers, and of radio and television writers and stations, is the danger of committing purely accidental invasions of privacy and of disseminating name similarities resulting in defamation. The fear is well founded as to defamation, for defamation is inherently dangerous. (See Section

26.) But it can be suggested that the common fear of accidental identification invading privacy is unfounded, certainly as to mere accidental identity of names as between fictional and actual personages.

Two different questions arise in deciding liability as to privacy invasion.

First: Would the public, or a substantial segment thereof, *reasonably* identify the fictional character with the individual who complains that he was portrayed or his personality so used? The word "reasonably", of course, is the law's usual indirection and means that a jury must decide the contested question.

If the answer to the first question is "yes", then the second question arises: Should the author be held legally liable for such identification of a fictional character with an actual person, *only* if the author intended to create the identification, consciously or subconsciously, or *also* if he portrayed his fictional character so carelessly that similarity resulted? In short, if the identification is purely accidental though actual in the public's mind, should the author be held liable for damages for privacy invasion and should his work be subject to prohibition of publication by injunction?

Where defamation is involved, the answer is that the author is subject to absolute liability. Intent or lack of care by the defamer need not be shown by the defamed complainant. A medieval rule of absolute liability is used in defamation: the test is "not who is meant, but who is hit". If the public, or a segment thereof, reasonably can be held to identify the plaintiff with the defamed person that fact ends the inquiry, and the publisher of the defamation is held liable even if he did not so intend and was in no way careless. This rule in defamation is like that applied to the one who keeps wild animals, or explosives; if the wild animal escapes, or if the dangerous explosives blow up, however careful the owner may be, the owner usually must pay. So, too, where a false statement gets away from a defamer and hits another. The liability imposed is rigid and harsh: lack of intent or carefulness is no defense if you defame, though it is if your automobile runs down and injures a pedestrian.

Should the same absolute-liability rule apply in privacy invasion? Though the courts have not definitively ruled, it can be suggested that in privacy invasion a less harsh rule applies—that of intent or carelessness—and that accidental identification creates no liability.

One case suggests a possible contrary result, i.e. that intent to invade privacy need not be proved. But it is believed that this ruling will not be applied generally in privacy because of the special circumstances therein.

Here,[24] a publicity employee of a motion-picture theater mailed a letter on pink stationery in a feminine hand to 1000 men in Los Angeles, which read:

Dearest:

Don't breathe it to a soul, but I'm back in Los Angeles and more curious than ever to see you. Remember how I cut up about a year ago? Well, I'm raring to go again and believe me I'm in the mood for fun.

Let's renew our acquaintanceship and I promise you an evening you won't forget. Meet me in front of Warners Downtown Theatre at 7th and Hill on Thursday. Just look for a girl with a gleam in her eye, a smile on her lips and mischief on her mind!

Fondly,

Your ectoplasmic playmate,
Marion Kerby.

An actual Marion Kerby, an actress and concert singer and the only Marion Kerby in the Los Angeles telephone directory, sued. The chief character in the motion picture thus advertised was also Marion Kerby. The publicity employee did not know of the actual Marion Kerby's existence and his employer pleaded lack of intent. Recovery was nevertheless allowed against the motion-picture theater for invasion of privacy. The court applied the defamation rule, "what controls is he who is hit, not he who is intended."

Here, however, the letter purported to be not fictional but actual. That purport was the censorable aspect of the overbold publicity idea, and the post-card invitation had defamatory implications. The success of the publicity stunt involved an effort to create the impression of reality. In a novel, everyone knows that the character is fictional. Thus this case scarcely applies to invasions of privacy in fiction. To apply defamation's harsh rule of absolute liability to privacy will cause the courts to restrict the area of recovery in privacy invasion, as has been the result in defamation. (See Sections 21 and 22.) The rule of absolute liability in defamation is a concept dating from medieval days. It is not applied generally by the courts as to personal wrongs. So it is unlikely that absolute liability will be applied in privacy invasions.

Where an author gathers character material from an actual person, he must not only be discreet about it—he must also resort to alteration so as to be able to negative identity and thus avoid liability. If he alters his material sufficiently, the possibilities both of reasonable identification and of intent can be averted. Alteration is a fiction writer's sole protection. Fiction writers must not rely only on the fact that they have given the character a name different from that of the actual personage used. No prudent writer, of course, would be so careless as not to alter the name of a person used as a model in fiction. But changing only the name is inadequate as a technique of protection. The writer also must carefully change physical appearance, locality, occupation, or sex of the person used. Changes of sex are the most decisive, yet of course the most difficult. If an author sufficiently alters the personality used, then vivid and vital action incidents observed from individuals, including character traits and motives, can safely be used. The drift of privacy protection, however, calls for persistent care and skill of alteration by fiction writers.

Where writers of fiction use even living *public* characters, unless they resort to these techniques of alteration, they are on dangerous ground. As to biographies, since the Jeffries and Koussevitzky cases, writers have a free hand. James J. Jeffries, since he was a news character, was held to have no right to object to a story of his life published in a newspaper running at the same time as an authorized biography.[25] So, too, to the same effect was the ruling in the case of Serge Koussevitzky.[26] Writers of biographies of living persons need fear no suit for privacy invasion from the public person they write about, if he be in the public eye as a musician, actor, artist, public athlete, or office holder. They need fear defamation suits only if they step into untruthful statements or libelous facts.

But in the use of living public characters as models for characters in fictional writing of a more imaginative form than comic cartoons or true-confession stories, privacy perils instantly arise. No freedom is granted to fiction writers comparable to that granted writers of a biography. The distinction may seem artificial and unfair, but it is fixed and so far final.

New York's Justice Shientag, one of the state's most discerning judges, who decided the Koussevitzky case, observed:

The right of privacy statute does not apply to an unauthorized biography of a public figure *unless the biography is fictional or novelized in character*. An examination of the book complained of clearly shows that it is not fictional. That it may contain untrue statements does not transform it into the class of fiction. [Italics added.]

The risk of privacy invasion, of course, is much greater in the use of actual persons as models for major characters than it is in the case of minor fictional characters.

If a living public personage (such as an office holder, military figure, artist, or actor) be not fictionalized but actually portrayed as part of the background in a story, that use would be akin to news reporting and would probably be permitted under the privacy statute. Even in fiction, fair comment and satirizing of public characters, if of minor space, is permitted. If no defamation be involved, no liability would arise against the author or publisher. But there are no decisions on the point.

But if such a living public personage be fictionalized and used as a minor character, what then? Technically the novelist and his publisher could be sued for privacy invasion. Yet since the use was only as a minor character, if no defamation be involved, the invasion of privacy probably would not be substantial enough to create liability. But that is as far as a prudent fiction writer dare go in dealing with living public personages. Unfortunately no decisions permit categorical conclusions.

The most urgent care, moreover, must be used in portraying "heavies" or villains. Here, if actual persons are used as models, the danger is overwhelming. Defamation added to violation of privacy can result in very heavy damages; even punitive damages may be imposed if there is a finding of malice. Malice in the law means improper motive; it includes calculated intention to injure. Ill will, or desire to injure, is the pith of legal malice.

Publishers, since they are liable for damages for privacy invasion and defamation by their authors (but usually not for punitive damages) will be wise to cross-quiz their authors closely as to the character material used in creating a Carmen or Uriah Heep type of character. If the author, in creating a "bad" character, is inspired by dislike for a living person, serious damages may arise. In the suit against Miss Rawlings, for example, imagine what would have been the result if Miss Cason had not been favorably depicted.

13. ACCIDENTAL IDENTITY OF NAMES

Unfortunately the brunt of privacy restrictions has now been placed upon fiction writers. Unjust though that result may be, it must be faced. The peril to writers and innocent publishers by privacy invasions as portrayals in fiction is more to be feared than the danger of privacy invasion by mere accidental identity of fictional names. Defamation by error in names is a definite peril in factual news reporting, but fortunately not in fiction. Yet publishers still shiver needlessly before the ghost of identity of names between a fictional character and an unknown actual personage. Here fiction "gets the breaks."

The source of the fear of liability by accidental identity of names is a colorful English news reporting episode.[27] The London *Sunday Chronicle* published a "gossipy" current news account of motor races at Dieppe, wherein its reporter added a curving quip:

There is Artemus Jones with a woman who is not his wife, who must be, you know—the other thing. Really, it is most surprising how our fellow-countrymen behave when they go abroad.

The reporter made up the name Artemus Jones to avoid pillorying an Englishman bearing a different name at whom he was actually looking as he wrote. But another and actual Englishman who happened to be named Artemus Jones, and who was not at Dieppe (incidentally a lawyer), bobbed up out of the correspondent's unknown world and claimed libel because the finger of philandering ignominy had falsely been pointed at him. He recovered heavy damages.

Since the story was a news account, readers who knew the actual Artemus Jones could reasonably believe the real Artemus Jones had been caught philandering. Risk from errors in names in news reporting thus is sharp and urgent. But such dangers are farfetched when fictional characters accidentally are labeled by the names of actual persons unknown to the author. The fictional element, as distinct from news reporting, then makes identification by name alone insufficient to create liability either for privacy invasion or for defamation. If sufficient other items of identification are added, then there emerge the improbabilities of accidental similarity and the likelihood of identification and of intent to copy an actual person when portraying a fictional character. An issue of fact as to intentional invasion of privacy then is raised for the jury to decide.

Take the recent suit [28] dismissed against James T. Farrell. In his novel *Bernard Clare*, Mr. Farrell etched his chief character, an unhappy newspaper man bearing that name, in acid tones. An actual Bernard Clare, unknown to Mr. Farrell and also a newspaperman, popped up and sued for libel, not for privacy invasion. The court exonerated Mr. Farrell and fiction writers in comforting words:

> It would be an astonishing doctrine if every writer of fiction were required to make a search among all the records available in this nation which might tabulate the names and activities of millions of people in order to determine whether perchance one of the characters in the contemplated book designated as a novel may have the same name and occupation as a real person.

Here Mr. Farrell was sued for libel, not for privacy invasion. And in Minnesota, where the case was tried, libel requires a showing of intent to defame, contrary to the usual rule of absolute liability in defamation requiring no showing of intent. Yet the ruling in the Farrell case is a suggestive and generally accepted authority for the conclusion that mere accidental identity of names between a fictional and an actual character creates no liability in privacy invasion.

Recently a complainant having the name of a leading character in *From Here to Eternity* was thrown out of Court in a long and informative opinion to the same effect (Maggio v. Scribners, 130 N.Y.S. 2d 514). The grandchildren of the composer Robert Schumann could not recover for the use of their name or stress upon Schumann's insanity (Schumann v. Loews, 144 N.Y.S. 27). Charles Chaplin's privacy, it was held, was not violated by an unauthorized television broadcast of a telephone conversation by a reporter (152 F.R.D. 134).

If the similarities between an actual personage and a fictional character be made by the author to consist of more than similarities of name and occupation, the question arises whether the similarities are actual or intentional. The answer is for the jury to determine, despite the author's denial, as a conclusion on the facts. If the jury believes the similarities are purely accidental and not intentional, then, if the law of privacy develops as seems likely, no liability will be imposed on the author.

Some overclever authors, or their publishers and agents, as a protective maneuver, find in the telephone directory the name of an actual person similar to their fictional character's name, and obtain the written consent of such person. If the author gets the consent of the *actual* person he models a character on, that consent, of course, is complete protection. But merely getting the consent of an otherwise unknown person, having a name similar to one's character, is futile. In fact, a trap for the author to fall into. For if another (third) actual person, having the same name as the author's character, bobs up and sues, then the issue is solely between the author and that third person having the same name as his character. The test then is that of additional similarities and proof of intent on the author's part. The consent previously obtained from another is of no avail against the third person, if he be damaged by invasion of privacy. Obtaining a protective screen in advance merely shows fear of wrongdoing, i.e. possible intentional invasion of the privacy of the person who sues and an overclever scheme of trying to sidestep liability.

14. A USELESS NOTICE

The custom has now become widespread, with publishers and authors, of inserting a notice, intended to protect themselves, at the beginning of a novel, motion picture, or other fictional creation. Such a notice typically states that the events and characters are all fictional and that no character appearing in the fictional narrative is drawn from or modeled on actual living personages, or that similarities are purely coincidental or accidental. This self-serving announcement in advance is unintendedly humorous, since it is of scant avail or use. It could well be omitted, for it is provincial and adds little dignity to publishing in the United States. The publication of a work as a novel itself proclaims that the work is fictional.

A denial of intent, particularly in advance, means little. Whether or not the writer of fiction intended to copy a living person is for the jury to decide. The writer's denial at the trial is more convincing and pertinent than a self-serving notice published in advance. Lack of intent is not a defense in defamation; in privacy invasion, the test is whether a reasonable person would identify the fictional character involved with the living person suing. Usually it is, as a practical matter, impossible for an invasion of privacy to arise and for a recognizable identity to occur if the creator of a fictional character did not intentionally or subconsciously note or copy the living personality; thus a self-serving denial of intent is of no avail. The jury must decide the issues of intent and identity on the facts, and a jury gives little heed to a formula declaration in advance. Even as a piece of evidence showing that readers should not reasonably identify the living person with the fictional character, such notice is of no avail. Stock notices are disregarded. As a defense against punitive damages, whereunder the notice technically is admissible in evidence to the jury, it is also of little practical use. Awards of punitive damages are rare; they are not allowed against innocent and reasonably careful publishers; direct evidence must be shown to prove ill will and a right to punitive damages. The self-serving defense in advance may even show a fear of privacy invasion, a consciousness that may increase liability. If an evil character be portrayed, based on a living personage who is thus defamed, a notice in advance of no intent to portray or defame will not persuade a jury that either intent or ill will is absent.

Since the notice may give publishers and writers ill-founded ideas of a possible defense in privacy and defamation liability, and in reality serves no useful legal purpose, the undignified legal futility should be omitted. The semiofficial Restatement of the Law puts it aptly: [29]

The fact that the author or producer states that his work is exclusively one of fiction and is in no sense applicable to living persons is immaterial, except as to punitive damages, if readers actually and reasonably understand otherwise.

In a famous English lawsuit over *Rasputin, The Mad Monk*, the motion picture portraying the career of the actual Rasputin, an actual Russian Princess Irina sued Metro-Goldwyn-Mayer for defamation.[30] The court considered the effect of a possible notice, and its use as a defense was rejected. So too in a recent vigorously

worded inference in a Federal District Court ruling in Massachusetts, this notice as a defense was in effect rejected.[31] It is to be noted,
however, that in both of these cases the motion pictures, in part,
were based on actual news events and personages, making the notice
less applicable than it might be in respect to pure fiction.

15. DAMAGES IN PRIVACY INVASION

The measure of damage in privacy invasion has not yet been
clearly defined. As in defamation, the determination as to the damages in privacy invasion is left to the jury. In defamation, the test
is that of the damage done to the defamed person's standing in the
community; damages for mental suffering also may be fixed in the
discretion of the jury. So too, if the fictional character be un-
favorably drawn in privacy invasion, the defamation test may be
applied. If the jury's award is clearly too high, the judge may intervene and cause a reduction thereof.

Invasions of privacy, of course, may arise without defamation or
harsh character portrayal. Where a fictional character, modeled on
a living person, is favorably described as was done in the lawsuit
involving Miss Rawlings' *Cross Creek*, considerable confusion has
arisen as to the measure of damages. In the case of a favorably portrayed character little destruction of social or public position results.
Mental suffering involved may be remote, even farfetched. Such
was the finding in the Rawlings case (see Section 2), where no
damages were allowed.

But another element of damage may be noted in privacy invasions, although it is not yet established by the cases: that of unjust enrichment. Personality, particularly merited favorable publicity, must be viewed as having property aspects. In the Binns case,
the substantial damages allowed could be justified only on the theory
that the motion picture, in depicting the heroism of Binns, profited
unjustly by using the publicity about and the personality of Binns
(as property) without compensation to him. What is the fair value
of the profit unjustly derived by the user of the personality of
another, in the light of the publicity that a person like Binns enjoyed? Such seems a fair element to be considered by the jury in
awarding damages. The motion-picture user of Binns' personality

and publicity clearly had unjustly enriched itself. Such a consideration is now coming to the fore in cases of unauthorized use or
exhibition in television of a performer or athlete as a publicity attraction. (See Section 192.)

It is possibly because New York courts do not desire to become
literary agencies that in the Molony case (see Section 10) the
court refused to find that any right of privacy was involved. For if
the right of privacy is to be reasonably protected, then the damages
granted should include an approximation of the amount of unfair
enrichment by a writer or publisher or radio or television station
or motion-picture producer who uses the personality of another as
a model for a story character without consent. Such damages would
be in addition to damages resulting from destruction of community
standing or from mental suffering.

Punitive damages are different. They are not awarded, in reality,
unless ill will or clear intention to injure or spite be proved. Thus
the usual publisher, or station, need have no realistic fear of punitive
damages.

The obscurity of the test as to damages in privacy is but a phase
of the undeveloped state of the entire concept of created publicity
as property. (See Chapter XXI.) A property concept emerges where
personality has values intertwined with publicity, or where the selling of fiction or television portrayal is helped by the use of an
actual, colorful personality as a character, and of his created publicity. That aspect is a rising and important aspect of privacy.

16. FUTURE OF PRIVACY PROTECTION

Unfortunately, the only definite result of this new right of privacy, aside from limits upon advertisers, is a marked limitation upon
fiction writers of the more meritorious, imaginative creations, in
their gathering of character material. For them the rule is regretta-
ble. The protection of ordinary persons from privacy invasion by
an over-aggressive press has not been sufficiently advanced by the
New York courts, who set the pace.

Yet the sixty years that have passed since Justice Brandeis first advanced the right of privacy have clarified the concept involved. The
essential conflicts involved are now apparent. The future evolve-
ment of the legal protection granted can perhaps be suggested.

Some courts still fail to glimpse the basic end of Justice Brandeis: the right of the individual to be protected legally from cruel and unnecessary abuses by a sensation-seeking press. That simple objective, however, in the end will control the right of privacy. Freedom of the press does not necessitate inhuman abuses. Liberty will not perish if a reporter's license be checked.

The dividing line, between freedom of the press and restraints on invasions of privacy in news reporting, realistically turns on the distinction between current and stale news. The free reporting of current events must ever be permitted. Public interest so requires. In reporting crimes and public events, the press must be allowed great license, though such reporting often is harsh, sensational, and intended to arouse improper emotions. Possible abuses by police and prosecutors, either as persecutions of the innocent or as corrupt protection of the guilty, can best be restrained by blazing publicity.

Even in the reporting of current news, many abuses can be checked. Reporting purely private misfortunes with undue sensationalism, such as the birth of malformed children to unfortunate parents, or the treatment, for humor-rousing purposes, of disease afflictions, such as a passion for overeating, properly has been restrained. The orbit of protection to "ordinary" or "little" people should boldly be enlarged.

And when news becomes stale and passes into the mercy of the past, the right of privacy should be more vigorously protected. The test then should *not* be merely the *means* or *form* of publication, but the *purpose* of the publication. The New York courts have lagged here. Their decisions center on the *means* used. The means of publication is a factor in determining purpose, but is far from controlling. Newspapers are not devoted solely to publishing current news; substantial sections are devoted to pure entertainment. The greater portion of the material in Sunday editions, and in many columnist forays, is comparable to that in periodicals and books purveying entertainment, not devoted to news. The test should not be whether the means of publication used is a newspaper, a motion picture, a comic magazine, a biography, or a novel. The purpose and nature of the particular story involved should be appraised separately and objectively; the form and means of publication may be factors in that appraisal but should not control. With these tests the right of

privacy would not be so difficult to apply. A late New York decision, as to the "Lady of the Rose",[5] follows that view.

The realistic test then becomes: Is the particular item published
an instance of news reporting or instructive news comment, in
which the public has a clear and definite interest? Or is it simply the
selling of entertainment, using stale and half-forgotten events,
wherein a profit-seeking publisher and entertainment seekers primarily are benefited? Entertainment is sold for profit, news reporting likewise. But, as to privacy rights, the public interest outweighs
the profit element in news reporting. It does not in entertainment
selling. The two distinctions between current and stale news, and
as to the purpose (news reporting vs. entertainment), should be
controlling. They constitute a rational and sharply edged line, not
too difficult for court and jury to determine. The distinction is
clearer than many distinctions in defamation.

Judged by these tests, the realities of privacy invasion are becom-
ing clearer. The public interest favors oblivion for stale news, except
where distinct educational ends and discussion are involved. The
public interest in putting a quietus on past unfortunate events is
fully recognized by the law.

In criminal prosecutions, where capital punishment is not involved (murder and treason), the law imposes a statute of short
limitation and of forgetting, generally seven to three years. After
this short time, the state can not prosecute for a crime though
provable. This statute of limitations as to crimes is a complete bar.
The same rule applies in civil litigation; the lapse of time and of
oblivion, varying from twenty years where real estate is involved
down to one or two years in cases of personal wrongs, intervenes.
Here the lapse of time ends the right to sue.

This limitation of the right to prosecute, or sue, accents the distinction between stale and current news in privacy invasion. Even
in the case of a criminal who serves a jail sentence, the public recognizes the humanitarian consideration that a convict, "having paid
his debt to society", is entitled to a chance to start life again. A few
states view truth as no defense to defamation involving publication
of his long-past offense in such circumstances.

In privacy invasion, this consideration of permitting the past to
bury its dead should be given fuller scope, as a distinction between

stale and current news. The California decision in the *Red Kimono* case (Section 10) seems obviously just; few will defend a motion picture's selling entertainment that drags back into sad publicity a wrongdoer who has rehabilitated herself.

The decision of the New York Federal Court in the case of Sidis, the prodigy who failed miserably, high-lights the injustice resulting from not distinguishing between current and stale news. It also stresses the fairness of the test of the *purpose* of publication as distinct from the *means* of publication. Newspapers and periodicals are not so sacred that they are above restraint, merely because they are newspapers or periodicals. The purpose of publication should control. A factual study of the failure of prodigies, if published in an educational magazine or in a journal directed toward parents, may well involve a purpose requiring an invasion of privacy. Medical journals publish case histories as instruction and discussion. But here the vital test emerges. In medical journals, the name and identity of the unfortunate patient are not given and he is described by a symbol (X); if pictures are used the face is covered. In *The New Yorker* articles about Sidis, the purpose was not education but attempted humor: salty wit and clever personality portrayal by cruel barbs. Public interest, other than that of entertainment, was completely lacking.

A thorough "going-over" of the most personal and intimate details of privacy is resorted to in such forays in order to create personality color. Sidis' promise and failure were items in the past and forgotten. To drag him out of his obscurity, merely for the display of wit, was akin to bear baiting in Elizabethan times. The right of privacy is predicated upon the humanitarian consideration that infliction and exhibition of human mental suffering are as barbaric as was the display of physical suffering of animals or of gladiators in ancient times. Publicity cruelties are indefensible. To permit them on the ground of public interest, when no public interest is involved, is a sardonic retreat to the Coliseum of Rome. That comparison is the nub of Justice Brandeis' idea.

Appraised by the double test of (a) the distinction between stale and current news, and (b) the distinction as to the *purpose* of the publicity and not merely as to the *means* used, the application of the theory of privacy comes into focus. Profit considerations, masking behind a nonexisting, falsely called right of the public to non-current news, emerge as a decisive factor. And the realities of personality publicity as property also emerge.

If a seller of entertainment wishes to use favorable publicity obtained by a hero like Molony, or Binns, after the current interest in the event has receded and is almost forgotten, such a seller of entertainment for profit should be required to obtain the consent of the hero or pay for the value of the publicity used. Publicity values by then have become property. Here it makes no rational difference whether the entertainment is disseminated by motion pictures or by comic magazines or by periodicals or by newspapers. Motion pictures sometimes report news as newsreels; sometimes they sell entertainment as features or serials. The purpose of the use should be decided by the jury. An advertisement using Molony's picture and name to promote the sale of cigarettes would not be permitted. Why to promote the sale of comics? Why shouldn't the publicity Molony justly enjoyed, in both instances, be viewed as his property?

In the writing of meritorious fiction, the burden of the restriction should and probably will be eased; but it also must be realistically appraised. To hold that the private life and events of a publicly known individual may be invaded in a biography but not in a novel is unfair to fiction writers. No sensible basis is revealed, other than technical indulgence. Since the usual purpose both of fiction and of biographies is the selling of entertainment for profit, therefore privacy, it can be urged, should not be invaded by either a biography or a novel. Comment, however, on the public aspects of a performer, musician, or artist is different and necessary.

An officeholder or one who seeks to advance by dealing in public affairs should be subject to biographical treatment; but not others, even though they are artists or performers seeking profit from the public. No public interest, as to either biographical or fictional treatment, then arises. Fictionalization of the personality of a living, public officeholder is on the borderline. Fictional use may well fall outside the needs of comment on a public official's motives and character.

As to fiction, a practical distinction in privacy invasion will probably be accepted in the future as between major and minor characters. Greater latitude may be given to using actual persons as models for minor characters, if defamation is absent, because little profit to the writer or harm to the model arises therefrom. The sacrifice demanded from fiction writers requires greater advance in the main intent in the theory of privacy: protection from abuses in news reporting, either as harping on cruel events, particularly about little people, or as "old chatter" and stale news.

Those fair and realistic ends are slow in coming to the fore in the concept of privacy, as a new shield for the individual. But hope can persist.

PART TWO

Defamation

—— IV ——

Realities of Modern Defamation

17. DEFAMATION DEFINED

DEFAMATION is the destruction of an individual's reputation and personality by the publication of *false* statements of fact or inference. It differs basically from privacy invasion, where the wrong arises from the truthful use without consent of an individual's personality, i.e. of his name, picture, or character portrait. In defamation the essential and basic issue is: does the *false* statement *injure* reputation? Thus truth is a complete defense in defamation, but not in privacy invasion, except in a few jurisdictions where malice (i.e. improper motive) may destroy the defense of truth.

Defamation thus is, in essence, the injury to or destruction of an individual's (or a corporation's) ties with other members of the community. Defamation results when false statements injure and lower the complainant's standing in his community so that others may refuse to associate, deal with, or accept him. The usual legal summary of a defamatory statement is that it holds the complaining individual "up to hatred, ridicule, or contempt."

Intent of the defamer need not be proved in defamation, nor a lack of care. Such is the basic medieval rigidity still prevailing in the law of defamation. This rigidity has created unfortunate counter-technicalities. These arise as to "secondary" publishers and as to the distinction between slander and libel, later discussed. One who publishes a false statement, however innocently, is liable for damages if the reasonably minded public, or a part thereof, concludes that the complainant has been hit. The one who unleashes the false and defamatory statement has no defense other than proving the statement to be true, or of establishing the limited defense of privilege, later outlined. The test in defamation is not "who is meant to be hit" but "who is hit".

Partly as a result of this harsh theory of absolute liability, absurdly technical distinctions between libel and slander still prevail, particularly in instances of defamation by television or radio.

18. MODERN ELEMENTS OF DEFAMATION

The realistic modern elements of defamation can be classified under five heads: (1) an extravagantly technical distinction between libel and slander, which has created ardent controversies in the application of the rules of defamation to modern means of publication, viz. television and the radio; (2) the realistic difficulties of determining who is hit by a defamatory statement, particularly when the defamatory statement is a general attack upon a class or a small group, or is conveyed by implication, inference, or innuendo; (3) the practical difficulties of determining what constitutes defamation by false statement, as distinct from the expression of opinion under the right to fair comment; (4) the defense of privilege, whereby certain persons who, although they have falsely defamed the complainant, nevertheless are excused because of public need and convenience; (5) the fixing of the damages, including punitive damages; particularly the medieval rule that courts will not enjoin, in advance of the injury, damage by the publication of defamatory matter.

19. LIBEL AND SLANDER

A hairsplitting distinction still prevails between slander and libel. This technicality defines slander as oral publication of a false statement, i.e. by word of mouth and by means that reach the ear. Libel is defined as false statements in writing or printing, means that reach the eye. This highly artificial distinction is of great importance.

One who has been slandered (that is, defamed by word of mouth) cannot recover damages, or even have a jury decide if he has been damaged, or estimate the damage, unless he can prove special damages. Special damages are difficult to show. The net result is that in the great majority of defamations by slander no recovery can be had; only four instances are excepted.

In libel, i.e. defamation by print, special damages need not be proved. If libeled (i.e. defamed in print), a complainant may have a jury appraise the damage, merely by proving to the jury that the false and defamatory statement was published about him, and by nullifying any defense of truth or privilege proffered by the defendant.

Since the majority of modern courts in the United States hold defamation by radio and television commonly to be slander, and not libel, this verbal medieval distinction in fact robs many a defamed person of any relief whatsoever.

By special damages is meant definite, concrete, and specific proof of injury. Moreover, the injury must result in specific monetary loss. Thus only in unusual instances can special damages be proved.

Because of this difficulty of proof, the medieval law made certain arbitrary exceptions to the rule that specific injury, i.e. special damages, must be proved in slander. If the slanderous statement (1) falsely accuses the complainant of suffering from a loathsome disease, or (2) of having committed a crime, or (3) if it harms him in his trade, business, or profession, then no proof of special damages is needed. In the case of women, another exception is added: (4) a false charge of unchastity. As to these four and artificially limited instances of slander, the defamatory statements then are held to be "slanders per se" or "actionable per se", i.e. without the need of further proof, explanation, or examination.

Outside of these four arbitrary exceptions, special damages must be pleaded and proved in all cases of slander before a complainant can submit his case to a jury and ask for damages. Thus in the larger orbit of defamation by slander, no relief in fact is allowed.

A New York Federal court has just held that defamation by television is slander, not libel. Here the defamatory statement was oral and spontaneous and not read from a script.[1] Miss Bentley, in a *Meet the Press* television program, was asked is she would identify Mr. Remington "as a communist". She replied: "Yes, I would certainly do that." Mr. Remington sued. The court held that the statement, if false, was slander, not libel, because not read from a written script. But it also held that since the charge would injure Mr. Remington in his occupation as a public official it was slander per se. That is, since it came within one of the four exceptions (damage to his calling), special damage need not be proved. If Mr. Remington had not been a public official, he might have been denied the right to go to the jury, i.e. recover.

The majority of the decisions today hold that defamation over the radio, where the false statement is made extemporaneously, is slander, not libel. But if a written script be read over the radio or television, the majority of our courts hold the defamation to be libel. The hearer of radio broadcasts, of course, seldom knows or cares whether or not a script is being read. This hairsplitting, verbal distinction seems an absurdity. Yet such is the unfortunate and solemn pronouncement of the modern law of defamation.

20. THE MEDIEVAL HAND

Why does our modern law cling to such a technical distinction between libel and slander? From habit. In the early nineteenth century, Parliament asked the judges of England to advise it whether or not the distinction should be abolished. The judges so advised. They characterized the distinction as outgrown. But Parliament, nevertheless, didn't end the medieval rule, nor have lawmakers in the United States. Those who conduct radio and television stations, of course, are eager to cling to the exemption from liability for defamation which this medieval survival grants them.

In the fourteenth and fifteenth centuries, the courts of the church, not those of the king, granted relief for all wrongs by defamation. The priest-judges, who administered relief for defamation, favored penance instead of money damages. The limited injuries involved in oral slander, they felt, could best be managed by patching up the personal quarrels involved. In medieval days, however, the written or printed word carried great sanction of authenticity. People believed that anything in print must be true. Print, obviously, had a much wider circulation than oral statements. So the Star Chamber, when it took over control of printed publications in the effort of the state to impose censorship upon thoughts dangerous to the Crown, viewed defamation in print seriously. To prevent dueling and public disorder, where libel was involved, the Star Chamber adopted the rule that if defamation was in print or writing damages would be presumed. It also held that libels of a serious type, since they tended to create duels and breaches of the peace, were crimes. It added that in criminal libel truth was no defense, as it was in civil defamation. Thus emerged the adage: "The greater the truth, the greater the libel." The modern law still views serious libels of specific limited types as crimes, but generally permits truth as a defense even in criminal libel.

When the Star Chamber was abolished by the Long Parliament and Cromwell in 1641, the king's courts took over control of all relief for defamation from the Star Chamber and the canonical courts. But the distinction between slander and libel was preserved. And all efforts to end the distinction thereafter have failed, even in modern law in the United States.

21. THE CONFLICT TODAY

Artificial and technical distinctions pile absurdities upon absurdities. Even in medieval times, defamation in graphic form, i.e. by drawings or cartoons or by statues or effigies, was held to be libel. Today modern courts make the absurd distinction, above noted, that the defamation is libel when a broadcaster reads a written script over the radio, merely slander if he speaks without a script. In television, it is probable that if the defamatory statement were shown on the screen by facsimile the defamation would be held to be libel. But no court has so ruled as yet.

A great many legal articles have argued trenchantly that any defamation by television or radio is libel, not slander. Legislatures have enacted statutes skirting the fringes of the distinction. Five states have enacted statutes imposing possibilities of criminal liability for defamation by radio. In two of these five states, Oregon and Washington, the statutes refer to radio defamation as libel; in California, Illinois, and North Dakota it is termed slander. But a realistic resolution of the controversy has not even been begun.

The dispute as to what is mere slander or libel over the air is complicated, and in fact controlled, by the dispute as to how far a radio or television station should be held liable for defamation broadcast. If the defamation is uttered by others who merely hire the stations' facilities, should the stations be held absolutely liable, i.e. as "primary publishers", or liable only for lack of due care, i.e. as "secondary publishers"? The distinction involved is an aspect of the medieval theory of absolute liability in defamation before noted. Also, since radio and television stations are not permitted, under the

Federal Communications Act, to act as censors in some instances, it is urged that they must be treated leniently, i.e. as slanderers and not as publishers of libels. It is doubtful if the federal interdiction against political censorship should prohibit refusal to broadcast defamatory statements. (See Section 179.) But all these arguments are used by radio and television stations eager to retain the special privilege the law grants them in holding that television or radio defamation is slander and thus imposes slight risk of liability.

22. PREVAILING DECISIONS IN BROADCASTING DEFAMATION

Since the earliest decision, that of Nebraska's Supreme Court, in 1932, holding that the reading of a script over the radio is libel, seven other American states and Australia have considered the question as to whether defamation by radio is slander or libel, with conflicting results. The prevailing view is that of New York's highest court. That eminent court considered the question exhaustively in the instance of a radio broadcast by the news commentator Walter Winchell.[2]

Here the commentator read from a script, using language which the court held was defamatory, concerning the complainant, who was head of a movement vigorous during World War II for "Peace Now". The broadcaster asserted that the complainant favored the Nazis and urged peace only because Hitler was losing the war. The court, in construing his words, held that this charge did not defame the complainant in his professional character, and thus if viewed as slander, it did not constitute "slander per se". The court followed the rule that a loss of $7000 in earnings to the complainant was not proof of special damages. This ruling illustrates the difficulties of proving special damage in slander. In short, the court held that if the defamatory statement was slander, the complainant's cause would be thrown out of court.

The court held, however, that since the commentator had read from a script, the defamation was libel and recovery could be had. The court laid great stress upon an earlier, dubious English decision holding that the reading of a libelous letter by the writer *orally* to a third person, without any mailing or further publication of the letter, constituted libel. In a notable concurring decision, not acceptable to a majority of the judges, Judge Fuld argued that the broadcast was libel, not because the commentator read from a script, but because the distinction was obsolete. He urged that the far-flung audience reached by a radio broadcast made the dissemination of a defamatory statement as harmful and convincing as defamation printed in a newspaper or in a letter. There special damages need not be proved.

In Pennsylvania, that state's able Supreme Court reached an advanced result, but not as clear-cut as that urged by Judge Fuld.[3] Here Al Jolson was the chief performer in a radio advertiser's broadcast performed from a carefully prepared script. But Mr. Jolson "ad-libbed" when the name of the plaintiff's hotel was mentioned, and interjected: "That's a rotten hotel." The court hesitated to decide whether the spontaneous interjection was not mere slander, because it was purely extemporaneous and not read from a script, or whether it was slanderous per se. The court hinted at a new right to sue, viz. radio defamation, obviating the distinction between slander and libel, but held back.

The categorical ruling of the court was limited to a holding that the broadcasting station was not liable for defamation since it merely leased its facilities to the sponsor-advertiser. The absolute rule of liability in defamation, in short, was relaxed. Since the radio station had not intentionally or negligently participated in the remark of Jolson, and had not employed Jolson, the court held that the radio station should not be held liable. The problem of primary and secondary liability is discussed definitively later, in Section 24.

The majority of the eight states that have considered the question, however, hold that defamation by radio, if the defamatory statement be read from a script, is libel. If not read from a script but uttered spontaneously, it is held to be slander. In Australia, it is slander whether read from a script, or uttered extemporaneously.

23. THE SENSIBLE APPROACH

Common sense, it would seem, would be to follow both Judge Fuld's and the Pennsylvania view. Defamation by radio or television should be viewed as libel, whether read from a script or uttered extemporaneously. The same liability for damages then would prevail as in defamation by a newspaper or magazine. Special damages would not have to be shown.

The ancient distinction that granted relief for defamation in print without proof of damage was based upon the widespread dissemination, by print and the conviction of its veracity. In a publication by radio or television, the coverage and conviction is as great as in printing, if not greater. The broadcasting or televising of a defamatory statement also carries the persuasion that the statement must be true, on the theory that where there is so much smoke there must be some fire.

But a still more sensible view would be to abolish entirely the distinction between slander and libel, as the English judges suggested. Then the jury could determine whether or not the damages sustained have been substantial enough to warrant any financial relief. Yet many fear that then our courts would be cluttered with petty spite lawsuits. Should every defamatory word, orally uttered in petty quarrels when few are present, be held a wrong permitting the complainant to go to the jury without proof of special damages? The ancient "frowning down" of petty slander suits has merit. Yet the answer seems that juries can be trusted to award no damages in purely petty squabbles.

Radio and television stations would be protected if liability for damage were limited to cases where the station is at fault by amending the old rule of absolute liability in defamation. Both aspects of the decision of the Supreme Court of Pennsylvania, above noted, seem essential to a revision of the law of defamation.

24. ABSOLUTE LIABILITY IN DEFAMATION

The ancient impulse in defamation was urgently to protect the injured. Thus as the second element in defamation, the rule in imposing liability still is "not who is meant but who is hit".

He who originates a defamatory statement cannot plead the lack of intent or of negligence. Innocence is no defense. Because of this harsh and absolute liability, limitations of liability have been added to protect those who are not the originators of the defamation.

The publisher of a newspaper, magazine, or book containing defamatory matter, however, is held absolutely liable. He is called the "primary publisher". Only the author or writer of the article may have known of the falsity of the statement, but such a fact is no defense to the publisher as the primary publisher. Only as to punitive damages, as distinct from compensating or ordinary damages, is the primary publisher protected. A primary publisher is not liable for punitive damages if he did not know of the falsity and intended no injury.

But a newsstand or bookstore that sells the newspaper, magazine, or book, or the lending library that rents it out, is not held to so harsh a standard of liability. The newsstand or bookseller or lending library is called the "secondary publisher". A secondary publisher is held liable only if he knows, or has reasonable grounds to know, or has notice, that the printed matter he is selling is defamatory. A secondary publisher, upon having notice that a suit has been brought for defamation or that a charge of defamation has been asserted, however, continues thereafter to distribute such assailed matter at his peril. Then he becomes strictly liable, like a primary publisher. Likewise, a telegraph company that transmits a defamatory telegram is not liable, unless its employees knew, or could reasonably conclude, that the message so transmitted contained defamatory matter.

Thus the operator of a radio or television station in some instances may be acting as a primary publisher of defamatory matter. In other instances, its position may be that of a secondary publisher. But the law generally makes no such distinction.

Where a broadcasting station leases its facilities to a sponsor or other user for a commercial or political broadcast only, the sponsor or direct user, not the radio station, should be deemed liable as the primary publisher if defamatory matter be broadcast. But the law seems otherwise. In a sponsored program, where defamatory matter is uttered, the following are, and should be, held liable as primary publishers: (1) the individual who uttered the defamatory matter; (2) the sponsor; and (3) even the advertising agent who arranged the program. As to the sponsor, even though he did not know of the libel, he is the employer, and like an employer whose chauffeur runs down another carelessly or intentionally in the course of the employer's business, he must be held liable. So too with the advertising agency that arranged the program; it too is primarily involved in the transaction. But the fair view would be that the broadcasting or television station, merely leasing its facilities, is not primarily involved, and should be viewed in the position of a secondary publisher. Like a bookseller or telegraph company, it should not be liable unless it knew that defamatory matter was going to be published or unless it had reason to so know. But the law is not yet so advanced.

In the case of a "sustaining program", where there is no sponsor, a different result should follow. The broadcasting station itself is the employer of those broadcasting the defamatory matter. The station can fairly be held liable as the primary publisher.

If that rule were followed, all defamation by radio or television could well be deemed libel, not slander. The obligation to pay damages would be fastened only upon those who are responsible for the defamation. Under such a view the need of proof of special damage, which is now required in slander, would not be needed to mitigate an absolute liability now imposed on radio and television stations.

25. THE TEST OF WHO IS HIT

The basic theory of absolute liability in defamation holds that, however innocent the publisher of defamatory statements may be, he is liable if he actually but unintentionally hits someone by a false statement, even someone of whom he never heard or knew.

The most striking instances of this result are shown by two leading English cases, both probably law in the United States: (1) the famous case of a supposedly nonexisting Artemus Jones, already discussed in the chapter on Privacy (Section 13), and (2) the heavy recovery for defamation granted Princess Irina against Metro-Goldwyn-Mayer in England, because she was unintentionally depicted and defamed in a very popular motion picture *Rasputin, the Mad Monk*.[4]

The Artemus Jones case need not be further noted. As before stated, it is too much feared by fiction writers or those who disseminate fiction. The legal result in the case of the popular picture *Rasputin, The Mad Monk* is arresting. Here an actual Princess Irina claimed she was "hit" by the fictional character "Princess Natasha" in the picture, who was by inference depicted in the picture as having been raped by Rasputin. Princess Irina, an actual member of the Czar's court and the actual wife of an actual Prince Yous-soupoff, rumored to have been the destroyer of Rasputin, asserted that the actual events depicted in the picture, other than the raping, pointed to her, for the motion picture depicting Rasputin and portraying the Russian court was based on actual events and, of course, on the facts of Rasputin's life. The picture producer and its writers pleaded they did not know of the existence of Princess Irina. But the Appellate Court allowed the heavy damages awarded by the jury to be recovered, holding that the sole test here, as in the Artemus Jones case, was whether or not reasonable members of the public would believe that the character described as "Princess Natasha" pointed to and "hit" Princess Irina. Lack of intent and innocence and the greatest of care on the part of the picture maker, it held, was no defense.

The court held that defamation by a motion picture is libel, not slander. Also, it rejected the clever and curious argument of counsel for the picture company, that a lady's chastity is not besmirched if she be depicted as raped, not as seduced, i.e. that Princess Irina being only slandered had to prove special damage. Also the court rejected brusquely any defense from the pleas of an implied notice that all the incidents and characters were fictional. Here many of the events were actual, stressing the fatuity of a "coincidental notice". The facts themselves speak.

The court stressed the distinction that rejects accidental defamation by errors in names in purely imaginative, fictional work, but sustains defamation by accidental identity of names in news reporting and in fiction that uses actual events or personages. For in wholly imaginary fiction, where accidental identity of names occurred, Justice Scrutton said, the accidental identity by names did not result in defamation under the rule of "who is hit", for the purely imaginary character "was a mere type and did not mean anybody." But in the *Rasputin* picture the characters were partly drawn from actual personages; here and in news reporting, error in names and thus accidental identity in names can be defamatory.

These results are in accord with the sensible aspects of defamation. The semifactual, semifictional character of "Princess Natasha" was unlike the wholly fictional character "Bernard Clare" in Farrell's novel. Fiction writers who use news material and historical living persons can be "hit" by damage verdicts both for defamation and for invasions of privacy. They must be very careful.

26. DEFAMATION BY ERROR IN NAME

In newspaper reporting one of the commonest and most dangerous forms of defamation is that arising from an error in a name. It is uniformly held that where such an error hits a person, even of whom the publishers of the defamation never heard, the publisher is liable. The courts of the United States follow the theory in the Artemus Jones case of accidental defamation by error in name.

The *San Francisco Examiner* printed a story about fraud in city contracts, referring to one of the contractors arrested as "*J. W. Taylor*". The contractor actually involved was *J. N.* Taylor. A contractor in San Francisco named *J. W.* Taylor, who also did work for the city, claimed that he had been hit by the error in the initials. He was allowed recovery though there was no intent to refer to him.[5]

In Washington, D.C., a newspaper, in reporting the arrest for forgery of Harry P. S. Kennedy, an attorney from Detroit, referred to the arrested man as "Harry Kennedy, an Attorney". Harry Kennedy, the only lawyer of that name in Washington and an entirely different person, was allowed to recover.[6]

In Missouri a newspaper published an article about a James Farley, as the "great strikebreaker", and by accident published a picture of another James Farley, the Recorder of Deeds of St. Louis. The Recorder of Deeds was allowed to recover.[7]

A news reporter telegraphed a story to his paper referring to a named individual as "a cultured gentleman." [8] The telegraph company in error changed the words to "colored gentleman"; the newspaper used the erroneous description. The individual so described was allowed to recover, for in the South it is often deemed defamatory to describe a white person as colored.

27. DEFAMATION AND PUBLICATION

Defamation can not result unless there is publication of the defamatory matter to someone other than the defamed person. And where the defamed person himself makes public or consents to the publication of the defamatory matter, it necessarily follows that there is no defamation. Consent has been given where the one assailed dares his accuser to state his charges publicly, and reveal the facts.

But where an assailed person dares a senator or congressman to repeat his charges publicly outside of Congress, and thus without his absolute privilege, the assailed person consents only to the waiver of privilege, not to the public statement of the defamation. Thus recovery probably can be had, if the defamatory statements are false and are uttered without privilege. These are nice, yet in this instance realistic, distinctions.

Mailing a handwritten letter containing defamatory matter only to the person defamed is not publication, for publication requires dissemination to a third person other than the publisher of the defamation and the defamed. Thus, if the oral slanderous charge is in a foreign language, and no one present understands the foreign speech used, no publication and no defamation result.

The decisions are filled with ironic twists in logical application of the rule that the test in defamation is "who is hit". If the writer of a defamatory letter mails the letter by honest mistake to the wrong person, instead of to the person defamed, and the erroneous recipient opens and reads the letter, publication arises and defamation results. The sender of the letter cannot plead that he did not intend to mail the letter to the third person or acted carefully. The same result arises if the servant of the writer of the letter, against his wishes, mails the letter to the wrong person—but not if a thief steals and reads it. If the utterer of a defamatory matter, by error in dialing his telephone, speaks to a person other than the defamed person to whom alone he intended to utter the charge, publication results. The dictating of a letter to a stenographer, or the sending of a message by telegram, is publication to a third person. So, too, if a person makes a defamatory oral speech or an oral defamatory statement to another, not expecting it to be printed in a newspaper or put in print, but it is, he is liable for libel as a proximate result. So too is the newspaper. A person is liable also for the defamation harm done by the unexpected newspaper publication of a private letter without his consent. The newspaper also is liable. These are examples of the harsh liability of a primary publisher for all of the proximately consequent results of his defamatory statement. Such examples stress the analogy to the keeping of wild animals knowing that they are dangerous. For absolute liability is imposed upon the originator of a defamatory statement. If the tiger or defamation gets loose, its keeper or first utterer is held absolutely liable. Accident, lack of intent, and absence of carelessness are no excuse. Defamation, because of this arbitrary rule, like an explosive, is a dangerous commodity to create or handle. If you are hit by an automobile, you must prove intent to hit you or lack of care in order to recover damages. But if you are hit by a published defamation, you need only show that you are hit.

V

What Is Defamatory?

28. DEFAMATION AND INSINUATION

THE GENERAL test of what is defamatory, as the destruction by false statement of another's personality or of his social ties in a community, in actual experience is at times difficult to state. The right of opinion and comment intervenes, as distinct from the right to assert facts. Where does free speech end and defamation begin?

As a practical aspect, the powers and discretion of the judge in defamation trials are unusually great. It is the judge's function to decide whether the words assailed may go to the jury. As a preliminary step, his decision is controlling as to whether the words set forth or explained in the complaint can be reasonably viewed by the jury as defamatory. The judge's ruling may be that there is no defamation possible, ending the case; or he may rule that the words, standing alone, without explanation or detailing of the circumstances involved, can be reasonably deemed defamatory. Then his ruling is that the words may be viewed as defamatory "per se", i.e. defamatory without further explanation. Thereupon the final decision is for the jury. Or again, the judge may rule that explanation, and circumstances as to the uttering, are needed. If so, it is for him to rule whether or not the additional statements set forth in the complaint are sufficiently illuminating to permit the plaintiff to have the jury decide. So two steps are involved in deciding what is defamatory: first, the judge's over-all preliminary decision; and if it be favorable to the plaintiff, then the jury's verdict. The big problem for a plaintiff often is to get by the judge. Thus the decisions of trial and appellate courts, often explained in opinions, are the vital guides as to what is defamatory. The leading decisions thereon are accordingly summarized as a guide, later in this chapter. (See Sections 33, 34, and 35.)

Words have different meanings in different situations. Innuendos, insinuations, and vocal circumstances must be appraised. A perfectly innocent description of a person, under special circumstances, may lose its innocence. Cunning is often utilized by those who defame. Also unreasonable offense is taken by sensitive persons criticized in a fair expression of opinion. Thus a detailed examination of what is defamatory in practice is essential.

Defamation is false and injurious statement in an item of fact, not of opinion. The fair expression of opinion, particularly as to matters of public interest, if it is not based upon or does not imply falsehood as to facts, must be permitted in a democratic community. Otherwise free speech and a free press would be ended. Newspaper editors and columnists, radio and television commentators, rival political candidates, critics of literary and dramatic works, and examiners of ideas must be allowed to express their opinions freely. Those who dislike the opinions so expressed can not be granted the right to complain that they have been defamed, unless the statement of opinion is so intertwined with false statements of fact that the false total stated constitutes defamation. Since opinion shades quickly into fact, the distinction between the two is often difficult to draw. For example, is the imputation of an improper or false motive an expression of opinion or a statement of fact?

29. OPINION

Obviously the publication of a false statement of fact by phrasing it in words of opinion or rumor will not bar liability. If a columnist carefully writes, "In my opinion and in my opinion only John Doe may be a Communist," or "Rumor has it that John Doe is a Communist, although we have no proof," the statement is libelous—if John Doe is not a Communist. For saying one is a Communist is defamatory in many states today. (See Section 33.)

The essential difficulty, moreover, in distinguishing opinion from fact arises from the reality that the privilege of fair comment is intertwined in the distinction. It is universally recognized that in matters involving the public interest there is a necessary right of fair comment. Sometimes this right is deemed a privilege, i.e. a defense that prevents recovery for a false and defamatory statement. The clearer appraisal of the right of fair comment, however, is that fair comment is not a defense but tends to control the distinction between opinion and fact. In short, if fair comment is not involved, opinion may come closer to false facts than otherwise. The motive and purpose of the commentator, as distinct from past or present objective facts, is the pith of the fair-comment privilege.

Public interest and the consequent right of fair comment arise in: (a) election contests where qualifications of candidates commonly are vigorously, even violently, discussed; (b) criticisms of public officers for dereliction in duty, including the conduct of public officers in hiring contractors, managing institutions and schools, and spending public funds; (c) criticism of literary works, art exhibits, plays, and entertainment; and (d) public discussion of ideas in general. Here a wide latitude of criticism and comment is necessary. This wide latitude permits the inference and use of facts as part of the expression of the opinion. Some error in the implication of false circumstances must be permitted if free discussion is to be protected. But that wider orbit given to opinion in matters of public interest does not prevail in purely private disputes.

It is now held that falsely to charge a person, particularly one in public life, in print with being a Communist or a Nazi is libelous. (See Section 33.) But it has also been held that, in a discussion involving public interest, falsely to accuse a writer of having attempted to make Communism seem "more reasonable", and "less hateful", or to "make black-face pearly white", is not libelous.[1] But to make inferential comparison of an individual with Communists, where no public interest is involved, purely to add fire to a private dispute, might well be held not to be an expression of opinion but an implication false as to fact and defamatory. (See Section 33.)

Election contests, in a democratic state, require wide latitude for violent expression of opinion. Hot charges and countercharges, and angry announcements by candidates that they are suing a newspaper or a rival candidate for libel, are common. But usually all the alleged libels are forgotten after an election. The suits that are tried for defamation involved in election contests are still numerous, yet experience shows that juries are not inclined to grant verdicts for election defamations; juries construe false statements in such situations as opinions and not as allegations of fact. Juries incline to the view that sensitive individuals should not venture into politics.

Thus, in distinguishing between opinion and fact, the circumstance of public interest and the occasion which calls forth the utterance control the practical result reached.

One of the clearest judicial notations of the difference between opinion and fact in defamation appears in a decision in New South Wales quoted with approval by a United States Federal court: [2]

The error which is usually committed by those who bring themselves within the law of libel when commenting on conduct is in thinking that they are commenting when in point of fact they are misdescribing. Real comment is merely the expression of opinion. Misdescription is matter of fact. If the misdescription is such an unfaithful representation of a person's conduct as to induce people to think that he has done something dishonorable, disgraceful, or contemptible, it is clearly libelous. To state accurately what a man has done, and then to say that in your opinion such conduct is disgraceful or dishonorable, is comment which may do no harm, as every one can judge for himself whether the opinion expressed is well founded or not. Misdescription of conduct, on the other hand, only leads to the one conclusion detrimental to the person whose conduct is misdescribed, and leaves the reader no opportunity for judging for himself the character of the conduct condemned, nothing but a false picture being presented for judgment.

30. DEFAMATION IN CRITICISM

A critic of a play, or a literary work, is given broad scope in expressing an adverse opinion. When, however, the critic goes into the private life of the author, he may pass from the realm of opinion to that of facts.[2a] A critic who states that the play or novel he is criticizing could only be written by a "sexual pervert", or that an author who could concoct such a work must have a "depraved moral character", is dealing with facts as well as opinion. Having gone beyond the orbit of opinion, his statement, if false and if the author has none of these depravities, is defamatory. The right of fair comment does not go that far. If in trying to prove that the play shows the author's depravity, the critic charges inferentially that the author's character is depraved, such a statement, if false, is not privileged as fair comment. Also the statement in a book review that a novel is a plagiarism of another work, if false, is defamatory.

Such a false statement of fact is not permitted as an expression of an opinion or deemed necessary to the writing of fair criticism.

Defamation may be stated in the form of a joke; humor is no defense. To print a man's picture beside that of a gorilla in a discussion of evolution may be libel.[3] A picture of a jockey carrying his saddle, but showing the saddle apparently attached to the jockey as a humorous, obscene deformity, was held to be a libel.[4] The right to satirize and burlesque, as included in the privilege of fair comment, permits a slight excursion into minor matters of fact as the statement of opinion. But it is a limited privilege.

31. INSINUATION

A defamatory statement may be so complete that, standing alone and without explanation, it clearly holds the complainant up to "ridicule, hatred, and contempt". Then the addition of any further circumstance or interpretation is unnecessary. Such a statement is held to be libelous "per se", and the jury may award damages without looking beyond "the four corners of the libelous statement".

But many statements of fact become defamatory only if explained by collateral circumstances or interpretive keys. Defamation by innuendo is a typical example. To call a lady a "cocotte", since the French word has a double meaning (poached egg or prostitute) requires her to prove to the jury that the opprobrious meaning would be taken by those who read the statement. The fair meaning of the words used, as held in the minds of fair people, is the test. When Horace Greeley wrote of James Fenimore Cooper, "He will not bring the action in New York, for we are known here, nor in Otsego, for he is known there", it was held that Cooper had been libeled, because a fair reader would conclude that Greeley said, by inference, that Cooper's reputation in Otsego was bad.[5] Cleverness is of no avail.

Often an explanation of the innuendo must be added by the complainant to show the libelous effect. Also, in many instances, collateral facts must be added to explain the full meaning of the statement. The complainant must add these explanatory facts or interpretations, or the definition of the innuendo, to his pleadings for the judge to rule on; also the plaintiff must prove them to the jury. A few courts add that special damage must be proved where a statement is not defamatory per se. That is neither the sensible nor prevailing rule. All that need be added to a statement not libelous per se, is sufficient explanation to permit a reasonable person to consider the statement defamatory. Proof of special damages is not needed.[6]

32. THE REASONABLE INTERPRETATION

The test of what is defamatory, and what is not, is what the reasonable public, or a part thereof, would understand in each instance. Here again emerges the lawyer's favorite fiction: the reasonable man, or the reasonably prudent man. He is, of course, nonexistent. What is meant is that the interpretation of the statement is left to the jury, and that the judge will not reverse the jury's findings unless the statement complained of could not, viewed by any rational person, be found to mean what the jury held it means. A jury may be motivated by whim, by capriciousness, or by arbitrary or prejudiced emotions. In that event the judge sets aside the verdict. If the challenged statement cannot be reasonably viewed as defamatory, of course then there is no need of submitting it to a jury. But judges do at times let the case go to the jury so as to obviate the need of a possible retrial, and then reject the jury's findings if whimsical or beyond the pale of reason; thus they facilitate the appeal. Similarly the jury may allow damages that are unreasonably high. The judge then may set aside the verdict unless the complainant voluntarily reduces the amount of the award.

A defamatory statement, of course, need not reach all of the public nor even a large segment of the public. So long as it reaches one or more persons, other than the defamer and the defamed, it has been published. In appraising whether it would be construed as defamatory, the conclusions that would be reached by this small segment of the public are sufficient.

The complainant need not be specifically named in the defamatory statement. So long as it points to him by fair inference he has a right to damages. If, to a small group of people one and only one of whom is a lawyer, a person says "all lawyers are crooks", the lawyer may sue for slander on the grounds that, since he was known as the only lawyer present, the false statement in effect accused him of being a crook. Since such a defamation injures the lawyer in the carrying on of his profession, it is slanderous per se; no special damages need be proved. Orally to call a nonprofessional person a crook, however, is not equivalent to charging him with having committed a crime, and so is not slanderous per se. There recovery for slander cannot be had without showing special damages. In libel the result is otherwise. Such are the artificial distinctions still prevailing in the law of defamation, as to slander and libel.

Defamatory statements about a large group of people do not entitle a member of that group to sue. Libelous falsehoods published against Catholics or Jews, or priests generally, do not permit a particular member of the religion or profession to sue, for the statement does not point with sufficient definiteness to a particular member of that group; the large group itself has no right to sue.

But a libelous statement may point to an individual without naming the individual. In a dispute between Eddie Cantor and radio editors, Mr. Cantor accused some newspaper radio editors in New York (New York then had twelve) of being "experts at log rolling * * * whose various rackets are a disgrace to the newspaper profession." One of the twelve radio editors, though unnamed, sued Cantor. Whether the accusation made by Mr. Cantor was libelous as to the particular editor suing was ruled a matter that could go to the jury to decide.[7]

Corporations, whether conducted for charitable or profit purposes, may sue for defamation. But the defamation must injure them as corporations; i.e. falsely besmirch their financial standing, their methods, or their objectives.

A newspaper headline may be defamatory because of a bold and bald statement made therein, even if the article itself is so "watered down" that it is not defamatory aside from the headline. The headline is judged alone. Modifications in the article do not nullify the libel in the headline.

33. PRINTED WORDS HELD LIBELOUS

Definitions of what is defamatory necessarily are general, and skip over difficulties of interpretation. Light on what is or is not defamatory can best be afforded by actual instances of words that the courts have held to be defamatory, if false. In many instances in the following, the objectionable language is summarized for brevity, and in such instances the quoted words are the substance involved.

The following words in print have been held to be a libel per se, i.e. without explanation being required, if false.

1. Falsely describing a public official as being a "Communist" or a "former Daily Worker employee" could go to the jury to rule if a libel.[8]

Ten years ago a contrary rule was reached.[9]

But statements in a newspaper charging an editor and writer with having defended Communism in Russia, and attempting to make its operations seem "more reasonable" and "less hateful," have been held not to be libelous.[10]

2. Falsely accusing a person of having been classified by his draft board as "pro-Nazi" is libelous.[11]

So too posting a sign after victory in a lawsuit over a debt, comparing the complainant with Hitler, was held a libel.[12]

3. Publishing an individual's picture as an "American Quisling" is a libel.[13]

4. In accusations of anti-Semitism, the decisions are in conflict. A syndicated column, charging a Congressman with opposing the appointment of a lawyer for judge of the Federal District Court "because he was a Jew and one not born in the United States," brought on a flock of lawsuits in various states. In a New York decision [14] the statement, if false, was held to be a libel. In Ohio and Tennessee decisions [15] it was held not to be libel.

5. False statements of marital separation and discord may be libelous. When a newspaper stated that a beauty-contest winner was secretly married before the contest, but was about to leave her husband as a result of her beauty award, the false statement was held as libel.[16]

6. Calling a man too educated to earn a living,[17] or desperately poor,[18] or a eunuch,[19] or illegitimate [20] is a libel.

7. Calling a hotel rotten may be libelous.[21]

8. Stating that a woman was served with a legal writ while in a bathtub is libelous.[22]

9. A statement that an unmarried woman is pregnant is defamatory.[23]

10. A newspaper article mentioning the complainant as the friend of an Arab who wanted a chief wife for his harem, and adding the Arab was willing to purchase her from her parents, and that the complainant would make contact with the Arab for any woman that might be interested, was held a libel of the complainant.[24]

11. In Texas, it was held a libel falsely to describe a white person as a Negro.[25]

12. A charge by a labor-union newspaper that a corporation falsified its earnings to the public and to its workers "all in the name of patriotism" was a libel of the corporation.[26]

13. Where a newspaper article has said that a labor union overcharged or was guilty of extortion, the statement if false is libel and the labor union may sue.[27]

14. A newspaper article with a headline "A Legal Racket," describing litigation brought by a parent against his son for injuries in an automobile accident, and stating that the readers could imagine who paid the bill in the "pleasant little family affair", was a libel.[28]

15. A statement that the complainant was in jail in connection with a murder, and that the body of the murdered man had been found in the complainant's cellar, was libel.[29]

16. A newspaper headline reading "Man held in jail since the fatal crash in December", with a story stating the fact that the complainant had received a suspended sentence for criminal negligence, was held to be libelous, since the headline was not a "fair index" of the facts of the story.[30]

17. The false attribution, to a well-known theatrical producer, of the production of an inferior work, was held to be libel for injuring his reputation in the theatrical world.[31]

18. A lawyer having been suspended from practice for five years in the Federal District Court, an article stating he had been disbarred for submitting false affidavits was a libel.[32]

19. A statement that prosecuting attorney shields criminal elements is libelous per se.[33]

20. Falsely stating that an assistant county engineer was "cashiered" is libelous, since it implies dismissal with dishonor.[34]

21. A newspaper article stating that the village attorney had taken sides with the railroad and had sold out the taxpayers was held to be libel.[35]

22. A false statement that the complainant, a candidate for public office, had charged a neighbor with peering through windows at a middle-aged Negro and that the woman had planted a row of trees to protect her privacy, where the candidate had never made such a charge, was held a libel.[36]

23. A newspaper statement charging a municipal court judge with granting a continuance in a criminal prosecution from political considerations, and charging further that since the criminal defendant had committed murder during the continuance the blood of the victim was on the hands of the judge, was held to be libel.[37]

24. A newspaper editorial stating that no one wants to spend the rest of his life holding his nose, as he would have to do if the com-

plainant was re-elected since the complainant was the defender for a vice ring, was held to be libel.[38]

25. A newspaper's description of a Congressman as serving the interests of a former client by having inserted a "joker" in a law, but carefully avoiding accusing the Congressman of acts constituting a crime, was allowed to go to the jury as libelous.[38a]

26. Newspaper charges against members of a political canvassing board, of falsifying the count of ballots, are a libel.[39]

27. A false statement that the owners of a house at a given address (which was the address of complainant who was not named) were evicting an ex-serviceman, his wife, and their baby, was held to be libel.[40]

28. A motion picture which portrayed a Navy officer as impetuous and undisciplined, in picturing a historical event in which the officer had participated, was held to be a libel.[41] Here the officer had waived his right of privacy in writing before the picture was made.

29. Falsely charging a person with insanity is libel. So too is an erroneous statement of suicide, but not an erroneous statement of death.[42]

30. A newspaper description of a complainant, as having bought her husband, found him disappointing as an editor and inadequate as a husband, and desiring another man, was held to be a libel.[43]

31. Charging a person with violation of confidence reposed in him or with treachery to his associates, is a libel.[44]

32. Where a jeweler sold a watch to the complaint on installment payments which were all made, subsequent dunning letters in unsealed envelopes sent to her at the address of relatives where she was not residing, plus a letter to her employer falsely saying the account was "delinquent", were held by the highest court of New York to be libelous and the case was sent to the jury.[44a] But a Georgia court has held that a statement about a complainant, who is not a merchant, that he has debts and refuses to pay them, is not a libel in the absence of special circumstances.[45] On this point the rulings are in conflict, some states holding that explanation and circumstances of injury must be pleaded to make the statement defamatory.

33. An article describing one as willing to lie to injure the church, as having a vile spirit, and as associating with another described as "one of Satan's choicest tools", was held to be libel.[46]

34. PRINTED WORDS HELD NOT LIBELOUS

1. An encyclopedia's statement that the claim of Cooke as the discoverer of the North Pole was "universally rejected" was held not a libel.[47]

2. Notice posted in a theater, charging the complainant, an actor, with having been "disloyal to the theater and the neighborhood", was not a libel.[48]

3. An article attacking a statement of a named psychiatrist about the harmful effects of soap operas, and saying that the psychiatrist's findings were "sensational", not "scientific approaches", and adding that "radio has no room for casuistry" and that the psychiatrist "has no evidence and has therefore proved nothing", was not a libel.[49]

4. A statement that the complainant had fled from a foreign country and was not an American citizen, is not libel.[50]

5. But a newspaper's true report of a government clerk throwing eggs at her superior, with additional unproved charges of an official's misconduct, was held libel and not privileged as fair comment.[50a]

6. A statement that a corporation is using the mail to defraud is not a libel as to a director of such corporation.[51]

7. A newspaper statement that the complainant's wife, who was suing him for divorce, was also the complainant's aunt, was not a libel. The relationship might have been by marriage not by blood.[52]

8. Newspaper charges implying that a congressman voted in opposition to the wishes of the majority of his constituents, that his opposition to lend-lease was motivated by greed, and that dictatorships took advantage of internal dissension such as that which he created were held not to be a libel.[53]

9. Accusing a candidate of raising religious issues and being a reactionary, and stating that his election would be a victory for fascism, were held not to be libel.[54]

10. Accusing a candidate for public office of not being qualified by education or training and of "being the man Friday of another", and saying that he is "shrewd but quick tempered", are not libels.[55]

11. A statement that an Association of Variety Artists was a company union was not a libel.[56]

12. A newspaper story that the complainant had died and was lying in state, at an address which was the complainant's tavern, was held not to be libel.[57]

13. A newspaper description of a governor's brother as dispensing patronage in the state and ruling it with an iron hand was not libel.[58]

14. A newspaper article stating that the complainant was a connoisseur in the art of collecting "steel engravings of past United States Presidents printed in subdued shades on United States Treasury paper", without further pleading of innuendo or insinuation, was held not to be a libel.[59]

15. A newspaper article criticizing vaudeville as such, and depicting the complainant, under a caption reading, "Whistler, crooner, and yodeler, imitates woodpeckers, owls and whistles Sanctuary of the Heart", with a notation stating that his price was $65, was held not to be a libel.[60]

16. A newspaper article describing a maritime labor union as a "creeping paralysis" was not a libel per se of the union.[61]

35. ORAL WORDS HELD NOT SLANDEROUS
WITHOUT SPECIAL DAMAGE

1. An oral statement by Mayor La Guardia referring to the complainant, a lawyer, as a "bum in a gin mill" picked by politicians to break up the Mayor's audiences, was held not to be actionable without a showing of special damages. The implication of intoxication did not reflect on a lawyer's ability to carry on his profession,[62] in the judge's opinion.

2. Even though an attorney exceeded his privilege in addressing a jury and falsely said, of the complainant, that "any man whose wife had eight miscarriages, is a brute", the statement was not slander per se.[63]

3. Where it is falsely stated from the pulpit that a religious man has been excommunicated from the church, the statement is not slander per se, and in the absence of special damages recovery cannot be had. But if the complainant be a merchant and his customers be members of the church, he can then establish special damages and recover.[64]

4. Orally calling a man a crook, a bastard, of canine ancestry, or accusing him of being dirty, is not slander per se and does not permit recovery in the absence of special damages.[65]

36. DEFENSES OF TRUTH

The most important defense in defamation is that the statement involved is true. Usually truth is an absolute defense. Originally, in criminal libel, since certain libels were held to be a crime because likely to create a breach of the peace (duels or private revenge) truth was held not to be a defense. Today truth is usually a defense even in criminal libel. But in a few states, truth still is no defense in criminal libel if malice (desire to injure or ill-will) be proved. Also in a few states, even in civil defamation, the humanitarian consideration is established that truth is no defense where a harmful but truthful statement is published out of malice.

In establishing truth as a defense, however, the truth proved must be precisely the statement published. The famous medieval illustration still is generally followed: truth is not a defense where the defamatory statement accuses the complainant of stealing a watch, if proof is offered that the complainant in fact stole a clock and from another person. Those who publish defamatory statements, relying upon truth as a defense, must be meticulously careful in making certain that they can prove precisely what they published. Though most courts do not allow proof of malice to destroy the defense of truth, he who publishes the truth without good reason to do so, or even with good reason, finds every possible technicality thrown at him.

This danger of relying upon truth as an absolute defense and privilege often arises in newspaper reports of court and other public proceedings. Most of the states have statutes providing that a true and fair newspaper report of what was said or done at a judicial or other public proceeding, even if entirely false words and charges are asserted in such public proceedings, do not constitute libel.

In New York the statute [65a] provides that a newspaper report of a court or public proceeding is absolutely privileged if it be "a fair and true report". A recent suit against a New York newspaper aptly illustrates the modern application of the ancient illustration about the report of one who stole a watch whereas the article stolen was a clock. Here the news syndicate gave the usual colorful tabloid account of a motion in a separation proceeding. This account stated that the plaintiff's wife had charged "yesterday in Supreme Court" "that the tycoon [husband] not only has been double dealing her with a lady in his employ but was also cheating on the corespondent." The facts were that a few days before the story was published the supporting papers making the above charges against the husband were withdrawn pursuant to a court order, the withdrawal papers being filed the next day and before the "yesterday" of the newspaper account. The New York Court of Appeals ruled that the above newspaper report was not privileged within the statute, holding that the article had said that the plaintiff's wife "made her charges against him yesterday—an assertion that was false." The article "made no mention of the fact that the charges were made as part of a motion which had hitherto been withdrawn—an omission that was unfair". It resulted that the article was neither true nor fair and consequently that privilege by Section 353 of the New York Practice Act did not attach to it.[65a]

An effort to have the legislators of New York amend the above statute to add the word "substantially" to "fair and true" failed. Such a ruling illustrates the meticulous accuracy, care, and caution that must be taken in a newspaper account of a judicial or public proceeding.

37. DEFENSE OF PRIVILEGE

In many instances other than those where truth is relied on as defense, no recovery can be had against the publisher of a false and defamatory statement. Two kinds of privilege, aside from truth, are recognized: (1) absolute privilege, wherein improper motive in making the false statement does not destroy the privilege; and (2) qualified privilege, wherein an improper motive may destroy the privilege.

Absolute Privilege

Absolute privilege for Congressmen is specified in the Constitution as to a ". . . Speech or Debate in Either House. State constitutions usually have similar provisions. The general belief is that this privilege is unlimited and that it covers committee proceedings. The Supreme Court has not so definitively ruled. Public executives, as to acts necessary to the performance of their duties, are also privileged. This exemption is deemed necessary in the public interest. A member of Congress can not be sued for any libelous false statement, relevant or irrelevant, whether made in good faith or maliciously or even venomously, if the statement is made in Congress or in any committee of Congress. The same rule applies to judicial proceedings. Judges, witnesses, lawyers, and parties to a proceeding (and their pleadings) are protected absolutely. Bad motive here does not destroy the privilege.

But a requisite of relevance is imposed in judicial proceedings though not in Congressional statements. A litigant, and his lawyer, for example, who in a legal complaint to collect payment of a note, add the false statement, irrelevant to the issue, that the defendant is an ex-convict, can be sued for libel. The test of relevance here, however, is not the technical test of the law of evidence. It is a wider test. If the defamatory statement can not, even remotely, be relevant to the issue involved, then the defense of privilege is absent. Thus a lawyer can not assert the privilege of a judicial proceeding when he says, of a defendant, in addressing a jury, to describe the defendant's character, "Any man whose wife had eight miscarriages is a brute", where the marital acts of the defendant are not the issue.

Communications between a husband and wife are absolutely privileged. The defense of privilege as to communications between a husband and wife originally was based upon the absurd assertion that they were one. The more sensible view, however, is that the privilege is based upon the character of the relation, which requires complete freedom of communication.

Conditional Privilege

Since errors often arise in the conduct of business, and in common communications between individuals, most relevant defamations which result as part of necessary or usual transactions are protected by a qualified privilege. If a prospective employer inquires of a former employer as to the character of an applicant for a job, then a false statement made by the former employer, without knowledge of its falsity and in good faith, is conditionally privileged. The privilege is conditional in that, if the false statement be made with knowledge that it is false, or for a bad motive, such as retaining the services of the employee, or to prevent him from getting a job, the privilege is destroyed.

The orbit of this conditional privilege is indefinite. It includes communications arising from all usual accepted relations. Included are situations where one defends one's own reputation against defamation; then anything relevant will be privileged, if in good faith— even the statement that one's accuser is a liar. Likewise when one is attempting to recover stolen property, or to discover the thief of one's property, or to collect money, or to protest against the mismanagement of a concern in which one has a financial interest, or is warning one's servants against improper conduct with those with whom they come in contact, one is protected by this conditional privilege exempting from liability for related defamation.

Also he who volunteers statements, as a good samaritan, to protect others or the public interest, is granted this conditional privilege. One who communicates with the authorities, for the prevention or detection of a crime or concerning the misconduct of public officials, is granted a conditional privilege. Many states, however, limit this privilege, in the protection of the public interest, to expressions of opinion and do not permit false statements of fact.

Usually the right of fair comment, or criticism on matters of public interest, is viewed as a privilege—conditional and limited. The more illuminating view, however, is one which holds that greater latitude is given in distinguishing an opinion, as distinct from a misstatement of fact, where the publication involves matters of public concern and value. This aspect has been noted in Section 29.

Newspapers that report legislative or judicial proceedings are granted a qualified privilege, provided the report be fair and accurate and not accompanied with headlines which do not fairly indicate the substance of the report.

The defense of conditional privilege, in its application, however, often proves to be slippery. It is lost if the means used to communicate the information are not reasonable and proper, or if the publisher be motivated by the desire to injure, or if the publisher cunningly seeks to profit personally.

38. DAMAGES

The measure of damages in defamation is solely for the jury to determine. If the jury fixes an unreasonable and extravagant amount, however, the judge may set aside the verdict unless a smaller amount of damages be accepted by the claimant. In fixing the damages and calculating their extent the jury may go beyond the financial injury and beyond the damage to the complainant's standing in the community; it may allow compensation for mental suffering caused by reason of the defamation, even though no physical injury results from such mental suffering. This rule is more generous than that which usually is applied in personal-injury actions. It is not clearly applied in invasions of privacy.

Exemplary or punitive damages are usually asked for by complainants, but seldom allowed. As to publishers of newspapers, books, and periodicals, and also as to radio and television broadcasters, punitive damages are almost a negligible risk. Punitive damages are not granted unless the publisher or station clearly has been motivated by malice or knows of the falsity thereof, or otherwise participates therein. Ignorance of the falsity precludes punitive damages, in the absence of malice.

A prompt retraction of a libelous statement, after discovery that it was false, can be submitted to the jury in mitigation of the damages. So likewise, evidence that the publisher acted with proper motives and a belief in the truth thereof. The test here is how far the jury will believe the publisher of the libel. Also the bad reputation of the complainant may be considered by the jury, to establish that the defamation did not result in much damage, and that the amount should be fixed accordingly. But the bad reputation of the complainant does not prevent his going to the jury.

Though substantial damages are allowed for defamation, the courts generally will not prevent, by issuing an injunction, the spreading of defamation. The fear of judicial censorship of freedom of speech intervenes. In the case of the unauthorized biography of Dr. Serge Koussevitzky, the court denied relief as to privacy, on the ground that a biography of a public artistic figure was not an invasion of privacy. (See Section 12.) When Dr. Koussevitzky asserted that many of the statements in the biography were defamatory and asked for an injunction against publication, the court denied that relief on medieval precedents saying: [66]

The present law of this State, however, is conclusive to the effect that a court of equity will not restrain the publication of a libel even though the alleged wrongdoer may be financially irresponsible. This doctrine is very old, and it goes back, in this State, to the leading case of Brandreth v. Lance [8 Paige Ch. 24 (1839)]. It has been criticized as archaic and outmoded; it results, it is urged, in a situation where a man's reputation lies at the mercy of the profligacy of others; that libelous imputations leave a stain which no after-repudiation can wipe out; and that "the traditional doctrine puts anyone's business at the mercy of any insolvent malicious defamer who has sufficient imagination to lay out a skillful campaign of extortion." * * *
Whatever the basis of the ancient doctrine may have been—whether it originated from any valid, reasoned conviction or from historical accidents of practice and procedure—it is deeply ingrained in our law.

Thus, though defamation involves a vital human right more important today than ever before, unfortunately the law refuses to modernize itself in this field. An able legal writer has well said: [67]

It must be confessed at the beginning that there is a great deal of the law of defamation which makes no sense. It contains anomalies and absurdities for which no legal writer ever has had a kind word, and it is a curious compound of a strict liability imposed upon innocent defendants, as rigid and extreme as anything found in the law, with a blind and almost perverse refusal to compensate the plaintiff for a real and very serious harm.

PART THREE

Copyright

VI

What Is a Copyright?

39. COPYRIGHT DEFINED

A COPYRIGHT is the right not to have one's mental work, as expressed in written or other objective form, copied or commercially used by another. It exists separate from the ownership of the tangible physical paper, or other medium, in which the intellectual labor has been set down.

The oldest and most common medium whereunder a copyright arises is a manuscript. The copyright in a manuscript is distinct from the property right in the paper and ink. It is entirely an intangible, law-made right. It assures to the author the exclusive control over and profit from any of the possible ways of expression and use of his intellectual labor as set down in his manuscript. This monopoly includes copying and transformations of his expression into other forms. It covers not only printing but also all changes into publication or use from the original form, such as a stage play, television, radio, or motion picture, and any new and now unknown device of expression created by tomorrow's inventions.

Copyrights thus originate from a fluid concept. They fall into three classes: common-law, statutory, and international. The similar purpose of all three kinds of copyright is to protect in the full fruits of the creation those who write manuscripts or express their intellectual labor in any other tangible form, also to protect those who buy and thereafter deal in, disseminate, or publish such intellectual creations. Since these varied forms of use are many and intertwined, and ever enlarging, a copyright is in reality a *bundle* of rights—to use Augustine Birrell's apt Victorian description.

For example, an author may lose a manuscript, or give it to another for reading, or other special use, without intending thereby to lose his exclusive control of the right of copying or publishing or otherwise using it. Whether he retains or gives up possession of his manuscript, his common-law copyright protects him, and does so more adequately than can the ownership of the manuscript itself as a piece of tangible paper as property.

For a copyright has always been and is conceived as a non-physical right entirely apart and distinct from the paper, writing, or other object which it protects. The drafter of our present Statute covering copyrights took time so to specify in its Section 27:

> The copyright is distinct from the property in the material object copyrighted, and the sale or conveyance, by gift or otherwise, of the material object shall not of itself constitute a transfer of the copyright, nor shall the assignment of the copyright constitute a transfer of the title to the material object; but nothing in this title shall be deemed to forbid, prevent, or restrict the transfer of any copy of a copyrighted work the possession of which has been lawfully obtained.

Recently a collector bought the manuscript of an unpublished story written by Mark Twain. The collector decided to publish it. The heirs of Mark Twain objected, because Mark Twain had concluded that the story wasn't finished or good enough to be published. His heirs still honored Mark Twain's wishes. The court held [1] that though the collector had gotten good title to the manuscript he had not thereby obtained the right to publish it. Ordinarily the sale of a manuscript or painting by an author or artist, without expressly reserving the copyright, impliedly includes and conveys the right of publication or copying.[2] A prudent author or artist therefore should cover that point carefully in writing when he disposes of his manuscript or painting. He should specify which of his bundle of rights he wants to retain. In the Mark Twain case under discussion, though no specification was made, the court held that the facts did not show that Mark Twain or his heirs had sold, or intended to sell, their common-law copyright. The collector therefore had the right to keep the manuscript forever, but never to publish it.

The sale of a printed book, if a statutory copyright be taken out, gives the purchaser the right to read it, but not to copy it or to turn it into a stage play or radio or television drama. For the author (or his publisher) after the sale still retains the statutory copyright as to all the other uses and possible transformations included in the bundle. Statutory copyrights are of greater value and use than common-law copyrights because statutory copyrights more adequately protect the bundle of rights and uses. Statutory copyrights arise when the author (or another, owning the created work) elects to take the protection of the copyright statute. Then a common-law copyright comes to an end. The common-law copyright also is destroyed by publication without obtaining a statutory copyright. This technicality is fully discussed later. (See Chapter IX.)

40. COMMON-LAW COPYRIGHTS ARE AUTOMATIC

Common-law copyrights today, though not as useful as statutory copyrights, still are very important. They are automatically created and automatically lost. They exist in every manuscript or other form of expression, such as a painting, work of art, or letter, automatically upon creation and without any required act or formality. They antedate copyright statutes. The holder of a common-law copyright, so soon as he sets down his expression, has this common-law copyright though he never heard of its existence. It can endure forever. But when the holder takes out a statutory, formality-created copyright, or publishes his manuscript without obtaining a statutory copyright, or publishes it and tries but fails to conform to the formalities of obtaining a statutory copyright, he destroys and ends forever his common-law copyright, even though he doesn't so intend or desire. Such are the law's arbitrary dictates.

The "great divide" separating common-law from statutory copyrights is the act of publication or of obtaining a statutory copyright. Publication or statutory registration destroys a common-law copyright. A statutory copyright must be obtained on publication. Otherwise the work is in the public domain and can be copied and used freely by anyone.

What constitutes "publication", a most important aspect of the "bundle of rights", is set forth precisely in Chapter IX.

41. COPYRIGHTS ARE MODERN

Copyrights, as bundles of rights, came into importance with the invention of printing. They are in essence modern and ever-enlarging rights. The coverage of a statutory or common-law copyright extends over each new invention or use that may be devised after creation of the work, and thus into the furthest corners of the entertainment industry. Motion pictures, the radio, and television have added new ways of use, but are all subject to every aspect of copyright law as much as is the older use of printing. These newer uses were unknown in 1909, when the present Copyright Statute of the United States was enacted. But the courts today subject all these varied uses to every provision of the earlier statute. And running through all the new controversies and new forms of use runs the same basic concept: a copyright is the right of the copyright proprietor not to have the expression of his intellectual labor copied or commercially used without his consent.

Before the invention of printing, authors needed only limited protection. Thus judge-made nonstatutory common-law copyrights were adequate. Copying of manuscripts by hand was a laborious way of reproduction and accordingly few problems of protection arose. In 1710, in the reign of Queen Anne, Parliament enacted the first copyright statute—the famous Statute of Anne. This obscure statute started much of the lawyer's hairsplitting about copyright technicalities which has continued down to date. Copyright statutes, including the present United States Copyright Statute of 1909, seem fated ever to be unskillfully written. But common sense and accurate statement can usually prevail as to the bundle of rights called copyrights.

42. THE THREE FORMS OF COPYRIGHT

The Statute of Anne and subsequent United States statutes have split copyrights within the United States into two kinds of domestic copyrights: (a) *common-law* copyrights, existing before the enactment of the Statute of Anne and United States copyright statutes (and in the United States after the enactment of the Copyright Statute of 1909 but only before publication or copyright registration); (b) another and different copyright created by the Copyright Statute enacted in 1909 by Congress. This statute for brevity is called the Copyright Statute and is cited as "C.S." It is officially codified as, and called, "Title 17, United States Code." It is printed in this book as Appendix B.

The two forms of copyright—common-law and statutory— never can exist simultaneously. Publication and registration under the Copyright Statute separate their existence.

This odd, logically unnecessary conclusion was reached by the House of Lords soon after the enactment of the Statute of Anne, in a hotly controverted, long, and labored decision.[3] The Supreme Court of the United States has made the holding of the English judges the law of this country.[4] Many able judges and lawyers have argued that this judicial ruling, that a common-law perpetual copyright is destroyed and ended forever if the author publishes his work, or if he takes out a statutory copyright, is erroneous. They insist that it is unfair to authors. The reasons, as set forth by Drone, our ablest United States writer on copyrights, are persuasive but unimportant today. For the rule now is categorical. The author must choose between a common-law and a statutory copyright. He can't have both.

In England, however, such common-law copyrights are expressly abolished and protection equal to a common-law copyright is granted by a statutory copyright. (Copyright Act of England, 1911, 1 & 2 Geo. 5, Chap. 46, Sec. 31.)

Today in the United States, statutory copyrights are the more important of the two forms of copyright.

43. COPYRIGHTS BY TREATY *

Copyright protection abroad is obtained by United States nationals under three multilateral treaties, affording what are called *international copyrights:* (1) the Universal Copyright Convention of 1955 (U.C.C.), to which the United States and eighteen other nations had adhered by June, 1956; (2) the Berne Convention, to which the United States has not adhered although most other civilized nations have; (3) the two Pan-American Conventions. Under United States copyright legislation pursuant to the U.C.C., certain formalities are relaxed for nationals of alien sovereignties adhering to it; it is no longer required that their books in the English language be printed in the United States; they need no longer obtain ad interim copyrights; and the five-year term of ad interim copyrights obtained prior to 1955 is automatically ex-

* See Section 83 in Chapter XII, concerning copyright treaties.

tended to twenty-eight years from the date of first publication abroad. But the U.C.C. does not end the need for United States nationals to obtain protection under the Berne Convention "via the back door."

44. LETTERS AND PHOTOGRAPHS

Letters

In protecting rights in letters, common-law copyrights still are the essential means. When one writes a letter, whether one be famous or humdrum, the person to whom one addresses and sends the letter becomes the owner thereof, i.e. of the manuscript and the paper and ink used. But, though the sender can't require the recipient to give the letter back to him, the recipient can't publish it without the sender's consent. The still-ruling decision so holding is that of Justice Story as to Washington's letters.[5] He who writes a letter—brilliant or pedestrian—retains the common-law copyright therein even after he mails it.[6] If the sender be an official and the letter be sent in an official capacity it is a public document in which there can be no copyright.[7] Then the recipient or anyone else can freely use and republish it. The government can publish or withhold unpublished official letters of any official without the sender's consent.[8]

But otherwise, no matter how obscure the writer of a letter may be, the common-law copyright belongs to him and his heirs, not to the recipient or to the public. The writer of a letter can publish it without the consent of the recipient, who has the right to retain it.[9] Some hold the mistaken view that the consent of a recipient of a letter is necessary before publication; the courts do not so hold. Of course anything defamatory in a published letter is at the sender's risk on publication. In a decision involving a group of Mary Baker Eddy's letters the Supreme Court of Massachusetts,[10] in an exhaustive opinion, followed the above rulings and added that the writer of a letter can require the recipient to permit copies thereof to be made by and for a sender. Unlike other property, copyright in letters cannot be levied on, or seized, by creditors or by a trustee in bankruptcy, and on death of the writer copyright passes to his heirs,[11] because of the personal nature of letters, analogous to privacy rights.

Photographs

When you go to a photographer to have your picture taken, the photographer is your employee for hire. Aside from the sweeping right of privacy as to pictures (see Chapter II), you own and control the negative and any prints made therefrom.[12] The photographer by custom may display it in his shop as an example of his excellent work—until you object. But unless you expressly consent, he cannot sell it for advertising or for any use. Though the law of common-law copyright is not expressly applied to photographs, the analogy between photographs and other created objects to which common-law copyright does apply has shaped the law. If the photographer is not hired and paid by you, but takes your picture as a photographic study, or for his own commercial purposes *with* your consent, then he, as the creator, can copyright or sell the picture,[13] unless you expressly stipulate otherwise or unless a right of privacy can be spelled out from the special circumstances involved.

Clearance of Photographs

The clearing of photographs for publication requires detail care because of the several rights that may be involved: (1) privacy; (2) common-law or statutory copyright in the photograph; (3) legal ownership of the common-law or statutory copyright by others than the ostensible possessor thereof.

If any recognizable individual appears in the photograph, it is necessary to make certain that the privacy rights of such individual will not be invaded by publication. If the photograph constitutes news reporting of a public event, such as an accident, a parade, a demonstration of athletic skill, or a public contest, the news-reporting right makes it unnecessary to get the consent of such bystanders. But if the photograph is merely of a street, or a scene not the place of any public event, the consent of recognizable bystanders is probably required because the news-reporting involved in a merely illustrative scene is remote. Pictures of public characters, such as public office holders, or those seeking office, entertainers, artists, actors, or public athletes of any kind, may be used freely without danger of privacy invasion if the photographs are used in reference to news reporting or public comment and do not involve aspects of advertising or private trade.

As to copyright, if the negative or the copy thereof involved does not bear the copyright notice, it is safe to assume there is no statutory copyright thereon.[13a] If such a photograph has been previously published or commercially sold, it is safe to act on the basis that the common-law copyright likewise has been destroyed.[13b] Otherwise care must be taken to ascertain who owns the copyright, common-law or statutory, and to obtain such copyright proprietor's consent. In the case of a statutory copyright, reliance can not be had solely upon the copyright certificate. There is always the possibility that the statutory copyright has been assigned, and to be absolutely certain a check must be made in the Copyright Office where such assignments are recorded.[13c] In the absence of such a record, the holder of a statutory copyright can be assumed to be the person in whose name the copyright certificate was issued.

As to the common-law copyright in photographs, it is necessary to make certain who is, in equity and in law, the owner thereof. The owner is not necessarily the photographer who made the photograph and who asserts title thereto. If he were a photographer for hire, he would not be the owner in fact of the common-law copyright therein; that would be held by the person by whom he was hired. The consent of such person must be obtained. In the case of photographs of animals this consent is important, for if the owner of the animal employs a photographer to make its picture the owner of the animal has the sole right to consent to the use of the picture.

Mere possession of the negative or photograph is not adequate proof of the ownership of the rights therein. Just as in the purchase of an automobile from a person who has possession, proof that title is held by the person in possession is advisable.

45. VITALITY OF COMMON-LAW COPYRIGHTS

The concept of a common-law copyright is still expanding. That concept was urged by Justice Brandeis (see Section 4) as the origin for the new right of privacy. And just as common-law copyrights are recognized to be property, though of an intangible nature, so the same view of privacy rights, as having property aspects in personality, is now emerging. Also, the analogy to common-law copyright in other creations favors recognition of created publicity also as having property aspects in situations where unfair competition is asserted. Just as an objectively expressed literary work is protected as property, so also created publicity, if such publicity is adduced into a definite form, is being protected. But the decisions are still vague on this aspect, and the theoretical bases of rulings as to unfair use of publicity as unfair competition have not yet become definitive. Yet such a concept is the clearest explanation of several decisions protecting rights in publicity. (See Section 165.)

Ideas, not of a literary nature, but as business plans, or as advertising or as selling, originations and plans, are now protected (see Section 170) by an unphrased analogy to the theory of common-law copyrights. First, such business ideas must be definitively set down, if not in the form of a manuscript then by resolution of the elements into specific and detailed data and forms. Second, they must be new and novel, a requirement akin to the requisites in patents. Then the courts will protect such a commercial idea. Here the impact of the concept of common-law copyright is definite, though as yet unphrased.

Despite the modern skill of drafting revealed in the British Copyright Act and in the copyright acts of Continental European countries, as contrasted to our United States Copyright Statute, British and European statutory protection is inferior to that of the United States as to common-law copyrights. Europe generally, like England, has abolished nonstatutory common-law copyrights. (See Chapter XII, Section 88.) The author's rights in unpublished works are preserved as an automatic statutory copyright. No formal act of the creator is required. But both in England and under the Berne Convention (see Section 83) the statutory right in an unpublished work is granted only to an author who is a citizen of (or to an alien if he be a resident of) the country wherein he claims a statutory copyright at the time of creating the unpublished work.

As to published works of resident aliens, no difficulties arise in foreign countries. The date of publication makes it possible to prove fairly easily, under the British and Continental European statutes, whether the alien author was a resident in the particular country at the time of publication of the work as to which he claims a statutory copyright. But the date of creation of an unpublished work is often difficult to establish. In England and on the continent of Europe, the question arises as to whether or not an alien author, claiming a statutory copyright in an unpublished work, was a resident of the country, under whose statute he claims a statutory copyright, at the date of the creation thereof.

Such difficulties do not arise in respect to the protection of common-law copyrights under the United States law. In the United States a statutory copyright can be obtained by United States citizens, or by aliens resident in the United States, or by subjects of countries that grant copyright protection to United States nationals, though such subjects are not resident in the United States. (See Chapter VIII, Section 58.) The same three classes of creators (including foreigners of most nations, never resident in the United States) are automatically granted a United States common-law copyright in their unpublished works [14] without any act on their part. Thus the date of creation of an unpublished work is not important in establishing a United States common-law copyright under the theory established in this country.

The granting by the United States of common-law copyrights to alien nonresident authors is thus much more liberal and much more satisfactory than the analogous practice of England or Europe. An English author of an unpublished work, denied a common-law copyright in England and limited there to a statutory copyright in his work, still has a common-law copyright in the United States. The liberality involved is of great importance to playwrights. If an English playwright had no such common-law copyright in the United States in his unpublished play, anyone could perform his play "for free" in this country. A United States playwright, not resident abroad, who does not publish his play as a printed work in Canada or England and thus obtain an international copyright, has difficulties in enforcing his performing rights abroad. (See Section 88.)

Common-law copyrights in the United States, in short, are not only valuable and generously granted and expanding in application; they are also persistently vital and markedly viable.

VII

How a Statutory Copyright Is Obtained: Term Duration and Renewals

46. THE COPYRIGHT STATUTE OF 1909

THE PRECISE distinctions between a common-law and a statutory copyright can best be understood after a description of statutory copyrights and the way they are obtained.

Statutory copyrights in the United States, as already noted, must be taken out under the provisions of the Copyright Statute of 1909. This Statute supersedes earlier copyright enactments of Congress, the first of which was passed in 1790. Our newer forms of entertainment—motion pictures, radio, and television—were largely unknown in 1909. Nevertheless the courts hold that they are governed by the rules stated in this 1909 Statute which, except as to minor details, has not been amended since 1909. In consequence, an improved and up-to-date statute is urgently needed. Most of the technicalities as to statutory copyrights arise from the inadequacies of the imperfect and dated Statute of 1909. But conflicts within the entertainment industry have so far frustrated all efforts to get a modern and more adequate statute. Only an optimist can be hopeful that Congress will soon enact one.

47. THE COPYRIGHT CLAUSE IN THE UNITED STATES CONSTITUTION

Exclusive power over United States statutory copyrights is vested in the Federal government, as distinct from the states, under the provisions of Article 1, Section 8, in the Constitution of the United States, which reads:

The Congress shall have power: * * * To promote the Progress of Science and useful Arts, by securing for limited Times to Authors and Inventors the exclusive Right to their respective Writings and Discoveries.

It is suggestive of the difficulties of copyright drafting, which seem the pursuing fate of copyright legislation, that all of the key words used even in this lucid constitutional provision have had to be enlarged as to coverage by the courts through intelligent interpretation and construction. The key words therein are now held to include more than they literally specify. Not only *authors*, but also employers, including corporations, who hire authors, and those who buy from authors the work created, are permitted under the Copyright Statute to obtain copyrights in an author's work in their own names and thus become the copyright proprietors. Also the word "authors" is held to include painters and sculptors, photographers, architects, and compilers of noncreative list material. Not only "writings" but also photographs, motion pictures, maps, paintings, statues, models, and designs for works of art can be copyrighted. Even purely mechanical compilations such as city directories and similar lists and commercial reference books, which one would not ordinarily say "promote the progress of science and *useful arts*", and which involve scant originality, may by judicial construction be validly copyrighted under the Copyright Statute enacted under the Congressional power granted under this copyright clause of the Constitution.

By reason of this constitutional provision, the Federal courts alone have court jurisdiction over statutory copyrights. The states and their state courts still have exclusive court jurisdiction over common-law copyrights, except where diversity of residence by the litigants, in different states, is involved, which diversity of state citizenship confers jurisdiction on the Federal courts under another constitutional clause. International copyrights, in turn, are created solely by formal treaties between the nations adhering thereto, thus requiring international sovereign accord.

48. OBTAINING A STATUTORY COPYRIGHT

An initial, rigid, and most important distinction arises, under the Copyright Statute, when one seeks to obtain a statutory copyright. It causes considerable confusion. This distinction is between:

(a) books, periodicals, and newspapers (and the articles and stories and material printed therein), which in order to be sold to the public and thus profited from, must be printed and copies thereof sold;

(b) plays and lectures, radio and television scripts, musical compositions, and works of art, which can be made public and commercial use thereof had, solely by being performed, delivered, or displayed in public, without the printing and selling of copies.

This rigid distinction is one of the unfortunate technicalities prescribed in the Copyright Statute and must ever be kept in mind.

As to the book and periodical class of works (including newspapers)—(a) above—the Copyright Statute requires the making of copies and the sale or issue thereof to the public, *before* a statutory copyright can be applied for and obtained. (C.S., Section 10, 11, and 13.) While such material is in manuscript form, and before copies are sold to the public, no statutory copyright thereof can be obtained. Many authors are unaware of this rigid prior requisite as to publication, and try to copyright, under the Statute, works in the book and periodical class *before publication*. Their purpose is to protect and prove their priority of creation, but the effort is in vain. How this protection can be obtained before publication is outlined in Chapter XXIV.

As to the unpublished class—(b) above—this procedure of prior printing and publication is not required under the Copyright Statute (Section 12), and a statutory copyright can be had therein *without publication.*

A detailed specification of these works, such as plays, lectures, and works of arts, comprising this unpublished class as distinct from the book and periodical class, appears later in this chapter in Section 52.

49. THE FOUR * ESSENTIAL ACTS

To obtain a statutory copyright in a book, periodical, or newspaper, the following four acts must be done in sequence by the applicant for copyright:

1. The manuscript must first be published, and the printing, binding, and illustration work thereof must be done in the United States. (C.S., Section 16.) By publishing and publication is meant "making public" by the sale, or putting on sale, of copies. Thus in a practical sense, both *printing* and the *selling* of copies, or offering for sale to the public, must be done prior to copyrighting. (C.S., Section 10.) What constitutes publication as to each type of work is further outlined in Chapter IX. Unfortunately the distinctions may be technical and labored. Gratis issuing may be publishing.

2. A copyright notice, simultaneous with the publication and sale of the work, must be put in a specified, prominent place in the book or periodical; in the case of a book, on or on the reverse side of the title page. If this requirement is not precisely performed, including the placing of the notice, no statutory copyright arises and the common-law copyright is ended forever by publication. Then all rights of any kind in the work in the United States are lost forever. (C.S., Sections 10, 19.)

3. Two copies of the printed book must be sent "promptly" after "1" and "2" have been done, but not before, to the Register of Copyrights in Washington, together with the registration form duly filled in, requesting a copyright certificate and accompanied by payment of a small fee to the Register. If a foreign publication one copy only need be sent. (C.S., Section 13.) (As to foreign publication and the obtaining of an international copyright, see Chapter XII.)

4. An affidavit under oath must also be sent to the Register at the same time as the registration form and the deposit copies, to prove

---

* The requirements of "1" as to printing in the United States, and of "3" and "4" are now deleted to conform to the U.C.C., but *only as to nationals* of foreign nations adhering to the U.C.C.; also, as to such nationals *only*, the requisites of "2" (the copyright notice) are reduced. As to all other nationals, including U.S. nationals, the technicalities of the Four Essential Acts are still in full effect. See Section 83.

that the book meets the requirements of the "manufacturing clause" (C.S., Sections 16 and 209). A book or periodical, to meet these requirements, must both have its text and illustrations printed and bound entirely in the United States. But this requirement is limited to books and periodicals in English, and thus does not apply to such other works as published plays, musical compositions, works in languages other than English, and foreign-printed works in English registered for ad interim copyright, which endures only for five years (see Chapter VIII). As to foreign-language works, the manufacturing clause applies if the author of a book or periodical is either a United States citizen or an alien resident in the United States; [1a] if the author is an alien and domiciled in a foreign country, the manufacturing clause does not apply.

Thereupon a copyright certificate (C.S., Section 31) is issued by the Register and the copyright is completely had by the recipient, who is called, in the awkward words of the Copyright Statute thereafter, "the copyright proprietor." (C.S., Section 19.)

Publication ("1" above) without the copyright notice ("2" above) destroys the common-law copyright and puts the entire work in the public domain in the United States forever.[1] By the phrase "being in the public domain" the law means that everyone forever thereafter is free to copy, use, and profit in any form from the work, without any limitations whatsoever. Unfortunately there are no ways of curing or regaining any rights thus lost.[2]

Details as to compliance with each of these four acts necessary to obtain a statutory copyright follow in Chapter VIII. But a precise notation of the second or unpublished class, i.e. works as to which a statutory copyright can be had without printing and publishing, will be clarifying before these details are noted.

50. WHEN PRINTING AND SALE OF COPIES IS NOT REQUIRED

Works which can be profited from, by permitting public use without printing and publication, can be copyrighted under the Copyright Statute without any printing or publication.

Only one act is required as to this unpublished class: the mailing of an unprinted or manuscript copy, or other legible reproduction thereof even in handwriting, to the Register, with an application duly filled in, plus payment of the small fee. Thereupon a statutory copyright is obtained in such works.

51. REGISTRATION DESTROYS THE COMMON-LAW COPYRIGHT

If a work, having been copyrighted as an unpublished work, is later published, it must be copyrighted again. The Copyright Statute prescribes as to this unpublished class in its Section 12:

* * * But the privilege of registration of copyright secured hereunder shall not exempt the copyright proprietor from the deposit of copies, under sections 13 and 14 of this title, where the work is later reproduced in copies for sale.

Considerable discussion has arisen as to whether registration of a work in the unpublished class with the Copyright Office destroys the common-law copyright. The common-law copyright clearly is destroyed by publication. Is mere registration, i.e. sending a copy to the Copyright Office for registration as an unpublished work under Section 12 (C.S.), publication? The rulings are that registration of an unpublished work with the Copyright Office is not publication; [3] but a high court has ruled that registration of an unpublished work with the Copyright Office, under an application for a statutory copyright, ends and destroys the common-law copyright.[4]

52. THE LIST OF WORKS THAT CAN BE COPYRIGHTED WITHOUT PUBLICATION

The works as to which a statutory copyright can be had without printing and publication—as distinct from books, periodicals, and newspapers, where publication is required before statutory copyrighting—are generally described in Section 12 of the Copyright Statute. But they are not expressly described in the list of "classification of works for registration", thirteen in actual number, set out in Section 5 of the Copyright Statute. That classification is not too specific. The regulations of the Copyright Office, hereinafter set forth, fill that need of concreteness.

Section 12 of the Copyright Statute, the basic general rule, reads:

Copyright may also be had of the works of an author, of which copies are not reproduced for sale, by the deposit, with claim of copyright, of one complete copy of such work if it be a lecture or similar production or a dramatic, musical, or dramatico-musical composition; of a title and description, with one print taken from each scene or act, if the work be a motion-picture photoplay; of a photographic print if the work be a photograph; of a title and description, with not less than two prints taken from different sections of a complete motion picture, if the work be a motion picture other than a photoplay; or of a photograph or other identifying reproduction thereof, if it be a work of art or a plastic work or drawing.

The general terms used in the section above and in Section 5 (C.S.) are amplified and specifically described in the Official Regulations of the Copyright Office, Library of Congress. Since a precise understanding is needed as to what works, unpublished, can be copyrighted under the Copyright Statute, these Official Regulations are clarifying. They read, as to unpublished works that can be copyrighted:

(a) *Lectures* (Form C of the Copyright Office application for copyright). Lectures or similar productions prepared for oral delivery. This class includes unpublished works such as lectures, sermons, addresses, monologs, recording scripts, and scripts for television and radio programs. When these works are published, registration should be made in Class A. (Books and Periodicals.)

(b) *Plays* (Form D). Dramatic and dramatico-musical compositions. This class includes works dramatic in character such as plays, dramatic scripts designed for radio or television broadcast, pantomimes, ballets, musical comedies and operas.

(c) *Music* (Form E). Musical compositions. This class includes all musical compositions (other than dramatico-musical compositions), with or without words, as well as new versions of musical compositions, such as adaptations, arrangements and editings, when such editing is the writing of an author.

(d) *Motion Pictures* (Form L). Motion picture photoplays. This class includes motion pictures, dramatic in character, such as features, serials, animated cartoons, musical plays, and similar productions intended for projection on a screen, or for transmission by television or other means.

(e) *Photographs* (Form K). Photographs. This class includes photographic prints and filmstrips, slide films and individual slides. Photoengravings and other photomechanical reproductions of photographs are registered in Class K on Form K.

(f) *Nondramatic Motion Pictures* (Form L). Motion pictures other than photoplays. This class includes nondramatic motion pictures, such as newsreels, musical shorts, travelogues, educational and vocational guidance films, and similar productions intended for projection on a screen, or for transmission by television or other means.

(g) *Art Creations* (Form G). Works of art—(a) In general. This class includes works of artistic craftsmanship, in so far as their form but not their mechanical or utilitarian aspects are concerned, such as artistic jewelry, enamels, glassware, and tapestries, as well as all works belonging to the fine arts, such as paintings, drawings and sculpture.

In the above Regulations are also included specifications of "published three-dimensional works of art"; "reproductions of works of art"; "drawings of a plastic or a scientific or technical character"; "prints, pictorial illustrations and commercial prints or labels." (The quotations are in each instance from the above Regulations.) These four specialized classes are discussed, together with the peculiar copyright problems they raise, in Chapter XVII. Thus these eleven types of works comprise what are called the "unpublished class".

Most of these works, or copies thereof, falling in this unpublished class can initially or later be published and then copyrighted as published works. They can be thus copyrighted instead of, or after, the copyrighting of them as nonpublished works. But upon subsequent publication the first three of the four essential acts specified in Section 49 above are required: (1) They must be published; (2) the copyright notice must be affixed; (3) new copies must be deposited with the Register. The fourth essential act, the affidavit of printing in the United States, is not required, even as to published plays, also not as to musical compositions. Section 16 of the Copyright Statute limits the United States–printing requisite to books and periodicals, i.e. to classes (a) and (b) specified in Section 5 of the Copyright Statute.

53. WHEN A COMMON-LAW COPYRIGHT
MUST BE RELIED ON

The author or owner of a manuscript for a book or novel, or for a work falling in the book-and-periodical class above noted, and of material used in a periodical, such as short stories, poems, and factual or critical articles (not in the literary form of a lecture, play, radio or television script, or other work in the unpublished class), cannot obtain a statutory copyright before printing and publication thereof. Authors, thus unable to publish and copyright their works, must rely on their common-law copyright until printing and publication. How they can protect themselves from piracy, during this interim period of hope while soliciting publication, is suggested in Chapter XXIV.

54. DISADVANTAGES OF A COMMON-LAW COPYRIGHT

The disadvantages of a common-law copyright are:

1. It is forever automatically destroyed on any even unintended act of publication. Publication by others than the author, with his express or tacit consent, likewise destroys the common-law copyright. Therefore the common-law copyright owner must know what constitutes publication and never step over the line thereof, or permit anyone so to do, without obtaining a statutory copyright.

2. An author fears he lacks adequate proof of the date and content of his creation in case of an infringement suit. This lack of proof, however, can be taken care of otherwise, as specified in Chapter XXIV.

3. The remedies, particularly as to recovery of minimum damages in case of piracy, are not as adequate in proceedings in a state court brought under a common-law copyright as they are under Federal court procedure enforcing the ample relief and damage provisions of the Copyright Statute.

4. The protection of an unpublished play, if performed or exhibited in foreign countries by a United States author, is difficult. (See Section 88.)

55. ADVANTAGES OF A COMMON-LAW COPYRIGHT

The duration of a common-law copyright is perpetual. A statutory copyright endures only for a limited term: two successive terms of twenty-eight years each, or fifty-six years in all. (See Section 56.) Thus dramatists and composers of operas, many of whom do not care to sell copies of their works, often prefer to rely on the perpetual common-law copyright.

56. TERM DURATION; RENEWALS

The duration, or term, of a statutory copyright in the United States is for twenty-eight years "from the date of first publication". (Section 24, C.S.) The statute does not specify the day when the twenty-eight years begin in the case of unpublished works copyrighted under the statute, for which there is of course no "date of first publication". The courts, however, hold that for such works the twenty-eight years begin on the date of registration.[4]

The first twenty-eight-year term can be renewed and extended for a second twenty-eight years, making fifty-six years in all, if application for renewal is made to the Register within one year before the first term ends. A dead author's "widow, widower, or children," and if they be not living at the time of renewal, then his "executors, or in the absence of a will, his next of kin," can obtain a renewal. (Section 24, C.S.) The Supreme Court has decided that the "or" in the statute means "and" and that the widow and children jointly have (a) the right of renewal and (b) its benefits.[4a] The Court left open for future decision the determination of how the benefits are divided between the two classes. It also ruled that in determining the rights of an illegitimate child under the statute it would follow the applicable state law. Difficult undetermined queries arise where an administrator for an author who leaves a will is appointed on the death of the named executor. The rigidity and imperfect drafting of this clause in the Copyright Statute is unfortunate. The courts enforce the clause with technical exactitude. An employer for hire of an author or of the compiler of a cyclopedic work, as the copyright proprietor, or one who copyrights a posthumous work, has the right to renew and extend the copyright term. If the publisher is the copyright proprietor as the assignee or licensee of the author, which is common, then the author has the right of renewal even though the publisher is the copyright proprietor. (Section 24, C.S.)

If the author so assigns, or holds the copyright in his own name and thus is the copyright proprietor, and if he also expressly conveys to a purchaser or assignee the right of renewal for the second twenty-eight years, the conveyance of the right to renew, however, is viewed by the courts only as the sale of an "expectancy". This limiting word "expectancy" means that, though the sale of the right to renew is validly executed, the assignment of the right of renewal fails and is void if the author dies before the end of the first twenty-eight years of the copyright term. If the assignment is voided by the author's death, then the right to renew passes to and is held solely by the widow or children or next of kin of the author, in strict order of succession, although the author has expressly already conveyed to others his right of renewal of the copyright.[5] But if the author who has sold the right of renewal is living at the end of the first twenty-eight years, then the right of renewal passes to and is owned by his assignee.[6]

This odd and complicated rule, the courts hold, is the intent and effect of Section 24 of the Copyright Statute. It is an interpretation intended to protect the improvident author against himself, as a phase of the author's moral rights. (As to moral and retained rights of the author see Chapter XVIII.) The limitation above noted means that if the author dies before the end of the first twenty-eight years he cannot by his prior conveyance deprive his widow and children of their "expectancy" of the right of renewal. He can do so only if he is alive at the end of the first twenty-eight years. This right of renewal is a very valuable right in the case of successful works, particularly highly popular songs and music. Publishers get around this limitation designed to protect the author by having the author's wife and children convey their expectancy at the same time when they buy the copyright from the author. Such an assignment of the widow's expectancy, by the wife or children of the author, is valid if there is independent consideration therefor. The courts scrutinize the adequacy of the consideration involved.[7] The wife and children should remember that their signing of the conveyance granting rights of renewal is not a mere formality. They are selling away a new and perhaps valuable right and should expect separate compensation therefor, or not sign.

In most European countries, and under international copyrights under the Treaty of Berne, copyrights endure during the life of the author plus fifty years after his death. In a few foreign countries the period of fifty years after the death of the author is shortened.

As before noted, common-law copyrights run on forever.

After a statutory copyright is obtained the chief thing to remember is never to publish or permit publication of the copyrighted work without the copyright notice. Publication without a copyright notice by an assignee or another engaged in a joint enterprise with the copyright proprietor is fatal. The definition of a "joint enterprise" is not too clear in the law. (See Chapter VIII.) Unfortunately the requirement of a copyright notice on publication is a technical phase of copyrights upon which the courts are most insistent and inflexible. The statutory requirements must be categorically and explicitly and rigidly adhered to or else the copyright is lost in toto. The Copyright Statute's Section 21 contains a clause preventing loss of copyright where the copyright notice is omitted "by accident or mistake * * * ," but this saving clause is not liberally construed by the courts. (See Section 57B.)

——— VIII ———

Details in Statutory Copyrighting;
Nationality; Ad Interim Copyrights

---

57. THE FOUR ESSENTIAL ACTS IN COPYRIGHTING
    ON PUBLICATION, AS ALTERED BY
    THE UNIVERSAL COPYRIGHT CONVENTION

VARIOUS details must be noted as to the four acts essential to obtaining a statutory copyright, noted in Chapter VII, Section 49.

a. Copyright Notice

The notice of copyright on a published work requires technical precision both as to form and placing. As to form, the Copyright Statute specifies:

[Section 19] The notice of copyright * * * shall consist either of the word "Copyright" or the abbreviation "Copr.", accompanied by the name of the copyright proprietor, and if the work be a printed literary, musical, or dramatic work, the notice shall include also the year in which the copyright was secured by publication.

Thus the usual form runs: "Copyright, 1951, by John Doe." The "by" is not required.

The place where the copyright notice shall be inserted and appear also is prescribed by the Copyright Statute:

[Section 20] The notice of copyright shall be applied in the case of a book or other printed publications, upon its title page or the page immediately following, or if a periodical either upon the title page or upon the first page of text of each separate number or under the title heading, or if a musical work either upon its title page or the first page of music. One notice of copyright in each volume or in each number of a newspaper or periodical published shall suffice.

97

The amendment to the Copyright Statute enacted in 1954 in order to conform to the requisites of the U.C.C. specifies:

(c) When the Universal Copyright Convention, signed at Geneva on September 6, 1952, shall be in force between the United States of America and the foreign state or nation of which such author is a citizen or subject, or in which the work was first published. Any work to which copyright is extended pursuant to this subsection shall be exempt from the following provisions of this title: * * * and (5) the requirements of sections 19 and 20: *Provided, however,* That such exemptions shall apply only if from the time of first publication all the copies of the work published with the authority of the author or other copyright proprietor shall bear the symbol © accompanied by the name of the copyright proprietor and the year of first publication placed in such manner and location as to give reasonable notice of claim of copyright * * *.

The provisions of this subsection shall not be extended to works of an author who is a citizen of, or domiciled in the United States of America regardless of place of first publication, or to works first published in the United States.

From the above amendment it follows that Sections 19 and 20 of the Copyright Statute specifying the form and placing of the copyright notice are considerably relaxed *only* in favor of nationals of any nation adhering to the U.C.C. (but *not as to nationals of the United States of America* or of nonadhering nations) in the following ways: (a) as to use of © instead of "copyright" as sufficient in *all* instances; (b) the place of insertion of such notice, the requisite being solely of "such manner and location as to give reasonable notice of claim of copyright" being sufficient.

This latter relaxation is of considerable importance. Nationals of the United States of America and of nations not adhering to the U.C.C., however, still must conform to the rigid requirement of form of notice (Section 19) and of placing thereof (Section 20).

In the case of works of art, models, maps, drawings, and photographs, the symbol © can be used, "accompanied by the initials, monogram, mark, or symbol of the copyright proprietor"; his name must then appear, permissibly elsewhere, in the "margin, back, permanent base, or pedestal." (Section 19, C.S.)

These requirements as to the form or the place of the copyright notice are enforced by the courts with rigidly technical and meticulous precision. Careful observance is essential, for they involve the most dangerous technicalities under the Copyright Statute.

Where, for example, the copyright notice in a portfolio book picturing clerical vestments was printed on the *separate* sheet immediately following the title page, the court held that the copyright notice was improperly placed and that the requirements as to copyright notice were not complied with.[1] Thus the portfolio book was not copyrighted and its entire contents were in the public domain in the United States, although otherwise the statute had been complied with. For the court held that the word "page" in the statutory requisite means "one side of a leaf of a book" and that the copyright notice must appear on that leaf. The court added: "Notice on any other page than that indicated by the Statute is ineffective, no matter how prominent, and courts may not dispense with this requirement."

As to periodicals or newspapers, the copyright notice can be "either upon the title page or upon the first page of text of each separate number or under the title heading."

The question often arises as to the position where the copyright notice should be placed when a copyrighted work is quoted from and the quotation extends beyond the scope of fair use and is with the express consent of the copyright proprietor whose work is quoted from. Where should the copyright notice as to the parts quoted from be placed? Clearly upon the reverse side of the title page of the work wherein such quotes are used. The same rule applies to compilations. Thus placing the copyright notice, as to quoted from and used works, at the foot of the page or the end of the chapter wherein quotations appear, is dangerous, though in fact such placing would seem an adequate notice of the copyright claim.

The test that must be applied is that of the classification of the work wherein the quotation, or other use, appears. If the work wherein the quotation appears is a book, the categorical requirement of the Copyright Statute must be conformed to. That requirement demands placing upon the title page or the reverse side thereof. Unfortunately the Copyright Statute provides for no other place, even if so many copyright notices are used that the title page (or its reverse side) is overcrowded. If no space be available thereon, the following page can, it seems, be used with a statement on the title page stipulating incorporation by reference of the following page into the title page. The courts recognize incorporation by reference in documents. This incorporation by reference seems the only way of conforming to the technical requisites of the statute, where space is lacking on the title page or on its reverse side. There are no court rulings on this technical point.

Likewise where the symbol © alone is used on works of art, maps, drawings, photographs, and prints, the © must not be printed so small as to be readable only with the aid of a magnifying glass. If the © can not be read by the naked eye, the copyright notice is defective and the content of the work is in the public domain.[2] Likewise the use of the © instead of "Copyrighted" or "Copr." must be rigidly limited to the works wherein the © is expressly permitted. It was recently held that a panel of prints, as a comic strip telling a story, is a "pictorial illustration", and that the word "copyright" or the letter © "will serve" therefor. The lower court had held use of © only, fatal.[3] But Judge Learned Hand, in reversing for the Appellate Court, indicated a more liberal trend as to the use of the copyright notice both generally and on comic strips.

Such rulings may seem the quintessence of technicality; but they are the law. The statutory requirements as to the copyright notice must be slavishly adhered to.

The copyright notice need not be affixed to works not reproduced for sale and copyrighted under Section 12 of the Copyright Statute.[3a]

b. Error in, or Omission of, the Copyright Notice

Omission or error in the copyright notice (in subsequent copies but not in the first copy), by accident or mistake, where "the copyright proprietor has sought to comply with the provisions * * * with respect to notice", will not invalidate the copyright. (Section 21, C.S.) But recovery can not be had against an infringer who had no actual notice of the copyright. Also an innocent infringer must be reimbursed for his outlay if his copies can not be used after he discovers the inadvertent error as to notice of the copyright proprietor. (Section 21, C.S.)

This saving provision applies only to copies sold and published after the first copy, not as to the first published copies by which copyright is obtained.[4] If on the first copies the error originates and occurs, then the error is fatal. Also, where an error in a copyright notice is one as to the year of first publication, if a later year is used than the actual year of publication, the error is fatal, and is not saved by Section 21, C.S., as above. The reason which impelled the courts to reach this harsh conclusion is that by falsely using a later year the copyright proprietor may be seeking to get an additional period for his copyright beyond the statutory term. That possible claim makes the error fatal.[5] If he claims in his copyright notice an earlier year than first publication, and thus shortens his copyright term, the error is not fatal.

c. Copies Deposited

The Statute (Section 13, C.S.) requires deposit with the Register, in the case of a published work, of:

1. Two copies "of the best edition thereof then published."

2. But if the work be published in a foreign country by an author who is a citizen thereof and not of the United States, only one copy need be deposited. In the case of an ad interim copyright, a second copy can be deposited in lieu of the $4 copyright fee. (See Section 215, C.S.)

3. If the author of a contribution published in a periodical seeks separate copyright registration of the article, one copy of the article must be deposited in its entirety.

4. If of a work "not reproduced in copies for sale" (i.e. under C.S. Section 12, being the class called unpublished works as noted in Section 52 of this book), one "copy, print, photograph", or other identifying reproduction must be deposited.

By amendment to the Copyright Statute approved March 29, 1956, the following was inserted in Section 13 covering the deposit of works classified in Section 5 as (g), (h), (i), and (k):

* * * or if the work belongs to a class specified in subsections (g), (h), (i) or (k) of section 5 or this title, and if the Register of Copyrights determines that it is impracticable to deposit copies because of their size, weight, fragility, or monetary value he may permit the deposit of photographs or other identifying reproductions in lieu of copies of the work as published under such rules and regulations as he may prescribe with the approval of the Librarian of Congress; * * *

Thus as to the above noted artistic works the Register of Copyrights may permit deposit of substitutes instead of actual works.

d. Time of Deposit

The Statute says the depositing shall be done "promptly". (Section 13, C.S.) Mailing to the Register with a proper address is sufficient. If the Register does not receive the mailed copy, the applicant has nevertheless complied with the requirement.[6] Postage costs need not be affixed; the postmaster must give a receipt for copies deposited for mailing. (Section 15, C.S.)

What does the word "promptly", as used in the Statute, mean? The courts have defined it. The Copyright Statute, Section 13, provides that an action to enforce a statutory copyright can not be brought until such "deposit of copies." The Supreme Court has held that, depositing and registration having been done fourteen months after first publication, with the copyright notice affixed, the performance is "prompt" enough and a suit can be maintained at that late date.[7] So the actual depositing can safely be done within fourteen months after publication; but a suit can't be brought without first depositing copies. What constitutes a fatal delay, if longer than fourteen months, has not yet been decided.

The Register can by notice demand deposit of copies if none have been deposited, and a claimant not so complying must pay $100 and costs. Failure to comply also means the voiding of the copyright. (Section 14, C.S.)

In 1954 a new section was added at the end of the Copyright Statute as Section 216 which reads as follows:

[Section 216] When the day for taking action falls on Saturday, Sunday, or a holiday.

When the last day for making any deposit or application, or for paying any fee, or for delivering any other material to the Copyright Office falls on Saturday, Sunday, or a holiday within the District of Columbia, such action may be taken on the next succeeding business day.

SEC. 2. The table of contents of chapter 3 of title 17 of the United States Code is amended by adding at the end thereof "216. When the day for taking action falls on Saturday, Sunday, or a holiday."

e. Affidavit of Printing in United States

The requirement of printing in the United States is the most unfortunate requirement in the Statute. It makes it impossible for this country to become a member of international copyright treaties (the Convention of Berne, as amended, also called the Convention of Rome; see Chapter XII). Most other nations do not impose this condition of local printing as to copyright of books published within their territory by anyone. Foreign nations, because of this requirement preventing copyrighting in the United States of books in English printed outside the United States, refuse to permit automatic international copyrights to arise within their territories by and on publication in the United States. Thus to get an international copyright under the Convention of Berne, publication must be made within a nation that is a member of the Convention, *simultaneously* with the first United States publication. The procedure needed and what "simultaneously" means are specified in Chapter XII.

The requirement of United States printing (Section 16, C.S.) expressly applies only to those classifications of copyrightable works itemized in C.S. Section 5 as: "(a) books * * * (b) periodicals * * * " No other of the thirteen classes of the works itemized in Section 5 of the C.S. need be printed or made in the United States.

Also exempted from the requirement of United States printing are the original texts of books "of foreign origin in a language other than English". Books in Braille for the blind are exempted.

The requirement as to printing includes binding, illustrations, and all forms of reproduction by typesetting machines, plates, lithographic process, or photoengraving. (Section 16, C.S.) If other later known ways of copying be invented, the requirement does not apply.[8]

The affidavit of United States printing (a Copyright Office form) requires a statement also of the place where and the establishment in which the manufacturing was done, and the date of printing or publication. (Section 17, C.S.) The affidavit must be by an individual; if the copyright applicant be a corporation, then by an individual as an officer or agent and on behalf of the corporation.

Books printed abroad but eligible for copyright under the Universal Copyright Convention do not require this affidavit.

58. NATIONALITY

All United States citizens, and aliens *who are living in the United States at the time of first publication,* can obtain a copyright under the Copyright Statute. (Section 9, C.S.) So also can citizens (not residing in the United States) of those foreign countries which grant to citizens of the United States the benefit of copyright within their territories on United States works on substantially the same basis as to their own citizens. Those nations which so grant rights to United States citizens are determined from time to time by the proclamation of the President of the United States. Most foreign countries, except the Union of Soviet Socialist Republics and perhaps other "Iron Curtain" countries, grant such reciprocal rights. Foreign countries also have no printing requirements. A detailed check-up of the President's proclamations is desirable whenever a foreigner not domiciled in the United States seeks a copyright.

Assignees and heirs and successors of authors may obtain a copyright. Thus an author's employer, whether corporate or individual, can copyright the work. (C.S., Section 26.) The requirements as to citizenship or domicile, or reciprocal-grant, apply to copyright privilege in the case of assignees, employers, and heirs.

Hitler, as an author, raised an interesting query as to the requisite nationality of an author under our copyright statute. The United States copyright in his *Mein Kampf* was assailed because Hitler, before he became a citizen of Germany, was a stateless person after he refused to serve in the Austrian army and before he acquired German citizenship. *Mein Kampf* was written in that interim. But a court held that a stateless person could obtain a United States copyright, also that the possession of the manuscript by the German assignor to the United States copyright proprietor was sufficient proof of Hitler's transfer of the copyright to the German assignor.[9]

59. AD INTERIM COPYRIGHTS

Ad interim copyrights have lost their importance. Interim copyrights endure for only five years (unless extended by U.S. printing under Section 23, C.S.). Under the U.C.C. the copyright term for U.C.C. nationals is twenty-eight years "from date of first publication abroad". Also the term of an ad interim copyright obtained by U.C.C. nationals prior to the U.C.C. is automatically extended to twenty-eight years. Nationals of nations not so adhering to the U.C.C., however, must still rely on ad interim copyrights. Except as to U.C.C. nationals, this ad interim copyright is obtained by making an application therefor and depositing a copy with the Register not later than *six months* after first publication in a foreign territory. No fee need be paid to the Copyright Office. (Section 215, C.S.)

The above provisions for ad interim copyrights are according to Section 22 of the Copyright State, providing for ad interim copyrights, as amended on June 3, 1949.[10] These amendments radically alter the previous provisions applying to ad interim copyrights. The provisions of Section 22 (old Section 21) covering ad interim copyrights previously had provided that in the case of a book or periodical first published abroad in the English language, an application could be made not later than sixty days after publication for an ad interim copyright which endured for four months after the deposit of a copy in the Copyright Office. Because of war conditions, making the short time requirements difficult to comply with, Congress on September 25, 1941, enacted a statute empowering the President by proclamation to extend and grant a moratorium on the above sixty-day and four-month periods respectively. On March 14, 1944, President Roosevelt issued such a proclamation (Proclamation No. 2608). Under this proclamation the time for applying for an ad interim copyright (sixty days) and the time within which the printing had to be done in the United States before the expiration of the ad interim copyright (four months) was indefinitely extended.

All these provisions have since been changed. In June 1949 Congress amended Sections 16, 22, and 107 of the Copyright Statute, making four important alterations therein: (1) Under the amendatory statute of 1949 the period within which an application can be made for an ad interim copyright on a book first published abroad in the English language is extended to six months (instead of sixty days) after its publication abroad. The term of such ad interim copyright is extended to five years (instead of four months). (2) A new addition to Section 16 of the Copyright Statute provides that 1500 copies of each such book or periodical printed abroad in the English language may be imported into the United States within five years after first publication in a foreign state or nation. (3) But such books so imported under the ad interim copyright must contain the copyright notice as above discussed and such permission to import such books prevails only if the ad interim copyright has been taken out in the United States. This notice requirement is a change from the previous provisions, which did not require a copyright notice on books and periodicals copyrighted under the ad interim copyright and under which, indeed, the insertion of such copyright notice in such books registered under an ad interim copyright prevented their importation. Now, however, the copyright notice must be inserted. (4) By proclamation of President Truman signed on May 21, 1950,[11] effective December 29, 1950, the earlier proclamation of President Roosevelt, No. 2608, of March 14, 1944, above discussed, was ended. Thus the moratorium placed upon ad interim copyrights came to an end as of December 29, 1950, and the more liberal 1949 statutory provisions as to ad interim copyrights, above noted, alone protect foreign authors and publishers of books and periodicals in English.

By amendment to Section 22 the words "or periodical" were added, conforming to the Copyright Office interpretation that the ad interim provisions apply to periodicals also. Also, as a minor appeasement of foreign resentment against the United States printing requirements, Section 215 of the Copyright Statute was amended to dispense with the $4.00 Copyright Office fee for each ad interim copyright. Only a second copy of the book so registered and a catalogue card in the form desired by the Copyright Office need be supplied in lieu of the $4.00 fee for ad interim copyright.

It is interesting to note that the Senate Committee in its report on these amendments noted that of 14,000 books published in 1948 in English abroad, largely in England, only 139 had been followed by ad interim copyrights in the United States.[12]

Before five years have elapsed the proprietor of an ad interim copyright may print the book in the United States and otherwise comply with the four essential acts noted in Chapter VII. Thereupon he obtains a copyright on such work (Section 23, C.S.) for the full remaining term.[12a] Otherwise, after the five years, the work is in the public domain in, and all rights are lost in, the United States.

60. FIRST PUBLICATION OUTSIDE OF THE UNITED STATES

What if a work in English is first published outside of the United States, and long afterwards the effort is made to secure a United States statutory copyright as a published work on the basis of the publication abroad? The query has often been raised by text writers. It presents many technical thorns. The importance of the technical thorns, in the advancement of international copyrights (see Chapter XII), is striking.

A recent decision,[13] by an able judge, Jerome N. Frank, an author in his own right and keenly aware of the realities of copyright protection, has cut away some of these thorns. His reasoning followed an earlier suggestive decision. A vigorous opinion in the same case, by another able judge, Charles E. Clark, however, indicates that the query has not been finally answered.

The query was formulated by Judge Frank's decision in a majority ruling, as to a song in Hungarian first published in Hungary in 1935 with a defective copyright notice, but copyrighted validly (so the court assumed) as to Hungary under the Hungarian copyright statute. Songs or works in a foreign language need not be printed in the United States (see Section 16, C.S.; see also Section 57e herein). In 1936 copyright registration of the song as a published work was completed under Section 10 of the Copyright Statute. A Hungarian national, by Presidential proclamation under Section 9 of the Copyright Statute, was entitled in 1936 to reciprocal United States copyright protection.

The court held that here the United States copyright was valid under the later registration in the United States in 1936 on the basis of the first publication in Hungary in 1935. The court further held that the first publication in Hungary did not require any copyright notice. The situation here was complicated, as to the lack of a copyright notice on the first publication in Hungary, because the copyright notice actually used when the song was published in Hungary was fatally defective under the United States law. For the year specified in the Hungarian copyright notice was a year later than the year of first publication. (See Section 57b.) Thus the error would have been fatal if the first publication had occurred in the United States, and if a valid copyright notice had been held necessary as to first publication in Hungary. So, to uphold the United States copyright, the court had to find that first publication of the song, if abroad, did not require any copyright notice at all.

The court noted that some copies of the Hungarian song bearing the defective copyright notice had drifted into the United States, saying: "The imported copies sold in this country were not shown to be authorized by the then proprietor." Yet the court held that the first publication of the song in Hungary, without a valid copyright notice, and the subsequent registration in the United States, gave a valid United States copyright. It held that no copyright notice was needed on first publication abroad in order to reach this result.

The need of the copyright notice on a first publication abroad was strongly urged by Judge Clark. Yet the decision of the majority and of the court seems admirable. Even if technically assailable, the advance in international copyright protection makes the decision a welcome step forward. The general view under the Convention of Berne, establishing international copyrights, is that if a work is first published in a country not a member of the Convention, without simultaneous publication within a country that is a member, the work falls into the public domain and never can thereafter be copyrighted.[14] The publication of a book in English abroad, without the taking out of an ad interim copyright within the United States, also, it is generally held, puts the work in the public domain.

This unfortunate result was avoided, in the case of this Hungarian song, by the courts holding that the first publication in Hungary was an act of first publication so far as the United States copyright was concerned. Thus the owner or his assignee could follow through and obtain a valid copyright later in the United States. The Supreme Court (see Section 57d) has ruled that if the act of registration and depositing of a copy with the Copyright Office occurs within fourteen months after the first publication, registration is in time for suit.

The ruling by Judge Frank cuts away technicalities that would prevent international copyright. It permits copyright protection in the United States on some works first published abroad. Theoretically it applies to books first published abroad not in English. What of books in English, first published abroad, if printed in the United States? That actual situation is very unlikely to arise. Under this interpretation, United States copyright law, for once, favors international copyright protection to a greater extent than does the Convention of Berne.

The decision in an earlier case,[15] though vague, also protected foreign publication abroad. Here a song lyric, in Italian, was first published in Italy, and validly copyrighted there. Four years later an assignee of the Italian copyright proprietor copyrighted the song in the United States. His copyright was held valid.

A sharp difficulty in the holding of Judge Frank arises from his ruling that no copyright notice is needed in a publication abroad. The logical implications of that ruling are perplexing. The court had to make that ruling because the copyright notice used in the case before it, as before noted, was fatally defective. It is often urged that the United States copyright statute can have no validity outside of United States territory. That unquestionably is so. But a United States statute validly can govern acts abroad as to consequences arising therefrom as to rights in the United States, i.e. the obtaining of a copyright valid in the United States. And why should works first published abroad need no copyright notice, while rigid requirements are imposed as to works first published in the United States? Section 10 of the Copyright Statute only requires a copyright notice "to be affixed to each copy thereof published or offered for sale in the United States." That section contemplates first publication in the United States as the basis of a United States copyright. The drafter of the provision did not contemplate first publication abroad. But if first publication occurs abroad, why should a lesser rule be imposed than if first publication occurs in the United States?

European and British copyright laws reject registration and the use of a copyright notice, i.e. all formalities in copyright protection, as dated and immaturely technical. But Congress had decided otherwise for the United States.

The theory of Congress is that those who copy works without a copyright notice are not to be sued. Should a United States national, so relying on this theory, be held liable when he believes a work, if a musical composition printed abroad, is in the public domain because of no copyright notice? Perhaps all technicalities, such as copyright notices, should be ended. But Congress alone can do that.

Some of these doubts were swept aside, however, in the above decision of Judge Frank as to the Hungarian song. Since the end result is to lessen international copyright barriers, the decision is cheering. But the decision raises an interesting query as to the rigid but never expressly adjudicated rule that publication and copyright registration in a domestic territory, if there not be simultaneous publication and copyrighting in foreign countries, places the work in the public domain in such foreign countries. No one has ever dared doubt that conclusion. Does Judge Frank's decision permit its being raised?

IX

Publication

61. WHAT CONSTITUTES PUBLICATION

CURRENTLY, because of decisions concerning phonograph records (see page 114), sharp controversy but not much new light has arisen as to what constitutes "publication".

A statutory copyright, in published works, can be obtained by publication with the copyright notice affixed. But in any event, on publication, with or without obtaining a statutory copyright, the common-law copyright is ended.

Thus a precise understanding of what constitutes publication is essential.

The British Copyright Act of 1911 has a lucid definition of publication: "Publication, in relation to any work, means the issue of copies to the public." (1 & 2 Geo. 5, C. 46, Sec. I [3].)

To the British definition there can be helpfully added and stressed the aspect of making copies as the practical first step involved: i.e. printing or other mass production of copies. The second step is the issuing or selling of copies. The second step cannot very well occur without the first; thus copying, by printing, is the decisive actual act.

The making and issuing (i.e. sale or giving away of copies to the public) is the common-sense and practical definition of publication.

The United States Copyright Statute speaks of publication and indirectly defines publication in Section 26 as follows:

In the interpretation and construction of this title "the date of publication" shall in the case of a work of which copies are reproduced for sale or distribution be held to be the earliest date when copies of the first authorized edition were placed on sale, sold, or publicly distributed by the proprietor of the copyright or under his authority, and the word "author" shall include an employer in the case of works made for hire.[1a]

Publication is sometimes defined as the act of "making public" or "dedicating to the public". Neither of these definitions is particularly helpful. A play when publicly performed is made public and dedicated to the public. So too with a lecture, when delivered in public. Yet the law uniformly holds that public delivery and thus making public of a lecture, or play, does not constitute publication. Nor is dedication clarifying as a definition, when pictures or works of art are publicly displayed in galleries. Such display is not publication under the law. The making of *copies* and the *sale*, or gratis giving of the copies, to the public, is the pith of publication. Gratis distribution of *copies* is equivalent to selling, but rarely occurs as to copies of a work of value. When the gratis distribution is for a special purpose, as books sent to reviewers or copies of plays furnished to actors, such distribution is not publication.

As a physical requisite, copying must precede publication. Printing thus is the most easily identified part of publication and without such printing, as a rule, there is no publication. What the statute, in reality, contemplates as the act of publication is the combined act of printing and selling (or giving copies) to the public. That constitutes the reality of the English definition "the issue of copies to the public."

It has been held that the sale of one of several galley-proof copies of a manuscript and in a private home [1] constitutes publication. The correctness of this decision can be questioned, for the court therein strained its reasoning in order to condemn a sharp newspaper trick. The *Atlantic Monthly* had arranged with Governor Alfred E. Smith, in 1927, to publish a letter from him about the prejudice against a Roman Catholic running for the Presidency. The *Atlantic* had arranged with Governor Smith to publish his letter first and then to release it to the press generally. A newspaper reporter bribed a watchman, working for the *Atlantic*'s printer, and got a copy of the letter from him, and published it, thus beating the *Atlantic*'s deadline. The *Atlantic* sued the newspaper for piracy, asserting that the *Atlantic* had obtained a valid copyright before publication of the issue of the magazine, by the sale of one galley proof of the letter, with the copyright notice affixed, to the *Atlantic*'s Treasurer for ten cents. The Treasurer had followed this sale by promptly mailing to the Register another galley copy, with its application for a statutory copyright. The court held this sale of the one copy to the *Atlantic*'s Treasurer was publication. Thus it held the newspaper an infringer of the *Atlantic*'s copyright.

The sale here was hardly a bona fide sale. Nor a sale or an actual distribution of copies to the public. Token or symbolical or other unreal sale to the public does not constitute publication. Yet, under this decision, a sale of even a manuscript copy, without printing, may be deemed publication. But in a practical sense mechanical reproduction and issuing, or placing on sale of several copies, is necessary to have publication.

As distinguished from works which can be copyrighted without being published (plays, lectures, and works of art), the realistic test is the essential need of copying or printing for public use. But printing of copies of a play for use by actors and others engaged in the production, and distribution to them alone, is not publication. (See Section 62.)

62. PUBLICATION AS TO DIFFERING MEDIA DEFINED

1. Books, Periodicals

Printing and public sale or gratis distribution of copies of books and periodicals constitutes the basic use and is the definition of publication. Unless there be publication, no statutory copyright can be had.

2. Dramas

Performance of a play, by acting before the public, whether or not for profit, does not constitute publication.[2] Thus the playwright or producer may rely on his common-law copyright before and after public performance for profit. For performance is not a publication destroying this common-law copyright. That rule is completely established. The playwright may take out a statutory copyright, without printing and publishing the play, under Section 12 of the Copyright Statute, or publish and copyright his play as a published work, or rely on his common-law copyright. He thus has three choices.

If the author desires to print and circulate copies of his play solely for use by the actors and others engaged in the performance, so doing does not constitute publication.[3] But if he prints and sells copies to the public he must copyright his play as a published work.

3. Delivery of Lectures

The rule and test here is the same as in the case of a play.[4] Delivery in public, whether or not for profit, is not publication.

4. Musical Compositions and Dramas

Singing or performing a musical composition in public is not a publication.[5] So too with operas, operettas, and musical comedies; public performance thereof is not publication.[6]

5. Paintings and Other Works of Art; Photographs; Drawings; Maps; Architectural Plans

Public exhibition in galleries, where permission is not given to the public to copy, is not publication.[7] Unless there be proof to the contrary, mere exhibition in a public gallery does not imply the right to copy and thus constitute an act of publication.[8] Nor does a sketch of a painting used in the gallery catalogue, with or without the painter's consent, constitute publication.[9] But exhibition of the statue of an elk, at a public Elks' celebration, in a judicial burst of humor, has been held to be publication,[10] because the right to copy the inartistic statue was deemed publicly given thereby.

When an architect files his plans to build a house, with a city building department, his plans are deemed published.[11] This ruling is often criticized.

6. Motion Pictures, Dramatic, Documentary, or Scenic

Copies of physical prints of a motion picture are rarely sold. Commonly they are only leased for the particular exhibition and distributed under short leases by the motion picture exchange. Leasing to and exhibition in a theater to the public is held not to be publication.[12] Yet motion picture companies invariably obtain a statutory copyright before public exhibition. If prints are sold, publication results.[13]

7. Maps and Prints

Prints and pictorial illustrations, including labels used for articles of merchandise, need not be published before a statutory copyright can be had. The rule is different as to maps. But copying and sale of copies constitutes publication. A statutory copyright of the reproduction as a published work must be obtained to keep the entire creation from falling into the public domain. Exhibiting copies is not publication.[14]

Maps must be published before they can be copyrighted: that is, copies must be made and publicly distributed (Regulations of the Copyright Office, Section 202.7).

8. Radio Broadcasting

Radio broadcasting of material is not publication thereof.[15]

9. Phonograph Records

Today one of the hottest questions in copyright law is the controversy of what constitutes publication, as to media other than print. The issue has become critical for phonograph manufacturers because of the two Federal decisions holding that the sale of phonograph records is publication of the contents thereof, thus ending any common-law copyright therein. Judge Igoe's earlier decision [16] has been followed by Judge Leibell in the Mills Music case (1954; 126 F. Supp. 54, p. 69).

Judge Igoe objected to the retention of a perpetual copyright of a musical composition after its recording on a record and the wide public sale of *copies* of the record, holding that records "are available for purchase in every city, town and hamlet" and that "the dissemination of the composition is complete and is as complete as by sale of a sheet music reproduction of the composition."

If the same reasoning be applied to radio broadcasting and television, where dissemination is equally wide, though copies of the broadcast or photoplay are not sold to the public, yet are widely available for use, startling results must follow. This decision indicates the precarious position of those who use the newer mediums of entertainment communication in reliance upon the analogy thereof to plays, i.e. that no publication results by performance or exhibition. Motion pictures are protected by specific Copyright Statute provisions.

If Judge Igoe's ruling be followed, the Copyright Statute must be amended. For it contains no provision for registering a copy of a musical composition, in record form, as a published work, with the Copyright Office. The creator of a musical composition, if he desires to have his composition recorded and copies of the record sold, must rely for copyright protection either upon (a) a common-law copyright; (b) a statutory copyright under Section 12 of the Copyright Statute as an unpublished work; or (c) a statutory copyright as a published work, i.e. of the sheet music or score.

If Judge Igoe's opinion be followed and the sale of phonograph records be deemed publication, then the common-law or statutory copyright under Section 12 is ended by publication, i.e. sale of copies, of the record. And the Copyright Statute has no provision for registering phonograph records as a published work after publication. But a statutory copyright of the score, if a copyright notice be put on the record, would save the copyright in the score.

10. Television

There have been no court decisions yet as to whether television broadcasting and exhibition constitutes publication. By analogy to the ruling as to plays, radio broadcasting, and motion pictures, it is generally believed, probably correctly, that television reproduction will not be held to be publication. But television permits facsimile reproduction of words on the screen in extenso. If that facsimile printing should cover a substantial part of the literary work, it could well be argued, by analogy to the printing of books, that such facsimile constitutes publication.

Judge Igoe's decision [16] as to phonograph recording, noted above, must cause concern among television broadcasters. The analogy of his reasoning partly applies to television use. The problem is considered in detail in Chapter XXV, Television Problems, Section 194.

An interesting recent case involving music is the ruling of a New York high court that a phonograph manufacturer could be enjoined from picking up from the air the broadcast performance of an opera by the Metropolitan Opera Company, recording it on tape, and manufacturing and selling a phonograph record thereof (Metropolitan Opera Company v. Nichols, 107 N.Y. Supp. 2d 795). The opinion is far from lucid but the ruling is sweeping.

X

What Can Be Copyrighted

63. COPYRIGHT AS THE PROTECTION OF EXPRESSION

AUTHORS often misunderstand the extent of the protection granted under a copyright, whether common-law, statutory, or international. Initially, a basic theoretical distinction separates the legal concept of copyrights as distinct from that of patents. Copyrights protect expression, not ideas. Patents protect novel ideas formulated into mechanical techniques. Thus patents are a wider right than copyrights.

At the start of copyright discussion (Chapter VI) a copyright was defined as "the right not to have one's mental work, as *expressed* in written or other objective form, copied . . .". The test of "expression" states the guiding rule as to the scope of a copyright monopoly, as distinct from a patent monopoly.

The right granted under a copyright is against *copying* of the *expression* set down, not against the use of the material and varied ideas created, or facts and information gathered by the author from the objective world of facts. The "Idea alone, apart from the means of expressing it, is not protected" by a copyright.[1] Nor can an author obtain a monopoly over common material open to use by everyone.[2]

The courts require some originality of mental labor, however slight and unimaginative.[3] Any form of expression, even in compiling or arranging humdrum commercial lists, is deemed a sufficient modicum of originality in expression or arrangement for copyrighting. When that modicum of mental work is set down, the copyright law protects all the forms and variations and transformations of the expression used by the author—but only to the extent of such ex-

116

pression set down. In piracy trials as to literary works of more merit the copyright protection granted likewise covers skill and form of expression and that skill and form only.

Ideas and imaginative thought and concepts, as well as the factual fictional material used, can not be copyrighted, in order to protect the public interest. If copyright monopolies were granted in ideas and in the orbit of objective material, freedom of thought and expression would end.[4] Therefore by social necessity, the extent of copyright protection of ideas is limited to the author's expression. But by the protection of expression is not meant protection only of a mere sequence of words. Paraphrasing or colored restatement or adaptation is copying and thus forbidden.[5] Forbidden copying also includes all forms of re-expression and imitated transformation and even arrangement. Treatment and development of the material used also is protected. This final facet of forbidden treatment copying is difficult to define. How far, and to what extent, such protection of treatment and arrangement, as a monopoly over expression, extends, constitutes the fluid and perplexing crux of copyright litigation. Where does expression end and the bare and naked material emerge? The decision is a matter of judicial appraisal. In reality, it is an affair of more or less.

64. LITERAL AND TREATMENT COPYING

A more detailed statement of the practical aspects involved in the copying of expression, as distinct from literal copying, may help to clarify the apparently technical distinctions in judicial decisions as to what is protected under a copyright.

Literal copying is a mere repetition of the words used by another, including minor variations, or slavish rephrasing (i.e. paraphrasing) thereof. Also the copying in music of prior literal expression, i.e. copying the musical notes, perhaps with slight variation, of another. Such literal copying is categorically forbidden under copyright law—except where a limited privilege of fair comment and of fair use (see Chapter XV) is involved. We term it herein literal copying.

But copying can be of a wider, more obscure, and cleverer form. It can consist of copying the treatment and development and larger items of creative expression of another. Ideas, plots, character portrayal and dramatic conflict, situation and surprise, narrative suspense and plot manipulation, are involved in this taking and copying of the larger expression of another. Such copying may or may not be piracy. Here arises the essence and difficulty of the bulk of piracy litigation. This secondary or wider form of copying can be termed "treatment copying" to distinguish it from "literal copying". Treatment copying is forbidden as rigorously as is literal copying. But it is harder to appraise.

Thus decisions as to what constitutes infringement must be the test and definition of what can be copyrighted. Such decisions become clearer when viewed as involving either literal or treatment copying of another's expression. But always the court limits itself to protecting the *expression* of the copyright, and the extensive right of transformation thereof into other literary forms, as distinct from protection of the *material* use.

65. DISTINCTION BETWEEN COPYRIGHTS AND PATENTS

It follows that the monopoly granted under a copyright is far more drastically limited than that granted under a patent. Though power to legislate as to both is lodged in Congress by the same constitutional clause, the theory as to the monopoly granted to the author and that granted to the inventor is basically different.

Under a patent, the law grants to the inventor the monopoly (but for a shorter term than in copyrights, i.e. for seventeen years) as to "any new and useful art, machine, manufacture of matter, or any new and useful improvements thereof", or of any "new variety of plant," [6] or as to "any new, original and ornamental design for an article of manufacture".[6]

Thus a patent is the exclusive right "to make, use and vend" the patented device or process [6] as against all others who independently, and in ignorance of the earlier patent, or with knowledge thereof, thereafter devise the same device or process. Not so with copyrights. The only prohibition granted by a copyright is against *copying* the prior expression. An independent, original expression and creation of the same work, in ignorance of the earlier copyright, and so without copying, does not violate a prior copyright grant. The new creator also can obtain a copyright in his independently created work.[7]

66. COPYRIGHT AND PATENT PROCEDURE

The basic distinction between a copyright and a patent is further shown by the governmental procedure under which patents and copyrights are obtained. The patent office examines all patent applications to see if the claim set forth involves something novel [8] and has not been anticipated. Only then is a patent claim allowed. Considerable delay is involved before a patent claim is allowed. All prior patents are carefully examined and analyzed by the examiner of the patent office, insofar as they may bear upon the claims made, as to novelty and prior invention.

The Copyright Office issues its copyright certificate instantly and automatically on any and all material submitted, without examining such material or similar prior material to ascertain if there are similarities or anticipations. The only facts checked by the Copyright Office are as to whether the material and application submitted come within the technical provisions and conform to the copyright statute as to what can be copyrighted. A copyright certificate when granted means only that the author has complied with the formal provisions of the Copyright Statute. The difference has been stated by an able judge (Woolsey) [9] as:

The Copyright Office does not, when a book is offered for copyright, study any prior art, as does the Patent Office when a patent is sought. It grants the copyright, thus putting the protection of the law not only over the copyrighted book as an entirety, but over the original content of the book. It is then left to the courts, if litigation ensues, to say what the original content is, and to define the zone in which the copyright owner is protected.

A prima facie case, or preliminary assumption, is created in favor of the patent holder by the grant of the patent.[10] But all the burden of proof is upon a copyright proprietor in litigation or otherwise to show that his copyright covers what he claims. His copyright certificate only creates a presumption as to technical acts of compliance with the Copyright Statute. The Copyright Office issues a copyright certificate without going into this basic issue of original creative expression.

67. PRIORITY

Authors, nevertheless, hope to get an exclusive right—in an idea, a dramatic situation, a plot, a historical or emotional incident, a concept or type of story or novel, or as to a locale or an atmosphere—either by obtaining a prior copyright or by prior use. They believe mistakenly that if they are the first in time to obtain a copyright therein, they thus obtain prior right thereto, and can prevent others thereafter from using the same idea, locale, atmosphere, plot, concept, or type. Most authors are eager to copyright their material for this reason as soon as possible.

But in fact, no legal right is obtained by mere priority. All the copyright proprietor gets is the right not to have his expression and his treatment of the material copied. The public and other authors still retain the right to use any and all of the same material.

If A writes a play or novel and copyrights it, and if B writes the same identical play or novel later on, word for word, but without knowing of the existence of A's play or novel, B does not violate A's copyright when he publishes his later independent creation. In patent law, the ruling would be just the opposite. B's later and independent creation and use of A's patent idea would violate A's patent monopoly. If B should attempt to make, vend, or use his later and independently created patent, he would be an infringer. But such priority of right is not granted under the copyright law. It is but an author's unfounded desire and hope.

Judge Learned Hand, one of our ablest and most distinguished judges, and particularly experienced and lucid in copyright decisions, has tersely phrased that result: [11]

Borrowed the work must indeed not be, for a plagiarist is not himself pro tanto an "author"; but if by some magic a man who had never known it were to compose anew Keats' Ode on a Grecian Urn, he would be an "author" and, if he copyrighted it, others might not copy that poem, though they might of course copy Keats' [i.e. after Keats' copyright expired].

Of course, it is highly unlikely that B would or could write a poem or play identical or almost identical with A's poem or play, without B's knowing of A's creation and copying it—so well-nigh impossible in reality that the theoretical distinction above noted is not as important as it seems. The law of evidence recognizes that improbability, and the result is that complete similarity, or a marked and too striking and substantial identity, between two works in itself constitutes evidence and proof of copying and of "access"—and thus of piracy. (By access is meant that B knew of, and had means of copying, A's play.) Even if the prior creator A can't prove that the later creator B had "access to" A's play, A can claim piracy and perchance restrain B from using B's later play on the ground of plagiarism, unless the court finds, despite the marked similarity, that B did not know of and did not copy A's play. (See Chapter XIX on Piracy Litigation.) Finding of no copying, where very great similarity is shown, is rare. In deciding whether or not there was copying, a court in practice usually deems it impossible for two literary works to be too markedly similar without copying.

Thus the possibility of two independent creations of a literary work like the "Ode on a Grecian Urn" is close to a mere theoretical statement. Yet it is basic as to what can and can not be copyrighted.

68. THE REALISTIC TEST AS TO COPYING

The short answer as to what is protected under a copyright is obtained by going backwards: from rulings as to what constitutes piracy, conclusions can be drawn as to what the copyright protection covers.

The distinction between copyrights and patents, above noted, controls in part the answer as to what constitutes piracy. In literal copying there is little difficulty and obscurity. Most of our litigation arises over treatment copying.

The realistic steps in determining what constitutes piracy in cases of treatment copying are three: (1) Is there a sufficiently marked similarity between the two works to raise an issue of copying, and what are the similarities? (2) Eliminating similarities of material and ideas in the public domain, are the similarities of treatment expression left (literal expression rarely is involved), as distinct from similarities of ideas and of material in the public domain, sufficient to raise an issue of copying? (3) Do the clues and evidence as to access and other copying circumstances involved, and the nature and extent of the similarities in treatment expression, add up to a conclusion that the similarities arose from treatment copying and not from independent creation?

Only if the answer to the first query is in the affirmative need the court go further. Then the second query must be taken up. And the answer to the third query is an affair of weighing access and similarities in treatment expression, and other incidental evidence, such as the slightest touches of literal copying, as against the evidence suggesting independent mental labor and creation.

The treatment copying found possibly to exist may be too slight, and not substantial enough, to constitute a holding of piracy. That consideration is part of the second query. If the possible treatment copying be at best but slight, then independent creation may be held the factual cause of the other similarities found under the first query.

In short, under copyright law, the evidentiary test involved is twofold: (1) internal and external expression similarity as shown by comparing the two works; (2) circumstantial evidence indicating whether such similarities are due to independent creation or to treatment copying. If traces of literal copying, or other fugitive clues, are found, these may be decisive and require a holding of piracy.

69. PUBLIC DOMAIN

If two copyrighted works are somewhat markedly similar, piracy need not be found, since the similarities may solely be similarities of material used. Even some copying of an earlier work is permitted, as a following of suggestions relating to material in the public domain. Where and when such suggestion and material copying of a copyrighted work is permitted is an important aspect of copyright theory. It requires a separation of substance from expression. Substance, as ideas and objective material (and distinct from the expression thereof) may be used by anyone.

The technical term "public domain" is used as descriptive of what may freely be used. This legal phrase "public domain", as denoting material which may be freely copied and used by anyone at any time, has a larger and a lesser scope.

In its larger scope, the phrase covers and includes ideas, concepts, material, historical events, news, and action episodes arising in the past and present in the external world. All these belong to everyone, i.e. to the public. They can be used by anyone. No part thereof can be withdrawn from public use by copyrighting. No one can obtain a monopoly as to that which belongs to everyone, i.e. exists in the public domain.

In its lesser significance, the phrase "public domain" describes the great mass of classic literary, dramatic, musical, and intellectual creations, written in the past. Literary and artistic creations created in the past, before copyrights existed, and which were never copyrighted, belong to everyone and are in the public domain. Also, copyrighted literary, musical, and artistic works of any kind upon which copyrights were taken out are in the public domain after these copyrights have expired by lapse of time. Included too within the public domain are current works upon which the creator has lost his common-law copyright by publication without obtaining a statutory copyright; and works as to which the author attempted to obtain a statutory copyright, but as to which the copyright is invalid by reason of technical flaws or failings.

Any created expression once in the public domain can not thereafter be copyrighted and withdrawn from the public domain. The Copyright Statute (Section 8) summarizes the rule: "No copyright shall exist in the original text of any work which is in the public domain."

70. ADAPTATIONS OF MATERIAL IN THE PUBLIC DOMAIN

If one uses material in the public domain, however, any expression or twists added, by way of adaptation, arrangement, or novel treatment, can be copyrighted. But the copyright proprietor does not thereby obtain any copyright over the material that he took from the public domain. His copyright covers only that which he added and his treatment expression. What previously existed is still open to use by everyone. The Copyright Statute, Section 7, provides:

> Compilations or abridgements, adaptations, arrangements, dramatizations, translations, or other versions of works in the public domain or of copyrighted works when produced with the consent of the proprietor of the copyright in such works, or works republished with

new matter, shall be regarded as new works subject to copyright under the provisions of this title; but the publications of any such new works shall not affect the force or validity of any subsisting copyright upon the matter employed or any part thereof, or be construed to imply an exclusive right to such use of the original works, or to secure or extend copyright in such original works.

Shakespeare's *Hamlet*, of course, is in the public domain. But an amended text can be copyrighted, the copyright covering only the new items. Also a new arrangement of the scenes in *Hamlet* might be made, or scenes therein be eliminated, or new stage directions or new lines added, and anything that is new and added can be copyrighted. When a work not in the public domain, but upon which there is an outstanding copyright, is adapted or changed, such adaptation or similar use constitutes piracy unless the consent of the copyright proprietor thereof be had. The Copyright Statute above quoted (Section 7) so expressly provides.

71. PUBLIC DOMAIN AS TO MUSIC

In music, extensive use of musical material in the public domain is common. Melodies, themes, and songs, including folk music, are constantly taken from the public domain. Lesser composers adapt, change, popularize, and use musical material taken from the works of classic composers. All this is freely permitted, if the copyright on the older work has expired. Such arrangements of, and additions to, or changes in, musical material in the public domain can be copyrighted, as to what is added or as to the arrangement or change made. But such copyrighting can not preclude others from using the same material found in the public domain. The copyright prevents only the use of the new arrangement or additions or alterations.

72. DEFENSE OF PUBLIC DOMAIN IN LITIGATION

One of the commonest defenses resorted to in literary and musical litigation is the attempt, by those accused of piracy, to show that the material which the copyright plaintiff alleges was stolen, already was in the public domain. In piracy litigation, particularly as to musical copyrights, a defendant often attempts to show either (1) that both he and the plaintiff took the melody or theme from a musical composition in the public domain; or (2) that since the musical material was in the public domain the second user had the right to copy it, even from the first user's work. The test then solely is as to whether or not the alleged pirate used only material in the public domain or whether he took any new material or arrangement covered by the copyright of the complaining litigant.

In litigation over literary works, the alleged infringer defendant often produces experts, who range through all past literature, seeking to show similarities between the writings of the plaintiff and of material found in the public domain. Here, too, the test reduces itself to whether or not the alleged infringer copied any new expression or treatment found in the plaintiff's works.

In short, a defendant, since he can use anything in the public domain, often uses as a defense either (1) that he copied from the public domain; (2) that the plaintiff did so too, and that the plaintiff's copyright does not include much of the material the defendant used and copied; or (3) that even copying of plaintiff's work was permitted copying, because the defendant could copy anything that the plaintiff himself took from the public domain.

These defenses are valid, if the defendant has not also used the complainant's expression, arrangement, or treatment of material in the public domain. Thus the issue as to what can be copyrighted and what can't be copyrighted is the distinction between the use of material on the one hand and literal or treatment copying on the other hand.

73. ILLUSTRATIONS FROM PIRACY TRIALS

As a preliminary factor, any copying must be substantial, not slight and negligible, to be piracy. If very slight and very minor, no infringement results. But this qualification seldom arises in practical experience. Almost always a pirate goes further. And the slight instances of copying may be clues to prove that the pirate's entire work was copied from the prior copyright and is not independent creation.

Material such as ideas, emotions, concepts, news events, atmosphere, locale, historical events, and even stock plots and characters, is not copyrightable. Thus the copyright law permits free use of them, wherever they are set down, provided that copying as literal copying or treatment copying is not also involved.

Miss Ann Nichols, for example, wrote a successful play entitled *Abie's Irish Rose*. It had one of the longest runs in Broadway history. Universal Pictures Corporation thereafter produced a similar motion picture entitled *The Cohens and Kellys*. Ann Nichols sued the picture company, alleging copying and piracy of her play.[12] Defendant admitted knowledge of and access to plaintiff's play, as it had to, by reason of the success of the play.

Abie's Irish Rose was based upon the dramatic idea of intermarriage between an Irish Catholic girl and a Jewish boy, humorously and sentimentally treated and developed. The idea of the defendant's motion picture was the same as that in the play. The plot action of the love story in both works largely involved the same stock kinds of love and religious and racial conflict, as items of action, all sentimentally and humorously treated. But the action and other incidents in each work, the court found, were different.

The court held that plaintiff and defendant both took their idea, plot, and situation from the public domain, and that similarities in dramatic expression, treatment, and character development were not sufficiently marked or substantial to show that the defendant had copied those phases and items of treatment expression in plaintiff's play that came under and were included within plaintiff's copyright protection. There was, of course, no literal copying.

In so holding for the defendant the court said: [12]

Emotions, like mere ideas, are not subject to pre-emption; they are common property. It is the incidents or elements, or grouping of them, which produce the emotion that are to be compared. Similar emotions may be caused by very different ideas. It is obvious that the underlying emotions reflected by the principal characters in a play or book may be similar, and yet that the characters and expressions of the same emotions be different. * * *

That the same emotions are found in plays would not alone be sufficient to prove infringement, but, if similar emotions are portrayed by a sequence of events presented in like manner, expression, and form, then infringement would be apparent. * * *

The fundamental plot in *Abie's Irish Rose* is not new and is common property in the "public domain". The theme of the secret marriage, meeting parental opposition because of prejudice, racial or otherwise, with an Irish-Jewish background, is not new. A similar idea is found in a number of plays, * * *.

The record discloses that in 1925 the defendant, the Universal Pictures Corporation, tried to purchase *Abie's Irish Rose* motion picture rights, and that, when the scenario of *The Cohens and Kellys* was being written, its authors "studied" the synopsis of *Abie's Irish Rose;* also that the Universal Weekly, a publication issued by the Universal Pictures Corporation, announced on the completion of its picture that its photoplay will be to the screen what *Abie's Irish Rose* is to the stage, and, while there is a fairly strong inference that the authors of *The Cohens and the Kellys* gained some of their ideas from *Abie's Irish Rose,* for the reasons discussed above, my conclusion is that such rights of the complainant as are protected by copyright have not been infringed.

Here, in short, the similarities in the two works were as to material in the public domain. Miss Nichols could not copyright such material and prevent its use later in defendant's motion picture.

Another famous case involved the successful Broadway stage hit *Marie Odile.*[13] Martinez Sierra, a Spanish author of repute, sent to Belasco a manuscript of a play entitled *The Cradle Song,* dealing with convent life and about a female foundling left with nuns. Belasco was admittedly slow in returning the manuscript. Thus access to the play by Belasco was established. Soon thereafter Belasco produced the play *Marie Odile,* which likewise centered around convent life and concerned a foundling girl left with nuns. The court held, however, that Belasco had not infringed upon the plaintiff's play, because similarities of dialogue and language and action were not such as to show any treatment copying by Belasco. The court's ruling on this point was: [13]

As has been frequently pointed out in reported cases, and as is matter of common knowledge, most of the incidents that happen in the world may be availed of in plays or books, and the question essentially is in what manner they are availed of. Except for some extraordinary developments, such as, for instance, have happened in the way of instruments of war in the present war, there is rarely anything that is physically new. Convents are old. The theme of a foundling in some relation or another is old. The conduct of persons in any given walk or department of life,—that is to say, the normal conduct,—is ordinarily old and well known. The task which is presented to the playwright is to weld together these old elements with some fundamental or controlling theme in such a manner as to make a successful appeal, either artistically or financially, or both. Except for the fact that the scene of both plays is in a convent, and that of necessity there are some similarities of dialogue and language, the two plays are essentially and fundamentally different.

Again a dramatist hit upon an idea of a play about convicts, in which the locale was the notoriously severe convict life at Alcatraz Prison. He copyrighted his play and sent it to defendant, a picture company; it was returned with a rejection slip. Later the picture company produced a motion picture entitled *Alcatraz Prison*, using the same locale and basic plot. The picture company asserted it had not used plaintiff's play. The court held that even if the picture company used the same locale and idea, sufficient treatment similarity was not involved in the motion picture to establish substantial copying by the picture company of the plaintiff's treatment and development. The court's ruling was sharply etched: [14]

I am convinced that while both authors consciously or unconsciously made use of a common fundamental plot, the stories told are not the same. There is a material difference in the characters and the episodes necessarily required in describing the gangster operations so familiar to the public. The fundamental plot, however, is the same, and of course is not copyrightable under the law. And the statute does not and can not give the plaintiff a monopoly of ideas, merely protecting the means of expressing the idea.

In another case [15] involving plots in the public domain, the court stressed the sparse number of plots, their availability, and the limited extent of copyright protection therein:

The dramatic situations which form the stuff of drama are few. The entire dramatic literature of the world can be reduced to some three dozen situations. In fact, an ingenious Frenchman has written a book in which, after analyzing the entire dramatic literature from the time of the Greek and Hindu dramas to the present time, he concludes that all these dramatic works present, in variant form, the few situations which he has analyzed. A rule, therefore, which would place originality not in the manner of treatment of theme, but in the theme, would place the "hack writer" upon the same footing with the genius. And so the law, realistic in this respect, places originality where it belongs. * * *
Even though there are characters in both plays having similarity and

some instances of similar phraseology, when the theory of the two plays is entirely different, there is no infringement. * * * A person may take the same fundamental idea as that of another work, and if in developing it the incidents in which it is developed are substantially different, if the idea is worked out on different lines, so that the two works bear no real resemblance to each other, there will be no infringement. * * * A copyright extends only to the arrangement of the words. A copyright does not give a monopoly in any incident in a play. Other authors have the right to exploit the facts, experiences, field of thought, and general ideas, provided they do not substantially copy a concrete form, in which the circumstances and ideas have been developed, arranged, and put into shape.

As to copyright priority, the court added:

The law of copyright has merely provided an additional method whereby an author by registering his work establishes his right as of the date of registration with the Register of Copyrights, so that he may be in a position to show by the official registration the date of the publication of his original composition. The right which the copyright law protects differs in no respect from any other form of personal property in the protection which the common law throws about it. Its basis is the right of every one to the fruit of his labor.

Using stock plots creates no copyright therein.[15a] Only if new and original treatment is added, and then copied by another, does treatment copying occur. And the piracy extends only to the new twists—if there are such. Then copying of a plot becomes treatment copying.

Judge Learned Hand has observed: [16]

We did not in Dymow v. Bolton, 11 F. (2d) 690, hold that a plagiarist was never liable for stealing a plot; * * * . We found the plot of the second play was too different to infringe, because the most detailed pattern, common to both, eliminated so much from each that its content went into the public domain; and for this reason we said, "this mere subsection of a plot was not susceptible of copyright." But we do not doubt that two plays may correspond in plot closely enough for infringement. How far that correspondence must go is another matter.

Copying stock characters is not piracy. But copying a cleverly or vividly developed and skillfully portrayed character may constitute

copying of treatment expression. The test, as in the copying of a
plot, is the skill used by the first user of the plot or portrayer of
the character. Judge Learned Hand has so observed as to the copying of well-developed characters, in holding that copying a character may be so extensive as to be treatment copying and piracy: [17]

Nor need we hold that the same [piracy] may not be true as to the
characters, quite independently of the "plot" proper, though, as far
as we know, such a case has never arisen. If Twelfth Night were copyrighted, it is quite possible that a second comer might so closely imi-
tate Sir Toby Belch or Malvolio as to infringe, but it would not be
enough that for one of his characters he cast a riotous knight who kept
wassail to the discomfort of the household, or a vain and foppish
steward who became amorous of his mistress. These would be no
more than Shakespeare's "ideas" in the play, as little capable of monopoly as Einstein's Doctrine of Relativity, or Darwin's theory of the
Origin of Species. It follows that the less developed the characters, the
less they can be copyrighted; that is the penalty an author must bear
for marking them too indistinctly.

So too, in the far-fetched attack upon Miss Du Maurier's *Rebecca*, the mere use by Miss Du Maurier and the complainant of a
similar "second wife" stock plot was rejected by the court as
evidence of treatment copying.[18]

A recent ruling that Warner Brothers, the assignees from Dashiell
Hammett of the copyright of *The Maltese Falcon*, could not enjoin
Hammett's subsequent grantee from using the leading character
therein, "Sam Spade", has caused great controversy. The opinion,
properly construed, means not that a character cannot be copyrighted, but that the copyright assignment, as drawn, did not assign
the exclusive right in the characters of the book, because of a defect
in the wording of the fine print (Warner v. C.B.S. Inc. 216 F. 2d
945).

74. DANGERS OF COPYING MATERIAL IN THE PUBLIC DOMAIN

Infringement arises, however, if the similarities in expression as
to mere idea, locale, and plot are so great that it is likely that the
defendant indulged in treatment copying. Copying even of ideas
thus involves peril. For those admitting the copying of material

as used by another are commonly accused of copying more, i.e. of treatment copying.

Usually in copyright litigation the defendant does not admit any knowledge of, or access to, the plaintiff's work. Thus he studiously denies any copying at all. Admissions to the contrary are dangerous. Where a defendant admits, or must admit, imitation or copying of only an idea or concept or material in the public domain used by a predecessor, he usually finds himself in a dangerous defensive situation. He must show clear difference of expression and treatment in his work as against the treatment of the prior work, to escape penalty for treatment copying, since there may be subconscious prejudice, even in the judicial mind, against one who admits copying, even of an idea or locale or plot.

Thus the rule that ideas, material, locale, and plots are not copyrightable does not mean in practical experience that imitators thereof are safe in admitting intentional use thereof, as copying from or getting ideas from such prior copyrighted work. For he who copies public-domain material from another, and hopes cleverly not to step over the line into treatment copying, submits himself to the uncertainty of judicial determination. A judge's judgment, like his discretion, varies with the size of his foot.

The risk in permissible copying of material in the public domain is shown in litigation over the famous Broadway play *Dishonored Lady*, by Edward Sheldon.[19] The idea and material for this very successful drama was obtained by the dramatist from a celebrated Scottish murder trial held in 1857. Thus the idea and material were in the public domain. The trial was so famous that it was described in a popular English book called *Notable Scottish Trials*. Later an English author, Mrs. Belloc Lowndes, used this trial material in the public domain for a novel, before Sheldon wrote his play. After the success of Sheldon's play, Metro-Goldwyn decided to make a picture out of this public-domain material. It negotiated with Edward Sheldon's agents for the purpose of the picture rights in his play, but an agreement could not be reached. Thus access was undeniable.

The picture company later produced a motion picture using the Lowndes novel, as to which it bought a license to make a motion picture, and also using the material in the public domain. Sheldon sued for piracy. There was, of course, no literal copying and no similarities of dialogue, though some similarities of dramatic situations. The picture company claimed this was all either public-domain material or independent creation or in the Lowndes novel.

The lower court [20] found that the defendant had not copied the treatment in the Sheldon play; and since the picture company was free to use the same material used by the plaintiff, it held that the picture company was not an infringer. On appeal the Circuit Court reversed,[21] saying, through Judge Learned Hand:

True, much of the picture owes nothing to the play; some of it is plainly drawn from the novel; but that is entirely immaterial; it is enough that substantial parts were lifted; no plagiarist can excuse the wrong by showing how much of his work he did not pirate. We can not avoid the conviction that, if the picture was not an infringement of the play, there can be none short of taking the dialogue.

For one of the main defenses raised by the picture company was that the dialogue in the two plays was entirely dissimilar, and since clearly there was no literal copying whatsoever from the dialogue which formed the dramatic essence of the play, there was no piracy. As to that the court said:

We have often decided that a play may be pirated without using the dialogue.

Thus one must be careful, if one uses material in the public domain, when one knows of a prior or recent use thereof. Otherwise one can get involved in a charge of treatment copying. For what constitutes mere use of material, and what constitutes copying of treatment expression, depends upon the delicate discretion of successive judges.

─── XI ───

What Can Not Be Copyrighted

In ADDITION to ideas and concepts and material in the public domain (as distinct from the expression thereof), which can not be copyrighted, many disparate items likewise can not be copyrighted. A grouping and detailing of these will be helpful.

75. TITLES

Titles are not included within the protection of a copyright.[1] They are deemed akin to ideas, of which the supply is limited and the pre-emption thereof by copyright would be too harsh a restraint upon the public.

Titles, however, in situations where they are associated in the public mind with the fame of a particular work, may be protected under the law of unfair competition. (See Chapter XXII.) How titles may be thus protected is there discussed in detail as an aspect of that subject. The theory by which protection is afforded to titles involves elements and limitations apart from and distinct from copyright, and peculiar to the concept of unfair competition.

But titles of periodicals and newspapers, and similar repeatedly issued publications, may be copyrighted under the law of trademarks, if "coined". (See footnote 12a to Chapter XXI.)

76. NEWS

News events, obviously, are in the public domain and can not be copyrighted.[2] However, expression thereof, i.e. "literary quality and style, apart from the bare recital of the facts or statement of news, * * * is protected by the copyright law." [3] Also, where unfair competition results from the unfair use by a rival news service of another's labor in collecting news, the law of unfair competition affords protection.[4] (See Section 164 hereafter.)

77. OBSCENE MATTER

Obscene or pornographic material can not be copyrighted; any attempted copyright obtained thereto is invalid. The reason, as held by the courts, is that the constitutional power granted Congress to enact copyright legislation (set forth before in Section 47) contemplates that copyrights will "promote the Progress of Science and the useful Arts". Obscenity does not carry out this purpose. What constitutes obscenity, particularly in relation to censorship, is discussed in Chapter XXV. But it is clear that obscenity may destroy a copyright duly obtained, [5] if it be a substantial enough part of the entire copyrighted work, or be striking enough in itself. Whether the assailed matter is obscene, and whether the obscenity so permeates the entire work as to destroy the copyright, are questions of fact to be decided by the court in each instance. The general result is clear: obscenity is not copyrightable. For the same reason, expressions of schemes which are designed to, or may, further fraud or deception, are denied copyright protection. Where a salesman's manual of advertisements for piano playing contained false and dishonest claims of untrue learning results, copyright protection was denied.[6] But a manual on horse racing was afforded copyright protection, probably on the attenuated ground that it was useful to breeders, not to gamblers only.[7]

78. MECHANICAL SYSTEMS AND METHODS

Since there is wavering of the dividing line between the expression of ideas in writing and by graphic designs or diagrams on the one hand, and ideas expressed and formulated as a mechanical process, on the other hand, futile efforts are often made to obtain copyright protection, instead of protection under patent law. Problems often arise as to the protection of original designs for useful objects which may, to a limited extent, be protected by design patents; also as to designs for dress styles or dress fabrics which cannot be protected by patent; also as to formulations of card games and novel creations of dolls and toys which likewise can not be patented.

The patent law is inadequate to protect many such commercial items. The copyright law, however, is not a substitute. New legislation is thus currently urged upon Congress.

The basic decision drawing the line between copyright protection of expression on the one hand, and attempted protection of substantive forms that can not be copyrighted on the other hand, is an excellently phrased decision of the Supreme Court in 1879, written by Justice Bradley. The question involved the extent of copyright protection on a copyrighted book of forms and schedules for book-keeping.[8]

The author had devised a simplified one-page method of book-keeping, thus avoiding the need of double entries. The copyrighted book consisted of (a) an explanation of his system and (b) a collection of ruled sheets or forms illustrating the new system as put into practice. The defendant copied and used the forms, varying them slightly. The court held that this *use* of the *forms* was not an infringement of the author's copyright in the book.

Justice Bradley lucidly set forth the reasons why such use was not piracy:

There is no doubt that a work on the subject of book-keeping, though only explanatory of well known systems, may be the subject of a copyright; but, then, it is claimed only as a book. Such a book may be explanatory either of old systems, or of an entirely new system: * * * But there is a clear distinction between the book, as such, and the art which it is intended to illustrate. * * * The same distinction may be predicated of every other art as well as that of book-keeping. A treatise on the composition and use of medicines, be they old or new; on the construction and use of ploughs or watches or churns; or on the mixture and application of colors for painting or dyeing; or on the mode of drawing lines to produce the effect of perspective, would be the subject of copyright; but no one would contend that the copyright of the treatise would give the exclusive right to the art or manufacture described therein. * * * To give to the author of the book an exclusive property in the art described therein, when no examination of its novelty has ever been officially made, would be a surprise and a fraud upon the public. That is the province of letters patent, not of copyright. The claim to an invention or discovery of an art or manufacture must be subjected to the examination of the Patent Office before an exclusive right therein can be obtained; and it can only be secured by a patent from the government. * * *

Of course, these observations are not intended to apply to ornamental designs, or pictorial illustrations addressed to the taste. Of these it may be said that their form is their essence and their object the production of pleasure in their contemplation. This is their final end. They are as much the products of genius and the result of compositions as are the lines of the poet or the historian's periods. On the other hand, the teachings of science and the rules and methods of useful art have their final end in application and use; and this application and use are what the public derive from the publication of a book which teaches them. But as embodied and taught in a literary composition or book, their essence consists only in their statement. This alone is what is secured by the copyright. The use by another of the same methods of statement, whether in words or illustrations, in a book published for teaching the art, would, undoubtedly, be an infringement of the copyright.

So too where a book on a new system of shorthand was copyrighted. The copyright of the book describing the new system did not cover the right to use that system.[9]

79. CARD GAMES

The above noted language also covers games. The rules, methods of play, and techniques in card or other games can not be copyrighted. That has been the express ruling as to books on bridge [10] and as to Acy-Ducy,[11] also as to Roller Derby contests.

The originator of the familiar Roller Derby contests ingeniously wrote and copyrighted a fictional story about Roller Derby shows. He attempted thereby to prevent others from operating similar Roller Derbies. The courts held he could not so do under the law of copyright.[12] District Court Judge Jenney ruled:

What Seltzer really composed was a description of a system for conducting races on roller skates. A system, as such, can never be copyrighted. If it finds any protection, it must come from the patent laws. * * * Included in his conception were certain stage devices which perhaps made the races produced under plaintiff's system more entertaining to an audience. But the authorities are insistent that a piece of scenery such as a penalty box amounts to nothing more than a mere mechanical device which cannot be copyrighted. It is clear also that the open-house or free-for-all feature is but a part of the system of rules, and cannot receive any greater protection than the system as a whole.

Even if plaintiff's books be held to describe a game or sporting event, the rules thereof, as ideas, are not copyrightable.

But later Seltzer gained an injunction in New York, on the grounds of unfair competition, preventing others from using the term "Roller Derby." [12a]

Where an author, however, copyrights a description of a game no one can copy his expression as such.[13] His expression and/or phrasing of the analysis or technique of playing is protected. The material involved, however, in the card or other game is not subject to copyright.

80. ADVERTISEMENTS CAN BE COPYRIGHTED

Advertisements and sales catalogues, as such, may be copyrighted and their text and pictures can not be copied. Such are the rulings as to advertisements of ladies' dresses; [14] also as to circus posters.[15] But the style and design of the dresses so copyrighted by advertisements or catalogues can be copied by others in making dresses.[16]

81. STAGE BUSINESS AND GAGS IN ACTING

Actors' "stage business" and actors' "gags" are not copyrightable. By stage business is meant the mannerisms, gestures, expressions and other acting devices improvised by a skilled actor to portray a role. By "gag" is meant a minor incident or sequence of minor incidents, usually of a humorous nature, closely related to and made vocal by gestures and intonations. These can be copied and taken by others,[17] unless the law of unfair competition intervenes. (See Section 161.) So, too, a sequence of dance steps and scenes can be freely copied.[18]

But where a sequence of incidents and action dramatically portrays and pictures action and produces a dramatic story, even in pantomime, the dramatic sequence can be copyrighted. A railroad-wreck scene depicted in a stage melodrama was held protected by a statutory copyright.[19] So, too, in motion-picture sequences. A dramatic sequence in a Harold Lloyd comedy scene in a silent motion picture was protected: [20]

The means of expressing an idea is subject to copyright protection, and where one uses his own method or way of expressing his idea, such adornment constitutes a protectible work. It is true that the mere motions, voice and postures of actors and mere stage business is not subject to copyright protection, but the sequence in question has literary quality in that it contains a story and is dramatic composition.

Pantomime is copyrightable. Judge Learned Hand has tersely said of pantomime: [21]

We have often decided that a play may be pirated without using the dialogue. * * * Were it not so, there could be no piracy of a pantomime, where there cannot be any dialogue; yet nobody would deny to pantomime the name of drama. Speech is only a small part of a dramatist's means of expression; he draws on all the arts and compounds his play from words and gestures and scenery and costume and from the very looks of the actors themselves. Again and again a play may lapse into pantomime at its most poignant and significant moments; a nod, a movement of the hand, a pause, may tell the audience more than words could tell. To be sure, not all this is always copyrighted, though there is no reason why it may not be, for those decisions do not forbid which hold that mere scenic tricks will not be protected.

The holding that "stage business" and "gags" and dance sequences can not be copyrighted seems quite unfair to the profession. Mimicry of leading actors, allowed as part of the right of fair comment, and constituting comedy and variety comedy by satirical or burlesque effects, is one thing. No one disagrees with the granting of that right of mimicry, which, within limits of not too great a copying of dramatic material, is clearly established. But to permit unlimited imitation of "stage business" and "gags" after they have been created by able actors is unfair. Some countries have attempted to protect actors' stage creations by statutory laws (e.g. Austria and England), but the United States law affords no protection, except under the law of unfair competition later discussed. (See Section 161.) So, too, with choreography. If it be only a sequence of steps interpretative of a mood or emotional effect, as noted before, it is not protected. If a dramatic story be told thereby it should be and is copyrightable as an unpublished work. The Regulations of the Copyright Office (b) (Section 49) permit registration of "dramatic scripts designed for * * * pantomimes and ballets * * * as plays." It is to be hoped that judges will respond in enlarging the protection for choreography. The steady expansion of the law of unfair competition gives hopes of relief. Even if a dance does not express a dramatic story, but merely a mood or a sequence of grace, it should be protected. It is protected in Europe under the Convention of Berne. (See Section 2 of the Convention of Berne.)

82. GOVERNMENT PUBLICATIONS

No copyright can be had ordinarily in a governmental publication. The Copyright Statute, Section 7, so specifies:

No copyright shall subsist * * * in any publication of the United States Government, or any reprint, in whole or in part, thereof; *Provided*, that copyright may be secured by the Postmaster General on behalf of the United States in the whole or any part of the publications authorized by Section 1 of the Act of Jan. 27, 1938 (39 U.S.C. 371).

The above exemption as to publications by the Postmaster General covers "illustrations in black and white of postage stamps" and "descriptive, historical and philatelic information with regard to such stamps." [22]

The exemption from copyrighting rights includes any record of any governmental department, also public records of state, county, or municipal proceedings and acts, although the Copyright Statute only speaks of the United States. Court rulings before the enactment of the Copyright Statute in 1909 so holding [23] can not be deemed overruled by the inartistic drafting of the above section.

When a government employee made a map of the Arctic and copyrighted it in his own name, the copyright was held to be held by the employee in trust for the government. Copying and publication of the map by *Collier's* was held not to be piracy.[24]

— XII —

International Copyrights

83. THE NEW UNIVERSAL COPYRIGHT CONVENTION

The most important recent advance in copyright is the adherence of the United States to the Universal Copyright Convention (U.C.C.; see Section 43 above). Copyright protection abroad for nationals of the United States for the first time is now on a firm foundation.

Each nation adhering to the U.C.C. covenants to afford to "the published and unpublished works" of the nationals of each "Contracting State the same protection . . . as it accords to the works" of its own nationals (Article II, U.C.C.).

The United States now has amended its Copyright Statute (*but solely* for nationals of U.C.C.-adhering nations except the U.S.A.): (1) to end the requisite of printing within the United States; (2) to end deposit of copies with the Register of Copyrights; (3) to liberalize importation of works from abroad; (4) to simplify the form and placing of the copyright notice (See Section 57 for details). Also, the U.C.C. practically ends the need of U.C.C. nationals obtaining ad interim copyrights.

Copyright protection will, nevertheless, also be sought under the two other great multilateral treaties; particularly under the Berne Convention "by the back door". The reasons are: (1) most civilized nations (except the United States) are members of the Berne Convention, but only eighteen (so far) have adhered to the U.C.C.; (2) minor technicalities may arise favoring protection under the Berne Convention.

A big gain by the U.C.C. is that objection no longer will be made abroad (e.g. in Holland and Canada) to U.S. nationals' obtaining protection under the Berne Convention, since the requisite of U.S. printing for aliens publishing abroad largely has been ended.

Thus copyright protection abroad for American nationals today involves three main treaties:

A. The U.C.C.

B. A European treaty, called the Berne Convention, first entered into in 1886 by nearly all the civilized nations except the United States and Russia. This Berne Convention was completed at Paris in 1896, revised at Berlin in 1908, "completed" at Berne in 1914, revised at Rome in 1928, and again revised at Brussels in 1948. Since the detailed order of changes made by these successive conventions is not pertinent, all reference in this discussion is to the final text as revised through 1948.

C. In addition to the Berne Convention, there have been three Pan-American copyright conventions or treaties: the Montevideo Convention of 1889; the Mexico City Convention of 1902; and that of Buenos Aires of 1910, called the Pan-American Convention of 1910. The important and controlling convention is the Pan-American Convention of 1910, to which the United States and twenty other powers, including all of the South American countries except Bolivia, have adhered.

84. HOW UNITED STATES NATIONALS GET INTER-
    NATIONAL PROTECTION UNDER THE BERNE
    CONVENTION

The United States is a member of the Pan-American Convention, but not of the Berne Convention. United States authors and publishers, however, manage to get protection under the Berne Convention by publishing their works simultaneously, at the time of publication in the United States, within a nation which is a member of the Berne Convention. This practice is permitted by tolerance under the provisions of the Berne Convention.

The countries in which this simultaneous publication is made, in order to obtain protection under the Berne Convention, usually are Great Britain or Canada. The procedure of simultaneous publication in both Great Britain and Canada is largely the same. Some have questioned the validity of simultaneous publication in Canada because of Canadian tariff prohibitions against importation of books. This difficulty, though often argued over in the past, was not enforced or actual. The U.C.C. probably has ended any objections by Canadian authors and publishers to simultaneous publication by

U.S. nationals in Canada since Canadian nationals no longer (after Canada adheres to the U.C.C.) will be required to print their books in the U.S. to get full U.S. copyright protection.

By publication in Canada (or Great Britain) simultaneously with first publication in the United States, two results arise: (1) a copyright is obtained in that country under either the Canadian Copyright Act of 1922 [1] or the English Copyright Act of 1911; [2] (2) since the United States publisher (or author) thus holds a Canadian (or a British) copyright, automatically he obtains full protection under the Treaty of Berne in each of the nations that are members of the Treaty of Berne, including all the members of the British Commonwealth and Empire. Thus the United States copyright and the Canadian or English copyright together substantially include all the civilized world, except the Union of Soviet Socialist Republics and possibly other "Iron Curtain" countries.

There has been some objection against permitting a citizen of the United States, which is not a member of the International Copyright Union, to obtain protection under the Berne Convention while the United States refuses to conform to the obligations of the Berne Convention. At one time objections were raised in England against permitting United States nationals to use England as a back door for obtaining copyright protection under the Berne Convention. But England has been very tolerant; nothing has come of these objections, although a commission with Lord Reading as chairman has recently submitted legislation concerning this and other copyright problems. England and Canada thus provide protection under the Berne Convention for United States nationals, by granting them a British Empire copyright.

85. WHAT IS SIMULTANEOUS PUBLICATION?

If a work of United States origin be published in the United States, without being published simultaneously in England or Canada, or in another sovereignty adhering to the Convention of Berne, the United States work, so far as England and other Berne Convention countries are concerned, is in the public domain. Then no copyright protection whatsoever can be had in foreign nations under the Convention of Berne.

British Publication

The necessity of first or simultaneous publication in England is specified in Section 1-A of the British Copyright Act of 1911, which reads as follows:

Copyright shall subsist throughout the parts of His Majesty's dominions * * * if (a) in the case of a published work the work was first published in such parts of His Majesty's dominions.

The British Copyright Act of 1911 also provides in Section 35, Subdivision 3, as follows, as to simultaneous publication:

For the purposes of this Act, a work shall be deemed to be first published within the parts of His Majesty's dominions to which this Act extends, notwithstanding that it has been published simultaneously in some other place, unless the publication in such parts of His Majesty's dominions as aforesaid is colourable only and is not intended to satisfy the reasonable requirements of the public, and a work shall be deemed to be published simultaneously in two places if the time between the publication in one such place and the publication in the other place does not exceed fourteen days, or such longer period as may, for the time being, be fixed by Order in Council.

The above two quotations from the British Act thus specify with precision the door through which a United States publisher or author must enter in order to get (a) a British copyright and (b) copyright protection under the Convention of Berne.

As to simultaneous first publication there are two precise requirements: (a) not more than fourteen days must elapse between publication in the United States and England; (b) the publication in England must not be "colourable only" but "intended to satisfy the reasonable requirements of the public" in England.

What constitutes publication in England not "colourable", satisfying the needs of the public? A convenient, lucid British decision blueprints the answer.[3]

Printing in England is not required. Issuing of copies to the public is required, by the placing of copies on sale, plus the sending of a copy to the British Museum and to the receiving agents of the University Libraries. This performance constitutes a "noncolourable publication" in England. Then a valid publication results. Such was the holding in a leading British case. The case so holding involved the copyrighting in England of a song of United States origin by a publisher in the United States. Twelve copies of the song were sent to the British publisher with instructions to copyright the song in England on May 15, 1913. The British publisher did so by sending one copy each to the above noted libraries and by exposing six copies for sale on the counter of its retail department in London. The song was not advertised. There was no immediate demand for it. The court held that the publication was complete, "not colourable", and that the acts above noted were sufficient to meet the reasonable demands of the public as such demands arose. No official registration or copyright notice is required under the British Statute.

The test thus is the placing on sale of an adequate supply, plus the sending of a copy to each of the leading British libraries. Upon such publication, without printing in England, full copyright protection is obtained in England, and thus in all the civilized countries of the world adhering to the Convention of Berne. The same result can be achieved by publication in any of the British Commonwealth nations. ·

Canadian Publication

Today the simultaneous publication of United States works in Canada is more usual than in England. Here the technical provisions as to simultaneous publication are the same. The Canadian Copyright Act of 1922 is modeled after the British Copyright Act. Common-law copyrights are abolished [Section 42 (5), Canadian Copyright Act], but unpublished works are granted statutory protection. The same fourteen-day provision appearing in the British Act appears in the Canadian Act in defining simultaneous publication [Section 3 (4) Canadian Copyright Act of 1922]. Canada adhered to the Convention of Berne on July 27, 1923. Canada also proclaimed its mutual copyright protection with the United States on December 26, 1927. [See Howard C. Fox, *Canadian Copyright Law* (1944), p. 550.]

Some publishers are unnecessarily concerned about arranging simultaneous publication in Canada instead of in England, because of certain academic provisions in the Canadian Copyright Act. Thirty years after an author's death, any of his published works can be published in Canada subject to payment of a royalty of ten per cent of the sales price. On the same royalty conditions, at any time, if sufficient copies of a work are not available in Canada, a Canadian publisher in Canada can print and sell the work after notice has been given to the copyright proprietor and after he has failed to procure the making available in Canada of 1000 copies.[4] Likewise records and perforated music rolls of copyrighted musical works previously recorded can be made in Canada upon payment of a royalty of two cents for each record side.[5] This Canadian provision as to manufacturing records is similar to that of Section 1(e) of the United States Copyright Statute.

None of these Canadian provisions, seldom availed of, need give concern to United States publishers. They are not averted by simultaneous publishing in England rather than Canada, since subsequent sales in Canada will in all probability occur and make the Canadian provisions applicable.

Some United States publishers print on their title leaf "Simultaneously published in the United States of America by ——— and in Canada by ———", naming both the United States and Canadian publishers. The notation of a Canadian publisher as one who puts the work on general sale in Canada is helpful but not necessary. The notice to the public of simultaneous publication in Canada and the United States is not conclusive. The fact of Canadian publishing must obviously conform to the notice [6] and can be established without the published claim. But the notice helps as evidence. The essential need is actual simultaneous publishing in Canada by the act of putting the work on general sale in Canada. It is desirable to have a Canadian firm, with or without the above notice, act as the publisher in Canada as an aspect of simultaneous publication in Canada.

Decisions in the Netherlands have required a publication within the Netherlands to have a Netherlands publisher, in order to constitute an act of publication in that country. But that requisite does not include printing within the Netherlands, even though its courts are not too co-operative in protecting foreign publishers.

The Canadian Copyright Act permits registration of a copyright claim with the Canadian Registrar of Copyrights, part of the office of the Canadian Commission of Patents. This registration is desirable and not onerous. In its absence only an injunction, not damages, can be obtained against an infringer who proves he had no actual notice of the Canadian copyright.[7]

86. PROTECTION GRANTED IN CANADA, ENGLAND, AND EUROPE

The chief differences between the copyright law of England and the bulk of the European nations on one hand and that of the United States on the other hand are three:

1. England, Canada, and Europe have now dispensed with all formalities in copyright procedure. Therefore there need be no deposit of copies with any public authority to obtain a copyright in Canada, England, or Europe, and there need be no affixing of any copyright notice of any kind. Article 4, Section 2, of the Convention of Berne reads:

The enjoyment and the exercise of these rights shall not be subject to any formality; * * *.

2. Common-law copyrights as such are abolished. There is a statutory copyright in unpublished works which comes into being automatically upon creation, without any disclosure, publication, registration, or formality. Thus Canada, England, and Europe are not perplexed by the issue as to the destruction of a common-law copyright by publication. But, oddly, a new host of difficulties have arisen under the European and British view as to common-law copyrights. These are later discussed. (See Section 88.)

3. The term of the copyright in England and Europe is the life of the author plus fifty years. If the work be by joint authors, then copyright endures for the life of the author who dies latest, plus fifty years. In some countries the fifty-year period is shortened.

87. STRUCTURE OF THE CONVENTION OF BERNE

International copyright treaties could either (a) adopt a uniform copyright law, which would apply uniformly in all countries; or (b) permit varying copyright enactments in each country, but provide that within a country adhering to the treaty the citizens of any foreign country adhering must be afforded the same copyright protection that is afforded to any citizen of an adhering country.

The first procedure would be more desirable, of course, but is too difficult.

Thus the Convention of Berne adopts the second method. It provides that each country adhering to the treaty agrees to afford all the protection of its copyright laws to copyrights originating in any other nation that is a member of the Convention of Berne.

88. TECHNICALITIES UNDER THE BERNE CONVENTION

The difficulties arising under the European and British common-law copyright concept originate from the basic distinction between published and unpublished works, in that the one category was formerly protected by statutory copyright and the other by non-statutory common-law copyright. Both categories have been brought under statutory copyright, and nonstatutory common-law copyrights on unpublished works are abolished in England. (Section 36, British Copyright Act, 1911.) Once a work is published, a copyright of it as a published work automatically comes into existence in England. When a work is unpublished, however, the statutory copyright arises automatically on its creation, but depends upon the nationality or residence of the author. Section B-1 of the British Copyright Act of 1911, for example, typically provides the test for copyright protection of unpublished works. It reads: "But if * * * (b) in the case of an unpublished work the author was at the date of making the work a British subject or resident within such parts of His Majesty's dominions," then a copyright arises in such unpublished work.

No question evolves if the author of any unpublished work is a British citizen, that is, a subject of the King. Citizenship changes, and the date thereof, are rare and furnish clear records. But as to a resident of England who is not a British subject, the question always arises whether at the time of the creation of the work he was a resident in England. And, of course, in the case of an unpublished work by an author who is not a British subject and who is not resident in England but resides say in the United States, no way exists of obtaining a British copyright on an unpublished work short of publishing simultaneously in England.

The question is not academic. A play, never published, written say by a United States author not residing in England (or in any country adhering to the Convention of Berne), at the time of writing enjoys no copyright protection within Europe or the British Empire. The performance of the play in England, or elsewhere in Europe, of course, does not constitute publication under British and European law. A copyright proprietor has the exclusive right of performance of a play under British and European law, as he has in the United States. But a United States playwright, residing in the United States, can get a British or European copyright on his unpublished play only by publication in England or Europe, not by performance.

Also, where an alien intermittently resides in England and elsewhere, and writes a play or other unpublished work, his English copyright is always open to attack on the ground he was not a resident in England at the time he wrote the work. United States producers using such plays may have difficulties.

United States authors must therefore consider the wisdom, if they want their plays performed in England or abroad, of publishing their plays abroad and in the United States simultaneously. A published play, to be copyrightable in the United States, need not be printed in the United States. (See Section 57E.)

Publication abroad, of course, need not mean printing within the country where the play is published. But difficulties nevertheless arise. Netherlands courts hold that mere distribution of a few copies in the Netherlands is not publication.[8] Nor is it sufficient merely to print a Netherlands publisher's name on the title page of a book sold in the Netherlands. Evidently there must be a bona fide contract, under which a Netherlands publisher puts out the book, but does not necessarily print it in the Netherlands.

89. COVERAGE UNDER THE BERNE CONVENTION

The scope of coverage of works under the British Copyright Statute and under the Convention of Berne (see its Article 2) is generally the same as that afforded under the United States Copyright Statute. The most noteworthy addition is the protection of "choreographic works and entertainments in dumb show, the acting form of which is fixed or otherwise" (Convention of Berne, Article 2). This is, of course, admirable. Also an author's moral or retained rights are protected. (See Section 138.)

The right of translating or of summarizing any work is fully protected in Europe as in the United States. The provisions as to the protection of works of art are quite broad. (See Section 2 of Article 2, Convention of Berne.) But considerable difficulties arise as to mechanical reproduction of music which need not here be noted. Also the provisions as to rights in lectures and speeches and press material are quite detailed and involved. Not being of practical urgency, they are not discussed in this book.

Articles "on current economic, political or religious issues" may be reproduced by the press "unless the reproduction thereof is expressly reserved." Article 9 of the Berne Convention reads:

(1) Serial novels, short stories, and all other works, whether literary, scientific or artistic, whatever their purpose, and which are published in the newspapers or periodicals of one of the Countries of the Union shall not be reproduced in the other Countries without the consent of the authors.

(2) Articles on current economic, political or religious topics may be reproduced by the press unless the reproduction thereof is expressly reserved; nevertheless the source must always be clearly indicated. The legal consequences of the breach of this obligation shall be determined by the laws of the Country where protection is claimed.

(3) The protection of this Convention shall not apply to news of the day nor to miscellaneous information having the character of mere items of news.

A provision similar to Sections 2 and 3 of Article 9 of the Convention of Berne appears in the Pan-American Copyright Convention (Article 11), which reads as follows:

Literary, scientific or artistic writings, whatever may be their subjects, published in newspapers or magazines, in any one of the countries of the Union, shall not be reproduced in the other countries without the consent of the authors. With the exception of the works mentioned, any article in a newspaper may be reprinted by others, if it has not been expressly prohibited, but in every case, the source from which it is taken must be cited.

News and miscellaneous items published merely for general information, do not enjoy protection under this convention.

It is for this reason that United States periodicals and most books usually carry a notice "all rights reserved". A further reason for this notice, as later noted, is another provision (Section 3) of the **Pan-American Convention** which reads:

* * * the acknowledgement of a copyright obtained in one State, in conformity with its laws, shall produce its effects of conferring full right in all the other states without the necessity of complying with any other formality, provided always there shall appear in the work a statement that indicates the reservation of the property right.

Under the Pan-American Convention there is a full reciprocal recognition of copyrights throughout the members of the Pan-American Union adhering to this treaty. The provision "provided always there shall appear in the work a statement that indicates the reservation of the property right" seems an unfortunate formality. What is probably meant is that there must be some form of copyright notice, upon which Congress has laid such stress in the United States Copyright Statute. In view of this provision, here is another reason for the use of the phrase "all rights reserved". That phrase is an adequate conformity with the above language of the Pan-American Copyright Convention.

This notice "all rights reserved" can for all the foregoing reasons well be used in United States books and periodicals. But its use is not necessary, as is the required copyright notice, failure to use which is fatal in the United States. Unlike nugatory efforts to limit by notice the rights of fair comment, and to avoid liability for defamation or piracy by self-serving declarations, the notice "all rights reserved" is desirable.

90. IMPORTATION OF BOOKS AND SHEETS

Except as to nationals of countries that are adherents of the Universal Copyright Convention, the Copyright Statute (in its Sections 106 and 107) prohibits the importation (a) of any "article bearing a false notice of copyright"; (b) of any piratical copies; (c) of "any copies" which have not been manufactured in the United States under the provisions for printing in the United States, *excepting* 1500 copies of a work in English published abroad and registered under an ad interim copyright. (See Section 59.) Also, (d) any plates of the same matter made from type not set within the United States or (e) any copies produced by a lithographing or photoengraving process not performed in the United States may not be imported.

The exceptions from the above provisions are, in order of importance: (a) a foreign newspaper or magazine containing matter copyrighted in the United States, with the consent of the authority of the copyright proprietor, may be imported into the United States but not if such copyrighted matter is not so authorized; also (b) the authorized edition of a book in a foreign language of which only a translation into English has been copyrighted in this country, and (c) works in Braille.

The exceptions also extend to any book (in English) published abroad with the authorization of the copyright proprietor but are limited to: (a) *one copy* at one time brought in for individual use and not for sale, but not including a foreign reprint of a book by a United States author copyrighted in the United States; (b) books imported for the use of the United States; (c) one copy of a book imported in good faith by an educational society or educational institution such as a college or free public library; (d) books forming parts of libraries or collections purchased en bloc for the use of educational societies and colleges or libraries; or (d) books in the personal baggage of persons or families arriving from foreign countries and not intended for sale. Books not in English, of course, are permitted to be imported, dehors the above exceptions.

The 1500 copies specified above as permitted to be imported under an ad interim copyright can be in the form of unbound sheets to be bound in this country, provided such books when published contain the copyright notice. There is no express provision so providing, but that seems included within the consent to import.

All these provisions are drastically enforced. They are designed to prevent any evasion of the provisions requiring the printing of books in the United States.

Books imported in violation of these provisions are subject to forfeiture in the same manner as property and obscene works imported into the United States in violation of the customs revenue laws. But where the importation does not involve willful negligence or fraud they can be returned to the country of export. (See Section 108, Copyright Statute.) A United States copyright proprietor can send notice on forms prepared by the copyright office to postmasters or customs officers at ports of entry into the United States designed to prevent importation of any copies of books in violation of such copyright proprietor's rights. (See Section 109, Copyright Statute.)

These drastic provisions are caused by the unfortunate requirement of printing books in the United States. The importation of 1500 copies above noted represents an effort to take a more considerate attitude toward foreign books in English in order to permit foreign publishers "to test the market"; but obviously they are not adequate to retain full reciprocity or to permit United States entry into the Berne Convention or to end the unfortunate effect of Section 16 requiring mechanical work to be done in the United States. The number of 1500 was fixed on the theory that the minimum commercially feasible printing of a book in the United States is 3000 copies. Thus it was decided by Congress that the importation of 1500 copies would not deprive printers in the United States of work. By importing and selling 1500 copies, the importing publisher could test the market and perhaps print more copies in the United States.[9]

——— XIII ———

The Copyright Proprietor's Bundle
of Rights

91. VARIED USES OF COPYRIGHTED MATERIAL

STATUTORY, common-law, and international copyrights all grant an exclusive monopoly over all the forms and ways of changed expression of the copyrighted literary work. Not only is literal copying, colorable rephrasing, or treatment copying prohibited. Transformations into all other forms of expression also are the sole right of the copyright proprietor.

A copyrighted novel, for example, can not be transformed into a play or a copyrighted play into a novel without the license of the copyright proprietor.

The most skillfully drafted section of the Copyright Statute is the first section specifying this exclusive right and control. Commonly it is called the "transformation section". It defines the different uses granted exclusively to the copyright proprietor:

Any person entitled thereto, upon complying with the provisions of this title, shall have the exclusive right:

(a) To print, reprint, publish, copy, and vend the copyrighted work;

(b) To translate the copyrighted work into other languages or dialects, or make any other version thereof, if it be a literary work; to dramatize it if it be a nondramatic work; to convert it into a novel or other nondramatic work if it be a drama; to arrange or adapt it if it be a musical work; to complete, execute, and finish it if it be a model or design for a work of art;

(c) To deliver or authorize the delivery of the copyrighted work in public for profit if it be a lecture, sermon, address, or similar production;

(d) To perform or represent the copyrighted work publicly if it be a drama or, if it be a dramatic work and not reproduced in copies for sale, to vend any manuscript or any record whatsoever thereof; to make or to procure the making of any transcription or record thereof by or from which, in whole or in part, it may in any manner or by any method be exhibited, performed, represented, produced, or reproduced; and to exhibit, perform, represent, produce, or reproduce it in any manner or by any method whatsoever; and

(e) To perform the copyrighted work publicly for profit if it be a musical composition; and for the purpose of public performance for profit, and for the purposes set forth in subsection (a) hereof, to make any arrangement or setting of it or of the melody of it in any system of notation or any form of record in which it may be read or reproduced * * *.

Section 3 of the Copyright Statute summarizes and adds thereto:

The copyright provided by this title shall protect all the copyrightable component parts of the work copyrighted, and all matter therein in which copyright is already subsisting, but without extending the duration or scope of such copyright. The copyright upon composite works or periodicals shall give to the proprietor thereof all the rights in respect thereto which he would have if each part were individually copyrighted under this title.

92. WHAT TRANSFORMATION INCLUDES

As provided in this transformation section above quoted, the copyright proprietor is granted by the Copyright Statute exclusive control over: (1) any form of copying, printing, publishing, or vending of the copyrighted work; (2) any translation into any other language; (3) any transformation into any other form of expression, i.e. dramatizing the copyrighted work into a stage play, motion picture, or radio or television performance; in reverse, any changing of a play into a novel or story. The additional exclusive right "to perform" the work publicly, if it be a play, or to perform it publicly for profit, if it be a musical composition, is granted. These additional performing rights are still retained if the copyright proprietor sells copies of his work to the public. In the case of plays, the copyright proprietor's retained right of performance includes all public performances, *whether or not for profit;* in the case of musical compositions the copyright proprietor retains, after he sells copies of the score to the public, only the right to perform the composition in public *for profit*. This added "for profit" limitation as to musical compositions is important.

93. TRANSLATIONS AND OTHER VERSIONS

An important minor right is that of translation and abridgement. The provisions of the Copyright Statute, Section 1(b) above set forth (Section 91), specify that the copyright proprietor has the exclusive right "To translate the copyrighted work into other languages or dialects, or make any other version thereof, it be a literary work; * * *".

The word "translation" needs no gloss. Translation includes obviously "free" translations or alterations or improvement in the text as part of the translator's skill. That right of translation belongs exclusively to the copyright proprietor. Where a writer of the life of Hans Christian Andersen translated Andersen's letters into English, a novelist who quoted extensive parts of these letters in writing a novel based on Andersen's life was held to have plagiarized, and gone beyond the limits of fair use.[1]

It is to be noted that the exclusive right of translation is limited to a "literary work", i.e. any work expressed in words, whether it be in the form of a story, poem, article, drama, lecture, or the lyric of a song. Where music notations are involved, the Copyright Statute, Section 1(b) provides that the copyright proprietor has the exclusive, related right, "to arrange or adapt it, if it be a musical work".

If the copyrighted work be a nondramatic work, the same section adds that the copyright proprietor has the exclusive right "to dramatize it if it be a nondramatic work".

94. ABRIDGEMENTS

Abridgements, condensations, summaries, or rearrangements are all reserved to the copyright proprietor by the phrase to "make any other version thereof" [C.S., Section 1(b)]. Under the earlier United States acts, the language of the statute did not expressly include the right to make "any other version thereof". Thus whether abridgements constituted piracy was open to doubt.[2] But now the right to abridge and condense and summarize clearly belongs exclusively to the copyright proprietor.

Can a summary by a stranger be *so short* and fleeting as *not* to constitute a violation of the copyright proprietor's exclusive right of abridgement? Three intertwined rulings, all involving a book containing hasty summaries of less than one hundred words each of the plots of operas, have held that very brief notations do not constitute abridgements or "other versions" of the operas, also that the copyright proprietor of the opera could not hold the publisher of the summaries for piracy.[3] These decisions might possibly be explained on the basis of fair comment (later discussed in Chapter XV), though that reason is not mentioned by the judge deciding these cases. Otherwise viewed, they are perplexing. The words "any other version" would seem to include even the most hasty summaries, if they are substantial enough to be more than fair comment.

95. DRAMATIZATION DEFINED

Before the right of public performance of plays, reserved exclusively to the copyright proprietor, can be understood clearly, a workable definition of the term "performance of a play" or "dramatic performance" must be supplied.

A drama or play, in legal concept, is a story told by action; to constitute a performance, those two elements (story and action) must be present. Dialogue, of course, is usually the device telling the bulk of the story of a play. But if words be not used, nevertheless a story told only by action (a pantomime) can constitute a dramatic performance. Sets and costumes commonly also are used; but, likewise, without sets and costumes, if a story be told in action, the result will be considered the performance of a play or drama. This legal definition of a performance of a play, or dramatic performance, as a story told in action, protects the copyright proprietor in a variety of situations.

A melodramatic stage scene, depicting a person tied to a railroad track by a villain, but handily rescued by the hero, though told with "very little dialogue" and largely by action, has been held to be a dramatic performance and therefore protected under a copyright as such.[4]

Performance of a drama has lucidly been defined by Justice Holmes,[5] in a suit where a silent motion picture appropriated, without license, scenes from Lew Wallace's copyrighted novel *Ben Hur*. The motion picture, though without words, was held to be a dramatic performance of parts of the novel and therefore piracy. This result was reached under the Copyright Statute of 1891, whereunder the litigation arose. This Statute made no mention of motion pictures. Justice Holmes ruled:

The subdivision of the question that has the most general importance is whether the public exhibition of these moving pictures infringed any rights under the copyright law. By Rev. Stat. Sec. 4952 * * * authors have the exclusive right to dramatize any of their works. So, if the exhibition was or was founded on a dramatizing of Ben Hur, this copyright was infringed. We are of opinion that Ben Hur was dramatized by what was done. Whether we consider the purpose of this clause of the statute, or the etymological history and present usages of language, drama may be achieved by action as well as by speech. Action can tell a story, display all the most vivid relations between men, and depict every kind of human emotion, without the aid of a word. It would be impossible to deny the title of drama to pantomime as played by masters of the art. * * * But if a pantomime of Ben Hur would be a dramatizing of Ben Hur, it would be none the less so that it was exhibited to the audience by reflection from a glass, and not by direct vision of the figures,—as sometimes has been done in order to produce ghostly or inexplicable effects. The essence of the matter in the case last supposed is not the mechanism employed, but that we see the event or story lived. The moving pictures are only less vivid than reflections from a mirror. With the former as with the latter our visual impression—what we see—is caused by the real pantomime of real men through the medium of natural forces, although the machinery is different and more complex. How it would be if the illusion of motion were produced from paintings instead of from photographs of the real thing may be left open until the question shall arise.

Songs can be dramatized by dramatic action telling the story suggested by the lyrics or otherwise. Such dramatization, unless permitted by the copyright proprietor of the song, is piracy. But most songs, as such, when sung or performed on the stage are not deemed dramatic performances, though they are held to be performances. The distinction involved was set forth in a dispute where the technical question involved was whether the plaintiff had assigned away so much of its rights that it hadn't retained the right to sue. The plaintiff argued that the performance of a song "Kiss Me Again" from *Mlle. Modiste* was a dramatic performance: [6]

The plaintiff claims that the song is a dramatic composition * * *. The plaintiff cites several English cases and one American case in support of the claim that the song in this case is a dramatic composition. It will not be necessary to review them all. The leading English case appears to be Russell v. Smith, 12 Q.B. 217. In that case it was held that a song called "The Ship on Fire," which related the burning of a ship at sea and the escape of those on board, describing their feelings in vehement language, and sometimes expressing them in the supposed words of the suffering parties, was dramatic, even though it was sung by one person only, sitting at a piano, giving effect to the verses by delivery, but not assisted by scenery or appropriate dress. But in that case the Chief Justice said:

"The song in question is stated in the bill to be founded on the loss of the Kent by fire in the Bay of Biscay. It represents a storm at sea, the burning of the ship, and the escape by boat to another ship, and so a safe return to land. It moves terror and pity and sympathy, by presenting danger and despair and joy, and maternal and conjugal affection. A witness of great experience in publishing music deposes that this was considered a dramatic song, and published with the title of a dramatic and descriptive song, and there was no evidence that any one considered it not dramatic. Thus the nature of the production places it rather in the representative than the narrative class of poetry, according to Lord Bacon's division of dramatic from epic (Advancement of Learning, book 11, Poesy), and the evidence states it to be known as dramatic among those who are conversant with such things."

In the present case there is no evidence that the song "Kiss Me Again" was ever considered by any one as a dramatic song, nor are there any dramatic features in it such as distinguish "The Ship on Fire" from ordinary songs.

The court added:

But, although this song is not a dramatic composition as it stands, it might conceivably be dramatized. The Copyright Act * * * gives the copyright owner the right "to dramatize it, if it be a nondramatic work". * * *

In relation to the right to sue for an infringement, a copyright is an indivisible thing, and cannot be split up and partially assigned either as to time, place, or particular rights or privileges, less than the sum of all the rights comprehended in the copyright.[7]

So, too, the use of comic-strip characters from the copyrighted comic strip "Mutt and Jeff", in a musical comedy called *In Cartoonland*, was held to be a dramatization of the comic character and strip and so piracy.[8]

But a copyrighted description of a dance in several tableaux, it has been held, does not tell a story and so is not a dramatic performance and is not entitled to protection from imitators.[9] This later ruling can be deemed limited by the scant dramatic material involved in this dance case. Pantomime will be a dramatic performance, if enough story is told, and then it is protected under the Copyright Statute.[10] A dance can tell a story as well as can pantomime. Creations of choreography are a rising art today and are entitled to copyright protection. But the rulings unfortunately do not yet so hold. These should be protected as interpretations of mood or patterns of grace, if sufficiently definite, even though no dramatic story be told. But no court rulings so hold.

96. PUBLIC PERFORMANCE

In the bundle of rights, one of the most important rights reserved to the copyright proprietor of a play is the exclusive right *to perform the play publicly*, even after copies of the play are sold to the public.

As to musical compositions, a somewhat similar but more limited right is granted the copyright proprietor; the exclusive right "To perform the copyrighted work publicly for profit" [C.S., Section 1(e)], even after the copies of the score are sold to the public. Thus in dramas and plays the exclusive right is broader; the exclusive right is "To perform or represent the copyrighted work publicly" [C.S., Section 1(d)]. In lectures the exclusive right granted is "To deliver or authorize the delivery of the copyrighted work in public for profit" [C.S., Section 1(c)].

97. RIGHTS RESERVED ON PUBLISHING COPIES

When a copyright proprietor sells or authorizes the sale of copies of his work to the public, he grants the purchaser, of course, the right freely to read it. What further rights does he grant? And what rights does he reserve and retain under the Copyright Statute and without specification?

In the case of a written work, including a drama, he grants, of course, the right to read it. In the case of a musical composition, the copyright proprietor grants the purchaser of a copy of the musical score or song the right freely to play it in the purchaser's home on an instrument or to sing it as often as the purchaser wishes. The copyright proprietor also grants the purchaser the right to play the musical composition in public, but only if no profit is derived from the performance by the purchaser. In the case of a play he grants the right to perform it *privately*, but not *publicly*, whether or not for profit.

98. POEMS AND NONDRAMATIC WORKS

In 1953, a great injustice, largely to poets but also to other writers, was ended by amendment to Subsection (c) of Section 1 of the Copyright Statute.

The amended section now reads:

(c) To deliver, authorize the delivery of, read, or present the copyrighted work in public for profit if it be a lecture, sermon, address or similar production, or other nondramatic literary work; to make or procure the making of any transcription or record thereof by or from which, in whole or in part, it may in any manner or by any method be exhibited, delivered, presented, produced, or reproduced; and to play or perform it in public for profit, and to exhibit, represent, produce, or reproduce it in any manner or by any method whatsoever. The damages for the infringement by broadcast of any work referred to in this subsection shall not exceed the sum of $100 where the infringing broadcaster shows that he was not aware that he was infringing and that such infringement could not have been reasonably foreseen; and

Under the provision existing prior to 1953 it was held that the exclusive right of publicly reading (as distinct from converting into a dramatic performance) all or parts of a copyrighted poem or a novel, or factual article, was not reserved to the copyright proprietor thereof. Even though the reading went far beyond fair comment, later defined (see Chapter XV), such public reading was freely permitted as of right. For the statute did not grant the exclusive right of public reading in respect to poems, novels and books to the copyright owner.

Before the amendment, an author wrote several poems, each of considerable length. He copyrighted the poems. Later he incorporated them in a drama which he copyrighted. Jimmy Durante recited and sang three of his poems in various public places, also over the radio. The court held the poet had no right to sue under his copyright.[11] The court ruled that "other copyrighted works [i.e. poems, novels, and nondramatic works] may be recited in public for profit without infringement". It also ruled that these particular poems were not dramatic productions, though other poems might be such; also that the later inclusion of the poems in the poet's copyrighted play did not change their original status under the first copyright as poems and turn the original poems into dramatic works.

The amendment alters all this. The poet or other copyright owner is granted the exclusive right "to deliver * * * read or present the copyrighted work in public for profit. Also "to exhibit, represent, produce or reproduce" it "in any manner or by any method". The words "in public for profit" have the wide meaning applied in the case of music performed "publicly for profit" under Subsection (e) of Section 1 of the Copyright Statute (see Section 122). If the reading be private (e.g. to a home gathering) then the author cannot object.

99. "PUBLIC" PERFORMANCE OF PLAYS DEFINED

As to plays, the Statute specifies the exclusive right in the copyright proprietor "to perform or represent the copyrighted work publicly." The sale of a copy of a published play, of course, does not result in the copyright proprietor's retained rights being destroyed. He retains all rights of *public* performance, whether or not for profit. What constitutes the *public* element in the performance of a play? No decision authoritative in the United States has been given. The clarifying decision will turn on several factors. Yet the results can be stated fairly definitively.

In a British case [12] a play was performed in a village, at a women's social and educational club, at which only members of the club were present. The women's club involved was one of 5000 similar women's clubs organized under an Act of Parliament; every woman in the village, under that law, was impliedly invited to and could become a member, on the payment of a small fee. The court held that the performance was public when given before such a club and was not a "domestic" or "private" performance. The court held that the performance was in fact and reality before a "portion of the public". The court noted that the audience seeing the play comprised a tenth of the female residents of the town. The semi-public nature of the club and the members present seemed the determinative factor in the court's mind.[13]

On the other hand, in a Maryland case,[14] where a film was exhibited at a private yacht club, but solely before members and their guests, the court held that the showing was not public. The Maryland case rejected the test of the number present, as stated in the English case. It held the club showing to be akin to an exhibition in a private home.

On reason, and from the standpoint of fairness, in determining the nature of a semipublic performance with or without admission charges, it must be concluded that the English ruling seems correct. Performance of a play in a private home is unusual. Though private performances are permitted by the Statute they are exceptional. Sometimes they become well publicized in the community and thus involve publicity. Any such performance of a play, gaining such publicity, may keep patrons from attending a public performance whereunder the playwright receives royalties.

Yet the Statute says "to perform * * * publicly." Performances in private homes not open to the public can not be called public. But those who run such private performances of a play without paying the author's royalties, run risks. The place where the performance is given is not the sole consideration. The fact that the performance is for charity or by a private group seeking no profit or acting for educational purposes, if the performance be open to many who may buy tickets, does not make the performance private. The Statute does not limit the playwright's monopoly to performances "for profit". Therefore those who arrange private performances, if wise, will not risk that the publicity involved may make the performance public. The difficulty of defining "public" should be a deterrent to private performances held without the consent of the playwright.

100. PROFIT IN MUSICAL PERFORMANCES

The words "for profit" added in the Statute as to public performance of musical compositions have been meticulously defined by the courts. "For profit", Justice Holmes has ruled, does not apply restrictively to a performance in public where the spectators are required to pay an admission fee.[15] The Supreme Court thus has held that a restaurant (where no "cover charge" was involved) performed "the copyrighted work for profit" by engaging an orchestra to play music for the pleasure of its patrons while eating. Also, it has been expressly held that performance of a musical composition, words or music or both, by radio, by television, in dance halls or other public places, is a public performance of the musical composition "for profit". A discussion of other aspects of performances of musical compositions (including the playing by mechanical means, such as phonograph records, juke boxes, broadcasting, and television) is concentrated in the discussion of musical rights appearing in Chapter XVI.

101. EXHIBITIONS OF MOTION PICTURES, AS PERFORMANCES

When a motion picture is exhibited, or when a play is publicly performed, the exhibition is not *publication*. (See Section 62, subdivisions 2 and 6.) But is the exhibition of a dramatic motion picture a public *performance* of the dramatic work?

The question has been litigated by motion-picture companies to prevent "bicycling". (By "bicycling" is meant the surreptitious, secret, and unauthorized exhibition of prints of motion pictures, to avoid payment of a royalty or license fee to the picture company, in which an exhibitor takes the film leased, from a theater licensed by the producer, to another unlicensed nearby theater and exhibits if there, collecting admissions but not paying the royalty or license fee.) In the early days of motion pictures, an exhibitor might lease a film for exhibition in his theater A. After it was shown there, he might rush it (by bicycle or automobile) to his theater B, as to which no license fee had been paid, and add a second exhibition at no cost to himself. If the exhibition of a film in a theater were held akin to the public showing of photographs or prints, the second showing would be permitted under the copyright law, once the film was leased. The picture company then would be limited to recovery on the limited and difficult grounds of fraudulent misuse of the rented physical print. If the unlicensed showing were held to be a public *performance* of the print, and thus *piracy*, then the motion-picture producers and distributors could automatically avail themselves of all the penalties set out in the Copyright Statute.

The first ruling handed down was that exhibitions of motion pictures were not performances.[16] The later and prevailing ruling now is that exhibitions of pictures are public performances thereof, thus following the *Ben Hur* case [17] (Section 95). Thus each such showing is piracy.

If a motion picture be a "scenic" or "newsreel", i.e. a film not picturing a dramatic story, the ruling is still the same.[18] The reasoning involved is not too logical as to "scenics" and "newsreels", but nevertheless it is definitive. The basis given for this later ruling is that the producer of the scenic retains the right to dramatize it and the unauthorized exhibition invades that retained right. But the same right is held by the maker of a group of prints, and yet once he releases them, anyone can exhibit them when and where he chooses. Thus the court's ruling as to "scenics" and "newsreels" is questionable.

102. THE RIGHT TO VEND

The Copyright Statute [Section 1(a)] grants the copyright proprietor the exclusive right to "vend the copyrighted work".

But the copyright proprietor who obtains a statutory copyright by publication, once he sells his work to a bookstore, can not impose, as part of his right to vend, a minimum price at which the book can be sold or resold to the public. In a suit by a publisher to restrain Macy's book department from selling the publisher's books at less than the fixed minimum price, as specified in print under the copyright notice, the Supreme Court denied the copyright proprietor any relief.[19]

The 1951 ruling rejecting minimum prices under the antitrust and fair-trade statutes confirms this holding as to books, as to the bookstore that has not signed an agreement with the publisher to establish minimum prices.

So also the right to copy and vend does not include the right to prevent purchasers of second-hand books from repairing, rebinding, and reselling copyrighted books previously sold;[20] or from rebinding such books with other or additional material;[21] or after buying unbound sheets, from binding and indexing them, using for the index copyrighted material in the sheets.[22] Also where a motion-picture film is sold, not leased, restrictions imposed as to the territory where it may be exhibited are unenforcible under the Copyright Statute.[23] In short, a copyright including the right to vend gives no rights to restrain the resale or use of the copyrighted book or work, once it is sold, or to fix prices or the terms of use,[24] by imposing conditions, by notice, or otherwise. This aspect of copyright is of importance as to the efforts of television stations to limit by notice the places where broadcast television programs, particularly of sports, may be exhibited. (See Chapter XXV.)

XIV

Assignments and Licenses

---

103. THE COPYRIGHT PROPRIETOR

THE PRETENTIOUS name "copyright proprietor" originates in the Copyright Statute (Sections 9 and 11). It means the person or corporation in whose name the copyright certificate is obtained and issued.

The copyright proprietor, i.e. the person who takes out the copyright, need not be the author. The Copyright Statute (Section 26) provides "the word 'author' shall include an employer in the case of works made for hire". Thus the author, as an employee or independent worker, may assign the created work to another who may take out the copyright on the actual author's creation and thereupon, instead of the author, become the copyright proprietor thereof.

At a trial, when the copyright certificate is introduced by the copyright proprietor as establishing his title and copyright, proof must be added by the copyright proprietor, if he is not the author, of such assignment or the other facts of such succession to the rights of the author or creator.

The Copyright Statute (Section 28) provides that copyrights may be "assigned, granted, or mortgaged by an instrument in writing signed by the proprietor of the copyright, or may be bequeathed by will."

Thus the copyright may be dealt with as transferable property. It may also be bequeathed by will; otherwise, it devolves on death to the copyright proprietor's heirs.

The Copyright Statute also provides (Section 30) for a recording of such transfers in the Copyright Office, similar to the procedure prevailing in the conveyance of land. The written instrument may be recorded in the Copyright Office. Valuable protection is acquired by such recording in that if the recording be within three months after the execution thereof in the United States, or within six months after the execution thereof outside the United States, it prevails over any other assignment not recorded. That is, the transferee can check the record of transfers in the Copyright Office and if he finds no such transfer, and has not had any notice of any prior transfer upon recording his transfer, his transfer will prevail over any other transfers made prior thereto and not recorded, or made subsequent thereto and recorded.

The time provision as to recording transfers means that by recording such assignment within such period of time protection is obtained against prior unrecorded assignments if actual notice of such unrecorded assignments be not shown.

104. ASSIGNMENTS AND LICENSES

But under the Copyright Statute as to transfers of the copyright an artificial rule arises which works hardship, and even financial loss, on unwary authors. Any assignment of the copyright is invalid unless all of the bundle of rights is transferred at one time thereby, throughout the United States, or for a specified fractional subdivision thereof, or of the world. An assignment of all the copyright proprietor's rights under a copyright as to and for a separate state or geographical division, or for all of the world, is enforcible. But an assignment of some of the rights included in the bundle for the world, or a part thereof, and retention of others is invalid and unenforcible, except as a license. For the various rights in the bundle are not separately assignable, but can only be licensed. In short, the copyright is not divisible. The rule involved runs: [1]

In relation to the right to sue for an infringement, a copyright is an indivisible thing, and cannot be split up and partially assigned either as to time, place, or particular rights or privileges, less than the sum of all the rights comprehended in the copyright.

To transfer any separate right in the bundle, as distinct from the whole bundle, the copyright proprietor must resort to the legal device and form of a license to the purchaser of the separate right he sells (such as the motion-picture rights) out of the bundle that he owns. The copyright proprietor then retains all the other rights and is the legal owner of all the rights in the copyright, including those he has licensed. The licensee is only the equitable owner of the rights in the bundle licensed to him. A licensee therefore can not sue an infringer in his own name for infringements of rights he holds as licensee. The licensor, i.e. the copyright proprietor, must sue for him. If the licensor refuses to sue to protect the licensee, the licensee can make his licensor a party defendant, together with the infringer, and thus force the licensor to sue.

All this seems terribly technical and awkward. It is—but it is also workable. Yet the actual hardships upon the author, which arise because a copyright is not divisible and assignable in part, are substantial and harrassing. The Copyright Statute should be amended so to provide for and permit divisible copyrights, i.e. copyrights whereunder separate parts and uses can be assigned completely. Because of this artificiality, many an author suffers and makes costly mistakes, unless alert. For the copyright proprietor, because of this unfair prohibition of partial assignments, usually is the magazine or book publisher; the author usually leaves the technicalities of copyrighting to the publisher and thus the publisher takes out the copyright in his own name. The Copyright Statute permits the creator, i.e. the author, to grant his entire rights and work to an employer or assignee, corporate or individual, who may validly apply for and obtain a copyright in his own and sole name.

105. GRANTS BETWEEN AUTHOR AND PUBLISHER

Take the case of an author who sells a short story or an article to a magazine. The contents of the entire periodical are copyrighted as one entity by the publisher of the magazine. The same practice usually applies as to newspapers and books comprising compilations or pieces from several authors. Books often are copyrighted in the name of the publisher to protect the publisher's right of first publication.

The author who sells a story to a magazine intends only to sell the right of first publication, as serial publication, to the magazine. He may want later to enlarge and publish his fictional creation as a novel. Or a digest magazine or other periodical may desire to republish the story. Or a motion-picture producer may desire to make a photoplay out of it. Or a playwright may desire to turn it into a drama. Under the Copyright Statute all those rights are owned by the magazine, for the copyright is indivisible. Only one copyright is issued or exists. And if it be in the publisher's name he is the owner of the entire bundle of rights, for he is the copyright proprietor.

Since that is not the fair intent of the parties, magazine publishers give the author a letter or printed form certifying that they retain only the exclusive right of first magazine publication and hold the other rights in trust for the author. For the magazine publisher can not assign the copyright on the entire issue of a periodical (which would include the copyright in all the stories and articles therein) to the author of a single piece. So he specifies in writing that he holds the other rights, i.e. other than of first serial publication, in trust for the author.

But in the printed form, so stating, a catch sometimes is hidden. A publisher of a magazine sometimes specifies that he retains a percentage interest in all of the rights, other than those of first publication, which he holds in trust for the author, and that only the percentage beyond that part retained by the magazine equitably is the property of the author. Most magazines retain a percentage interest in digest publication, which seems just. But too often authors don't read the fine print and thus suffer unanticipated financial deprivation.

Some magazine publishers and most book publishers believe that, since they are bringing the story into public existence and notice by publishing it, they have a right to receive a portion of the returns later derivable from reprinting or from motion-picture or television or dramatic uses.

In the case of books, in general, the publishing contract sets forth the division as to transformation uses, as the result of the "trade" between author and publisher.

Publishers of books, except in the case of prominent or insistent authors, often take out the copyright of a novel or book in their own names. Then they may retain, by their contract acknowledging they hold the other rights in trust, a sizeable share of the royalties that arise if the novel later be made into a motion picture or play, or be used in radio or television broadcasting. If the copyright of a book is taken out in the author's name, the publishing contract may specify the percentage of the transformation rights the publisher will receive.

Whether or not the publisher is the copyright proprietor, once the author signs or accepts the contract or letter of the publisher, the contract prevails. The author thus surrenders and limits his power to assert his full equitable rights. Unless the author agrees otherwise by entering into a publishing contract or letter agreement, he can have equity hold the publisher, if he is the copyright proprietor, as a trustee who holds all the other rights in trust for the author. But he can do so only if he can convince the court that this was the deal between himself and his publisher, or if a fair construction of a deal not actually made or expressed in writing so requires. Publishers ordinarily have their rights set forth in full in the publishing contract and so do not need to rely upon the aid of a court of equity.

Thus a prudent author should always read the fine print and bargain before he sells his manuscript to a magazine or book publisher or to a television or radio station.

Prominent authors often copyright a story or article in a magazine in their own names. This procedure is permitted,[2] but seldom practiced, because authors do not so insist or do not wish to pay the small copyright fee chargeable or do not know how to copyright.

It has been held that a magazine publisher, as the copyright proprietor, can validly assign the entire copyright on one picture to the photographer of a picture.[3] Such assignments are seldom made, because the publisher desires to protect his license of first publication by continuing as copyright proprietor. Also there has been a ruling holding to the contrary in the case of a story.[4]

106. UNIFORM CONTRACTS

Authors' leagues and dramatists' guilds try to require fair and uniform contracts reserving to their members the benefits accruing to publishers and producers under the Copyright Statute's limitation to only one, indivisible copyright grant. The Dramatists' Guild formerly required their members and producers to sign a uniform production contract, preserving for the playwright a uniform part of the motion-picture sale price, if a motion-picture company should buy the motion-picture rights from the producer. But the courts have ruled that the Dramatists' Guild's uniform contract is a restraint of trade and so a violation of the Sherman Antitrust Act.[5] Labor unions, under the Sherman and Clayton Antitrust Acts, are exempt from those provisions of antitrust laws. But according to the courts, dramatists and authors are not. The ruling is that the exception exempting labor unions from the restrictions imposed by the antitrust statutes "will not apply unless an employer-employee relationship is the 'matrix of the controversy'." [5] Thus authors and their League, since authors are not employees, are subject to the provisions of the federal antitrust statute. Their League is deemed not to be a labor union. Thus the situation is muddled. Individual dramatists still commonly require stage producers to sign contracts identical in large part with the prior uniform dramatists' contract. Yet such a practice is dubious as "conscious parallelism". This phrase in antitrust law is based on court rulings that identity of conduct by possible competitors is sufficient evidence to warrant a court's finding of conspiracy. In other words, insistence by an individual author upon a stage producers' signing a contract substantially similar to other contracts involves danger of a court finding that such insistence implies an unlawful agreement as to identical conduct. The antitrust laws should be amended to hold that dramatists' guilds are exempt from antitrust prohibitions, as are labor unions.

Meanwhile authors and dramatists or their agents individually must protect themselves by reading "the fine print" with great care and thus protecting themselves from the consequences of indivisibility of copyrights and awkward license customs.

107. LICENSES

Since under the Copyright Statute a copyright proprietor may validly assign and transfer his entire copyright only as one entity and only by one act and at one time, licenses, as before noted, as grants of separate rights in the bundle, are the common technical form of transfer used. Licenses of the separate rights contained in the bundle are very common. Even if the copyright proprietor retains only one of the bundle of rights comprising a copyright (say the right of first magazine publication) and transfers all the other rights (reprint, novel, drama, radio, television and serial, etc.) to another, the transfer then is only a license, the grantee is only a licensee, and the grantor in law remains the copyright proprietor. So the licensee can not sue in his own name.

As a result, licenses are long and technical, often being only obscure grants and reservations of rights. They usually can be understood adequately only by legal experts; and even lawyers make dangerous mistakes in respect to them.

108. DURATION OF LICENSES

A situation calling for special care by an author, and for vigorous legal skill, arises where an author as copyright proprietor grants a license to another to make a play or motion picture out of his work, or to televise it. Great financial loss to the author often arises from his not limiting the duration of such license. Unless the author specifies otherwise, he grants the licensee an exclusive license as to such granted right for the full or unexpired part of the twenty-eight years of the copyright term.[5a]

Also, without specific limitation and qualification, a license of the motion-picture or television rights includes the right by the licensee or his assigns to make several motion pictures or an unlimited number of television showings under the license.

The late Rex Beach, who was ably advised, when his novels were bought in the early days of motion pictures, carefully provided in the licenses he signed that he granted a license to make one motion picture only from each novel, and that license endured only for seven years from the date of grant. He thus specified that he retained the sole right to make a second motion picture, i.e. a remake. Other prudent dramatists and authors in dealing with motion-picture companies have followed the same procedure. The remake rights, i.e. the rights to make a second or third motion picture, out of very successful fictional works, can become very valuable after the making of the first picture, particularly if the first picture is a success.

Thus by carefully limiting the duration of a license to a short period of time, and by specifying the number of uses in motion-picture production or television production which may be made under such license, the author retains a very valuable residual right which may bring him more in royalties than received under the original license. Such protection of an author's interest is all a matter of knowledge, care, and bargaining. It is not too difficult for an author to limit the duration and extent of the rights granted. The producer usually is as anxious to get a license for the use he desires in a desirable work as the author is to get the royalties. If bargained for, much can be retained by the author. Unfortunately the author often does not read the fine print, or act with the benefit of an understanding of what he is granting and what he can reserve. Hollywood producers have accumulated a great quantity of renewal rights in valuable copyrighted properties by reason of the lack of skill of the authors who sold such licenses originally. This has become a matter of controversy between the producers and the Federal Communications Commission.

109. OBSCURE LANGUAGE IN LICENSES

Unskillful and unimaginative drafting of motion-picture, television, and other licenses has caused many costly lawsuits. The subject is highly technical and too detailed for full discussion here. But a few examples may be of use.

When an author grants the right "to dramatize" his copyrighted work, does that grant include the right to make a motion picture as well as a stage production? Ordinarily one would think that the right to make a motion picture was not included. But the courts have held otherwise. The decisions hold that the grant of a right to dramatize or produce dramatically includes the right to make a motion picture. Yet the rulings are conflicting.[6]

The inclusive holding, moreover, is subject to two qualifications: (1) limiting language and special provisions as to details may require a contrary result; (2) the query of whether or not the contract was drawn at a time when motion pictures were in existence.

In Manners v. Morosco,[6] Judge Holmes held that the right to dramatize a work, under a contract executed in 1912, would ordinarily include the right to make a motion picture therefrom. But in that case, since the contract provided that only seventy-five performances of the dramatic production were to be permitted within a year, the court held that the parties did not intend to include motion-picture rights in this instance. Later, when motion pictures became common, Judge Learned Hand held [7] that where Rex Beach granted the right to dramatize one of his novels it could not be held that he intended to grant the motion-picture rights. Other rulings are conflicting.

A further important qualification has been added by the courts. If an author be held not to have included the license to make a motion picture when he licensed a producer to make a dramatic production, nevertheless, although the producer did not get the right to make a motion picture, it may be held that the author himself can not use his right to make a motion picture or to permit others to do so during the term of the grant to dramatize the work. [8] The reason given for this result is that, since the author granted the earlier producer the exclusive right to "dramatize" the author's copyrighted work as a stage production, the parties at that time did not intend to permit the author *later* to destroy the value of the *stage production rights* that he licensed, by authorizing some one else to make a *motion picture* thereof, or by doing so himself. The courts recognize the fact that the making of a motion picture of a play may destroy the public appeal thereof as a play. They therefore hold, in certain instances, that where the author grants the right to dramatize his work, even if that grant did not include the right to make a motion picture, neither the author nor the dramatic producer can produce a motion picture during the term of the license to dramatize. Thus the motion-picture rights are not usable either by the author or by his first licensee of the right to dramatize his work. In short, a motion picture can not be made until the author and his licensee to dramatize reach an agreement.

This same construction recently (1949) was applied to a license granted by the owner of a sports arena in 1943 to "broadcast" boxing matches held therein. A Maryland court held: (a) that the grantee could not televise the matches, since the word "broadcast" when used in 1943 meant and specified radio broadcasting only and did not also include television; but (b) that the arena owner, because of his implied covenant not to destroy his licensee's right to radio broadcasts, could not televise or permit others to televise the boxing matches. As a consequence, only by mutual consent of grantor and grantee could the matches be televised. [9]

Considerable litigation has also arisen as to whether the grant of the rights to make a motion picture, at a time when only silent motion pictures were known, included the right to use dialogue in a sound motion picture made therefrom. The general rule is that the right to make a silent motion picture includes the right to make a talking motion picture.[10] Judge Swan ruled:

Nevertheless, we can entertain no doubt that the words used, "the exclusive moving picture rights," were sufficient to embrace not only motion pictures of the sort then known but also such technical improvements in motion pictures as might be developed during the term of the license, namely, the term of the copyright. The development of mechanism making it possible to accompany the screen picture with the sound of spoken words was but an improvement in the motion picture art. As the plaintiff well says, "talkies" are but a species of the genus motion pictures; they are employed by the same theaters, enjoyed by the same audiences, and nothing more than a forward step in the same art. Essentially the form and area of exploitation were the same. The mere fact that the species "talkies" may have been unknown and not within the contemplation of the parties in their description of the generic "moving pictures" does not prevent the latter from comprehending the former.

All this seems involved. And now that television productions as well as motion pictures and plays can be made out of successful novels or short stories, the situation is more complicated—too complicated for a layman to deal with. But he must be aware of the dangerous ground he treads on when he grants a license and ask questions.

Certain suggestions can be given. Great care must be taken, in drafting a license, particularly to dramatize a fictional work, that the particular right from the bundle of rights, and only that right, is precisely specified. Also the license must contain specific provisions expressly negativing any implied covenants. This precision can be effected only by: (1) a precise definition of just what particular right is licensed; (2) careful language specifically excluding any unknown and future inventions which may be utilized to express in any form the copyrighted work, expressly reserving such rights of expression by future inventions to the grantor or the author; (3) an express provision that there is no implied covenant preventing the grantor or author from utilizing at any time any of the rights which he retains, although that use may impair the license granted. If the licensee objects to this third specification, then the author, as grantor, must and will know what he is granting away before he signs.

Only by such care and imagination in drafting licenses can an author or copyright proprietor protect himself. The author must exert imagination. He must remember that few expected the invention of motion pictures; that after motion pictures were common, few expected the addition of sound to motion pictures; and that after sound motion pictures were common, few expected the invention of television.

110. STAGE PRODUCTIONS BY STOCK COMPANIES

Care must also be taken by a playwright when he grants the right to produce a play, to specify whether or not the playwright intends to permit production by stock companies. It is not clear, in the absence of express language, that the right to produce in a *stock* company is not included in a license to produce; [11] careless language may result in granting the right to produce a play by stock companies. The only safe rule is for the playwright, when he grants stage rights, expressly to set down whether or not he includes stock rights.

111. FINE PRINT IN LICENSES

Provisions permitting the divisibility of copyright are a highly desirable alteration in the Copyright Statute. They have been long urged by authors. Everyone is awaiting a new copyright statute, but no progress has been made. And the niceties of language, when authors grant rights to others, will always be with us, particularly since new inventions will persist in the future as they have in the past. The one safe rule for the author to follow is not to await changes in the copyright law but to read and brood over the "fine print", and then to make certain, by the full play of his imagination, that he has carefully defined the use he grants, and still more carefully specifies that he fully retains all the rest, expressly negativing any implied covenants to the contrary. Then the author can't go wrong. For who knows what price a copyright may have tomorrow?

XV

Fair Comment and Fair Use

112. FAIR DEALING

A QUERY which arises constantly concerns the right to use parts of a copyrighted book without liability for infringement under a right of fair use or fair comment.

The United States Copyright Statute makes no mention whatsoever of these rights. The British statute does. It specifies that a copyright is not infringed upon by "any fair dealing with any work for the purposes of private study, research, criticism, review, or newspaper summary." [1] The British proviso states generally the rule prevailing in the United States.

Accurate understanding, however, of what is meant by "fair dealing" (the British phrase) or "fair use" and "fair comment" (the United States phrases) requires an understanding of the four different aspects of the use involved.

First, there is the right of fair *comment*, i.e. a critic's right, (1) in an appraisal and discussion of a copyrighted work, whether a criticism of a novel, a factual work, a play, or a poem, to set forth literally any reasonably needed illustrative parts thereof; or (2) in a discussion of a writer's skill generally to quote and copy literal parts of the writer's work. This is the most familiar aspect of the general right involved here.

Second, there is the right to satirize and to burlesque, by mimicry or humorous criticism or comment, using therefor copyrighted matter. This is often viewed as an aspect of fair comment above noted.

Third, there is a different and more extensive right of fair *use*. This has an accepted aspect as the right to use parts of a literary work, not in criticism or satire but for atmosphere and incidental purposes and effects. For example, a writer of a short story may copy literally parts of a copyrighted song or poem or novel, either to establish atmosphere and to date the action and characters he is writing about, or to illustrate a factual article. This copying is permitted as fair use. The cases establishing this right are later more fully discussed. (See Section 117.)

Fourth, "fair use" is also sometimes incorrectly described as the right to copy ideas, concepts, and material in the public domain, when and as used in a prior copyrighted work. This use of the term is confusing. Here the ideas and material copied from a prior work are not susceptible of copyright in such prior work, because they are in the public domain. A clearer view is to deem such a use not as a qualified and limited right of fair use of copyrighted matter, but rather an absolute right of use of uncopyrighted matter. For the matter copied can not be copyrighted, and so can be freely used by anyone, without qualification. (See discussion before in Chapter X, Section 69.)

In the discussion herein, we use the phrase "fair comment" as meaning the first itemization above; also as including the rights of satirizing as noted in the second itemization. The phrase "fair use" is used to cover the third itemization only. "Fair use" is not used as denoting the fourth itemization, i.e. as to the copying of ideas and matters in the public domain. That right is absolute and wider than the right of fair use.

113. LEGAL BASIS OF FAIR COMMENT AND FAIR USE

The theoretical legal basis of fair comment and fair use in the United States, since the right is not specified in the Copyright Statute, has not yet been fully and accurately explored. Although there are many cases determining that the right exists, and fixing the extent thereof, there are no cases fully exploring the legal basis involved.

As a result, a provincial custom has arisen among United States publishers (including many prominent ones) of inserting a notice at the beginning of the book which either denies entirely the right of fair comment and fair use (without express consent in each instance by such publisher) or attempts drastically to limit the right of fair use. A typical example of such notices is:

All rights reserved. No part of this book may be reproduced in any form without the permission of the publisher (named).

Other forms, in common use, permit short quotations only in critical reviews published in *newspapers* and *periodicals*. Evidently they attempt to prohibit critical use by quotation in factual books or as background material in books.

This purported limitation is contrary to the law of copyright, and annoying because unfounded in legal right. An insertion of such a useless notice in a book is as undignified as it is futile.

The legal basis of fair comment given by the courts in the United States, since the right of fair comment or fair use is not granted in the Copyright Statute, is that it is implied. The implication arises from the act of the author or publisher in securing a statutory copyright, i.e. in publishing his book under a copyright notice.

Since the Constitutional grant of authority to Congress to enact copyright legislation specifies that copyrights are granted "to promote the Progress of Science and useful Arts", it must follow that the right of fair comment and fair use arises in the public, as part of the grant implied in the obtaining of a copyright. Except to fulfill this Constitutional end, Congress could not grant copyrights.

The usual judicial language as to implying the right of fair comment runs as follows:

In such cases the law implies the consent of the copyright owner to a fair use of his publication for the advancement of science or art.[2]

No further exploration has been undertaken, because no publisher has ever dared rely upon a notice denying or limiting the right of fair comment in any reported litigation.

The conclusion inaccurately drawn by publishers who use this futile notice, because of the given reason that it is *implied*, is too simple. It runs: Since the basis of the right is implied by the copyright proprietor's act of publishing and copyrighting, he can negative that implication by a flat statement to the contrary, at the time of publishing and copyrighting. Thus an effort is made to destroy the right before it comes into existence.

The error is complete. It is true that in some cases in contract law, an agreement may be implied in fact, i.e. the conduct of a party may indicate an agreement without the use of words stating the agreement. Such an implication in fact can be negatived by express words. (See Section 109.) But the implication as to fair comment here is not such an implication in fact. It is an implication in law, arising from the Constitutional condition.

The right of fair comment, in short, is imposed by the courts upon copyright proprietors who sell to the public, in order to protect the public's interest. Since the right is implied in law and in order to carry out the Constitutional provisions, in the public interest, it cannot be negatived by notice harming the public interest. Once the book is published and copyrighted, the law imposes the right of fair comment in the public as against the copyright proprietor. It is for the court, not the copyright proprietor, to define the extent and limits upon fair comment and fair use. No copyright proprietor can destroy that right, or limit it e.g. to a newspaper or periodical. Other book writers have the right of fair comment and criticism upon the ideas or literary merits of a copyrighted work, also the right to copy extracts thereof to buttress and illustrate or to corroborate that comment. And the use of quotations, to create background atmosphere or illustrate points, is a right of fair use that cannot be withheld by any copyright proprietor or publisher.

No court, by any decision or opinion, has ever given the slightest hint that the right of fair comment can be denied to the public by the copyright proprietor, through a notice denying it. Neither has any court ever suggested that the copyright proprietor has the right to define and so to limit the public right of fair comment and fair use. All the cases indicate that the definition of fair use and fair comment is for the court, acting in the public's interest, not for the publisher as the copyright proprietor. Thus the use of such futile notices could well be dispensed with.

In a recent case [3] on fair comment, a high court defined the right as follows:

Fair use has been defined as a privilege in others than the owner of a copyright to use the copyrighted material in a reasonable manner *without his consent*, notwithstanding the monopoly granted to the owner of the copyright. [Emphasis added]

Here it is to be noted that the court uses the words "without his consent", which we have italicized. This indicates a rejecting of the right to withhold consent by notice.

114. FAIR COMMENT UNDER A COMMON-LAW COPYRIGHT

It is generally said that no right of fair comment or use exists as to unpublished work protected by a common-law copyright.[4] Since the copyright proprietor has not published his work, and thus has not destroyed his common-law copyright, the public interest imposes no right of fair comment or of fair use. Even though the work be registered and copyrighted as an unpublished work, since such registration is not publication (see Section 51) it is doubtful if the right of fair comment or fair use should be held to arise in the public interest, for a work registered with the Copyright Office as an unpublished work is not open to the public under the Regulations of the Copyright Office.[5]

This result is particularly just where the work is made available to a critic or reviewer by subterfuge, or without the consent of the owner of the unpublished work, i.e. without publication.

But what happens when a play is publicly performed? Has a critic at such performance the right to note down from memory (or use shorthand) and quote literally a few of its lines in his criticism? Since performance of a play is not publication, if the play has not been copyrighted as a published work, at first glance it would seem that the critic has no such right because of the common-law copyright involved. But the better view would seem to be that by the act of public performance of the play the playwright has submitted his work to the public for fair comment. Public interest then can be said to intervene. So soon as the playwright elects to perform his work publicly, the public's rights intervene. The same rule should apply to musical works publicly performed under a common-law copyright and to works of art exhibited in a gallery open to the public.

Such is the view of an eminent British text writer on copyright as to British law.[6] His view is easily sustained by the express provision in the British Copyright Act granting the right of fair comment, both as to published and unpublished works. It would seem to be a fair interpretation of the public interest in the case of a public performance of a play protected by the common-law copyright in the United States. But there are no decisions on the point.

115. TESTS AS TO FAIR COMMENT AND FAIR USE

Fair comment and fair use are flexible rights. The right and the extent of literal copying thereunder permitted, both in fair comment and fair use, depend upon four factors. These are: (1) the nature of the work in which the copyrighted material is copied and the honest intent of criticizing or incidentally quoting and so using the part copied; (2) whether the two works are in competition and thus the copying by one claiming the privilege of fair comment will compete with the copyright work copied from, and thus reduce its public appeal and sale; (3) the quality or value of the parts copied; (4) the quantity or extent of copying, judged by the comparative length and nature of the work copied from and also of the publication in which the part copied is inserted. Educational and scientific works are granted a more extensive right of copying as fair comment, than are works which are sold solely for entertainment and which may be directly competitive in a purely financial sense.

If the copying be very slight and not substantial, though not fair comment, on the theory of "de minimis lex non curat" ("the law does not concern itself with trifles") no piracy results. Where a publisher of a French textbook copied a list of French words for preparation for Regents' examinations, obtaining these words from public lists of the State Education Department, but admitted that he had copied the article prefixes to four French words from the complainant's work, the lower court held that this could not be considered so substantial a copying of the plaintiff's work as to be deemed an infringement.[7] But the Appellate Court reversed on other grounds, finding that "although the word lists constitute only a small proportion—less than 15% of the printed matter * * *", piracy results and the defendant could not assert fair use.[8]

116. RULE-OF-THUMB TEST

Publishers often are told that a rule-of-thumb measure, of fifty to two hundred words copied from a book and not more than four lines from a poem, is a safe guide to fair use. The decisions show that such a purely quantitative test is far from safe or accurate. The quality of the parts copied and the nature of the copied work in which the copying appears are more important considerations than the quantity copied. The decisions permit a more extensive use than does this rule-of-thumb formula, particularly as to poems, but in certain cases fifty words may be too much for fair use and thus be fatal copying. (See Section 117.)

Clearance and obtaining consents, when use is made of copyrighted material, has become involved and exacting. Delays and expense are considerable. Authors do not know when they must, and when they need not, obtain clearances. Clarification of the rule as to fair comment, by a definite provision in the Copyright Statute, would be quite helpful. But that is too much to expect.

Interpretation of the cases indicates that the following guide can be stated as to what constitutes fair use and comment, and thus requires no clearance by consent of the copyright proprietor: Quotations of not more than 300 words, with credit noted, from a copyrighted work, provided the words copied do not exceed 1 per cent of the complete word content of the book quoted from, is legally permitted as fair comment if the copying appears in a text of a criticism, comment, or factual or news reporting. Of poems or short sketches quoted in criticism or news reporting, a far more liberal percentage may be used. If short passages are copied for advertising or commercial purposes, even a very small quotation requires clearance. Giving credit does not enlarge the right to copy; omitting the credit may be fatal.

117. EXAMPLES OF FAIR USE

The right of fair comment, as to satire or burlesque, has seldom been openly questioned. Only the extent of use has been questioned. Also there are few clear cases expressly covering the precise right of a critic or reviewer. No publisher has ever wished to defend a notice denying or limiting the right of fair comment.

There are many cases, however, passing on the right of fair use, which, like the cases on satire, sanction the right of fair copying. The general rule as to fair comment has been stated as follows: [9]

A copyrighted work is subject to fair criticism, serious or humorous. So far as is necessary to that end, quotations may be made from it, and it may be described by words, representations, pictures, or suggestions. It is not always easy to say where the line should be drawn between the use which for such purposes is permitted and that which is forbidden.

In a suit brought against *The Saturday Evening Post* [10] the author of a copyrighted song complained that the *Post* had published the entire chorus of his song, consisting of eight lines. The song, entitled "Go! You Packers Go!", was dedicated to the Green Bay Packers, a professional football team. The *Post*'s article narrated the history of this football team. The court held that the use of the entire chorus was a fair use, basing its decision upon the consideration that the article was not competitive with the song, that the music of the song was not used, and that therefore the use was not unfair to the copyright proprietor.

It is to be noted that the defendant used almost one-half of the copyrighted song in the article (a very extensive use by the test of quantity) and that the defendant's article was not a mere news comment or literary critique.

In another instance a copyright proprietor of a song entitled "Poor Pauline" sued *The New Yorker* for using most of the lyric of his copyrighted song, some fifteen lines, in a comment upon the death of Pearl White. [11] The plaintiff's song was written about Pearl White when she was famous as the flamboyant heroine of the *Perils of Pauline*. Over half the article in *The New Yorker*, in fact, consisted of quotations of the plaintiff's poem. The court held that the defendant, in literally copying so much of the plaintiff's poem, had not infringed because of its right of fair use. The court was guided largely by the test that there was no competition between the song and the magazine story. The article would not be used as a substitute for the song since there was no music. Thus the article would not affect the sale of the song.

A writer of a fiction serial in *Collier's* used extensive snatches of a copyrighted song (ten out of eighteen lines of the chorus) to establish atmosphere and date the characters of his story. The court denied relief to the copyright proprietor of the song, applying the tests above noted and holding that the story writer was protected by the defense of fair use. [12]

The *New York Herald Tribune* sued when one of its leading

copyrighted editorials, about Wendell Wilkie when he was nomi-
nated for the presidency, was copied in full. The defendant, an in-
vestment banker, mailed copies of this editorial widely. The court
held that whether or not the use of this entire editorial was fair use
depended upon the trial judge's judgment at the trial and could not
be decided on a motion for summary judgment.[13]

Recently an author of a novel copied extensively from letters of
Hans Christian Andersen translated from the Danish by a biographer
of Andersen and used by the biographer in his prior biography of
Andersen and appearing therein. Twenty-four passages from the
biography, largely from the translated letters, were used. Credit
was given to the author of the biography. The court held, however,
this use exceeded fair comment,[14] for the author of the biography
had a copyright in his translations. The defendant had the right to
use Andersen's letters which were in the public domain, in Danish,
by using them or translating them, but no right to copy the biographer's translation thereof. Here the court stressed the test as to
the quality and value of the extracts rather than as to their length.
The court added that if "a material and substantial part has been
copied, even though it be but a small part of the whole," the use may
be infringement.[14]

When Sigmund Spaeth in a history of popular songs copied the
entire lyric of a song and the melody line, such use was held more
than fair comment, the court noting that the Spaeth book was, according to its introduction, "intended for the amateur performer as
well as for the reader". Here Spaeth had obtained a license from the
assignee of the author, but failed to note that the renewal rights in
the copyright, entered before the license was granted to him, had
ended the assignee's claim as the copyright proprietor and that the
license granted by such assignee therefor was void. This holding of
infringement against Mr. Spaeth indicates the need of checking the
copyright date and the possibility that there is a renewal right resting
in others (see Section 56) when clearing rights.[15]

Again, where a cigarette manufacturer used three sentences from
a copyrighted authoritative medical book on the human voice, in the
effort to show that its cigarette had no effect upon smokers' throats,
the court held that the brevity of the quotation did not make it fair
use. The court stressed the fact that the cigarette manufacturer's use

was not of a scientific nature, and that works of educational value will be treated more leniently than advertisements. Here the value of the whole advertisement depended upon the three sentences copied.[16] The same test of quality was stressed in quotations from one history book in another history book.[17]

And where a professional group tutor at Harvard used parts of Taussig's *Economics* on sheets and in lectures preparing students for college examinations, the use was condemned as exceeding fair use.[18]

118. PARODY AND SATIRE

The right to satirize a copyrighted work is a recognized aspect of fair comment.[19] Considerable confusion often arises by the failure to ascertain the precise issue involved in mimicry and burlesque.

The precise question of fair comment in burlesquing or mimicking arises usually if the words and music used by the mimic or satirizer are copyrighted; it does not arise as to mere imitation of mannerism of actors or as to stage business. If the words used by the satirist or mimic be from a poem, the mimic has a right to use these words in public since the copyright proprietor of a poem has no exclusive right of public performance. (See Section 98.) But in the case of a song, where the copyright proprietor has the right of public performance for profit, small parts or snatches of the copyrighted words and music commonly used by the person mimicked or satirized may be used for burlesque or satire by an actor giving such a public performance only under the right of fair comment.[19] Here again the test involves the same four elements noted above as a limitation upon fair comment, particularly the quality and value of the lines used as well as the quantity. Another test is whether the substance of the act in question be mimicry or satire, as contrasted to mere entertainment by the delivery and use of the copyrighted material. The element of good faith is essential in parody,[19] i.e. it is essential that the use involved be humorous and be limited to satire, and that it not be plain copying as a device to sell entertainment by copying another's material.

Recently a Federal Court so held, quoting the above statement as the proper rule. (Loew's v. C.B.S. 131 F. Supp. 165, 1955).

119. INDEXES

It has been held where the defendant rightfully bought unbound, printed sheets of Kipling's works, and rebound and sold them, the defendant could add an index which used the words and phrases found in the copyrighted text. The copying of these words in an index is not piracy and comes within fair use, even though the user could not copy the pages from which they were taken.[20]

120. PROCEDURE AS TO FAIR USE

The author of a novel or of factual description, in order to obtain period atmosphere or to date his characters, often desires to quote or have one of his characters quote extracts from popular songs or poems. Not knowing of, or not wishing to rely on the extensive right of fair use as above noted, and out of caution, he often requests permission (or his publisher requires him to) from the owner of the copyright of the song or poem. Then an odd result occurs. The permission granted is noted on the title leaf. If several songs are used, the result is an annoying long list of copyright notices on the title leaf, where copyright notices must be placed. These are out of all proportion to the importance of the use involved. Is such procedure necessary?

Requesting such permission is not necessary. But authors and editors who request permission, out of an excessive caution, create a boomeranging situation. If the copyright proprietor consents, he fears his authorizing of publication of his song, if his copyright notice is not used, will be fatal. Under the extremely rigorous provisions of the Copyright Statute as to use of the copyright notice, noted before, publication of a copyright proprietor's work, or substantial parts thereof, with his consent and without the copyright notice, puts the work in the public domain. Thus if the copyright proprietor of a song consents to the use of parts thereof, caution requires him to require the copyright notice be used. Otherwise his only defense is that the parts quoted were not substantial.

The proper procedure therefore is for the publisher or author using parts of a copyrighted song to rely upon the right of fair comment. Or if the publisher is so cautious as to require consent from the copyright proprietor, and is not willing to rely upon his right of fair use, he should ask only for a letter from the copyright proprietor of the song confirming that the copying of the lines of the song is fair use. Then a copyright grant need not be used, for the copyright proprietor signing the letter is forever estopped from asserting that the use is not fair. This distinction will seem technical. But the exactions as to a copyright notice, even in permitted copying, are both technical and rigorous. By this procedure, any risk from not using the copyright notice is avoided completely.

—————— XVI ——————

Musical Compositions; Mechanical
Reproductions

121. MUSICAL FORMS

THE COPYRIGHT Statute uses varied descriptions of music: a "musical work" [Section 1(b)]; "a musical composition" and "parts of instruments serving to reproduce mechanically the musical work" [Section 1(e)]; "dramatic or dramatico-musical compositions" [Section 5(d)]; "mechanical reproduction of musical works" [Section 101(e)]. These are all descriptive of the various forms of music, protected as musical compositions, under the Copyright Statute.

The common uses and forms of musical composition include: (a) words (lyrics) of a song, together with the musical melody thereto; (b) operas and operettas and musical comedies; (c) orchestral and instrumental compositions; (d) choral, religious, and other group compositions; (e) phonograph records and mechanical piano rolls and juke boxes; (f) music recorded for reproduction in motion pictures, on film, wire, or tape; (g) music broadcast by radio or television, either by playing directly or by playing from recorded transcriptions on film, disk records, wire, or tape. These extensively varied uses have created a complicated and involved pattern of copyright protection in music.

In the music trade, distinctions are also made between: (a) sale of sheet music of songs and of instrumental and orchestra scores; (b) dramatic production of a song, where the song is featured, or acted out, as a miniature dramatic production with or without sets; (c) performance and musical production of a score and libretto as an opera, operetta, musical comedy, or musical revue; (d) performance of musical compositions by orchestras, bands, and choruses; (e) use of music where it is played or sung, or reproduced, or used as incidental or background music, in films, radio, television, places of entertainment, or commercial assemblies.

The Copyright Statute extends protection to all these varied uses and forms by granting to the copyright proprietor a valuable and far-flung and exclusive right "of public performance for profit". For Section 1(e) of the Copyright Statute provides that the copyright proprietor shall have "the exclusive right to perform the copyrighted work publicly for profit if it be a musical composition; and for the purpose of public performance for profit, and for the purposes set forth in subsection (a) hereof, to make any arrangement or setting of it or of the melody of it in any system of notation or any form of record in which the thought of an author may be recorded and from which it may be read or reproduced * * *."

This right of public performance for profit is retained by the copyright proprietor even after he has printed, published, and sold to the public the sheet music of the musical composition. This retained right after publication and sale, to control performance, is a valuable right. A playwright retains a broader right as to all public performances (without the qualification "for profit") after publishing his play; but with lectures "for profit" is added. Plays, when printed and sold, are not easily or commonly performed or delivered. Printed sheet music is available for and is designed—except as to the very few who read music without playing it—solely for performance. So a limitation imposed on the performance thereof, in view of the basic purpose involved when sheet music is publicly sold, is a unique retained copyright use granted the copyright proprietor of a musical work. Even after selling and releasing his musical composition to the public, he is permitted to control a major aspect of the use of the printed score he publicly has sold, to wit, its public performance for profit.

122. THE MEANING OF "FOR PROFIT"

The courts have defined "for profit" as meaning any public performance for financial gain, indirectly or directly derived. A performance is for profit even though no admission payment be charged to the place where it is performed.

This basic interpretation was reached as to a restaurant that employed an orchestra to play popular music for the enjoyment of its patrons while they dined. No cover charge, or charge for admission to the restaurant, was made. The Supreme Court ruled that the playing of music by an orchestra, under such circumstances, in the restaurant was a public performance for profit of the pieces played. Judge Holmes stated the decision in his customary lively phrasing: [1]

If the rights under the copyright are infringed only by a performance where money is taken at the door, they are very imperfectly protected. * * * The defendant's performances are not eleemosynary. They are part of a total for which the public pays, and the fact that the price of the whole is attributed to a particular item which those present are expected to order is not important. It is true that the music is not the sole object, but neither is the food, which probably could be got cheaper elsewhere. The object is a repast in surroundings that to people having limited powers of conversation, or disliking the rival noise, give a luxurious pleasure not to be had from eating a silent meal. If music did not pay, it would be given up. If it pays it pays out of the public's pocket. Whether it pays or not, the purpose of employing it is profit, and that is enough.

Today, the playing of music in a dance hall, hotel, skating rink, rodeo, excursion boat, or any other public gathering arranged for commercial gain is held to be public performance for profit. Also broadcasting copyrighted music over the radio or television, or reproduction of music in motion-picture film theaters, or the playing of it from phonograph records in any public place, or on coin-operated machines in places where an admission charge is made, constitutes a public performance for profit. Thus the description of uses "for profit" is almost all-inclusive as to public places.

123. MECHANICAL REPRODUCTIONS

In the case of "mechanical reproductions" or "instruments serving to reproduce mechanically the musical work" [Section 1(e)], the Copyright Statute imposes a special limitation upon the copyright proprietor. He is free to refuse and to prevent any mechanical or record reproduction of his musical work. But if he licenses such a right to another, or himself so mechanically reproduces the work, then everyone has the right to reproduce his music mechanically, upon payment to the copyright proprietor of "two cents on each part manufactured". The longest section of the Copyright Statute covers detailed phases of such enforced mechanical use. It even provides ways of collecting the royalty specified [C.S., Section 1(e)].

This odd provision was inserted to assure free competition and protect smaller record makers when the Copyright Statute was enacted. It suggests how clauses creep into statutes.

124. GRAND AND SMALL RIGHTS

The terms "grand right" and "small right" (or "small performing right") often are used as a rough twofold classification of all the varied rights involving performance of musical works. The terms are not clearly defined, and often are used with different meanings and inclusions by those in the trade. In fact, the use of these two terms is often confusing.

"Grand rights" usually include performance or stage rights of an opera, operetta, musical comedy (i.e. as "a dramatic or dramatico-musical composition"); also formerly all rights other than the "small rights" as those commonly granted to ASCAP or BMI. The use of the term is derived from Europe, is dated and no two lawyers seem to agree thereto.

"Small rights" in musical compositions include most of the incidental, nondramatic and small rights of public performance for profit and are usually assigned by the composer and lyric writer (and confirmed by the copyright proprietor where the copyright is registered by and in the name of a musical publishing firm as the copyright proprietor) to the American Society of Composers, Authors, and Publishers, and thereafter are licensed by ASCAP only. ASCAP is described in Section 125. The distinctions between the two rights, that is as grand rights and small rights, fluctuate in practice and change by reason of changing practices in the trade. Enforcement of the small rights by ASCAP and BMI has resulted in much litigation. Usually the small rights are deemed to be the uses in public performance for profit over the radio, by television, in motion-picture theaters by use of film or records, in dance halls, hotels, and other similar public places. Where phonograph records are played in such public places, the right to the public performance for profit of the music thereon recorded is likewise deemed a small right. But in the playing of records or other recordings (piano playing rolls or tape) in coin-operated machines such as juke boxes in public places, an additional distinction must be noted. Section 1(e) of the Copyright Statute provides that if an admission charge is made for entrance to the place where the coin-operated machine is in use the playing of the musical composition is a public performance for profit. If no admission is so charged the playing of the coin-operated machine is not a public performance for profit. Thus the small right as to the playing of phonograph records includes only playing where an admission charge is made at the place where the coin-operated machine is played.

When a song or other musical composition is briefly dramatized, either on a stage or by television or by radio performance, it is not clear whether or not the license so to dramatize is deemed a grand right to be licensed by the copyright proprietor, or a small right to be licensed by ASCAP. Such performance may consist of short scenes from a musical comedy or operetta, or the acting out of a song by sets and costumes in a brief tableau form. Whether the performance be by television, by radio, or on a variety stage, the only safe procedure is to get a license from both ASCAP and the copyright proprietor holding and retaining the grand rights.

In the use of musical productions in motion-picture theaters when reproduced from film, a novel situation has arisen which has only recently been changed by court decree. When a musical production is made into a motion-picture musical the motion-picture company has to obtain a license therefor from the copyright proprietor holding the grand right. But a great deal of music is used in motion pictures for background, incidental, and minor purposes in non-musical or musical pictures. As to such background music, previously the motion-picture producer paid a synchronization fee either to ASCAP or to the proprietor of the musical copyright. But that fee covered only the right to record the music on the film, not to perform it from the film. When it came to the playing of the music from the film in a motion-picture theater, the exhibitor had to obtain another, distinct license from ASCAP to permit the music to be played from the film, though already licensed as to recording to the picture producer. Thus two licenses had to be obtained for the same completed act. A Federal court in a New York district has condemned as an antitrust violation [2] this double licensing for the right of public performance for profit. Now under a consent decree the motion-picture producer obtains a right to record the music by paying a fee either to ASCAP or to the copyright proprietor of the song and musical composition, and in turn licenses the motion-picture theater to perform the music in the theater publicly for profit. The motion-picture theater will not under this decree, when it is finally worked out, have to get an ASCAP license for the right to perform music from the film. But since motion-picture theaters may use other music for incidental purposes, from phonograph or other recordings, they still may have to get licenses from ASCAP.

Since the commercial use of music is so widespread and the right so involved, the practices are constantly changing. The licensing of the right of public performance for profit of musical compositions has created more controversy than almost any other clause in the Copyright Statute. The functioning of ASCAP, which holds this right of public performance for profit from a myriad of song writers and composers (also confirmed in most instances by music publishers), has long been a subject of running litigation.

125. ASCAP

As soon as this right of public performance for profit was established by the Shanley decision of the Supreme Court, defining profit as any commercial use, difficulties arose as to enforcement of this right by the host of copyright proprietors holding such rights. The composers of songs and authors of lyrics who held the right of public performance, and the music publishers to whom they sold the right of printing sheet music therefor, organized for the task. They quarreled among themselves as to who got the "small right" thus created; and also on how to split the profits derived from licenses.

It was impossible for any individual publisher or composer to ascertain when and where his music was played. In view of the countless places where popular music was being played and performed for profit, that effort required policing. So an association was formed to enforce the "small right" of public performance for profit, as representing all the copyright proprietors of music who joined the association.

The organizers found a model in Europe. There elaborate organi-

zations had been established to enforce this right of public performance of music for profit, which has been long established by
European copyright law. As a result a membership corporation was
formed in New York, which comprised composers of music, authors
of lyrics, and the publishers of the sheet music thereof. The "small
right" of public performance for profit was and is licensed completely and exclusively to this membership corporation, by the
creators or copyright proprietors of musical compositions who join
the society. This organization is named the American Society of
Composers, Authors, and Publishers; the abbreviated name is
ASCAP, so familiar to all today.

ASCAP grants licenses to restaurants, hotels, dance halls, bands,
radio and television stations, and motion-picture theaters, and other
similar public places where such music is performed for profit. These
general licenses gave the licensee the right to perform in public for
profit any music included within the ASCAP catalogue, and to
perform it as frequently as desired. An annual fixed fee is collected.
The fixing of this annual fee is a matter of bargaining between
ASCAP and its licensees.

Difficulties have constantly arisen because of the opposition of
licensees. Varied users of music claim that ASCAP is a monopoly,
since it controls the greater part of copyrighted popular music.
The claim is made that ASCAP is exacting excessive charges in
fixing its annual license fee. Broadcasters formed a competitive co-
operative music society of their own. The government is constantly
intervening in ASCAP affairs, under the provisions of the Sherman
Antitrust Law. Thus the history of ASCAP has been the history of
one bitter suit after another. Also some states have attempted in
various exercises of state legislative powers to prevent ASCAP from
operating within their borders. Nevertheless ASCAP goes on and
prospers. The members of ASCAP have greatly benefited by annual payments graded according to their importance and success as
music and song creators.

126. SPLITTING OF THE RIGHT OF PUBLIC PERFORMANCE FOR PROFIT

This right of public performance for profit has been split in divers
and increasingly minute ways. In the case of motion pictures using
music, for example, a United States district court, as before noted,

has held ASCAP's motion-picture theater licenses invalid as violations of the Sherman Antitrust Act because of this splitting aspect. New controversies are likely to arise in the future. Yet the splitting technique persists.

Writers of novels, particularly of mystery stories, despite all the legal difficulties ASCAP is subject to, look with envy upon the composers of music because composers of music enjoy this right of public performance for profit. If an analogous right could be inserted in the Copyright Statute covering renting of books by lending libraries, fiction authors might enjoy some of the financial profits of musical authors. That aspect is discussed under protection of manuscripts. (See Section 186.)

127. PUBLIC CONTROL

The constant antitrust litigation directed against ASCAP indicates that some element of public control of the indubitable monopoly held by ASCAP seems required. To deny composers and lyric writers the right to profit from the public performance of their musical works would be unjust. It would be a reversion to the days when Mozart and Schubert died in poverty because they could not gain a livelihood merely out of the sale of their musical manuscripts to music publishers, or from payments from rich patrons of music who ordered special compositions to be composed.

Yet to let ASCAP charge any fee that it can get, because of its control of the great bulk of popular music, means constant agitation. The only solution possible, much as one may oppose public control, is to recognize that the granting of this right—of public performance for profit of musical compositions—inevitably creates a monopoly against which the public is entitled to protection. If the Register of Copyrights, or some similar public authority, were to be given the power (a) to pass upon the fairness of the basic terms and clauses of ASCAP license contracts and (b) to pass upon the fairness of the amount of the license fees exacted, the right both of the public and of composers would be protected. It will be difficult, of course, for such a public body to ascertain a measuring rod by which it can fix the amount of the ASCAP fees to be charged, because no standard of cost of creation, or value in free sale, is present. But comparison with other royalties prevailing could enable a public

administrator to determine if the ASCAP fee charged exceeds the
limits of fairness.

128. COLLABORATORS AS JOINT AUTHORS

Musical compositions commonly are created by the joint effort
of a composer of the music and an author of the lyrics. Collaboration in the writing of plays and other works is common, but it is
particularly marked in musical composition.

When two or more persons collaborate in the creation of a copyrighted work, they become joint authors owning the copyrighted
work as tenants in common. Unless by specific agreement they
divide the ownership otherwise, each of the joint authors owns an
equal half interest in the copyright.

To establish joint ownership of a copyright by collaborators, all
that need be shown is that the creation of the copyrighted work was
carried on jointly in the prosecution of a preconcerted joint design.[3]

In an English ruling,[4] it was held, however, where a play producer hired an author to write a play and suggested certain minor
changes therein after it was written, that the producer had not collaborated to the extent of being a joint author. On the other hand,
the parts and work contributed by two joint authors need not be
found to be of equal amount or value. Substantial contribution, both
of a qualitative and quantitative nature, is sufficient to constitute
joint and equal ownership of a copyrighted work. Unless the joint
authors agree otherwise, even if there be a disparity of contribution,
the profits and ownership are divided into equal shares by the law.

129. WHAT CONSTITUTES JOINT AUTHORSHIP

In the case of such collaboration, it is held that "physical pro-
pinquity of the authors and consultation while this [writing] was
being done" is not essential.[5] Here a composer of popular music,
while traveling with a show, was engaged by a musical-comedy
producer to write the music for an operetta. He did so while en
route by sending sheets of music to the author of the lyrics. He
never conferred otherwise with the writer of the lyrics and of the
book. One of the songs thus created was "I Wonder Who's Kissing
Her Now". The author of the music, on the expiration of the first
twenty-eight years of the copyright, through an assignee, renewed

the copyright. The court held that the renewal of the copyright by the assignee of the composer of the music, one of the joint authors, was for the equal benefit of the other author who wrote the lyrics. Thus it ruled that the renewal certificate, taken out by the assignee of the author of the music in his own name solely, was held in trust for both. In short, the assignee of the composer of the music and the author of the lyrics each had a half interest therein. Yet the two joint authors had never physically met.

A similar result was reached as to a different song in the same case, where the author of the lyrics of a song turned them over to a publisher and asked the music publisher to obtain someone to write the music for the lyrics. This was done. The author of the lyrics never met the composer of the music until the lyrics and the music had been copyrighted as a song. The court held that the two were joint authors and that they had collaborated in a common design.[5]

In this latter instance, after the copyright was renewed by the assignee of the writer of the lyrics, he contended that since the author of the music was alive when the copyright expired, and had taken no steps to renew the copyright of the music, the renewal copyright protected only the words.[6] He argued that the music was in the public domain. By this view of their joint authorship, the holder of the renewal copyright hoped to avoid sharing the profits under the renewed copyright with the composer of the music. He relied upon the fact that, though only the lyrics were copyrighted, no one could use the music without the lyrics.

This overclever contention the court rejected. It decided that when the joint owner (the assignee of the author of the lyrics) renewed the copyright in his own name solely, he renewed the copyright on the entire work, music and words. Also that the renewal copyright was held in trust, the profits of one-half thereof to be paid to the composer of the music. The courts protect joint owners vigorously.

130. TRANSFERS BY ONE JOINT OWNER

Where two joint owners own a copyrighted work the usual rules, prevailing as to ownership in common of any sort of property, control when it comes to the sale thereof. Either one of the joint owners acting alone may sell, or use the copyrighted property (i.e. produce it if it be a play), or license others to use it in any form. The non-consenting joint owner is entitled to receive an equal share of the profits derived from such use, but he can not prevent his co-owner from selling or using the property for their joint benefit unless he can show in due time that such sale or use involves a fraudulent or unfair diminution or diversion of profits.[7] Thus it is common to obtain licenses for particular uses from only one of two joint owners. The danger of litigation renders it advisable, however, though not necessary, to have the consent of both owners.

Where one joint author obtains profits from the use of the jointly owned work, the other joint author-owner can obtain an accounting and require payment to him of one-half of such profits, unless a definite other division has been agreed upon.[8] Formerly this right of accounting was doubted because it has been held in the law of patents that one joint owner of a patent could use the patent without paying the other joint owner for such use. But that rule, by express court ruling, now does not prevail as between joint owners of copyrights.

──── XVII ────

Works of Art, Maps, Commercial Lists, Advertising Media; Originality

131. COPYRIGHT PROVISIONS

THE COPYRIGHT Statute, in Section 5, itemizes thirteen classifications of "works for registration," i.e. works which may be registered with the Copyright Office for copyrighting.

The section prescribes that the application for registration shall specify to which of these classes the work to be copyrighted belongs. It also provides: "nor shall any error in classification invalidate or impair the copyright protection secured." In short, the classifications in this Section 5 are only an express recognition that such classes of works are subject to copyright and are for the convenience of the Copyright Office and copyright applicants.

Graphic writings or works, not expressed in words, are defined in six of the thirteen classifications of Section 5 of the Copyright Statute as:

(f) Maps.
(g) Works of art; models or designs for works of art.
(h) Reproductions of a work of art.
(i) Drawings or plastic works of a scientific or technical character.
(j) Photographs.
(k) Prints and pictorial illustrations including prints or labels used for articles of merchandise.

The official Regulations of the Copyright Office amplify these classifications and further define them. These official descriptions and amplifications of works pictorially represented must be borne in mind. The Register's official descriptions of prints, art creations, and maps are copied in full in Chapter VII, Section 52. In addition, the Regulations of the Copyright Office, U.S.C.A., Title 17, Section 202, Subdivisions 8, 9, 10, 11, and 12, specify:

Sec. 202.8. Works of art (Class G)—(a) *In general.* This class includes works of artistic craftsmanship, in so far as their form but not their mechanical or utilitarian aspects are concerned, such as artistic jewelry, enamels, glassware, and tapestries, as well as all works belonging to the fine arts, such as paintings, drawings and sculpture. Works of art and models or designs for works of art are registered in Class G on Form G, except published three-dimensional works of art which require Form GG.

(b) *Published three-dimensional works of art.* All applications for copyright registration of published three-dimensional works of art shall be accompanied by as many photographs, in black and white or in color, as are necessary to identify the work. Each photograph shall not be larger than nine by twelve inches, but preferably shall be eight by ten inches, nor shall it present an image of the work smaller than four inches in its greatest dimension. The title of the work shall appear on each photograph. * * * [Here follow detailed instructions as to the copies to be sent to the Copyright Office. See the Regulations, Section 202.8 (b), 1, 2, and 3.]

Sec. 202.9. Reproduction of works of art (Class H). This class includes published reproductions of existing works of art in the same or a different medium, such as a lithograph, photoengraving, etching or drawing of a painting, sculpture or other work of art.

Sec. 202.10. Drawings or plastic works of a scientific or technical character (Class I). This class includes diagrams or models illustrating scientific or technical works, or formulating scientific or technical information in linear or plastic form, such as an architect's or an engineer's plan or design, a mechanical drawing, or an anatomical model.

Sec. 202.11. Photographs (Class J). This class includes photographic prints and filmstrips, slide films and individual slides. Photoengravings and other photomechanical reproductions of photographs are registered in Class K on Form K.

Sec. 202.12. Prints, pictorial illustrations and Commercial Prints or Labels (Class K). This class includes prints or pictorial illustrations, greeting cards, picture postcards and similar prints, produced by means of lithography, photoengraving or other methods of reproduction. These works are registered on Form K. A print or label, not a trademark, published in connection with the sale or advertisement of an article or articles of merchandise, is also registered in this class on Form KK.

132. PICTORIAL WORKS

Section 12 of the Copyright Statute, in its specifications of those works which may be copyrighted "of which copies are not reproduced for sale", provides for the deposit of one copy only thereof with the copyright office. The Statute specifies, "a photographic print if the work be a photograph; * * * a photograph or other identifying reproduction thereof, if it be a work of art or a plastic work or drawing". Copyright notices are not required on unpublished works registered under Section 12 of the Copyright Statute.[1a]

It is to be noted that maps are the only form of graphic work not included under Section 12 of the Copyright Statute. Maps cannot be copyrighted if not first published and if copies are not reproduced for sale. When maps are reproduced for sale, they can be copyrighted after the publication of a copy thereof, with a copyright notice attached thereto and a deposit of a copy made in the Copyright Office.

As to all the other works noted in Section 12, they can be copyrighted without publication but also can be published. But after publication with the copyright notice, if copyrighted already as unpublished works, they must be copyrighted again as published works following the procedure specified in Chapter VIII.

Section 12 of the Copyright Statute specifies:

> But the privilege of registration of copyright secured hereunder shall not exempt the copyright proprietor from the deposit of copies, under sections 13 and 14 of this title, where the work is later reproduced in copies for sale.

133. COMMERCIAL LISTS AND ORIGINALITY

Some show of originality, the courts hold, must be involved in a work to make it copyrightable, because the Constitutional provision in Article 1, Section 8, grants the power to Congress to grant copyrights "to promote the Progress of Science and Useful Arts * * *"

But the courts have so narrowly construed this requirement that no exertion of imaginative originality in fact is required. The most humdrum commercial lists and compilations can be copyrighted.[1] The court, in fact, seldom closely examines and scrutinizes a copyrighted work to ascertain if the originality involved is sufficient to make the work capable of copyrighting. So long as it is not obscene or in furtherance of fraud, and is extensive enough to be substantial and involve some mental labor in the making, it is copyrightable.

The minimum mental labor and expression required is that of the hack compiler, who collects material and compiles and sets it down objectively in written form.[1] Thus the merest mental labor, such as used in the compilation of a city directory, is protected by copyright. What is protected is not the exclusive use of the material collected. That material is in the public domain. Merely the compiler's labor in collecting and setting down his list is protected. Anyone can make a similar list. But if the list be copyrighted, no one can copy the labor of the compiler by copying his list; instead, the second list maker must go out and make a list of his own by independent labor in collecting the material.

The Copyright Statute expressly recognizes the right of a mere compiler in Section 7 where it says: "Compilations or abridgements, adaptations, arrangements, * * * or other variations of works in the public domain * * * shall be regarded as new work subject to copyright under the provisions of this title; * * *."

Also Section 5 of the Copyright Act, in its classification of works that may be registered for copyright, expressly specifies "Books, including composite encyclopedic works, directories, gazetteers, and other compilations."

The test in claims of piracy of such lists is solely whether the second list was copied from the first list. As to a legal digest or legal text, for example, one may not merely copy the list of cases found in such a copyrighted legal text or digest. That would be copying the labor of the compiler. But the writer of a second digest or text may use the list of cases in the first digest as a reference indication to the cases in the law reports.[2] It is held that the purpose of the list or compilation is to direct the public to the sources which are in the public domain. Thus in taking cases from a legal digest or text, the second author if he goes to the original books and examines them is deemed not to be copying or infringing upon the copying in the earlier legal text.[2] Also the compiler of a second directory, although he may not copy the names from the city directory, but must go to the same sources and indulge in the same labor involved in collecting the list of his names, may use the earlier directory as a check for errors and omissions in his later directory.[2]

Under United States Copyright Statutes prior to 1909, abridgements were not subject to copyright. But under the provisions of Section 7 of the 1909 Copyright Statute they are now subject to copyright. However, for making an abridgement of a work, if the work so abridged and summarized is not in the public domain, the consent of the copyright proprietor thereof must first be had. If the work abridged, however, is in the public domain the abridgement may freely be made. It may be copyrighted as an alteration of or change in the work in the public domain.

134. IDENTITY OF ERROR IN COMPILATIONS

In determining whether or not there has been literal copying of a compilation, directory, digest, list of citations or of names, the courts have been quick to see the significance of identity of errors. Where a second maker of lists denies that he has copied a prior list, demonstrations that errors in the first list appear in the second list, if of a substantial number, are held to be conclusive proof of copying.[3] Identical errors do not occur by accident. Identity of error clearly indicates copying. It is almost the most convincing of all possible circumstantial evidence to prove literal copying.

135. PROTECTION OF ADVERTISEMENTS

The fact that a work of art or photograph or print is used for advertising does not in any way prevent its being copyrighted, provided it show some originality; but the amount of originality and artistic merit required, as above noted, is very slight.

If an advertising print or photograph or article meets this slight test it can be copyrighted. For example, an advertising catalogue of marine hardware is copyrightable.[4]

Again, a manufacturer of suits [5] copyrighted a book of pictorial illustrations of ladies' garments. The defendant copied these printed designs. It was held that the plaintiff had a valid copyright and could prevent the defendant from copying the prints of the women's dresses in its catalog. But it was also held that anyone could use the designs for patterns in making dresses, because the copyright of the picture of a dress only prevented the copying of that picture in another print or pictorial representation, but it did not prevent others from making dresses out of the designs. Here is an illustration of the previous discussion of what can be copyrighted. An idea, plan, or concept can not be copyrighted. Any protection therefor, if obtainable, must be obtained under the patent laws.

Likewise, where a manufacturer of artificial limbs copyrighted a catalog of pictures illustrating its products, such pictures showing artificial limbs, a competitor could not copy the pictures. But, except insofar as the artificial limbs so shown were subject to patent, the court held that the defendant could make artificial limbs from the illustrations.[6]

The scope of prints and commercial pictorial illustrations, which can be copyrighted, covers a wide area. The design of playing cards can be copyrighted.[7] Pictures of statues holding a candle for religious purposes can be copyrighted.[8]

136. THE COPYRIGHT NOTICE REQUIRED ON WORKS OF ART

In the case of maps, works of art, reproductions thereof, photographs and prints, etc., the Statute (Section 19) provides for an abbreviated notice which:

* * * may consist of the letter C enclosed within a circle, thus ©, accompanied by the initials, monogram, mark, or symbol of the copyright proprietor: *Provided*, that on some accessible portion of such copies or of the margin, back, permanent base, or pedestal, or of the substance on which such copies shall be mounted, his name shall appear.

It is to be noted that this provision does not require the year of copyrighting. Nor does the provision apply to comic strips.[9]

Where use is made of C in a circle, the © must be of sufficient size to be distinguishable by the naked eye. If it can not be seen, except by the use of a magnifying glass, or if the initial or symbol of the copyright proprietor is omitted, the error is fatal and the work is in the public domain.[9]

——— XVIII ———

Moral or Retained Rights

---

137. EUROPEAN PROTECTION OF CREATORS' MORAL RIGHTS

A SHARP disagreement over the protection granted authors against their own acts exists between Europe and America. The right of an author to be so protected is often called the author's "moral rights." Europe recognizes the right. America rejects it in large part.

The issue arises after an author, particularly a painter or sculptor, sells the copyright (statutory or common-law) in his work and completely divests himself of any ownership therein. Has he the right thereafter to seek legal relief (a) if his work be mutilated or changed, or (b) if his name be suppressed as the creator of the work?

Europe recognizes this right in authors and artists, despite any contracts that they may have signed. The retained rights are called "moral rights". The word "moral" is unfortunate, because the issue involved is different from one of ordinary morality. A more fitting name would be "retained rights" since the essential issue is whether the author or writer retains any rights, by judicial implication, after he has sold his copyright and his work without expressly reserving any rights at all.

138. EUROPE'S PHRASING OF THE RIGHT

The retained or moral right is codified in Article 6 bis of the Convention of Berne:

(1) Independently of the author's copyright, and even after the transfer of the said copyright, the author shall have the right, during his lifetime, to claim authorship of the work and to object [to] any distortion, mutilation or other alteration thereof, or any other action in

relation to the said work, which would be prejudicial to his honour or reputation.

Most European countries have legislation protecting this right. England has not. The United States formally rejects it, although there are curious hints of conformity in this country.

The essential right involved is the right not to have a painting or sculpture mutilated after it is sold. Also involved is the right not to have a creator's name suppressed from a successful work.

As to the right against mutilation, one's instinctive sympathies are with the creator. The alteration or mutilation of a painting or sculpture, particularly if it has definite artistic merit, can not be defended. The purchaser of the copyright therein should hold his rights in trust for the public benefit, so far as destruction or mutilation is involved. But in the United States no moral obligation is directly recognized, except as concerns renewal rights in a copyright and as concerns the right of an author as to the use of his name in most circumstances. As to alteration of the work no moral obligation is recognized in the United States.

A painter painted fresco murals on the wall of a New York church and sold all his rights therein to the church. The parishioners of the church did not like the mural, so they had it completely painted over. The artist sued. The court held that the artist's contract, as written, should be enforced; and since the contract conveyed all the rights to the church, the artist had no grounds to complain. The court completely rejected the artist's moral or retained rights.[1]

The situation here presented, of course, is considerably different from that where an acknowledged work of art is mutilated. To require a church to retain a work of art which was objectionable to its worshipers, or differs from their artistic views, is hardly sensible.

In another case, where certain Russian composers (Shostakovich, Prokofieff and others) sued a motion-picture company because a picture entitled *The Iron Curtain* used their music (which was in the public domain) as background music for a picture hostile to the composers' political views, the court held that there was no moral right involved.[2]

Another facet of the same problem arises when a novelist licenses the motion-picture or television rights in his creation and agrees that the producer thereof may make any changes that he deems advisable when dramatizing the work. If the changes are a mutilation of the novel, should the author have any retained rights, despite his express contract? The situation arose as to Theodore Dreiser's *An American Tragedy*, the motion-picture rights of which Dreiser sold to Paramount. The court inferentially rejected Mr. Dreiser's claims, denying his request for a preliminary injunction against the showing of the picture. The grounds of denial were that only on a trial could it be determined whether or not the changes were a mutilation, not on a preliminary hearing. The case was then settled. But the court evidently was not impressed by the claim of moral or retained rights in Dreiser.[3]

139. A SUGGESTED APPROACH

Motion-picture companies and television stations, which use large quantities of copyrighted material, make violent objection to any theory of moral or retained rights by an author. This objection is a lesser barrier against adherence by the United States to the Treaty of Rome. Licensees assert that if they are not permitted to change material, when by express agreement the author who sells such material to them so expressly consents, they can not function.

Yet the realities involved as to these moral or retained rights of the author are not too difficult to formulate as a sensible application of United States judicial principles.

1. In the case of meritorious paintings or works of art, alteration or mutilation should be frowned on. Here arises an essential difference between the alteration of a novel or drama and of a painting. The mutilation or alteration of a work of art, such as a painting, does not leave the original in its prior form. Alteration of treatment in the dramatization of a novel in a motion picture does not impair the original. There seems no possible excuse for the mutilation or alteration by the purchaser of a painting or work of art possessing artistic merit. When an artist paints a mural on the walls of a building he runs the risk of having it moved or painted over if the purchaser does not deem it worthy of preservation. That seems a necessary though harsh result.

But that reasoning does not mean that a movable work of art should be subject to mutilation or alteration. Though there is no

obligation that can be imposed upon the owner to exhibit and safeguard works of art, in fairness he should be required to attempt to
return it to its creator before he destroys or mutilates it. He should
be required to make a fair effort to notify its creator to come and
take it.

2. Such protection against mutilation of works of art and of
writings can be established by the courts under a theory of implied contract rights, as distinct from an expressly stated grant.
Where an author sells his copyright in his literary work to a motion-
picture company, or licenses its use, for a large sum of money, and
expressly agrees that his work can be changed or altered by the
motion-picture company as the company wishes, it is difficult to
find grounds for a retained right in the author in view of his elaborate agreement. Here the sole test should be whether or not the
author has clearly and expressly granted a right of alteration, and
how extensive a right. Implied rights should not be relied on to
protect a writer against his own acts.

3. But uninformed creators and artists should be protected by a
rule that the right to alter or change a work should not be implied
by the court. Unless the contract of sale between the author and
the purchaser expressly grants the right of alteration in very definite
terms, the purchaser should not be deemed to hold thereby the
right of alteration. Few artists, selling a picture, would expressly
grant the right to alter or change the work in express words. The
point is seldom raised at the time of sale. Thus the pith of protection
to an author in his retained rights really is a requirement that the
right of alteration, to be enforcible, must be clearly specified, with
all the presumptions and interpretations to the contrary in favor of
the creator. Such a recognition of the retained rights of an author
would be advisable in any revision of the copyright law.

140. UNITED STATES ASPECTS OF RETAINED RIGHTS

The limitation imposed upon the right of assigning a renewal term
of a copyright, under Section 24 of the Copyright Statute (see
Section 56), is a recognition of this retained or moral right of the
author. Here, even though the author in express writing grants away
the second or renewal term of his work, if the author be not living
at the expiration of the first twenty-eight years, his express assignee

can not renew the copyright. Only the widow, children, executor, and next of kin of the deceased author can do so.

141. RIGHT OF AN AUTHOR IN HIS NAME AND NOM DE PLUME

Similar leanings toward retained rights are found in United States rulings as to the use of an author's name or pen name. Most of the rulings turn either upon the failure of the purchaser to use the author's name in publishing a work, or upon the unauthorized use of an author's name. The rulings are in conflict but the courts generally protect an author's right not to have his name, as author, suppressed.

Bret Harte sued a publisher in New York on the ground that the publisher had used four chapters of a Bret Harte story (which the publisher had obtained lawfully) and then had hired someone to finish the story, publishing all under the name of Bret Harte as author. But a note in the book added that Bret Harte had written no more than the first four chapters. The court granted Bret Harte an injunction, on mingled theories of unfair competition and common-law implications as to moral right.[4]

In another case, S. L. Clemens sued a publisher of Clemens' uncopyrighted works in the public domain. Clemens asked that the publisher be enjoined from using Clemens' nom de plume "Mark Twain" on his public-domain works. The court held that Clemens had no exclusive right in such name and the publisher could proceed in his dubious ways.[5]

Where an author published uncopyrighted material under a nom de plume, and a publisher republished it, using the author's real name, it was held that the author had no right to complain under either the privacy statute of New York or the copyright law.[6]

In another case a motion-picture company bought a dog story by J. O. Curwood, but did not use the story. Instead it attached the plaintiff's name to an entirely different northwestern outdoor picture, similar to those for which Curwood was famous, and having nothing to do with dogs. The picture story was not written by Curwood. Here the court held that Curwood could enjoin the use of his name on this entirely different literary material.[7]

When the artist Vargas sold drawings by him to *Esquire*, under a contract which gave *Esquire* all the rights therein and without any specification as to the use of Vargas' name (or as to mention of Varga girls), it was held that *Esquire* had the right to use the pictures without putting Vargas' name on them.[8] The court proceeded on the narrow ground of denial of any retained or moral rights. Here, since the contract did not expressly permit *Esquire* to publish the Vargas drawings without using Vargas' name, a different result could have well been reached, as before noted, by implying rights to protect the artist if no express words prevent such implication.

When an author of a mystery story sold it for $200 to a publisher, without definitely specifying that his name had to be used as the author, the court held that the publisher could not refuse to pay the $200 and not publish the story when the author objected to publication thereof without the use of his name as author.[9] In holding that the author could recover the $200 from the publisher, even though the story was not published, the court reached a result contrary to the Vargas ruling and fairer to authors. For the pith of the ruling here was that an author's right to have credit as the author must be upheld.

In another case, where a writer named Stokes was engaged to prepare material for an encyclopedia to be called *Stokes Encyclopedia of Music*, which the publisher was permitted to copyright in its own name, it was held that the publisher had no right to merge the copyrighted material into a new publication, *University Encyclopedia of Music*, and suppressing the use of the author Stokes' name.[10]

A lecturer, some of whose lectures were in the public domain in a garbled and incorrect form using the lecturer's name as the author, was allowed to restrain the publishing of those lectures.[11]

Charles William Eliot, as the editor of *Eliot's Harvard Classics*, was granted an injunction preventing the use of his name on a rival, similar publication.[12]

In cases of law articles published in law encyclopedias, it is generally held that the author has no right to require the encyclopedia to use his name as the author of the articles.[13]

Thus moral or retained rights, particularly when it comes to denying to a creator the right to be known as the originator of his work, though formally denied as part of copyright law in the United States, constantly keep creeping back around the corner. The lack of such rights in our Copyright Statute is another instance of a needed revision.

XIX

Piracy Trials

142. PIRACY TRIALS, AS THE ACID TEST

THE ACID test as to what can be copyrighted and thus is protected by a copyright, as was noted in Chapter X, is found in decisions determining what constitutes piracy. Piracy trials define what can and can not be copyrighted. Determination by piracy trials, as to whether there has been independent creation or copying as either literal or treatment copying, realistically fixes the scope of copyright protection.

A summary of what actually takes place at a typical piracy trial therefore is illuminating as to the value of all the theories involved in a copyright. Trials cast light upon what are the realities of the right granted to an author, also upon the latitude allowed an author in using the ideas and works of others who have preceded him.

The dominant problem in piracy trials arises from the difficulty judges experience in determining whether or not there has been treatment copying. If the wrong alleged is one of literal copying, a determination usually is quickly reached. The issue in literal copying is simple to phrase and decide. If the literal copying of copyrightable material be substantial, then generally the court need only determine if the copyright statute has been complied with, or if the defense of fair comment or use is valid. But if the issue be one of treatment copying, many difficulties arise. The distinction between literal and treatment copying has been set forth in Section 64. Piracy, as treatment copying, if of a purely factual work, is easier to appraise than is piracy by treatment copying of fiction. Treatment copying often is difficult to determine. Obscurities and guesses intervene. The distinction between expression and substance

213

tends to be artificial. This artificiality creates many of the difficulties that arise in judicial determinations as whether or not there has been treatment copying of fiction, which constitutes the bulk of piracy trials.

143. PRELIMINARIES AT A PIRACY TRIAL

The trial of a piracy suit is usually by a judge without a jury. If damages are sought, either party may demand a jury trial. But usually the complexities involved persuade the parties to prefer a judge alone. Appeals, too, are usually important. Theoretically, an appellate court can overrule a trial judge only if legal error or clear error of judgment in appraising facts is found. But in no branch of the law do appellate judges act more freely in reviewing lower-court decisions than in copyright matters. Interest in the issues and the clarity of the record induce this freedom to reverse.

Preliminary matters first are disposed of at the trial. These preliminaries commonly are four. (1) Putting the copyright certificate in evidence, and the facts of creation, and the plaintiff's copyrighted work, usually are the first steps if the plaintiff's work involves a statutory copyright. (2) If the plaintiff relies on a common-law copyright, then the first step is the introduction in evidence of the original of the manuscript or other work which constitutes the creation of the complainant. Evidence also must be introduced in common-law copyright actions showing the time of creation. If the complainant's creation was completed later than the defendant's, or if serious doubt arises as to the time sequence, then the complainant has no case. How to establish in advance of litigation the date of an unpublished, uncopyrighted work is discussed in Chapter XXIV, Protection of Manuscripts. (3) Next, copies of the defendant's alleged infringing work are identified and introduced into evidence. (4) Finally, evidence as to access is introduced by the plaintiff.

Details of these four preliminary steps must be noted.

144. THE COPYRIGHT CERTIFICATE

The copyright certificate, issued to the copyright proprietor by the Copyright Office under Section 209 of the Copyright Statute, when introduced in evidence creates only a prima facie, i.e. preliminary, proof in favor of the copyright proprietor as to due and full performance of all acts required under the Statute, including compliance with the four essential acts noted in Chapter VII. The Copyright Statute provides that "Said certificate shall be admitted in any court as *prima facie* evidence of the facts stated therein." (C.S., Section 209; emphasis added.)

But the prima facie case thus made can be rebutted by actual proof to the contrary by the defendant, i.e. that the copyright proprietor in fact has not done all or any of the required registration acts. Then the judge decides whether or not the acts have been duly done. The copyright certificate is of no avail on the big issues: has the defendant copied the plaintiff's work?

In addition, where the copyright proprietor is not the author or creator but is the employer or assignee of the author, proof must be given of the facts of creation by the author, and the time thereof. This proof is usually short and documentary. Also the chain of title running to the copyright proprietor from the creator, entitling the copyright proprietor to obtain the copyright, must be proved.

145. COPIES OF THE TWO WORKS

The basic issue as to whether there has been piracy starts with the precise identification of the two works, i.e. of the complainant's alleged infringed work and of the alleged copy thereof by the defendant. These usually have been identified before the trial, by copies attached to the pleadings, i.e. to the plaintiff's complaint. Rule 2 of the Rules of the Supreme Court of the United States, applicable to copyright, provides:

A copy of the alleged infringement of copyright, if actually made, and a copy of the work alleged to be infringed, should accompany the petition, or its absence be explained; except in cases of alleged infringement by the public performance of dramatic and dramatico-musical compositions, the delivery of lectures, sermons, addresses, and so forth, the infringement of copyright upon sculptures and other similar works and in any case where it is not feasible.[1]

146. ACCESS

The technical term "access" means the submission of proof that the defendant had knowledge of the complainant's work, access to it, and thus an opportunity to copy it, i.e. access for copying. Usually the question of access is the first big litigated issue in a piracy trial. Rarely does the defendant admit, or find himself forced to admit by the circumstances involved, that he (the defendant) had knowledge of the plaintiff's copyrighted work or used it in any way. In the bulk of cases the defendant stoutly denies knowledge of, and therefore any use whatsoever of, the plaintiff's copyrighted work. Purchasers of copyrighted material, such as motion-picture producers and big broadcasting stations, studiously try by a preventive office procedure to bar any proof of access. They assert, and try to prove, that their readers read only literary material submitted by well-known authors or by accredited agents. The works of others, they assert, they mail back without reading; and their employees often testify at the trial that this iron-rigid rule was adhered to in the instance in question.[2] This practice, of course, works great hardships upon unknown authors. Also, at times, such evidence is doubted.

In many copyright cases, evidence as to access is detailed and hotly controverted, also quite farfetched. In fact the issue as to access is not too important realistically, though often it is ardently fought over.

In a recent famous piracy case,[3] the defendant was Miss Daphne Du Maurier; her novel *Rebecca* was claimed to be an infringement of the plaintiff's story published in *Hearst's International Magazine* in 1924, later appearing as a novel called *Blind Windows*. Both the plaintiff's short story and novel were published in the United States. Miss Du Maurier lived in England. *Rebecca* was published ten years after the plaintiff's works and was also made into a highly successful motion picture. The evidence as to how an English author would and did know of an unimportant earlier United States work was gone over in great detail. The contest suggests the farfetched stress laid upon access, as contrasted to the vital issue of treatment copying against independent creation.

Both the plaintiff's and the defendant's stories here involved the familiar second-marriage theme; in both works, the memory of the deceased first wife haunted the second wife and the husband's outlook.

The plaintiff's proof of access consisted of the bare possibility

(1) that Miss Du Maurier, who was seventeen when the plaintiff's story was first published, might have read either the magazine story or else a review of the plaintiff's novel in the *Times Literary Supplement* published *in London* in 1928, (2) or that Miss Du Maurier, having later sold stories to *Hearst's Cosmopolitan* in New York, might through her agent have been advised of the plaintiff's story. Also the plaintiff stressed that Miss Du Maurier was often in the home of Edgar Wallace, the English writer of mystery stories, Miss Du Maurier being a friend of Wallace's daughter. Mr. Wallace's mystery books had contained back pages, advertising other books, including the plaintiff's *Blind Windows*. Thus the plaintiff argued that Miss Du Maurier, while in Mr. Wallace's home, must have seen Mr. Wallace's books, noticed the advertisement of the plaintiff's novel, read it, and finally copied it.

Out of such fugitive threads is proof of access often spun. The court here rejected such evidence and held that such facts did not establish any access by the defendant to the plaintiff's work. But the time consumed thereover and the plaintiff's ingenuity were great.

The most common proof of access by the complainant is that the copyrighted work of the plaintiff was mailed to and offered to the defendant for purchase. Thereby the effort is made to establish, by mailing and rejection, that the defendant had knowledge of the plaintiff's work and could have copied it.[3] (See Section 182.)

If the similarities between the two works are very great, and the likelihood of independent creation thus is eliminated, the court will hold that *markedly great similarity in itself proves access*. Thus even the issue as to access in reality is usually decided by the vital issue of similarities between the two works.

147. DEFINING SIMILARITIES

After these preliminaries the court passes to the central issue, by the test of similarities and of internal circumstantial evidence, as to whether there was copying.

If the similarities found involve substantial instances of literal copying the determination of the case is easy. Then the usual defense of the defendant is to prove a technical defect in the plaintiff's copyright, or to establish a defense of uncopyrightable material, fair comment, or fair use as above noted. In the difficult piracy trials, as before noted, and in the great majority of cases, instances of literal copying are absent and the issue is one of treatment copying.

When the issue involves primarily treatment copying, the real difficulties begin. Then the first basic step of the court is carefully to ascertain and appraise the similarities between the two works involved. After the similarities have been noted, the second step is taken: that of eliminating similarities as to material not copyrightable.

This process of exclusion or elimination of similarities of material is difficult, because it involves an artificial distinction between material and expression. But material in the public domain must be earmarked and eliminated before the similarities involving treatment expression can be appraised and compared. Then only can the vital issue involved be brought into clear view. Similarities of ideas, of historical events, of historical and stock personalities, or familiar action incidents, of common human character traits, of stock plot and locale, first must be noted and excluded; what is left, then, is the similarities of treatment.

148. PUBLIC-DOMAIN MATERIAL AND FAIR USE

Confusion commonly arises as to the legal basis of this process of exclusion of material. A theory of fair use of material in the public domain is often inaccurately given as the legal basis of this exclusion, for it is sometimes said that a second author may copy the material in the public domain as used by a prior author, under a right of fair use. (See Section 112.)

A clearer and more helpful statement, as to the right of copying by a second author of material in the public domain used by a prior author, is that such material could not be copyrighted and was not copyrighted in fact by the prior author. The prior author's copyright did not include or cover any material in the public domain. The use by the second author of material found in the prior author's work, when such material was taken by the prior author from material in the public domain, is *of right*. It is not an invasion of a prior copyright. Thus the defense of fair use is not needed or pertinent.

The distinction involved may seem technical and narrow. But unless it is pinpointed confusion inevitably arises.

This right to copy work in the public domain is in reality based upon the fact that, since the material was in the public domain when the first author took it, such material, being in the public domain, could not be copyrighted by the first author. Thus it is not included within the protection of his copyright as obtained. That reason is categorical, complete, and sufficient.

Even if a subsequent writer gets from a prior copyrighted work his *idea* for a play or novel, or for the use of an obscurely known historical character or locale, the prior author can not claim copyright infringement.[3a] The prior copyright includes only the *expression* involved in the use of such material.

Much of the protracted discussion, in decisions determining whether or not there has been piracy in literary and musical works, since so much of any literary or musical work is in the public domain, turns upon the question of whether or not the similarities found arise from the use by complainant and the asserted pirate of public-domain material as distinct from the treatment thereof. Thus the initial task of the court is to separate public-domain material from the expression thereof. Only when the trier of the facts then finds that there are substantial similarities in expression and treatment, as distinct from material in the public domain, does any issue arise for decision.

149. SIMILARITIES IN TREATMENT

If the identities found in treatment also involve fugitive instances of literal copying, the determination of the case is made easier. But if there are no identities of literal copying but only identities of treatment expression, then the trier of the facts must appraise the skill in expression displayed by the complainant and the defendant, to decide the controlling issue now presented: are the similarities in the two works due to treatment copying or to independent creation by the alleged infringer?

If the plots of the defendant and plaintiff are similar, the prior creator can not complain of use of the same plot if it is a stock plot. But if there are similarities of details and twists of skill involved in the manipulation of the plot, or as to the technique of narration (treatment and use of suspense, conflict, surprise, and denouement), the plaintiff has acquired the right, as to such additions, not to have them copied.

150. INDEPENDENT CREATION AGAINST TREATMENT COPYING

After the trier of the facts thus has narrowed the orbit of similarities down to similarities in treatment expression [i.e. (1) has appraised the similarities, and (2) has determined the similarities of expression remaining after the elimination of identities of material in the public domain], the bulk of appraisal has been accomplished. The issue now is defined. The trier of the facts is now ready to proceed to the third and decisive step: comparison of the residuum of similarities of treatment expression in each work, in order to determine if similarities of treatment expression are due to independent creation by the asserted pirate or to treatment copying.

In reaching a conclusion on this third and final aspect of the issue, the trier of the facts finds himself in the situation of a detective in a "whodunit." Fugitive clues become important. Often the similarities in treatment expression are not of a nature, or are not sufficiently marked, or are not sufficiently illuminating, to enable the trier of the facts to reach a decision solely by the extent or nature of the similarities in treatment expression.

A numerical adding up of the number of treatment similarities is not decisive or very helpful. The quality of a few of the treatment similarities is far more important. One or two clear similarities in treatment expression, revealing high imaginative and creative skill, may be decisive. The trier of the facts appraises such paramount similarities in the light of the demonstrated skills of the plaintiff and the defendant.

But usually the trier of the facts relies more upon clues of a more humdrum nature. If there be a few fugitive traces of literal copying, the probability of copying becomes persuasive. If there be no such traces of literal copying, the court may be guided markedly by accidental similarities or by coincidences of error as to minor facts.

In a protracted trial involving two works dealing with the life of Clara Barton, the founder of the Red Cross, the complainant asserted that the writer of a short story in *Cosmopolitan* had copied the plaintiff's novelized rendering of the life of Miss Barton. The complainant had given a name to Miss Barton's lover which was not the name of the actual personage involved in Miss Barton's life. The defendant's work used the same name. Since the name was not that of an actual personage involved in Miss Barton's life, the court was greatly persuaded by this isolated similarity of names. For here the name was not actual but created.

So too in the copying of commercial lists, where there are no similarities of literal expression involved in the two lists, similarities of error in the names are held by the courts to be the most persuasive evidence of literal copying, for similarities of errors seldom occur in independent creation. (See Section 134.)

Another "whodunit" clue, used by the courts, is that of persistent and extensive similarities of material in the public domain. Historical facts and events in actual life, as before noted, are not copyrightable. But if the defendant admits that he got his idea, concept, or guide to material from the plaintiff's work, or if the abundance of such similarities indicates the defendant must have so used the plaintiff's work (even though the defendant stoutly denies that he did), a persuasive clue arises. In using the plaintiff's work as leads to public-domain material, the defendant was within his rights. But the admission by the defendant that he did so use such material, or the conclusion by the court that defendant did so use the plaintiff's work, tends to make the defendant's claim of independent creation less persuasive.

In determining the issue presented by the final and third query, i.e. treatment copying against independent creation, the court examines all the circumstantial evidence. This circumstantial evidence usually consists of the following: (a) evidence of access; (b) isolated traces of literal copying; (c) isolated items of identities by minor alterations of actual, though insignificant facts; (d) evidence as to leads to public-domain material found in the complainant's work; (e) the quality and value of the identities as distinct from the quantity thereof, especially in the light of the test of imaginative and literary skill; (f) the comparative skill of the complainant and defendant, as indicating whether or not the defendant could have independently created the similarities revealed and determined to exist.

From an over-all appraisal of all of these clues and items of evidence, the trier of the facts determines the answer to the final and third query: are the similarities of treatment expression due to independent creation or to treatment copying? If the trier of the facts finds that they are due to treatment copying, the finding is one of piracy.

151. INTENT AND SUBCONSCIOUS COPYING

It is not necessary for the plaintiff to establish that the defendant intended to copy the plaintiff's work, or even did so consciously. If the plaintiff subconsciously copied the plaintiff's work, piracy results. The courts recognize the possibilities of subconscious copying, particularly in musical works: [4]

Impressions register in our memories, and it is difficult at times to tell what calls them up. If the thing covered by a copyright has become familiar to the mind's eye, and one produces it from memory and writes it down, he copies just the same, and this may be done without conscious plagiarism. In this case, in all the essentials of the thing copyrighted, similarity amounts to identity, and the evidence establishes infringement.

152. USE OF EXPERTS

Often experts are placed upon the stand in copyright cases, particularly in piracy suits involving musical compositions. The courts, however, have repeatedly held that the test is not that of the judgment of an expert mind. In ascertaining whether there are marked similarities between works the test is that of the ordinary lay mind—whatever that may be.

On the question of infringement, I think the plaintiff's case must fall, because of the admission of both her experts that the two melodies, if played on the piano, or the two songs, if sung by any person, would not convey identity to the average listener. The courts have said that, ultimately, it is not the dissection to which a musical composition might be submitted under the microscopic eye of a musician which is the criterion of similarity, but the impression which the pirated song or phrase would carry to the average ear. [5]

The law has a passion for setting up the standard of the ordinarily prudent or reasonable mind as the standard to determine issues of fact. That same standard applies in copyright determinations.

Experts, however, may give opinion thereon which can be considered by the court or jury. Also they are allowed to give tabulations or "dissections" showing the quantity of similarities, in the form of numerical comparison. These tabulations, however, are not very effective. They usually are quantitative enumerations. Experts usually also list how much of the work used by each party is in the public domain, and thus is not subject to protection—facts of which the court itself is aware.

153. SUMMARY JUDGMENT

Most piracy lawsuits accent the expense and extended duration of piracy cases. The great bulk of piracy claims are decided in favor of the defendant. Unfortunately, many writers have an inaccurate understanding of the copyright law, and believe that they have established priorities as to material though such priorities are not recognized. And a few writers are too imaginative. As Judge Learned Hand has observed: [6]

Apparently the conviction of which authors and composers cannot be disabused, extends to their assignees; that the finest gossamers of similarity can be made to serve. The prizes are large; the security of the foundation often seems to be in inverse proportion.

The interests of authors generally would be advanced if unfounded piracy cases could be quickly disposed of. In order to discourage unfounded lawsuits, the Copyright Act has a provision reading that in copyright suits "full costs shall be allowed, and the court may award to the prevailing party a reasonable attorney's fee as part of the costs." (Section 116, C.S.) Unlike the British procedure, where the successful party is allowed to recover from the unsuccessful litigant his actual costs of suit, including heavy attorney's fees, the rule in the United States is that in ordinary litigation the costs awarded to the winner are nominal. The provision in the Copyright Statute is an adaptation of the British procedure. The courts interpret this language as permitting them *in their discretion* to allow attorneys' fees of a successful party to be paid by the unsuccessful adversary. Generally the court will not award attorney's fees where the court believes substantial and reasonable grounds existed for the claim or defense. Too often, however, the unsuccessful complainant is not able to pay heavy attorney's fees. Courts, in fact, are reluctant to award even against "strike suit" plaintiffs the full and large attorney's fees actually paid by successful defendants.

To protect parties, therefore, a procedure for summary judgment without trial is usual. In the Federal courts, if a judge finds "no genuine issue as to any material fact" is present, and that a party thus "is entitled to a judgment as a matter of law" (R.C.P. Rule 56), no trial need be had. If the judge, on examining the two works and other claims, rules that sufficient similarities are not established for a triable issue, costly litigation can be avoided. But our courts, unfortunately, are very reluctant to grant summary judgments against complainants in copyright suits.

When Cole Porter was sued by a composer for piracy, two issues were raised by his motion for summary judgment: (1) no substantial similarities of musical expression in the two works; (2) no access to the plaintiff's songs by the defendant. The lower court granted summary judgment against the complainant. The Appellate Court, after hearing records of the two songs, decided that the similarities "standing alone * * * did not compel the conclusion or permit the inference that defendant copied." [7]

The court held, however, that since the issue of access involved the credibility of the complainant and of Porter, and of their witnesses, the complainant was entitled to the jury trial he demanded, as to that issue of access and credibility.[7] Therefore the lower court was reversed for granting a summary judgment and a trial was ordered, which ended in a complete victory for Cole Porter.

Judge Clark, dissenting, in a vigorous opinion said: [7]

* * * the defendant did make one fatal tactical error. In an endeavor to assist us, he caused to be prepared records of all the musical pieces here involved, and presented these transcriptions through the medium of the affidavit of his pianist. Though he himself did not stress these records and properly met plaintiff's claims as to the written music with his own analysis, yet the tinny tintinnabulations of the music thus

canned resounded through the United States Courthouse to the exclusion of all else, including the real issues in the case.

Likewise, in the suit against Miss Du Maurier as to her *Rebecca*, the lower court was reversed for granting her a summary judgment. Here the reversal was on a technical aspect as to how the issue of copying was raised. The courts suggested that, on a different form of motion, summary judgment might have been proper. Thus the rule as to summary judgment is not clear. The usual conclusion is that summary judgment can not be granted in a copyright suit. That conclusion seems unfounded.[8] To force a defendant to suffer a long trial in an unwarranted lawsuit (in both the Du Maurier and Cole Porter lawsuits, above noted, the final decisions were vigorously for the defendant) imposes great practical hardships upon the great bulk of unestablished authors. Theoretically it is desirable to grant every humble author the right of a full trial. But such a rule tends to result in the rigid refusal by our most important buyers to read the works of unestablished authors, to prevent unfounded claims of access.

If summary judgments were granted, piracy litigation would be abbreviated. Then purchasers of literary material might relax these most unfortunate protective measures of never examining an unsolicited literary work and always sending it back unread.

154. INJUNCTIONS AND DAMAGES

The most elaborate provisions of the Copyright Statute, some sixteen sections in all, deal with enforcement by injunction and damages. This elaborateness of relief, so superior to that in state equity suits on common-law copyrights, makes it desirable to obtain a statutory copyright where possible.

The Copyright Statute permits an injunction against a continuing infringement. [C.S., Section 101(a).] Also, an award of the profits derived by an infringer is allowable under the statute to a successful copyright complainant. [C.S., Section 101(b).]

The details as to damages that can be allowed in the discretion of the Court under Section 101(b) of the Copyright Statute run:

(a) The plaintiff, to establish his loss of profits by the defendant's piracy, can recover the profits made by the defendant. The plaintiff, moreover, need only prove the amount of the defendant's sales and the defendant then must prove "every element of cost which he claims", as a proper deduction from his gross sales to guide the court in its fixing of the defendant's net profits to be paid to the plaintiff.

(b) As to a piratical use by a newspaper of a copyrighted photograph the maximum recovery is $200; the minimum $50. This, of course, is apart from privacy damage in the use of pictures.

(c) As to the piracy of undramatized or nondramatic works by motion-picture production, where the motion-picture producer *can* show "he was not aware that he was infringing" and "such infringement could not have been reasonably foreseen", the maximum recovery is $100. This defense of complete innocence, however, is rarely available to a defendant.

(d) In other cases, the court in its discretion can award to the plaintiff as damages a maximum of $5000 and a minimum of $250, and an Appellate Court may not reverse the trial court's reasonable discretion.[9]

The Supreme Court has held, in the case of unauthorized broadcasting of a musical work, that a hotel proprietor who provided radios for his guests must be deemed publicly to perform each musical composition played over the hotel's loudspeakers; that lack of intent to infringe such rights of the copyright proprietor is no defense; and that the minimum damages under Section 101 (b) therefor, where there is no proof of actual damages, must be $250.00.[10]

155. PROFITS

What happens, as to profits, if pirated material be mingled with unassailable material? Profits are defined as the gross sales of the infringer, less the infringer's costs of production and distribution. The Statute places upon the infringer the burden of completely establishing all of the costs and disbursements. [Section 101(b), C.S.] In the fixing of damages as to the pirated picture *Dishonored Lady*, the Supreme Court ruled that the complainant could recover only one-fifth of the profits made from the picture by Metro-Goldwyn-Mayer, the pirating picture company. The court noted the testimony of experts, appraising the value of the material taken from the complainant's play, as against the unpirated material and the value of the star actors used. This ratio was reduced by the Court to one-to-five, permitting the motion picture company to retain four-fifths of its profits from the picture. The Supreme Court rejected the view that where a defendant was found to be even an intentional plagiarizer the plaintiff was entitled to recover all the profits resulting from the mingling of complainant's copyrighted material and plagiarizer's skill and material.[11]

156. STATUTE OF LIMITATIONS

As to all legal claims, after a lapse of years (from twenty years to one year, depending on what is involved), there comes a time when the law permits no litigation, by imposing a statutory rule of limitations. One of the defects of the Copyright Statute is that it has no such limitation-on-suits clause. Piracy, of course, can continue during the full term of a copyright. But there is a time limitation in the damages recoverable.

The statute of limitations in the state where the Federal Court sits is imposed. Difficulty arises as to determining which among the various time limits of state laws on bringing suits should be imposed. The statutory copyright seems to be basically a right arising under a statute, and the section of the state law of limitations applying to suits under a statute can well be resorted to by the courts. A recent ruling has so held.[12]

157. PIRACY AND MUSICAL COMPOSITIONS

As to musical compositions, the difficulties in piracy trials are greater than as to literary works. Few genuinely and entirely original melodies and themes emerge today. Reworking of old material is very common. Subconsciously stored-up melodies and themes and musical accents taken from other's works constantly bob up out of the unknown. The number of melodies and themes and twists is limited. Similarities to those in the public domain are seldom absent. Lesser twists and the total effect of arrangement must prevail.

Thus the ascertainment of the issue in musical compositions, as a distinction between stock musical ideas and themes, which are in the public domain, and the new expression thereof, is difficult. In musical compositions the court is usually confronted with several difficulties: (1) The number of musical notations is limited. The art is largely one of delicate touches and nuances in the use of common material. The difficulties between substance and expression are most difficult to bring into the open. (2) The judge usually is not a trained musician and can not read or perform the works. In literary works, of course, this difficulty does not arise. The judge, in music-piracy litigation, is dependent upon others to perform the work or upon phonograph recordings. Thus he is more dependent upon the opinion of experts than in the case of literary material. The testimony of experts is often farfetched and too prone to mere artificial desiccation or professional analysis, as enumeration.

Courts, therefore, are hostile to expert testimony in music-piracy suits, although they receive it. The impression of two melodies or musical compositions upon the *ordinary lay ear*, not upon expert sensitivity, is the test in determining piracy similarities in music. But, since the court must take it all in by the ear, and usually in group gatherings, the test of the ordinary lay ear is difficult to apply.

PART FOUR

Unfair Competition

Expanding Protection against Unfair Competition

158. TWO FACETS OF UNFAIR COMPETITION

PROTECTION against unfair competition is a rapidly growing right with two facets, one ancient and one sharply modern. The ancient facet protects against the "palming off", by fraudulent implication, of the entertainment or goods of A as the entertainment or goods of B. It is intertwined with protection of trade names and trade marks. The protection analogy of trade marks, where a registered trade mark is involved, stems from this broader theory of "palming" or "passing off" of goods as unfair competition where registered trade marks are not involved.

If A's goods are "palmed off" by A as B's goods through results from false advertising by A, or through A's inducing confusion in the minds of the public, then B as the wronged person is entitled to an injunction and damages. Here we have the *first* or ancient facet of unfair competition. The basic theory here is often phrased as one of protection to the public. But B, who has created publicity and good will for his goods or entertainment, is likewise injured where A sells A's goods or entertainment as if they were those of B, thus using the good will and publicity B has created for his goods. The relief granted, in result, protects B rather than the public. But the courts usually add that the purpose is to protect the public from the deception involved, as well as to protect B.

The more modern and *second* aspect of unfair competition, which is not fully recognized in all courts and states, and as to which there is considerable confusion, arises from the concept that it is unfair to permit one to utilize the publicity of B, as property created by B, even if the goods of A and B do not compete, e.g. where A sells cigarettes and B sells songs. Here there is no palming off of A's goods as B's, no competition use. The unfair aspect is brought into clear focus only when created publicity is viewed as property. But the courts are reluctant frankly to recognize so fugitive a value as publicity as being property. Thus various obscure theories condemning unfair methods of competition are resorted to, when there is no direct competition as between A's and B's wares.

Where B creates publicity for his literary or entertainment property, it seems unfair for A to utilize that publicity and good will, to sell his own product, even though it be a different and noncompetitive product. Even though there be no public confusion involved, and no "palming off" or direct competition, and even if the public does not believe it is buying the entertainment or goods of another, an aspect of unfairness arises. Where one who has not created publicity uses the publicity appeal of another he seems to act unfairly. Such a user of another's publicity values is said to get a "free ride" or to "unjustly enrich himself" at another's expense. These commonly used phrases, however, do not lucidly describe the wrong. He who gets on a "free ride" or "unjustly enriches himself" acts unjustly only if and because he is thereby using another's publicity, viewed as property, and so is "hitchhiking".

This modern aspect of the law of unfair competition, as the recognition of created publicity as property, is still in the process of development. Much confusion commonly arises as to when and where this second rule of unfair competition should be applied.

159. IMPORTANCE OF UNFAIR COMPETITION

Unfair competition is of particular interest to those engaged in publishing, advertising, and entertainment because of the great value of publicity therein. Increasingly, new and novel means are used to create good will and to sell merchandise. Many of these represent a constantly expanding effort to gain public attention and patronage by giving away entertainment, or by utilizing the publicity of popular entertainers and of literary works and shows. Our radio and television broadcasting is made possible by sponsors who give away entertainment in order to gain publicity, good will, and patrons. Huge sums of money are spent to create such good will and publicity. Also clever schemes are constantly devised by outsiders to snatch up the publicity values of others.

Publicity and created good will, though fugitive and highly perishable, are in reality property. They are so intangible and evanescent, however, that the courts hesitate to be candid about their status as property. Yet in a rapidly increasing number of decisions the courts are protecting fleeting publicity values, on a variety of grounds, where no palming off is involved.

160. TRADE MARKS AND TRADE NAMES

The ancient right against unfair competition as palming off is partially codified in statutes protecting trade marks and trade names. In the United States trade-mark protection has been reduced to a modern statute, passed in 1946, called the Lanham Trade-Mark Act.[1]

Congress has power to enact a Federal trade-mark law, not under the Copyright Clause of the Constitution, but under the Interstate Commerce Clause thereof. The states also have jurisdiction over trade marks for goods never leaving their borders. But since most merchandise today is sold in interstate trade, the federal statute usually prevails. The Lanham Trade-Mark Act, like the law of unfair competition where registered trade marks are not involved, recognizes that it is impossible to grant a monopoly in the use of a common word, phrase, name, or geographical designation. All these are in the public domain. As in copyrights, no one can get an exclusive right in anything in the public domain for trade-mark use.

The distinction between a trade mark and a trade name, though both are closely interconnected, is sharply etched. A "trade mark" is used in relation to a particular article or price of merchandise, while a "trade name" is used "in relation to a *business*, and is an insignia and symbol of its reputation and good will." [2]

A word of general use and significance, i.e. a word or name which is merely descriptive, can not be monopolized and taken from public use by registration as a trade mark under the Lanham Trade-Mark Act. Neither can a name that is primarily descriptive of a geographical location. The name of a living individual can not be so used except by his consent. Neither can the name of a deceased president of the United States be used during the life of his widow except with her express consent. Trade names, unless they have acquired distinctiveness, are limited to coined words which do not preempt words in general use. Examples of such words are "Kodak" and "Philco". Symbols and etchings, of course, may be used as trade marks. Section 6 of the Copyright Act permits of registration under the Copyright Statute of "all prints and labels published in connection with the sale or advertising of articles of merchandise." (Section 6, C.S.) These, of course, must have some novelty or variation from ordinary material.

The law of unfair competition, so far as the "palming off" facet thereof is concerned, grants in effect an exclusive use, analogous to trade-mark rights, in names which have acquired a secondary meaning (apart from the general descriptive meaning) by reason of being used in connection with specified goods or literary property under names which have not been and can not be registered as trade marks or trade names.

So in unfair competition "palming off" cases, where the complainant relies upon a name that has not been or can not be registered under the Lanham Act, he must show that such name has acquired a secondary meaning, i.e. that it is not merely descriptive, but by established usage has acquired a fanciful or arbitrary significance as applied to his goods or business. Wide publicity and public notice, when attached to an ordinary name or word, creates this secondary meaning. This secondary meaning becomes the property of the person who has created it. This property in secondary meaning has particular value as to titles to literary and musical properties. These can not be copyrighted. But their secondary meaning is protected by the law of unfair competition.

The phrases "gold diggers" or "gold diggers of Broadway" are combinations of ordinary words. No one can withdraw these words from public use by obtaining a monopoly thereof, by copyright or by trade mark. But the phrase *Gold Diggers of Broadway*, when used as the title of a successful play or motion picture, acquired a secondary meaning. The wide publicity of such a successful play or picture causes the phrase, in the minds of the public, to have a secondary meaning: i.e. the designation of a successful particular play or motion picture. Thus it has been held that one who used that title for a different play or picture could be enjoined from such use of that title, unless he added an explanation of differentiation.[3]

161. TITLES AND STAGE BUSINESS

Instances of protection of the secondary meaning of titles of literary properties are common. Protection against use of an actor's "stage business" and techniques of mannerism by competitors, however, is in a "creeping stage".

The effort to protect the public, as distinct from the prior user of a title or other publicity property, still is partially pursued by the courts in these matters. This view is shown by the fact that the relief often granted is merely a requirement that the second user affix a notice equal in prominence to his title, specifying that his literary work is not the same work as the one with which the title has been commonly and previously identified. This is not always the only relief granted. But in many close cases such a differentiating notice is often the substance of the relief given. Sometimes other circumstances involved are controlling.

An actor produced movie shorts, imitating the dress and mannerisms of Charlie Chaplin, and using the name "Charlie Aplin". Later he offered to drop the name "Charlie Aplin". But he was prohibited by the court from imitating the mannerisms and technique of Charlie Chaplin, in such a way as to deceive and defraud the public, even though he dropped the name "Charlie Aplin". [4]

This case indicates that though "stage business" (as an actor's technique, devices of gesture, mannerisms, and other aptitudes of indirect expression) can not be protected, nevertheless the imitation may go too far. Then stage business can be protected under the law of unfair competition. It is all a matter of degree. Even in satire and burlesque and mimicry as fair use and comment, there are limits to the right.

The assignee of the producer of the play *Gold Diggers* produced a picture entitled *Gold Diggers of Broadway*. It was granted an injunction against the producer of a motion picture entitled *Gold Diggers of Paris*. But here a proviso was attached to the injunction that it would not apply if the second user, in type as large as the title *Gold Diggers of Paris*, stated his picture was not based on the play or the motion pictures of such prior user, Warner Bros.[3]

The author of the ballad "Yukon Jake" was granted an injunction against the use of the title *Yukon Jake* on a motion picture by a different author.[5]

The author of a play entitled *Sherlock Holmes, Detective* successfully enjoined a subsequent play under the title *Sherlock Holmes*.[6]

The publisher of the *Social Register* was permitted to enjoin the publication of a competitor work using the name *Howard's Social Register*.[7]

The publishers of the *Harvard Classics*, edited by Charles William Eliot, were allowed to enjoin a rival publisher using the title *Dr. Eliot's Five-Foot Book Shelf of the World's Best Books*.[8]

The author of the Frank Merriwell stories was granted an injunction against the distribution of a motion picture using, in the title thereof, the name "Frank Merriwell." [9]

The publisher of Pocket Books was denied an injunction against another publisher who copied some items as to the style and format of such Pocket Books. The lower court held that, although the complainant could not claim a trade monopoly with respect to the word "pocket", or as to the size or other elements composing the format of such books, an imitator could not combine these arrangements and thus deceive the public.[10]

The New York Court of Appeals reversed the lower court on the ground that the defendant had "given reasonable prominence to the legend AVON pocket-size BOOKS and to the medallion adopted by the defendant as a hall-mark. * * * Such identifying information, we think, serves adequately to exclude belief by a literate purchaser that the reprints are those of the plaintiff." Thus the Court of Appeals held that since the public was not deceived, the defendant's combination of plaintiff's markings and defendant's use of the plaintiff's publicity as to Pocket Books was not unfair competition. This ruling is perplexing: two judges of the high court dissented on the basis of the Associated Press case. (See Section 164.)

The Academy of Motion Picture Arts and Sciences (an organization of those active in Hollywood's motion-picture industry, and the bestower of "Oscars") was granted an injunction against the use of the name "The Hollywood Motion Picture Academy" to designate a dramatic and coaching school. Though the two enterprises were not directly competitive, the implication of deception to the public caused an injunction to issue.[11]

The author of the novel *Stella Dallas* successfully enjoined a radio broadcast using the name "Stella Dallas", although the broadcast did not use any of his copyright literary property. Aside from copyright infringement, the court held that the use of the name was unfair competition.[12]

Ernest Hemingway was allowed to enjoin the exhibition in the United States of a motion picture using the title *Fifth Column Squad*, because such title was similar to a play Hemingway had produced, as *The Fifth Column*.[13] The court noted Hemingway's play had not been a success. Nevertheless, the court held it had acquired a secondary meaning which the defendant could not appropriate.

Bud Fisher, as the originator of the comic strip "Mutt and Jeff", was granted an injunction against publication of an imitation of his strip using the "Mutt and Jeff" title.[14]

The Navy Club of the United States of America, when it sought to enjoin the use of "All Navy Club of the United States of America" by another, was denied an injunction on the ground of copyright and trade-name infringement, but was granted an injunction on the grounds of unfair competition.[15]

The radio program *The Author Meets the Critics* was denied an injunction against a rival radio program called *Books on Trial*.[16] Here the court held that the names of the two programs were not sufficiently close to cause any public confusion.

The author of a book entitled *We Who Are Young*,[17] which dealt factually with the economic problems of youth, was denied an injunction against a motion picture bearing the same title, the motion picture being a love story depicting financial difficulties of a young couple.

162. COMPETITIVE USES

No difficulty arises in registered trade marks, or in unregistered trade names which have acquired a secondary meaning, as against use by another selling entertainment or products directly competitive with those of the complainant who has established a prior right. Here an injunction is freely granted.

Where there is no such direct competition in the product or

entertainment involved, and no palming off of the goods of one as those of another, conflicts in decisions arise. What should be the rule if the two products sold are entirely different?

In the majority of cases the courts grant injunctive relief in such circumstances, indicating the modern departure from the theory of palming off. There may be, however, some trace of palming off even in such instances by the implication that the manufacturer of one product, using the trade mark or unregistered trade name which has a secondary meaning, also is the manufacturer of a different product produced by another and sold under the same name. That is, the trade-name aspect may be involved, as implying that the manufacturer of the two products is the same by implication as to the identical or similar trade names of the producer of both products.

Tiffany & Company, the jewelers, were granted an injunction against a motion picture company using the name "Tiffany" as its corporate name and as the trade name of its motion pictures. The motion-picture company had been using the name "Tiffany Productions" for twelve years, yet it was enjoined.[18]

The Bulova Watch Company was granted an injunction against the use of the name "Bulova" for shoes.[19]

The manufacturer of Rolls-Royce automobiles was granted an injunction against the use of the words "Rolls Royce" on radio tubes.[20]

The manufacturer of Yale locks obtained an injunction against the use of the word "Yale" for flash lights.[21]

The manufacturer of the Waterman Fountain Pen successfully enjoined the use of the name "Waterman" on razor blades.[22]

The manufacturer of a vegetable-juice cocktail, sold under the name "V-8", was allowed to enjoin the seller of vitamin pills from using the name "V-8".[23] Here the court did not note that "V-8" on automobiles antedated both products.

Colorable changes in the name are of little avail. The manufacturer of the trade-marked "Nu-Enamel" was permitted to enjoin the manufacturer of a similar product called "Nu-Beauty Enamel".[24]

The New York World's Fair successfully enjoined an unlicensed magazine publisher from using the name *World's Fair* or *Illustrated Fair News* for a publication.[25]

The Stork Club of *New York* was permitted to enjoin the use of its name for a small bar and grill in *San Francisco*, the court holding that the disparity in size, and the lack of competition between the two businesses, did not permit the use of the name by the second user.[26]

But the publisher of a book entitled *Vizualized American History* was not permitted to enjoin the publication of a similar textbook entitled *Vizualized American History*. The court viewed the word "Vizualized" as merely descriptive, as a word in common use which had not acquired a "secondary" meaning.[27]

The publisher of *Wow Comics* was not permitted on the ground of copyright infringement to prevent another publisher from buying second-hand copies of such comics, rebinding them, and then selling the rebound periodicals under the trade name *Double Comics*. But it was allowed to enjoin such reselling on the ground of unfair competition.[28]

In an old case, open to question, the publisher of the Nick Carter detective stories was not permitted to enjoin the use of the words "Nick Carter" on a motion picture. The court, in an elaborate opinion, ruled that the "Nick Carter" copyright was invalid for error in copyrighting, and that the copyright gap could not be filled by a claim of unfair competition.[29]

Where a complainant corporation, J. A. Dougherty Sons, had manufactured whiskey for ninety-one years under the name of "Dougherty's," an injunction was granted against a competitor of the actual name of Dougherty, using his own name for his whiskey. The court held that although a trade mark could not usually be had in a surname, and that a manufacturer usually had the right to use his own surname, nevertheless the result here would be "the stealing of the good will of another's business." [30]

In a vigorously contested case, a music publisher who had revived an old song called "Gambler's Blues", using the title "St. James' Infirmary", was denied an injunction against the use by another publisher of the name "St. James' Infirmary" on the same song. The unsatisfactory opinion held that the complainant could get no property in the name "St. James' Infirmary", which merely described the song.[31]

Such is the orbit of rulings where palming off, the first facet of unfair competition, is involved directly or inferentially. The cases at times are in conflict and apparently reach somewhat contradictory results in some instances. Each case has to be analyzed according to its specific circumstances. But the cases follow, in substance, a generally accepted theory. Unfair competition arises where a palming off results, directly or indirectly, because the defendant creates intentional similarities between his and complainant's advertising and exploitation and publicity creations by the use of complainant's publicity items and values. If the name or designation or slogan description used by the complainant is general and uses words and names in general use, he can not complain of the defendant's use of such name, designation, or descriptive phrase. These are in the public domain and open to use by anyone. But if a registered trade mark or trade name, or an unregistered designation, name, or description, is unique or results in a specific and direct "pointing at" and designation of complainant's goods or entertainment property (i.e. has or has acquired a secondary meaning and connotation), then the complainant can prevent possible palming off of his goods through possible confusion of plaintiff's earmarked wares with those of the defendant. And this prohibition includes implications of an identity as to the *producer*, as well as the *product*.

XXI

Publicity as Property

163. UNFAIR COMPETITION WITHOUT PALMING OFF

THE MOST obscure and hotly contested aspect of unfair competition today arises where the public is not deceived, or likely to be deceived, by palming off, but where protection is asked on grounds of unfairness. In essence the basis of the unfairness recognized in this modern aspect of unfair competition is that the seller is using publicity values which are, in reality, the *property* of another.

Advertising that utilizes publicity values, values existing apart from the wares advertised, is so common today that the issue has become acute. Sellers of merchandise widely use personality and entertainment publicity values of actors, athletes, and prominent people as impelling advertising. To avoid privacy violations, advertisers pay the persons whose names or photographs or personalities are used. May other advertisers by evasive cleverness seek to "cut in on" and use "for free" the publicity thus created for an advertised product?

Large sums of money are spent in entertaining the public "for free" in order to create good will and publicity for merchandise. But giving away entertainment by radio and television as a means of obtaining good will and thus sales for their goods is only one way in which sellers of merchandise use publicity property. Efforts constantly are undertaken to link merchandise to entertainment-personality appeal, by having entertainment personalities recommend or puff the wares advertised. This linking takes on many familiar forms. Persistent effort is made by competitors to snatch up some of this appeal. Thus in recent years the courts have been cluttered with litigation concerning what is fair as to the taking of such created publicity by others who have not paid for the dissemination thereof.

164. THE ASSOCIATED PRESS CASE

A great impetus was given, by a decision of the Supreme Court of the United States in 1918, toward the control of unfair use of publicity in cases where no palming off at all is involved.

Here the Associated Press asked for an injunction against the International News Service's unfair methods in copying and using news items gathered by the Associated Press. It was claimed by the Associated Press that its competitor, the International News Service, offended in three specific ways: (1) by bribing the employees of the Associated Press to give to the International News Service news that had been gathered by these employees exclusively for the Associated Press; (2) by inducing the subscribers of the Associated Press to do the same; and (3) by copying the news on the bulletin boards of subscribers of the Associated Press and disseminating the copied items as news gathered by International News Service.

The Supreme Court in an elaborately reasoned decision granted an injunction to Associated Press. In so doing it gave great impetus to this new and modern concept in the theory of unfair competition.

The decision is notable because here there was no palming off whatsoever. The news which the International News Service took from Associated Press was disseminated, inferentially or directly, as news gathered solely by the International News Service. Thus there was no implication of distributing the news gathered as Associated Press news.

The court held also that there was no question of copyright involved. News, as before noted, is in the public domain and can not be copyrighted. (See Section 76.)

The sole question before the court was whether the unfair means used by the International News Service, standing alone, should result in an injunction on the theory of unfair competition solely because of the unfair methods used. The court answered in the affirmative.

An unfortunate metaphor was used by Justice Pitney, who wrote the decision, which has created difficulties for subsequent courts. The metaphor runs that the International News Service was "endeavoring to reap where it has not sown".[1] The wrong, the court added, was "an unauthorized interference with * * * a * * * legitimate business, precisely at the point where the profit is to be reaped, in order to divert a material portion of the profit from those who have earned it to those who have not."

The broad doctrine thus enumerated has been looked at askance by subsequent courts. Law-text writers favor it as a prohibition of a "free ride" or of "unjust enrichment". But able judges have called it "a now discredited theory." [2] Justice Learned Hand has called the doctrine confusing and limited to the precise facts revealed in the Associated Press case, observing of the case that, "We think that no more was covered than situations substantially similar to those at bar" (i.e., printed news dispatches).[3]

Aside from these doubts, the Associated Press case today is questionable law because of an odd judicial quirk that will make laymen wonder. The Supreme Court took jurisdiction of the case solely because of diversity of citizenship. In 1918, when the case came to the Court, the theory was that our Federal courts, situated in the various states, should reach their own interpretations of substantive common law, even if no Federal question (i.e., enforcement of the Federal Constitution or of Federal laws enacted thereunder) were involved. In short, the Federal courts ruled that they were not obligated to follow the state court's interpretation of the common law, i.e. the decisions of the state court thereto, where the Federal court sat.

The Supreme Court in the Associated Press case thus laid down a rule of unfair competition to be applied in all states in the Federal courts, and did not follow the decisions of the separate state courts on this point, although no Constitutional or Federal law question was involved in such unfair-competition litigation.

Twenty years later the Supreme Court itself changed the general rule as to what courts state the common law. Where a Federal court acts because of diversity of citizenship, the Supreme Court said, a Federal court generally is obligated to follow the law of the state where it sits, as interpreted by that state's highest court.[4] Only where a Federal question is involved do the views of the Federal court prevail as supreme.

Under this decision the interpretation of unfair competition in the Associated Press case seems no longer to be the law of even our Federal courts. What prevails is the law of the supreme court of each state where an unfair-competition suit is brought. Since the state courts, as yet, have not generally followed the holding in the Associated Press case, the authority of that case is open to grave question. But insofar as the reasoning therein seems valid, the decision is persuasive.

Some state courts accept and others reject the holding of the Associated Press case. Conflict is common. But the law as to this second modern facet of unfair competition, where no competition commonly is involved and only the unfair use of publicity is complained of, is rapidly evolving.

165. PROPERTY IN PUBLICITY

The difficulty creating today's confusion is the strange reluctance of modern courts to recognize publicity as property.

In the Associated Press case the court did imply that publicity was property. The Court described good will and publicity, as that "which complainant has acquired at a substantial cost," and ruled that the defendant "cannot be heard to say that it is too fugitive or evanescent to be regarded as property. It has all the attributes of property necessary for determining that a misappropriation of it by a competitor is unfair competition because contrary to good conscience."

But here publicity, as advertising good will, was not involved, only news and the public value of gathered news. Most cases in unfair-competition issues usually involve not news but publicity as advertising values.

Why shouldn't publicity created by mental labor be viewed as property? Today favorable created publicity may have great and definite financial value. The publicity value of "puffing" of a ware by a successful stage or screen actor, by a singer, ball player, pugilist, or other performer enjoying the public's favor, is tremendous. One need only glance at current advertisements to see how commonly that value is used in selling merchandise. The publicity pull of a successful song or play or performer is tremendous. Such publicity is not accidental. It is created by skill and labor. It goes and comes quickly. But it is the result of labor.

If publicity be viewed as property, then its protection by the law is fair and necessary for obvious reasons. But unfortunately the courts have tended to stress the vague words "unfair" or "unfair competition" as the key involved, rather than the aspect of protection of property as such. Competition in using publicity values can not be deemed "unfair" unless that which is used is in some sense the property of another. Only if it is property and is recognized as such, without invasion of the public's rights, can the use thereof by a stranger be deemed legally unfair. For the particular means of use assailed is unfair only if the result is the taking of the property of another. If this view of this unfair competition be accepted, the conflicts between the decisions become clear.

The recognition of created publicity as property is merely an extension of the theory of a common-law copyright. In a common-law copyright the mental labor of the creator is deemed property. The law requires that such mental labor must be expressed in tangible form, such as a manuscript or painting, to permit legal protection. Modern entertainment and advertising publicity, when created, is not so evanescent that it can not be deemed sufficiently objectively expressed to be appraised as property. It takes tangible form. In the Associated Press case, the court said: "It is no answer to say that complainant spends its money for that which is too fugitive or evanescent to be the subject of property." In publicity, the act of the creator or the money spent results in definite objective forms of reality. The monetary value is clear-cut. No one can doubt the definiteness of publicity arising from the success of an actor or an athlete. The public by its response leaves no doubt.

In privacy law, the use of another's personality in advertising and entertainment is beginning to be viewed as the use of the property of another. By such a test the measure of damages, as before noted (Section 15), becomes clearer. For though a human being is not property and can not be bought and sold, the personality of living persons is bought and sold in the market place. The pictured face or figure of a pin-up, a living beautiful girl, is dealt in as property. The public interest is not contravened thereby.

It must be added that Justice Brandeis, in his dissenting opinion in the Associated Press case, insisted that the practices condemned in that case were within the law. He rejected the analogy of a common-law copyright in the values resulting from the gathering of news, although years before he had applied the analogy of a common-law copyright to personality when he advocated a modern right of privacy. (See Section 4.) His argument in the Associated Press case was closely legalistic in that he noted and refused to depart from ancient precedents. But his main objection to the majority ruling in the Associated Press case was the need of legislative action instead of judicial protection. He insisted that the courts could not adequately phrase the rights involved in unfair competition by extending the theory to new and novel situations such as news gathering. The public's rights in news he deemed paramount. That view is scarcely followed today and is hardly consistent with the views Justice Brandeis advanced as to privacy.

This aspect of privacy as property rights in publicity has now become acute in the efforts of television stations to limit those who can pick up and use their television broadcasts. This needed advance in the law of unfair competition is later discussed under television problems. (See Chapter XXV.)

Once publicity is viewed as akin to property, two dubious qualifications, which some courts apply in relief in unfair competition, no longer arise.

The two qualifications are: (1) relief can be granted only where there is competition between the complainant and defendant in the businesses they are carrying on, and (2) those who create good will by created publicity have no right to split the uses thereof and to grant the right to use such publicity to some and to withhold it from others. This last qualification has become acute today in the effort to limit the right to exhibit a televised sporting event to a particular class of owners or to a particular class of places. The question likewise is later discussed in reference to television. (See Chapter XXV.)

166. RECENT CASES ON PUBLICITY VALUES

In New York, the Madison Square Garden Corporation sued a motion-picture company which used actual shots of a hockey game in the Madison Square Garden in a feature motion picture. The dramatic action of the feature picture centered around the Stanley Cup hockey playoffs in Madison Square Garden. The motion-picture company had taken these shots from a newsreel thereof which it was licensed by the Garden to distribute. The court held that such use of these pictures of the Madison Square Garden, in the feature picture, was unfair competition.

The court was perplexed by the element of palming off, but recognized the property right involved:

> "The plaintiff [Madison Square Garden] clearly had a property right in its good name, its reputation, its good will built up at considerable expense, and its business in licensing genuine moving-picture photographs to be used in feature films from which it derived a substantial revenue * * *.
> There may be unfair competition by misappropriation as well as by misrepresentation. Both elements are here.[5]

Here competition between complainant and defendant was not required. The right of splitting the publicity right as a property right was also recognized. Madison Square Garden was permitted to grant the right to photograph its arena for use in a newsreel, without being held thereby to have granted the right to use such pictures for use in a dramatic feature. These results seem logical and lucid when the pictures taken of and the publicity enjoyed by the Garden, like the building itself, are viewed as property.

Two important decisions in conflict present another aspect of this same right of publicity as property.

The publisher of the magazine entitled *Seventeen* sought an injunction against the manufacturer of women's girdles who sold its wares as "Miss Seventeen Foundations".[6] The court held that the use of the word "Seventeen" for a magazine was "fanciful" and "arbitrary", not merely descriptive; i.e. the word "Seventeen" here had become known as more than a mere numeral but also as the name of the complainant's teen-age periodical. Thus the word "Seventeen" had acquired a secondary meaning and was entitled to legal protection. Here both the plaintiff and the defendant had registered the words "Seventeen" and "Miss Seventeen" as trade marks for their respective wares, but the court properly did not consider that aspect determinative. In short, the court held that, although there is no competition between the publisher of a magazine and the manufacturer of women's girdles, the use of the prior and favorably known magazine's name as the name of a girdle constituted unfair competition. Here there was no palming off; obviously no one would mistake a magazine for a girdle.[6]

A precisely opposite result was reached in a case involving the magazine *Vogue* by another high court. The Vogue Hat Company sold hats, labeling them with a large letter V and the picture of a girl. The letter V and the picture of a girl was the plaintiff magazine's trade mark. Here the court held that the word "Vogue" had not acquired a secondary meaning, but was merely a descriptive word and that there was no competition between the seller of the hats and the seller of the magazine.[7] It denied relief to the plaintiff. This decision seems unfortunate. Here the court refused to view publicity as property.

Another court granted an injunction in favor of the same magazine *Seventeen* against a manufacturer of dresses for junior teens, sold under the name "Seventeen".[8]

167. USE OF PHONOGRAPH RECORDS

Another sharp disagreement between two high courts has arisen as to band publicity as property. The litigation arose from the use of phonograph records for broadcasting.

The Supreme Court of Pennsylvania allowed Fred Waring an injunction against a broadcasting station using for broadcasting purposes records sold by Waring's Pennsylvanians Orchestra, recorded solely for home use.[9] Each record sold bore a notice "not licensed for radio broadcast". Despite this notice, the broadcasting company used the records over the air, announcing them as Fred Waring's recordings.

The court, in granting relief, wavered between a common-law copyright in the performance of the music, and an invasion of privacy. But here the broadcasting station had a license from ASCAP (as the licensee, from the copyright proprietor, of the right of public performance of the music recorded), and so the broadcasting station was free to broadcast the music as such. It is difficult to see, under the copyright decisions, how there is any common-law copyright in the skill only of Waring's orchestra as performers aside from the music played. Such skill, like stage business and gags, can not be copyrighted. Also it is difficult to see how there is any invasion of privacy. But the decision becomes clear if publicity is viewed as property. The broadcasting station announced the performance as that of Waring's Pennsylvanians. The orchestra's name formed the value of the broadcast and the record was used because the orchestra made it. Waring had a property right in that publicity value, arising from the fame of his orchestra, which Waring had created as publicity property.[9]

A flatly contrary decision was reached by a high New York Federal court.[10] Paul Whiteman sold phonograph records with the notice "not licensed for radio broadcasting." The court held that having sold the records, he lost any right to limit their use under his copyright. That view seems correct under copyright law. But the court, in effect, ignored the view of publicity as property. As a result, it refused to recognize any right to split the use of the property—to sell the records and publicity for use in homes and retain the publicity when it came to broadcasting uses.

A North Carolina high court has followed the Pennsylvania ruling. It enjoined the use of Waring's records bearing the above noted restriction in broadcasting.[11] A Massachusetts court, however, has refused to recognize any restriction on the use of records against playing thereof in a night club, holding that the record disk bore no such restrictive notice but implying that an injunction would have issued had it done so.[12]

168. UNFAIR USE OF NAMES OF PERIODICALS

When the name of a periodical is copied, the question of palming off is usually involved. If the name is distinctive and has obtained a secondary meaning descriptive of complainant's magazine, the court will grant relief.[12a] But where the name of the magazine is not descriptive only of the complainant's publication, relief is denied.

The publisher of *Modern Screen* was permitted to enjoin the use of the name *Modern Movies* for a similar magazine. Here there was considerable copying by the defendant of the makeup and form of the complainant's magazine.[13]

The publisher of a magazine called *Ranch Romances* was not permitted to enjoin the publication of another magazine called

Rangeland Romances, the basis of the decision being that "ranch romances" was a common phrase, the pulp field was overcrowded and the differences between the two magazines were such that the public was not likely to be confused.[14]

Likewise the publisher of a magazine entitled *Aviation* was not permitted to enjoin the use of the name *American Aviation*.[15]

169. *Hit Parade* CASES

A novel group of cases, involving a centralized aspect of unfair competition, centered about the weekly rating of the popularity of songs in a radio program known as the *Hit Parade*. This weekly publicizing of the ten most popular songs is carried on by a cigarette manufacturer in order to gain publicity and sales promotion of its cigarettes. The complainants against this tobacco company were two of the largest publishers of sheet music of popular songs. They complained, in two different suits, that the choice of the week's ten most popular songs on the *Hit Parade* was not fairly arrived at but was grossly inaccurate. They contended that songs published by the two complainants as music publishers, were among the ten truly most popular, but were passed over by the tobacco company in favor of less popular songs, because such less popular songs were favored by the artists on the program, or by the agents of the tobacco company. The fairness and accuracy of the polling and appraisal of comparative popularity, in short, were assailed.

The issues raised were novel and of importance to entertainment and advertising. The arguments went through four courts. Five lengthy decisions, one unreported, were handed down: three in favor of the complainants and two against the complainants.[16] The final decision, that of the Court of Appeals of New York, sustained the complaint in part.

The long-experienced senior judge of the United States District Court for the Southern District of New York, Judge John C. Knox, decided for the complainant, but postponed his decision until the controlling final decision of the New York state court. He noted:

That the theories on which plaintiff comes into court are unusual and have about them the elements of novelty, cannot be gainsaid; but these characteristics, in and of themselves, are far from meaning that wrong, however indirect and devious in its impact upon the business of an honest trader, cannot be rectified.[17]

The issue involved the second aspect of unfair competition. Obviously there was no issue of palming off or passing off of competitive products, either cigarettes or songs. Trade defamation was involved as a possible ground of relief for the complainants. But an ancient rule in trade defamation prevented the complainants from relying on that right.[18] In trade libel, i.e. where the sale and value of goods are damaged by false statements, recovery is not permitted unless special damages are shown. Special damages here did not mean merely the loss of revenue from the sale of the songs; more specific damages peculiar to these songs was required. Such proof was difficult to obtain. Thus the complainants had to rely upon unfair competition and not upon trade defamation for relief.

The defendants argued that the sale of sheet music and of cigarettes is not competitive. The defendants also asserted that the popularity of songs was news and belongs to the public; hence they had the right to use and publicize news. They denied any duty to song publishers, as strangers, to rate the songs accurately. The three decisions in favor of the complainant were on varying grounds: that of the New York Court of Appeals on the narrow ground of alleged intentional malicious harm. Thus no final theory has been formulated.

The complainants' partial victory, in the author's opinion, was due to a recognition of publicity values as property. Other theories can be given. These, however, are neither satisfactory nor in accord with the realities of this second facet of unfair competition. Here the music publishers, by their skill and the merit of their songs, had created a wide publicity for their particular songs. That publicity, though fleeting and fugitive, is as undeniable as it is commercially valuable. The creators of this publicity, the music publishers, were entitled to enjoy the fair benefits of that publicity as property. The defendants could increase the sales of their cigarettes by commenting on and fairly using those publicity values, as news, but only without damage thereto. Their right of fair use of that publicity had limits. Though the tobacco company's broadcasting station had a right to perform the songs publicly under an ASCAP license, its rating of popularity was a collateral use of the song publishers' created publicity values in the songs. Thereby the cigarette maker was using complainant's property. That use, if it damaged the property values of publicity involved in the songs, exceeded fair use as a news-reporting right, and was a taking of the song publishers' property. Inaccurate rating of the songs resulted in damage. The element of unfair competition involved arose from the use of another's property by the defendants in a manner beyond their rights, as members of the public, to comment upon and use the complainants' publicity as property. Upon these grounds the three prevailing decisions can be deemed to represent an advance in and an acceptance of the second modern facet of unfair competition as a recognition of property rights in created publicity. With the increasing number of public ratings of popularity of best-seller books and novels, songs, and other works, the *Hit Parade* cases raise legal issues that are likely continuously to reoccur.

Thus this second facet of unfair competition, as a modern and persistently advancing recognition of property rights in publicity created by success in entertainment and publication skill or by advertising expenditure or by skill, represents a vital, evolving right in publishing and entertainment. It affords legal protection to intangible items which have a distinct pecuniary value. For created commercial publicity values are no more fugitive and evanescent and vague then is commercial good will, which the law always has been quick to protect by legal writ.

PART FIVE

Television, Ideas, and Censorship

PART TWO

Television, Ideas, and Censorship

—————— XXII ——————

Protection of Commercial Ideas

---

170. IDEAS AS PROPERTY

OCCASIONALLY an idea becomes a vehicle for a swift ascent to wealth. Dreams come true when ideas click. Some commercial ideas are original and novel and can really be put into successful commercial effect. In common experience, however, most ideas lack originality and are impractical of application. But the fascination of ideas is persistent, more marked today than ever, in our age of prodigal advertising and publicity ingenuity and merchandising adventure.

The practical problem posed by an idea to one who originates it is how to protect it while selling it. The idea once disclosed, what protection remains? On the other hand, to those who need and buy ideas, the principal problem posed is that of separating ordinary from original ideas, so that the buyers or users of ideas may not be unjustly sued.

The protection of ideas is a much litigated problem. The experience of the courts has reduced protection of ideas to definite forms. Ideas under certain limited circumstances are recognized as the property of the creator. But in other instances they are the property of everyone. The sensible experience of judges has charted the dividing line, as between ideas that can be protected and ideas that can not be removed from general use.

Two basic considerations, one taken from the law of copyrights and the other from the law of patents, comprise the pattern of protection for commercial ideas. Under the copyright law literary ideas, as mere concepts, can not be copyrighted. That rule applies to commercial ideas. They all are in the public domain and open to use by everyone. Yet the expression of a literary or artistic idea, when reduced to definite form as a manuscript or drawing, is protected by the law of copyright. The expression, not the idea, becomes the property of the creator. The ancient and still-growing right of a common-law copyright protects literary ideas, when definitively expressed, but only as to the expression thereof. That rule extends to purely commercial ideas.

Under copyrights, the idea need not be novel or original. Since only the expression of an idea is protected under common-law copyright, and independent creation of the same idea is not barred, the test of originality is not dominant. But as to patents, an original and novel mechanical idea, when reduced to concrete functional or mechanical processes and operations, assures the creator of an exclusive monopoly in the process into which the idea has been embodied. Thus as to patents, the idea protected must be original, as well as reduced to a concrete functional form.

The ideas we are considering here are not of a literary or artistic nature, such as those embodied in common-law copyrights, or of a mechanical nature such as ideas resulting in patents. Ideas as to methods of selling, of business operations, of advertising and sales promotions, of creation of publicity, and of arousing public interest for merchandise generally, are of great commercial value. These are worthy of careful consideration. But they are of a class by themselves.

The courts have recognized the importance of such commercial ideas, if novel, and have laid down definite tests as to when and how such unusual ideas, not entitled to protection by copyright or patent law, may be regarded as property subject to legal protection. The courts have evolved a composite test for commercial ideas.

171. VALUE OF COMMERCIAL IDEAS

Applying the law both of copyrights and patents (by analogy although not by express iteration), judges have laid down two basic tests in the protection of commercial ideas. First: the idea must be new and novel and original, not an idea commonly known and already in circulation. Here the requirement of patent law is followed. Second: applying the theory of common-law copyrights, the courts require that such a novel idea must be more than a mere concept and must be reduced to concrete, detailed actuality. Reduction to concreteness, however, need not be elaborate, though elaboration of detail is usually required. The circumstance and details and operations of the idea must be concretely and specifically formulated so that the idea is no longer merely abstract but is reduced to formulated reality.

If these two requisites are fulfilled the law will protect an idea, even when it is disclosed, against unfair use by the one to whom it is disclosed. The law implies a promise on the user's part to pay the fair value thereof, though no express promise was made by the user before the disclosure.

172. DISCLOSURE OF IDEAS

If the creator of an idea obtains an express contract for payment, before the idea is disclosed by him, he will be protected under such a contract, provided the idea proves to be novel and worth while. If his idea is commonplace, however, a definite contract will not be enforced, unless the contract expressly calls for payment under such circumstances.

If, however, the creator of an idea discloses an idea without an express contract, relying upon an implied commitment to pay for the idea if it is worth while, the courts will recognize the implied commitment to pay only (a) if the idea is novel and original and (b) if the idea has been reduced to concrete and definite form. He who discloses an idea to another, without getting a definitive promise to pay, before he has formulated it into substantial detailed concrete form, loses all rights in his idea. His situation is akin to one who releases a wild animal he has captured. After he has released it he loses all rights therein.

The creator of an original idea must either (1) enter into an express contract for payment before he discloses his idea, or (2) if he is willing to rely upon a vague understanding, he must rely upon his idea's being novel and must reduce it to full and complete concreteness before he dares disclose it.

173. THE DECISIONS

Since the great majority of ideas are neither original nor reduced to concrete form, most of the decisions deny recovery. But a few protect the idea creator.

A feminine reporter interviewed the *Sunday News* about employment in writing society articles. She disclosed to the editor the plan and substance of her proposed articles, and all her ideas thereto. She was not employed by the *News*. Later that newspaper published a story of the interview, including her portrait, and added all disclosed ideas in article form as part of the interview. The court held that the plaintiff had a common-law copyright in the material which she had disclosed and granted her relief.[1] Here the reporter's ideas, though not expressed to the newspaper in manuscript form, were deemed sufficiently concrete by the court to be protected, by analogy only to a common-law copyright.

When a script for a motion picture was submitted to a motion-picture company, in general form, and the picture company used the title and the plot stated therein, recovery was allowed against the picture company, on the theory of a common-law copyright.[2]

A color engineer furnished the officers of the New York World's Fair a complete color plan and map, setting forth an arrangement of colors for all the buildings of the Fair. The color plan was detailed and complete and unified. The court here held that such a formulated idea should be protected. But it also held that the World's Fair had not used the color plan, and recovery was denied.[3]

A detailed plan for using surplus war material, then on sale, for the making of canvas-soled shoes, and details of how to put the plan into operation, were considered by a Missouri court sufficiently concrete and novel to permit recovery, despite the absence of any express contract for payment before disclosure.[4]

Where a concretely stated idea was submitted to the Columbia Broadcasting System for a radio program *Hollywood Idea*, involving a new combination of ideas, recovery of $35,000 was allowed by the Supreme Court of California.[5]

The cases in which protection of an idea have been denied are many. The frequency of litigation over ideas indicates the large number of ideas marketed which are not original. Also it indicates the failure of those who market original ideas, through ignorance, to safeguard their property rights.

An idea for a plan of "radio representation" was submitted in manuscript form to a Boston network, which later used the idea as a broadcast called *Spreading New England Fame*. The creator had not obtained an express contract from the broadcasting chain before he disclosed the idea. Also, he had failed to reduce his idea to sufficiently concrete form. So he was denied all relief. Here the claimant's general idea for a radio presentation had been used by the network. The creator's failure was due to his neglect to reduce his idea to more concrete form, or to get in advance a promise from the network to pay a definite sum for the idea if used.[6]

Most of the early idea cases arose in New York. The earliest of these denied relief to a life-insurance agent who submitted to the Equitable Life Assurance Society a plan to sell life insurance. The court ruled: [7]

Without denying that there may be property in an idea, or trade secret or system, it is obvious that its originator or proprietor must himself protect it from escape or disclosure. If it cannot be sold or negotiated or used without a disclosure, it would seem proper that some contract should guard or regulate the disclosure, otherwise it must follow the law of ideas and become the acquisition of whoever receives it.

A plan for ship-to-shore radio communication was disclosed to the Western Union Telegraph Company. The court denied relief because no promise in advance to pay, and no reduction to concreteness, permitted recovery.[8]

A plan for a miniature railway to be used by a railway at a world's fair, although used, permitted no recovery, the court holding: [9]

The letters between the parties upon which the plaintiff's claim is predicated do not constitute an express contract to compensate the plaintiff. An implied contract to do so does not arise therefrom, because they merely contain an abstract idea which may not be made the subject of property right in the absence of protection thereof by an express contract prior to disclosure. * * * Plaintiff's idea never took on concrete form at the time of disclosure so as to give rise to a property right such as occurs where a literary or artistic creation available for advertising use or otherwise is involved.

An idea creator sent a letter to a defendant, offering to make money for him, if the defendant would pay the idea creator one half of the money so made. A definite contract was signed. The idea creator then revealed an old savings-bank account in the defendant's name which had been publicized by the bank as a forgotten bank account. The defendant proved that he already knew of the existence of this account. The court denied any relief, holding that the idea disclosed was not original, i.e. not novel and valuable.[10]

A graphic chart was submitted to a safety-razor company, describing the way the hair grows on the human face, as an idea for an advertising campaign. The court held the chart not sufficiently concrete and denied relief.[11]

A plan submitted to a motor company for installment selling of automobiles, and for improving designs for the bodies of automobiles, was held not sufficiently novel nor sufficiently reduced to concrete form to permit inference of an implied obligation to pay.[12] In a lower-court decision in Pennsylvania, where a claimant suing the producer of *Fantasia* alleged that he had submitted the idea to use cartoons as illustrating music, the court rejected any protection of his ideas on vague grounds, probably because plaintiff had not put the idea in concrete form.[13]

In California, a section of Civil Code (980) for a while was deemed to give protection to ideas as a "product of the mind" to a greater extent than above stated. The legislature, however, amended the code and now ideas are given no greater protection in California than under the Common Law as above noted. (See Weitzenkorn v. Lesser 256 P. 2d 947, p. 955; Taylor v. Metro 115 F. Supp. 156.)

XXIII

Obscenity and Censorship

174. THE WIDE STATUTE COVERAGE

THE STRIKING thing about obscenity is the abundance of statutes, both Federal and state, prohibiting its publication, and the unavoidable generality of definition by the courts as to what constitutes obscenity. Also striking is the frequent refusal of the courts to find well-intentioned publications obscene.

Every state makes the publication of obscene matter a crime. Many of the states impose censorship upon motion pictures in their effort to prevent obscenity. Congress has also been most insistent in its detailed statutory enactments against sending obscenity through the mails, importing obscene books or matter, or generally sending obscenity into interstate or foreign commerce. And, since much of modern publication involves interstate commerce, constitutional conflicts constantly arise as to the rights of the state to censor for obscenity.

But out of all these efforts have resulted only a rule-of-thumb definition of obscenity, phrased in oddly limited brevity. The idea of obscenity is too basic to permit of definition in sharp precision. Thus reformers complain and prosecute, though enemies of censorship fume. Meanwhile sincere literary efforts in general are not condemned as obscene though spiced or interfused with obscene sex matter and terse Anglo-Saxon directness—except in Massachusetts.

175. OBSCENITY NOT COPYRIGHTABLE

Obscenity, as before noted, can not be copyrighted. (See Section 77.) If all the formalities of copyrighting have been gone through, and no objection has been raised by the Copyright Office to the matter copyrighted, nevertheless the copyright certificate obtained is open to attack at any time on the ground that the work copyrighted is obscene or reveals undue doses of obscenity. When obscenity bobs up under copyrights, another query instantly arises: whether obscenity in small amounts by itself renders the entire copyright invalid. The decision is a practical affair of "more or less". Usually the entire copyright is not invalidated because of small admixtures of obscenity, for the courts are not quick to condemn for obscenity where pornographic intent is not dominant.

The courts usually hold that the test of obscenity to be applied in copyright matters is the same as the test of obscenity under the Federal postal statutes.[1] Moreover, the Federal courts apply the same definition of obscenity (i.e. the test as to forbidden use of the mail) to all issues of obscenity under any of the Federal statutes whereunder the question arises. Thus the test as to whether obscenity tends to emerge is uniform as well as sparse. Generally the test applied by judges is realistic and practical and sensible.

176. THE FEDERAL STATUTES

All Federal laws against obscenity recently were collected and codified into one chapter (Chapter 71) of the new Statute of Federal Crimes and Criminal Procedure, enacted in 1948.[2]

The four controlling statutes found therein prohibit:

1. Use of the mails for sending, or knowingly receiving, obscene matter.[3]

2. The importation into the United States, from abroad, or the sending from the United States abroad, or distributing through the states, of obscene matter by any express company or common carrier; i.e. importation or sending of obscene matter by public means other than the mails.[4]

3. The displaying of any indecent matter on wrappers, envelopes, or post cards sent through the mails, or in commerce, to and from the United States or between the states.[5]

4. The use of obscene language in broadcasting.[6]

In addition, Section 1305 of the Tariff Act of 1930, still in force,[7] prohibits the importation into the United States of:

* * * any book, pamphlet, paper, writing, advertisement, circular, print, picture, or drawing containing any matter advocating or urging treason or insurrection against the United States, or forcible resistance to any law of the United States, or containing any threat to take the life of or inflict bodily harm upon any person in the United States, or any obscene book, pamphlet, paper, writing, advertisement, circular, print, picture, drawing, or other representation, figure, or image on or of paper or other material, or any cast, instrument, or other article which is obscene or immoral, * * *.

The procedure provided under this Tariff Act is that the Collector seizes the article, the United States attorney of the district then brings an action for forfeiture and destruction, and the person importing the article is permitted to appear (in person or by attorney, of course), and is granted the right to demand that the issue of obscenity be decided by a jury, with right of review by a higher court.

The key or *controlling section*, in all this recent codification of obscenity, is Section 1461. It prohibits the sending of any obscene matter through the mails, the pertinent language (emphasis added) reading:

Every *obscene, lewd, lascivious, indecent, filthy* or *vile* article, matter, thing, device * * * is declared to be nonmailable matter and shall not be conveyed in the mails or delivered from any post office or by any letter carrier * * * The term "indecent" as used in this section includes matter of a character tending to incite arson, murder, or assassination. * * *

Whoever knowingly deposits for mailing or delivery anything declared by this section to be unmailable, or knowingly takes the same from the mails for the purpose of circulating or depositing thereof, or for aiding in the circulation or deposition thereof, shall be fined up to $5000 or imprisoned up to five years, or both.

A new section (Title 18, Section 1465) was added in 1955:

Transportation of obscene matters for sale or distribution. Whoever knowingly transports in interstate or foreign commerce for the purpose of sale or distribution any obscene, lewd, lascivious, or filthy book, pamphlet, picture, film, paper, letter, writing, print, silhouette, drawing, figure, image, cast, phonograph recording, electrical transcription or other article capable of producing sound or any other matter of indecent or immoral character, shall be fined not more than $5,000 or imprisoned not more than five years, or both.

Here information as to contraceptive methods is included in the basic provision as to the mailing of obscene matters, and such are the oddities of the statute. The prohibition of any information as to, or means of, furthering of contraception is so broad that no interpretation, exception, or evasion is practicable.

Section 1463 likewise is very broad and sweeping in prohibiting the use of any obscene matter on the outside of envelopes or via postal cards.

And finally, Section 1466 reads:

Whoever utters any obscene, indecent or profane language by means of radio communication shall be fined not more than $10,000 or imprisoned not more than two years, or both.

Television is not specifically mentioned. Would it be deemed included as a phase of "radio communication"? Broadcast by radio is technologically a part of modern television, yet it is doubtful whether the statute would apply in a case of obscenity by television, because prosecution under a criminal statute requires explicit and definitive language. But Congress probably won't be far behind the purists in amending the statute.

177. INTERPRETATION OF THE FEDERAL STATUTES

Since the same test as to obscenity applies to all the phases thereof—importing, sending through the mail, distribution thereof by a common carrier or express company, or copyrighting—the general test of obscenity reached by the courts under the basic section (Section 1461, covering use of the mails) constitutes a complete definition of obscenity. The states today tend, in a few instances but not in all, to follow this interpretation of the federal courts as to what is obscenity. State judges are prone to rely upon the particular wording of their state statutes. And Massachusetts courts are ever Puritans.

The key words in the key section, Section 1461, are "obscene, lewd, lascivious and filthy". What do they include?

The addition of the word "filthy" is due to a decision by the Supreme Court, under a prior statute where the word "filthy" was absent, holding that a newspaper sent through the mails containing a tirade against an individual, which used almost every Anglo-Saxon word of vulgarity and profanity imaginable, was not "obscene, lewd, and lascivious".[7a] These three words, the court held, connoted sexual impurity; absent sex, under the old statute, there was no obscenity. For the court held that a criminal statute had to be construed strictly. So Congress promptly amended the statute, adding the word "filthy".

The courts in defining these four words stress and hold that: "Obscenity is not a technical term of the law and is not susceptible of exact definition, * * * ."[8] Also that the test of obscenity is not the effect upon *immature* or *distorted* minds into whose hands the publication might fall. Also that obscenity of a publication can not be fairly determined solely by viewing, or submitting to the jury, its obscene parts *alone*. The whole work must be submitted and the whole result appraised by the jury.

In an early English case,[9] a harsh rule was reached: the test of obscenity was by the standard alone of weak minds susceptible to immoral influences. The obscene parts of the book could be considered alone in determining obscenity. But this English view has been rejected by the courts in the United States, as is stated in a now controlling decision: [10]

But more recently this standard has been repudiated, and for it has been substituted the test that a book must be considered as a whole, in its effect, not upon any particular class, but upon all those whom it is likely to reach.

But the English test of "minds open to such influences" was recently (September 1951) adhered to in California.[10a]

An excellent summary of the present rule is found in the words of Judge Learned Hand: [11]

* * * the work must be taken as a whole, its merits weighed against its defects; * * * if it is old, its accepted place in the arts must be regarded; if new, the opinions of competent critics in published reviews or the like may be considered; what a court determines is its effect, not upon any particular class, but upon all those whom it is likely to reach. Thus "obscenity" is a function of many variables, * * * .

The above tests, laid down by further decisions in particular cases, result, as a practical matter, in two further guiding principles in determining what is obscene:

1. The meritorious purpose of a publication as a whole, i.e. if the objective of the publication be educational, scientific, or medical, or the advancement of the graphic arts, saves the publication from being condemned as obscene, by reason of minor yet even considerable obscene parts, such as description of obscene acts, or use of nude pictures, or portrayals of abnormality.

2. If the purpose of the publication is entertainment, as meritorious, creative skill, with a commendable literary theme (confirmed by public approval or the approval of critics), apparently such literary merit will save a book from being condemned as obscene merely because of patches of profanity or even of excursions into sex.

State courts, where profanity or sex is involved, do not take as liberal a view of obscenity as do the Federal courts. Grief constantly arises to authors and publishers in Massachusetts by reason of the tendency there to focus upon the use of a very few words of profanity or a brief flight of sexual vividness.

178. RULING DECISIONS

A high Federal court has firmly ruled against the destruction of a book imported into the United States entitled *Nudism in Modern Life*. This book contained twenty-three illustrations depicting nude male and female figures. The court in holding that the book was not obscene shrewdly observed: [12]

Probably the fundamental reason why the word obscene is not susceptible of exact definition is that such intangible moral concepts as it purports to connote, vary in meaning from one period to another. It is customary to see, now, in the daily newspapers and in the magazines, pictures of modeled male and female underwear which might have been shocking to readers of an earlier era. An age accustomed to the elaborate bathing costumes of forty years ago might have considered obscene the present-day beach costume of halters and trunks. But it is also true that the present age might regard those of 1900 as even more obscene.

James Joyce's *Ulysses*, when condemned by the customs authorities and denied importation into this country, was rescued from that obscenity condemnation by two decisions. One by Circuit Judge Hand on the appeal, gave a clear definition of obscenity protecting literary vividness, and rescuing *Ulysses:* [13]

* * * his book shows originality and is a work of symmetry and excellent craftsmanship of a sort. The question before us is whether such a book of artistic merit and scientific insight should be regarded as "obscene" within Section 305(a) of the Tariff Act.

That numerous long passages in "Ulysses" contain matter that is obscene under any fair definition of the word cannot be gainsaid; yet they are relevant to the purpose of depicting the thoughts of the characters and are introduced to give meaning to the whole, rather than to promote lust or portray filth for its own sake. The net effect even of portions most open to attack * * * is pitiful and tragic, rather than lustful.

* * * in the administration of statutes aimed at the suppression of immoral books, standard works of literature have not been barred merely because they contained *some* obscene passages, and * * * confiscation for such a reason would destroy much that is precious in order to benefit a few. * * *

It is settled, at least so far as this court is concerned, that works of physiology, medicine, science, and sex instruction are not within the statute, though to some extent and among some persons they may tend to promote lustful thoughts. * * * We think the same immunity should apply to literature as to science, where the presentation, when viewed objectively, is sincere, and the erotic matter is not introduced to promote lust and does not furnish the dominant note of the publication. The question in each case is whether a publication taken as a whole has a libidinous effect.

Judge Woolsey's description of the book for the lower court is also lucid: [14]

The words which are criticized as dirty are old Saxon words known to almost all men and, I venture, to many women, and are such words as would be naturally and habitually used, I believe, by the types of folk whose life, physical and mental, Joyce is seeking to describe * * *.

* * * but although it contains, as I have mentioned above, many words usually considered dirty, I have not found anything that I consider to be dirt for dirt's sake. Each word of the book contributes like a bit of mosaic to the detail of the picture which Joyce is seeking to construct * * *.

* * * It is not sufficient merely to find, as I have found above, that Joyce did not write "Ulysses" with what is commonly called pornographic intent. I must endeavor to apply a more objective standard to his book in order to determine its effect in the result, irrespective of the intent with which it was written.

The meaning of the word "obscene" as legally defined by the Courts is: Tending to stir the sex impulses or to lead to sexually impure and lustful thoughts * * *.

Whether a particular book would tend to excite such impulses and thoughts must be tested by the Court's opinion as to its effect on a person with average sex instincts—what the French would call *l'homme moyen sensuel*—who plays, in this branch of legal inquiry, the same role of hypothetical reagent as does the "reasonable man" in the law of torts and "the man learned in the art" on questions of invention in patent law. * * *

But my considered opinion, after long reflection, is that whilst in many places the effect of "Ulysses" on the reader is somewhat emetic, nowhere does it tend to be an aphrodisiac.

A book dealing with "married love" was held to be not obscene by Judge Woolsey: [15]

"Married Love" is a considered attempt to explain to married people how their mutual sex life may be made happier * * *. I cannot imagine a normal mind to which this book would seem to be obscene or immoral within the proper definition of these words or whose sex impulses would be stirred by reading it.

A book entitled *Sex Side of Life*, for sex education of children, was held not to be obscene: [16]

The statute we have to construe was never thought to bar from the mails everything which *might* stimulate sex impulses. If so, much chaste poetry and fiction, as well as many useful medical works would be under the ban. Like everything else, this law must be construed reasonably with a view to the general objects aimed at * * *.

We have been referred to no decisions where a truthful exposition of the sex side of life, evidently calculated for instruction and for the explanation of relevant facts, has been held to be obscene.

The defendant's discussion of the phenomena of sex is written with sincerity of feeling and with an idealization of the marriage relation and sex emotions. We think it tends to rationalize and dignify such emotions rather than to arouse lust. While it may be thought by some that portions of the tract go into unnecessary details that would better have been omitted, it may be fairly answered that the curiosity of many adolescents would not be satisfied without full explanation * * *. Any incidental tendency to arouse sex impulses which such a pamphlet may perhaps have is apart from and subordinate to its main effect. The tendency can only exist in so far as it is inherent in any sex instruction, and it would seem to be outweighed by the elimination of ignorance, curiosity, and morbid fear.

If a book, however, contains much obscene matter and yet can be sustained as having a scientific purpose, the method of advertising may control. A book describing the sexual practice of savages, admittedly of use to anthropologists, was unwisely advertised by thousands of circulars sent out at random. One even was unwisely addressed to an assistant United States attorney. Prosecution followed, and the court held that the purpose of the advertising was "plainly designed merely to catch the prurient"; also that "no sensible jury could have failed to pierce the fragile screen, set up to cover that purpose. * * * The books were not obscene per se; they had a proper use, but the defendants woefully misused them, and it was that misuse which constituted the gravamen of the crime." [17]

The courts are ever alert to prevent obscenity for pornographic reasons. If the general quality of the book makes it apparent that the book has no artistic skill, no scientific, medical, or educational purpose, the courts have no difficulty in condemning the book. A collection of "waggish tales" gathered from all over the world, but constituting merely smoking-room jests, was quickly held to be obscene.[18]

179. CENSORSHIP

Great advances against censorship have occurred currently in three notable U.S. Supreme Court decisions [19]: the Burstyn "Miracle" case (N.Y.), the Gelling case (Texas), and the "M" case (Ohio). The Court held that motion pictures come within the protection of free speech assured by the First Amendment to the U.S. Constitution, and hence that: (1) the N.Y. censor could not ban *The Miracle* as "sacrilegious"; (2) the Texas censor could not ban a race-relations picture as "prejudicial to the best interests of the people"; (3) the Ohio censor could not ban "M" as "harmful" and the N.Y. censor could not ban *La Ronde* as "immoral."

In the *Esquire* case (327 U.S. 146) the Supreme Court held that the Postmaster General could not act as a censor, saying:

But the petitioner's predecessor found that the objectionable items, though a small percentage of the total bulk, were regular recurrent features which gave the magazine its dominant tone or characteristic. These include jokes, cartoons, pictures, articles, and poems. They were said to reflect the smoking-room type of humor, featuring, in the main, sex. Some witnesses found the challenged items highly objectionable, calling them salacious and indecent. Others thought they were only racy and risqué. * * *

An examination of the items makes plain, we think, that the controversy is not whether the magazine publishes "information of a public character" or is devoted to "literature" or to the "arts". It is whether the contents are "good" or "bad". To uphold the order of revocation would, therefore, grant the Postmaster General a power of censorship. Such a power is so abhorrent to our traditions that a purpose to grant it should not be easily inferred.

It is plain, as we have said, that the favorable second-class rates were granted periodicals meeting the requirements of the Fourth condition, so that the public good might be served through a dissemination of the class of periodicals described. But that is a far cry from assuming that Congress had any idea that each applicant for the second-class rate must convince the Postmaster General that his publication positively contributes to the public good or public welfare. Under our system of government there is an accommodation for the widest varieties of tastes and ideas.

Likewise, the Federal Communications Commission held that under Section 315 of the Federal Communications Act (U.S.C.A. Title 47) a broadcasting station was not permitted to censor the script of a political candidate, to whom it had licensed the use of its station, for fear the script contained libelous matter. In a lengthy decision the Commission held that a station could not exercise the powers of censorship over the material of a political candidate. The Commission said: [19a]

The assumption of a right to censor "possibly libelous" matter, or statements which "might subject the station to suit" would give to radio stations a positive weapon of discrimination between contesting candidates which is precisely the opposite of what Congress intended to provide in this section.

Accordingly, we are of the opinion that the prohibition of Section 315 against any censorship by licensees of political speeches by candidates for office is absolute, and no exception exists in the case of material which is either libelous or might tend to involve the station in an action for damages.

The Commission also added a view as to which there must be considerable doubt:

* * * as we read the provisions of Section 15, the prohibition contained therein against censorship in connection with political broadcasts appears clearly to constitute an occupation of the field by federal

authority, which, under the law, would relieve the licensee of responsibility for any libelous matter broadcast in the course of a speech coming within Section 315 irrespective of the provisions of state law.

But the Supreme Court of Nebraska held a radio station liable for defamatory words in a broadcast political speech, thus rejecting the above views of the Federal Communications Commission.[19b]

180. STATE PROVISIONS

A great number of obscenity cases arise under state penal and censorship statutes. Some states are more liberal than others. Massachusetts, for example, where the Watch and Ward Society is powerful, is very strict. New York in a number of cases has favored the liberal rules of the Federal courts; in other cases the decisions of lower courts have been quite severe. Unfortunately, under the broad and general words of the New York Penal Statute, the views of a judge as to what is obscene, like the discretion of a chancellor where fraud is involved, enter into what is found obscene; thus the criterion of obscenity varies with the size of the judge's foot. One can never tell.

The controlling prohibition in New York appears in the New York Penal Law.[20] This provision makes it a misdemeanor to sell or generally to distribute or advertise "any obscene, lewd, lascivious, filthy, indecent or disgusting book, magazine, pamphlet, newspaper * * * phonograph record, picture, drawing, photograph, motion-picture film, figure or image." Under this provision and previous forms thereof, the New York courts have reached somewhat conflicting decisions. The general rule is that a literary work to be subject to condemnation must "invite to vice or voluptuousness" or tend "to excite lustful and lecherous desire." [21] In a case so stating the rule, the New York Court of Appeals held that a play entitled *Frankie and Johnnie* was not a violation of a section of the Penal Law as to dramas which uses language similar to that of the section as to books. The court said: [21]

The production of such a play may be repulsive to puritanical ideas of propriety as would "Camille" and may be offensive to the more liberal minded as lacking in taste and refinement, as would the morally unobjectionable "Abie's Irish Rose". The play may be gross and its characters wanting in moral sense. It may depict women who carry on a vicious trade and their male associates. It cannot be said to suggest, except "to a prurient imagination", unchaste or lustful ideas. It does not counsel or invite to vice or voluptuousness. It does not deride virtue. Unless we say that it is obscene to use the language of the street rather than that of the scholar, the play is not obscene under the Penal Law, although it might be so styled by the censorious.

In People v. Eastman,[22] the Court of Appeals of New York held that a scurrilous attack upon clergymen was not obscene within the prohibitions of the New York Penal Law, and the test was again laid down that it is necessary to show that an assailed work tended to excite lustful and lecherous desires.

In applying these tests, the City Magistrate's Court of New York held the novel *The Gilded Hearse*, the fictional material of which concerned the publishing business with sex addenda, not a violation of the penal provision.[23] The magistrate here accepted as relevant evidence, in appraising the obscenity of the book, the published literary opinions of professional critics as evidencing the author's sincerity of purpose and the book's literary worth. The magistrate declined, however, to receive in evidence unpublished letters in defense of the book from literary critics in the community. The magistrate lucidly specified the test which caused him to refuse to condemn the book as follows:

> To determine whether a book falls within the condemnation of the statute, an evaluation must be made of the extent to which the book as a whole would have a demoralizing effect on its readers, specifically respecting sexual behavior. * * * Various factors should be borne in mind when applying the judicially accepted standards used in measuring that effect. Among others, these factors include the theme of the book, the degree of sincerity of purpose evident in it, its literary worth, the channels used in its distribution, contemporary attitudes toward the literary treatment of sexual behavior and the types of readers (particularly with respect to age and intellectual development) reasonably to be expected to secure it for perusal.

The same magistrate held that the book entitled *End as a Man*,[24] in which the scene was laid in a military academy, by the same test likewise was not a violation of the Penal Law. The magistrate stated the following test as to language:

> The test of whether a book comes within the condemnation of the statute depends not upon the choice of language used in it, nor upon

the content of minor passages, but upon the effect of the whole book on reasonably normal readers both young and old.

Another New York City magistrate has held D. H. Lawrence's *The First Lady Chatterly* an obscene work within the prohibitions of the Penal Law.[25]

In an older case the Court of Appeals sustained a judgment against the New York Society for Suppression of Vice on the grounds of malicious prosecution for the arrest of the plaintiff for selling an English translation of Théophile Gautier's *Mademoiselle de Maupin*.[26]

Hands Around by Schnitzler has been held to be obscene in New York.[27]

A magistrate refused to find *The Well of Loneliness* not obscene and left the issue for the jury to decide.[28]

The autobiography *If I Die*, by André Gide, was held not obscene.[29]

Madeleine, the autobiography of a prostitute, likewise was held not to be obscene.[30]

The state courts recognize sincerity of artistic purpose, as contrasted to purveying dirt for dirt's sake, as an important distinction. But in the application of that distinction, some state courts are influenced greatly by scarlet patches of profanity and of Anglo-Saxon explicitness.[31] Thus indulgence therein is both imprudent and sorrow-creating for authors and publishers alike. The safe and profitable rule is firm exclusion thereof. The risks are great for pioneering.

181. CONSTITUTIONAL PROTECTION

Constitutional questions constantly are raised as to obscenity statutes. A state statute empowering a state board to censor motion pictures has been held by the Supreme Court not to be an unlawful burden on interstate commerce.[32]

Another subdivision of the before-noted Section of the New York Penal Law [Section 1141(2)], prohibiting the publication and distribution of a book, pamphlet, magazine, or newspaper "devoted to the publication and material made up of criminal news, police reports, lust or crime", was held unconstitutional by the Supreme Court of the United States. This ruling was reached despite the fact that the prohibition was construed by the highest state court of New York to consist merely of an effort to prevent the inciting of crime. The Supreme Court of the United States held that the prohibition in the state statute, even as narrowed and construed by the highest state court, "was too uncertain and indefinite" and thus a violation of the Fourteenth Amendment to the Federal Constitution.[33]

This decision is quite important because about twenty states have statutes similar to that of New York making the publication of works devoted to crime a misdemeanor.[34]

In the protracted litigation against Doubleday and Company involving Edmund Wilson's *Memoirs of Hecate County*, an unfortunately obscure result as to constitutional rights was reached. But the work was finally condemned as being a violation of the above-noted section of the New York Penal Law. A two-to-one judgment of the Court of Special Sessions of New York [35] held the work a violation of the Penal Law; the Appellate Division of the Supreme Court of New York [36] unanimously confirmed; the New York Court of Appeals [37] likewise confirmed the decision of the Court of Special Sessions, but noted that a constitutional question of freedom of speech under the Fourteenth Amendment to the United States Constitution was involved, and ruled adversely to the publisher on that point.

The summary of the reporter of the Court of Appeals decision suggests that the main argument of the defendant Doubleday and Company before the New York Court of Appeals was on constitutional grounds, because the standard applied by the lower courts "took into account only the effect of the book on the immature or the depraved, and not its effect on the minds of the mature and those not subject to such influences".[37] This argument, it seems, raised the constitutional question. The case was carried to the Supreme Court of the United States on this constitutional question of freedom of speech and that court, by a decision of four judges to four, failed to reverse the decision of the New York Court of Appeals on the constitutional question and in effect affirmed the decision of the state courts condemning the work.[38] Mr. Justice Frankfurter, who in a dissenting opinion in the Winters case [33] had sought to uphold the New York statute, did not participate in the decision in the

Memoirs of Hecate County case. His abstention caused the even division of the court.

Since the above-quoted language from Section 1141 as to obscenity contains so many specific and all-inclusive words defining obscenity, one must speculate concerning the reasoning of the four judges in the Supreme Court of the United States who voted to reverse the ruling of the Court of Appeals of New York in the *Hecate County* case, on constitutional grounds. Were they impelled by considerations of free speech in the condemnation of this particular literary work, or did they reason on grounds of generality in the statute, or were they impressed by the improper test asserted to be used by the lower courts (i.e. "the effect only on the immature and depraved")? The fact that the justices of the Supreme Court were evenly divided in their decision might raise hope that the court will interfere on constitutional grounds in unfounded condemnations of works of clear literary merit as obscene. But since the memorandum opinion of the court gave no reasons for the equally divided votes of the justices, one can only speculate.

The United States Supreme Court has held a Minnesota statute unconstitutional, as a violation of the due-process clause of the Fourteenth Amendment of the Federal Constitution, where such statute provided for the suppression by public officers, as a public nuisance, of any "malicious, scandalous and defamatory" newspaper published within the state.[39]

It is generally concluded that television and radio broadcasting, since they cross state borders, can be censored only by the Federal government under the interstate-commerce clause of the Constitution, not by the states, particularly since Federal control of both has been imposed by Congress, as to many aspects, in a Federal commission. But the Supreme Court has not so conclusively ruled as yet, although state courts have so intimated.

—————— XXIV ——————

Protection of Manuscripts and
Rights of Authors

182. MANUSCRIPTS AND PRIORITY

THE ASPECT of the Copyright Statute which seems most unfortunate to unestablished authors is that it does not permit copyrighting of novels, books, short stories, and articles before publication. Only works usable without publication (plays, lectures, motion pictures, radio and television scripts, and works of art) can be copyrighted under the Statute without publication. Therefore as to the great bulk of literary creations the author must rely upon his common-law copyright. (See Section 50.)

A common-law copyright arises only when the author's intellectual labor is reduced to objective or written form. Therefore preservation and identity of a manuscript and proof of date of its completion, making possible a common-law copyright, are vital to authors. Where litigation is based upon a common-law copyright, an essential preliminary step, as noted in the discussion of piracy litigation (see Chapter XIX) is proof of the date of completion of the original manuscript.

Also authors must do more than merely preserve the original manuscript. They must be ready to prove the date of the writing of that manuscript. It is always essential, in a piracy trial, to prove that the manuscript under which the complainant asserts a common-law copyright was completed prior to the infringing work. Otherwise the contention is possible that the complainant copied the work of the defendant.

Some authors mistakenly believe that if they could copyright their unpublished works they could establish a priority of creation which would prevail over subsequent independent creation by others, particularly as to use of an uncommon locale or novel historical characters or events. That belief is wrong. Authors of unpublished works lose nothing, so far as this phase of priority is concerned, by being denied the right to copyright unpublished books and periodical material.

But copyright registration of unpublished fiction and books would (a) establish irrefutably the date of creation and (b) identify beyond attack the contents of the manuscript. Thus registration is desirable in the case of works which can be copyrighted without publication. (See Section 52.)

What can the author do, however, as to literary works that must be published before a statutory copyright is permitted? How can he establish, beyond attack, the date of completion of his unpublished manuscript and the contents thereof?

Some authors resort to the device of mailing a copy of the manuscript to themselves. The envelope bears the date of mailing and thus establishes the time factor. But as was shown in the *Alexander's Ragtime Band* litigation,[1] the mailing of a manuscript may not irrefutably establish the contents of the manuscript, unless the envelope be opened only in open court after litigation has been started, or in the presence of defendant's counsel.

The cumbersome mailing of a manuscript to the author by himself is an unnecessary act. An easier means is afforded. All the author need do, after he has finished his manuscript, is to bind it (or a carbon copy) firmly and have the manuscript identified in writing by two or three witnesses. This identity is accomplished by having these witnesses write their names (and their addresses) on the first and last pages of the manuscript, followed by the date. If the author desires to be very careful, he can then place the manuscript within an envelope, seal the envelope, and have the same witnesses again write their names and the date across the sealed flap of the envelope and state, in writing, what the envelope contains. If litigation ever arises, the author then takes care to break the seal and open the envelope only in open court, and he can thereupon have the manuscript marked in evidence as an exhibit in the case.

Such procedure is fully as effective as copyright registration would be, and as effective as mailing a copy to oneself, and simpler. The procedure used is similar to that prevailing as to wills, where claims of alteration often are made. The testimony of the witnesses who have written their names upon the manuscript and envelope is completely competent to identify the manuscript, just as witnesses "prove" a will. Also such witnesses can establish the date noted on the manuscript, or envelope, as the date of creation. Such procedure is common in identifying patents, and the date thereof, by witnessing the patent drawings. If the witnesses die, evidence can be introduced identifying their signatures. Thereupon the signatures and the notation of the witnesses themselves will be accepted in court as proof when the envelope is opened or the manuscript introduced in evidence. If the author prefers to mail the manuscript to himself, the greatest care must be taken never to open the seal of the envelope except in open court or before counsel or agents of the adverse side, also to make certain that the flap is very firmly sealed.[1]

Production of the earliest copy of a manuscript, where reliance is made upon a common-law copyright, is important. For a complainant relying on a common-law copyright, failure to produce the original manuscript, or a copy made before the defendant's work appeared, may be fatal.

In the tumultuous litigation [2] against Richard Walton Tully, over his highly successful Hawaiian play *The Bird of Paradise*, the complainant asserted that Tully's play was plagiarized from her unpublished play *In Hawaii*. But she was unable to produce the original manuscript of her play, only "copies * * * concededly typewritten after this suit was begun." Although she won in two lower courts, the Court of Appeals of New York reversed, holding that there was no plagiarism. It noted the inability of the plaintiff to produce the original manuscript of the play as a significant item of evidence.

Those who rely upon a common-law copyright must carefully preserve the original manuscript, or an early and exact copy. Also they must prepare means of being able to prove the date of completion, as above suggested, to escape the fate of the author of *In Hawaii*.

183. AFTER THE MANUSCRIPT IS SOLD

The chief protective steps an author must take arise after he has sold his work. Since he desires to retain all of the rights other than the particular right that he has sold, he must make certain that such retained rights are agreed to by the purchaser—and in writing. Since copyrights are not divisible, usually the publisher of the work, if it is included in a periodical, takes out the copyright in his name. Thus he becomes the copyright proprietor. The statute permits the author to obtain a separate copyright upon his contribution to the periodical. (See Section 105.) Energetic and successful authors often do so, others rarely.

As to a book there is no good reason why the copyright should not be taken in the author's name, subject to the rights of the publisher. Otherwise, great care should be taken in making certain that the author retains all the rights under the transformation section of the Copyright Statute (C.S., Section 1) by the written agreement. The fine print of any letter or agreement should be carefully read by the author before signing. Other notations appearing in the chapter on assignments and licenses should be carefully kept in mind. Licenses today are wondrous documents. They include many provisions that are obscure to anyone except a lawyer expert in copyright law. Authors should not execute licenses without understanding every clause, or obtaining professional information upon every clause they do not clearly understand. Obscurity in a license often means that the author is sacrificing a valuable right. He will thereafter regret such a sacrifice if his work is as successful as his dreams contemplate. An author should not sell himself short.

184. NEEDED CHANGES IN THE COPYRIGHT STATUTE

The Copyright Statute needs revision. A long list of necessary amendments could be enumerated. A few glaring defects and lacks are outstanding.

It is too much to hope for the deletion of the requirement of United States printing of books and periodicals, so that international copyrights can be directly obtained by United States authors. The ending of all technical requirements of registration and copyright notice, advancing United States copyright procedure to the European form of copyrights without formality, is also too much to hope for.

Passing over these major desirable changes, other definite lacks in the Copyright Statute should be remedied. Copyrights should be freely divisible. The status and details of television use should be established and recognized. Poets, probably the most unfairly used group of authors under the present Copyright Statute, should have more protection. Their creations are usually short in length. As such they are usable in radio and in nonfacsimile television without penalty for literal copying. Such public use is permitted under the present Copyright Statute, except where using the poem in public can be deemed a dramatic performance. That protection is slender. Books of poems are sold in contemplation of reading by private persons or of reciting in private or school groups, and not for use for profit. The free right to recite a poem for profit in any public gathering, or over the radio or television, without extra compensation to the creator is markedly unfair, and proper remedial legislation is now pending.

Choreographic works, under the rulings of courts in the United States, are protected only when they tell a sufficiently definite story to be deemed dramatic productions. Choreographic works, increasingly popular today, interpret moods and impulses. These often can not be brought within the requirements of storytelling as dramatic representation. Choreographic representation, when definitely described in a script, even though storytelling and dramatic representation be absent, should be protected. Such is the European rule. But the difficulty is to record the sequences of the dance in sufficiently explicit written form to have something substantial that can be copyrighted. Choreographers have attempted to develop a notation analogous to musical notation, which will afford greater protection to their creations.

185. PLAYWRIGHTS AND THE ANTITRUST STATUTES

The Dramatists' Guild's effort to impose a uniform contract upon producers has been held a violation of the Sherman Antitrust Statute.[3] (See Section 106.) That statutory inhibition of monopolies expressly exempts labor unions. But such organizations as authors' leagues and dramatists' guilds are not considered labor unions in antitrust law, whereas organizations of many types of workers not manual workers are considered labor unions. This distinction is artificial. Authors and dramatists should have the right to band together to protect the weaker members of their group in disposing of their works to producers, by amendment to the antitrust statutes.

186. LENDING LIBRARIES

The contrast is marked between the fortunate status of composers of music and the writers of song lyrics, with their retained right of public performance for profit even after the sale of sheet music to the public, and the different status of authors and publishers whose royalties and sales are sharply decreased by lending libraries. The composers of music gained a great advance when they persuaded Congress to grant them, in 1909, the right of public performance for profit.

As to books, a use roughly similar to that of public performance for profit of music arises when lending libraries rent out such copyrighted books. This practice of lending, without sharing the lending fees with the copyright holder, works especial deprivation on writers and publishers of mystery stories since readers of these books are prone to rent rather than buy them. Authors and publishers of other fiction are likewise deprived of what might be significant amounts of income, since a large number of readers take such books from lending libraries who might otherwise purchase them. The author should have the right to decide whether his work shall be sold or rented.

If the copyright law were amended by adding after the word "vend" in Section 1(a) of the Copyright Statute the single word "lease", the copyright proprietor of books would enjoy a right analogous to that of public performance for profit prevailing as to musical compositions. Then the author could prevent lending libraries from renting out books, except on the payment of a license fee to him, or on other fair terms. The original insertion of that one word "lease" would greatly have increased the rewards of writing. Today an amendment to this effect would be no more than a fair protection to authors. But after all these years a longer clause than "to lease" may be necessary.

Objections, of course, can be raised to granting the copyright proprietor a control over the leasing of a copyrighted book. Efforts by the copyright proprietor to limit the resale price of his book have been held invalid,[4] and if an author controlled the leasing privilege the public might have to pay more to the author. Once the book is sold the publisher or author, as the copyright proprietor, can not control the price of sale by retailers. But the right to control leasing of the book is not price fixing or even restraint on circulation; if it is, it is a right the author should be permitted to retain and profit from. Congress can give authors that right.

Authors and playwrights, unfortunately, fail to press their rights upon Congress persistently. Composers of musical compositions did not get the benefit right of retaining public performance for profit by the pure beneficence or wisdom of the drafters of the Copyright Statute of 1909. They owe that right largely to arduous work of composers like Victor Herbert, who appeared, year after year, before House and Senate Committees and pleaded for that right. After composers obtained it, the right was constantly assailed before Congressional copyright committees. The enormous effort put forth by prominent music composers to obtain and then to retain that right is now forgotten. It was persistent and very marked. Composers concentrated upon this one demand with astounding vigor. Not until authors and playwrights exert similar vigor in obtaining relief from Congress will they receive benefits comparable to those enjoyed by composers of music.

187. AUTHORS AND TAXATION

An advantage that authors, as copyright proprietors, previously enjoyed as to income taxes, has just been ended by the Revenue Act of 1950. Prior to 1950, some successful authors were able to sell their copyrights and report the profit they received as capital gains, paying 25 per cent only of their receipts or profits. Authors with large incomes could thus escape the higher income-tax brackets. But the Revenue Act of 1950 expressly ends that practice. The Internal Revenue Code [5] is now amended by adding the following clause, Section 210, which excludes copyrights from being the basis of capital gains, by excluding them from capital assets:

(1) Capital assets.—The term "capital assets" means property held by the taxpayer (whether or not connected with his trade or business), but does not include * * *

(C) a copyright; a literary, musical, or artistic composition; or similar property; held by

(i) a taxpayer whose personal efforts created such property, or

(ii) a taxpayer in whose hands the basis of such property is determined, for the purpose of determining gain from a sale or exchange, in whole or in part by reference to the basis of such property in the hands of the person whose personal efforts created such property; * * *."

Likewise certain benefits to play producers and playwrights, and to those who invest in shows, as to income-tax savings, have been ended by this same Revenue Act of 1950. Prior to then it was customary to organize a show-production company in the "collapsible" corporate form. If the play was successful the corporation was dissolved and profits were distributed as capital gains; the income then was subject only to a 25 per cent capital gain tax and was not treated as ordinary income. The Revenue Act of 1950 (Section 212) ends that practice. It provides that income gained from "collapsible" corporations, after the dissolution of such corporations, shall not be deemed capital gains, but merely ordinary income. The only exception is as to stockholders owning not more than 10 per cent of the stock of the collapsible corporation. This exception is retained from past practice to help the raising of "angel funds" for shows. Rich "angels" can still claim capital gains if they own no more than 10 per cent of the play's corporate producer and such corporation is later "collapsed," i.e. dissolved and its assets distributed to its stockholders.

When a playwright or author, as a copyright proprietor, grants licenses for exclusive motion-picture rights in his play or novel, the price received therefrom can not be considered a capital gain. It must be considered as ordinary income. All licenses under a copyright are held to be ordinary income.[6]

The payments received by even a foreign author, from the grant of a license to use his copyrighted work in the United States as a motion picture or otherwise, likewise are held to be ordinary income to the foreign author, upon which an income tax must be paid to the United States, even though the foreign author never sets foot within the United States.[7]

Gross receipts derived by an author under a statutory copyright are subject to taxation by a state. Such receipts are not exempt from taxation by the states as the taxation of instrumentalities of the Federal government.[8] Even though the copyright exists only by virtue of Federal grant, the states have full right to tax it.

But the author does have a limited privilege under the income-tax law. Where he spends more than one year in the writing of a literary work, when he sells the work or receives royalties therefrom, if he receives not less than 80 per cent of the gross income (which is difficult to predict) in a taxable year, he is entitled to apportion the price or royalties he receives ratably as taxable income, over the time he was engaged in the writing of it, but not for more than the previous thirty-six months.[9] By spreading the income over "that part of the period preceding the close of the taxable year, but not more than thirty-six calendar months" in which he received not less than 80 per cent of the gross income, the author may benefit through escaping "high bracket" tax rates. But the author must establish for the tax authorities the years during which he was engaged in the creation of the specific work. The first draft of a manuscript is helpful evidence as to the years consumed, by dating the time the author started working on his creation.

But the 80 per cent minimum provision as to receipt of income in any one year, together with the limitation to thirty-six calendar months, limits the benefits derived and thus this tax provision is not too often helpful. But it has advantages and can be used beneficially by some successful authors more often than is done.

Publishers sometimes, by contracts with their authors, limit the amount of royalties the author can receive in the first year of publication as a device for distributing author income over an advantageous time period. But valid reasons for such delay in payment, other than tax savings, must be available as proof of the need of this limitation, otherwise the tax rule of "constructive receipt" may be asserted by the collector as to such postponed revenue.

——— XXV ———

Television's Problems

---

188. DIFFICULTIES OF A NEW ART

TELEVISION, as a recent means of communication, is not mentioned in the Copyright Act, nor is it even mentioned in the recent statute [1] prohibiting profane language over the air. It has been judicially determined, however, that defamation over television, when extemporaneous and not read from a script, is slander. (See Section 22.)

Under the Federal Communications Act, 1934,[2] jurisdiction over television stations is vested in the Federal Communications Commission, which has exclusive control over granting the license to operate a television station, and thus controls the functioning of this new means of communication. But apart from the specified questions of administrative control, the Commission has no control over the legal rights of individuals or corporations arising therefrom. Television thus has various difficulties under the general law which must be considered. Motion pictures were granted the right of copyrighting films, in 1912, by an amendment to the Copyright Statute. As yet no amendment of the Copyright Statute has recognized or clarified the copyrighting of material initially or subsequently transmitted by television. Thus difficulties arise, because of the lack of provisions in the Copyright Statute as to use of literary property in television. These are not grave, but they are perplexing. Other legal difficulties also have emerged.

Two chief problems confront television today. The first involves the right of a television station to limit the use of the pictures it broadcasts, as by issuing a notice limiting the exhibition of these pictures generally to places and for purposes not forbidden by the television station's notice, unless the station shall have granted such places specific authority to exhibit. The second problem involves the consequences of failure to insert a copyright notice by facsimile when copyrighted matter is reproduced on the television screen.

189. PROHIBITIONS BY NOTICE AS TO THE USE OF TELEVISION PROGRAMS

The effort of television stations to limit the reception and use of their programs to specific places began contemporaneously with the art. Television stations broadcast, in facsimile, notice that the television program may be received and viewed only in private homes or similar places. Express prohibitions are added against the reception and viewing of the televised program in public places, particularly where admission charges may be exacted. Television programs are now commonly exhibited in taverns and bars, but no efforts have yet been made to prohibit the exhibition there. Litigation has been successfully prosecuted, however, in lower courts, against the exhibition of athletic and sporting events (particularly prize fights, baseball and football games) in hotels and other public places of large assembly or in motion-picture theaters where admission charges are imposed. No authoritative ruling by any Appellate Court has yet been handed down as to the effect of such prohibitions by notice. There have been several lower-court decisions which are not too clear or comforting.

190. EFFECT OF THE NOTICE

Notice by a station, limiting the place of exhibition of a television program, obviously is not valid unless a definite and recognized legal right in law can be adduced as the basis of such notice. One who sells or releases property or words and images into the channels of trade and use can not ordinarily restrict by any notice the use of the things so set free or sold. A copyright proprietor who sells a book, for example, can not prohibit the resale of a book at less than a specified price. (See Section 102.) No such retained right is granted under the Copyright Statute. A restriction (called in the law a servitude) upon the resale or subsequent use of an article once sold, in the case of personal property, is generally held invalid. Efforts at price fixing or tying the use of one article to another, or similar restrictions upon the circulation of material or property, are condemned usually as a violation of the Federal antitrust acts. Is there any legal basis for the notice as to use and exhibition of a television program?

191. LEGAL BASIS OF THE NOTICE

Two grounds are commonly advanced as the basis of this notice of restriction used by television stations: first, the rights under the Copyright Statute; second, rights against unfair competition, particularly in reliance upon the Associated Press case. (See Chapter XXI, Section 164.) Neither of these grounds seems effectively adequate to implement the notice used. But a third and more realistic basis can be suggested: privacy.

So far as copyrights are involved in television reproduction, the television station (as the copyright proprietor or the licensee of the copyright proprietor) has a clear right to specify where and how the copyrighted matter may be used to the extent that the Copyright Statute so permits. But the use forbidden must be within the power of retention of the copyright proprietor as granted under the Copyright Statute.

Most of the current disputes have arisen over sporting events, prize fights, baseball and football games, which generally are not copyrighted or in fact copyrightable. So far as the performance of music for profit is concerned, the right of public performance of music in any public place can usually be obtained from ASCAP by those who control the forbidden places of exhibition of the television program. As to the use of literary material, such as novels or poems, in a form other than that of dramatic production, the copyright proprietor has no right of control over reading in public, even by television. (See Section 98.) Only when the use is that of a dramatic performance in public is the right of such use retained under a copyright. Thus in a great majority of cases where efforts are made to restrict the reproduction of copyrighted material by television in forbidden places, copyright protection as a practical matter is not very helpful and controlling.

The restriction of use of television programs arising from athletic contests (prize fights, baseball, football, basketball, and similar events) can therefore be taken as involving the typical and usual issue presented. The right of televising a prize fight or similar event is usually sold by the promoter to a sponsor. The television station is only indirectly involved in the deal, but sometimes a station is the promoter (as the Columbia Broadcasting System has been). The desire to restrict the place and purpose of reception of the program, in fact, usually originates with the promoter and is imposed upon the sponsor to whom the rights have been sold. If the promoter of a prize fight can restrict the reception solely to those uses the sponsor desires, the promoter may sell the television rights at a higher price. Also the promoter is vitally interested in restricting the places of reception of television because of the possible effect upon his box-office receipts. The television station indirectly is interested because any restriction upon reception, if it results in a higher monetary return and value to the sponsor and to the promoter of the prize fight, results in a wider use of television and creates possibilities of higher returns for the leasing of the facilities of the station.

Those who seek to pick up the television broadcast and exhibit the picture upon a screen in a hall, hotel, or motion-picture theater where admission charges are collected directly or indirectly are, in reality, selling something which they did not create and which they pick out of the air "for free". Even where a hotel puts a screen in its lobby without admission charge, but thus attracts a crowd and gains good will, it profits markedly though indirectly.

Has everyone a right to take out of space a transmitted program, once it is released? Is a fair analogy, as to such television transmission, that of wild animals, in which an individual gains a property right by capturing the animal but loses that property right instantly if the animal is released or escapes? Or is there a more stable property right in the television station that makes possible the protection of the money-making entertainment possibility involved? Restrictions on the reception of television programs require a viewing of the content of the television broadcast as involving more than publicity as property. It is not only publicity about the broadcast athletic event that is involved. Those who seek to pick up and exhibit the broadcast are using the program and the portrayal of the events, not merely the publicity about such events. News reporting and news comment and news publicity about an athletic event are open to all.

What is involved here is something far more valuable: picturing the actual event itself. More is involved than publicity as property, as suggested in Chapter XX on Unfair Competition.

A property right of the promoter can possibly be spelled out of his act of arranging the event, say the prize fight. The promoter, to be sure, controls the place where the prize fight is maintained. He can forbid the setting up of the television camera on his premises. But the forbidden reception and use we are considering does not require a television camera being placed on the premises. The actual events of the prize fight, once released into space, can be picked up and exhibited or even retransmitted to a motion-picture theater and displayed on to a screen therein. Ordinarily they may be captured for display on a television screen set up in a hall or a hotel. Thus, though there may be a property right in the place where the prize fight is held, or in the arrangements of the prize fight itself, the picking up of the television program out of space involves a different legal element.

The effort to limit television reception as unfair competition, as enunciated in the Associated Press case, also is difficult to rely on. Merely stressing the unfairness of the "free ride" is too vague and general. The forbidden use does not become unfair unless the television station and the sponsor and promoter can be said to retain some rights after they have broadcast the fight. Unfairness is too vague a word to be helpful, unless the lack of equity involved arises from the use of some property element not in the public domain and thus not open to use by all. That is the reason why courts tend to limit the Associated Press case to the news aspect therein involved. Moreover, the Associated Press case is now of doubtful validity, because of the decision in Erie Railroad vs. Tompkins, noted before in Section 164, holding there is no general Federal common law. For these reasons, grounds other than mere iteration of words ("unfair" or "free ride" or "unjust enrichment") must be found to justify restrictions on the reception of television programs. The notice and the assertion of legal unfairness must hang on a surviving legal right, other than a copyright, generally to be ascertained as existing immediately after the broadcast release.

192. PRIVACY AND ATHLETIC EVENTS

A realistic legal basis for restraints on the use of television broadcasts, where persons are pictured, or described, which is almost always the case, can be established under the right of privacy. Then the right involved is that of the persons portrayed—prize fighters, players in a baseball game or football game, actors, singers, musicians, or performers in any nonpolitical event—not to have their pictures and personalities used in the manner and form and in the place prohibited by the notice. Such personalities can assign that retained split-part right of privacy to the promoter, sponsor, or television station. No such right of privacy arises, of course, as to individuals participating in a public state event, such as the inauguration of a president, the parade of an army, or the meeting of any public body. But athletes and actors in nongovernmental events may retain a definite right of privacy, in whole or in split part, even when they perform in public. They may grant to some and not to others the right to invade their privacy as to their pictures or names. They may grant the right of privacy for use in one commercial class of places but not in other commercial places.

Pictures of performers and the facts of their lives, of course, may be used as news. But the current picturing of a particular performance, in which performers engage as commercial personality individuals, i.e. in a fight or game or show, is something that can be retained by them, in whole or part. They have a right to refuse to appear and perform, and also a right to impose conditions upon their doing so.

To say that they have lost all such rights of privacy because they elected to become professionals, as athletes or actors, is not fair. As professionals, who in the past earned a livelihood from past appearances, they have not deprived themselves of the right of privacy as to future performances or as to the use of their names, pictures, or personality in future events. If a girl has long made a livelihood as a model, and has sold her picture to numberless publications, she has not lost her right of privacy as to any future use of her picture. Her face and figure have not been put in the public domain because she is a professional model. She may be subject to news comment, but she is not subject to free use of her privacy by anyone even though she is a professional model. The right of a model to sell her picture in the future, and the right of a prize fighter to sell the reproduction of his personality in future events, thus is always retained.

The recent decision of the New York Appellate Division (First Department) in Gautier v. Pro Football [3] (June 29, 1951) expressly denies any privacy protection to entertainers and others in such circumstances. It is doubtful if this backward-looking decision will be followed outside New York; if it is, it is difficult to spell out legal justification for restrictions on the reception of television programs except under the holding of the court that entertainers may have property rights in such circumstances other than under the law of privacy. Oddly, under the narrow viewpoint of this decision, a professional model could not sue if a magazine used her picture on its cover page, no advertising appearing thereon.

It would seem therefore that the prize fighter has a clear right expressly to forbid in advance any television reproduction of his personality when he agrees to fight in public. These retained rights are assignable. Also he can split his privacy into segments, i.e. grant its use to some and deny it to others as a class. We have already noted that the right of splitting publicity as property is a reality beginning to be recognized by the law, just as the right of splitting copyright uses is recognized. Specialized licenses to use a copyrighted work, as a detailed splitting of copyright use by transformation, have become an elaborate process and are freely recognized in copyright law. The same right of splitting arises in the case of privacy. The recognition of this right of division, or splitting, is eminently fair and fully in accord with basic theories of property use.

A prize fighter thus can assign all his privacy rights as to a particular fight to a promoter or television station or sponsor. He or his assignee can split that right, granting it to some, denying it to others. A promoter or sponsor, having acquired the right of privacy of the prize fighter, therefore can give it away "for free" to those who own screens in their private homes or operate them in taverns. Such a promoter can retain and restrict the right as to all other uses, particularly where admission charges are imposed.

So likewise as to the right of an actor appearing in a motion picture, or of a musician portrayed while playing in a motion picture. He can prevent the exhibition by television of the motion picture portraying him. An actor has a right to assign his right of privacy, as a reproduction of his picture and personality in a performance, for the limited exhibition in a motion-picture theater only and not by television. He can forbid its use for all other uses except news comment. This right of limitation was recognized in the Madison Square Garden case. (See Section 166.) Here the court held that a license to a picture company to photograph hockey games in the Garden, for use in a newsreel, did not carry with it the right to use those same pictures in a feature motion picture.

Spectators at public events, however, seem to fall within a different class. By attending a public event, a spectator probably consents to the television use of his picture as part of the show. Limitations on his consent, however, can be suggested. The courts in the future will have to pass upon varying and nice modifications of a spectator's consent by attending. A spectator at a public sporting event may not want to be forced by an advertiser's representative into an intermission act, centered around him, the spectator. If the spectator objects and the television men persist, or if a man is stopped on the street for a "candid camera" interview and objects, his consent, by attending the public event or by walking in a public place, may not then be impliedly granted, and the television crew will proceed in using his picture at their peril. Even those who attend public places may be deemed to limit their consent to be televised. But usually, it would seem, appearance in a public place by a spectator carries considerable consent by waiver of privacy. But overextensive use of a well-known personality's picture, even if he attends a public place or consents to an advertising use of his personality by a particular grantee, can well have a sharply drawn limit regarding to whom and to what extent his waiver of personality has been granted, by implication or by express contract.

It follows therefore that the splitting of the right of privacy must be carefully specified in every license granted by the persons portrayed. Reliance upon the retention of rights by implication alone involves difficult questions of interpretation. Negative covenants may creep in by judicial implication. The court may well hold that rights of privacy have not been impliedly retained. But where the license granted by the performer is carefully drawn, and the splitting of the right of privacy carefully specified, making explicit the retention of certain parts thereof or use thereof in specified places and expressly prohibiting specified uses, it seems clear that on the basis of privacy the notice given by the television station can well be held valid if it conforms thereto. Yet no clear and carefully argued decisions so hold as yet.

Any retention of privacy rights, however, can not prevent publishing the performer's picture or sequences of pictures in a newspaper. That publication involves the right of the public to news; the right of newspapers to benefit as purveyors to the public is established by the courts. Here newspapers and periodicals, because of the public's interest and right, are a favored and fortunate group. Periodicals, enjoying the right of fair comment, can go quite far. Their portrayals, however, are after the event, and do not give a contemporaneous extensive picturing of the event. The limited extent of news reproduction of personality, however, can be exceeded. A fighter can grant a motion-picture company an exclusive right to exhibit after the event his performance in a fight. A periodical's picture reproduction seldom is, and can not be, that extensive. In college amateur athletic events, the college, by implication or express agreement, can be viewed as the assignee of its athletes' complete rights of privacy. The college authorities are permitted to control their athletes' rights of privacy, just as they can charge admission to the contest and give the athletes participating no part thereof except their expenses. A college amateur athlete, of course, can always refuse to participate and thus to grant to his college control of his right of privacy.

The notice of television stations restricting exhibition to limited places and uses, under this theory, thus becomes merely an aspect of the splitting of the privacy rights of the performers as granted and enforced by the television station. The performers can assign all or part of their split rights to the promoter or sponsor or television station. The promoter or sponsor can authorize the television station to use such partially granted privacy rights and to give notice of those retained by it on behalf of the performers or promoter. Here the law is merely conforming to the practices of the market place in the use of personality as an invasion of privacy.

Inherent in any enforcing of retained television privacy restriction, as to the place or manner of exhibition of such programs, is a recognition of privacy as a property right. To say that in such instances a prize fighter or performer can recover damages for violations only if he has therefrom suffered mental anguish or damage to his health (as was held in Cason v. Rollins; see Sections 2 and 15), or because he has been defamed, borders upon the absurd. Even in Gautier v. Pro Football,[3] the court recognized as an element of damages "a so-called property interest inherent" in one's personality involving more than mental distress. Unless property rights or personality damage can be shown, an injunction can not issue. Right to injunctive relief because the money damage involved is not ascertainable arises only where a right of property, or personality, is involved. Here the injury involved is in reality a diminution of the moneys to be received and earned by the performer, as an injury to his occupational rights. The realistic aspect is that of personality as a positive right, i.e. as property, not as a negative right of an individual merely not to be mentally disturbed by unwanted publicity. The publicity is wanted, if the price is right. Money, as property, is involved, not mere hurt feelings or physical injury.

Other property rights may be suggested, in addition to property rights based on privacy, as the basis for unfair-competition restrictions as to the place and purpose of reception of television programs. The owner of the arena, or a promoter as the lessee thereof, may be deemed to have a property right to prevent the photographing of this structure for commercial publicity purposes. The Madison Square Garden case suggests this right. (See Section 166.) If the arena owner or lessee has this property right in the photographic publicity use of his property, he can split the right and by notice permit its reception and exhibition by some and deny it to others.

Another property aspect lies in the fact that a promoter or arena owner, if the local franchise holder and member of a national league, owns all the local right in the name, league membership, and consequent publicity property values of the baseball, football, hockey or other professional athletic teams which he controls under his franchise. In amateur athletics, colleges may be deemed to hold such rights or to grant them to others. This franchise property value may be urged as the basis of a property right in the publicity created by the public performances of the team so franchised. Thus the promoter has a right to grant the use of these publicity property values to some and deny them to others. This right, of course, can not be used to limit the public's rights in having freely reported the news and events about such a team, as news events. To forbid some uses of televised picturing of such teams in continuous action, however, can not be deemed restriction upon news reporting.

To raise still another property question, can a promoter, having arranged say a prize fight, be deemed to have a property right in the promotion, event, idea, plan, and arrangement itself, and apart from the privacy rights of the fighters and referee, and of the property right of the owner of the arena? Here the property right is getting thin and insubstantial. By analogy to the property right in a league franchise, such a property right of a promoter in a mere planned contest and performance might be urged. But more substantial grounds exist when privacy, ownership of the arena, and league franchise rights are advanced.

Thus the prohibition, by notice, of the reception and exhibition of television programs for commercial purposes unsanctioned by the television station, can be sustained on four disparate or united property rights as unfair competition, since a television station retains property rights in a televised program, even after release thereof by broadcast. These four grounds all view publicity as property. The four bases of property rights in publicity are: (1) the property right in privacy; (2) the property right in a building, or arena; (3) a property right in the franchise as to a team; (4) the property right in a promotion itself.

The novelty of these legal theories as to privacy herein noted, stresses the need of protection through a statutory formulation of television law by Congress. Television is completely an interstate affair. It is a revolutionary new means of communication. The Copyright Statute should be amended to affirm and define the copyright protection allowed where television use is involved. Privacy, because of the interstate aspects of television, radio, and publishing, today has become essentially an interstate right. Since we have no Federal common law, we need a uniform Federal formulation and codification of the right of privacy. The privacy rights of those performing in broadcasts by television, as well as the rights of the public therein, can adequately be specified only by Congressional intervention. Meanwhile the courts hesitantly must carry on.

It is indeed extraordinary that so great an industry as television has not made a greater effort to protect its vital rights by obtaining the clarifying consideration of Congress under the interstate commerce clause of the United States Constitution.

193. COMPARABLE RULINGS IN RADIO

Several decisions as to exploitation of sporting events involve questions of restriction upon radio broadcasting and collateral uses. None of the decisions are exhaustive or satisfactory.

The earliest decision (1932) involved motion pictures taken of a boxing exhibition held at Ebbets Field in Brooklyn. A motion-picture camera was placed on a building overlooking the field. Without opinion, the Appellate Court of New York sustained an injunction.[4]

The promoters of a Joe Louis fight, in 1937, were permitted to enjoin a press service from broadcasting an account of the fight. Here the defendant's announcer listened to a broadcast of the promoter's licensee, and rephrased and rebroadcast each round.[5] Although the court granted an injunction, the reasons in the opinion are not clarifying as to the theory upheld.

A New York Federal court refused similar relief to the promoter of baseball games. Here a play-by-play description of the game was obtained and broadcast by methods unknown to the promoter. In an unsatisfactory decision the court denied any relief and permitted such unlicensed broadcasting.[6]

A year later, a Pennsylvania Federal court refused to follow this earlier New York decision.[7] Here a broadcast, play by play, of the complainant's Pittsburgh Pirates baseball games was carried on by the use of telescopes placed on the roofs of a building situated next to the ball park. The court granted an injunction on the basis of the Associated Press case. (See Section 164.)

In 1940 a Pennsylvania District Court, however, refused to enjoin the sale of score cards (outside the gates of the park) for baseball games.[8] The sale was by a vendor not licensed by the baseball club. The complainant had obtained such a license. The court held that no theory of unfair competition permitted its intervention.

Thus the radio and motion-picture cases do not cast too much light on the subject. Though a privacy theory is involved, the courts do not as yet go extensively into that aspect. Legislation by Congress clearly is needed.

194. SHOULD COPYRIGHT NOTICES BE USED IN TELEVISION?

It is generally believed (see Section 62) that the reproduction and exhibition of copyrighted matter by television is not a publication thereof, but merely involves use akin to public performance of plays. There are no decisions so holding as to television. The conclusion that television broadcast is not publication is based upon the rulings holding that performances of plays, dramatizations by radio broadcasting, and the exhibition of motion pictures all are not publications of the material used. Since a common-law or statutory copyright thus is not destroyed, no copyright notice is required in a program, or by notice, or elsewhere when a play is publicly performed. Thus it would seem at first glance that no copyright notice need be put upon the screen in the case of television use, even where the title and list of actors is reproduced in facsimile.

But perplexing doubts persist. The decisions as to radio broadcasting and motion pictures, that the use of literary material therein is not publication, are few. And they are not by high courts, nor in cases where the question was carefully argued and examined by the court. And unlike the basic analogy of stage performances of plays, where the dissemination and public release is sparse and the spectators numerically few, television broadcasting reaches vast numbers.

The recent, surprising decision of a Federal court (see Section 62) that the public sale of phonograph records is publication of the music recorded thereon shows how fragile and tenuous is this assurance that television broadcasting is not publication. As to phonograph records, the court stressed the wide public sale and use thereof. Television broadcasting involves an even wider dissemination, distribution, availability, and use. No physical copies of the television program, to be sure, are sold, as phonograph records are sold. But recordings of television shows are almost always made and often are sold or licensed within the trade. In Remington v. Bentley,[9] previously discussed on the point as to whether defamation in television broadcasting is slander or libel (see Section 22), the complainant alleged, in the attempt to establish that the defamation was libel, that many recorded (i.e. written) copies of the television broadcast had been made for later use. Wide use of facsimile in television adds a direct similarity to printed books; the widespread printing and distribution to the public of written, or printed, copies of television programs is indubitable then, though the printing is momentary and fugitive and copies are not placed physically in the hands of the public. And, since it is difficult to know where or when facsimile reproduction occurs in a television program, the courts may hold that facsimile possibilities require a holding of publication generally in television uses of literary material in a program. In short, television use is uncomfortably close to publication.

The Copyright Statute was fairly promptly amended to permit statutory copyrighting of motion pictures as unpublished works. Uniformly, motion-picture producers copyright their works under this provision (Sections 5 and 12, C.S.) and do not rely upon a common-law copyright or upon the theory that the exhibition of motion pictures requires no copyright notice. But television stations uniformly rely upon common-law copyrights or on registering scripts as unpublished works, and thus risk all on the belief that television broadcasting is not publication. For copyright notices commonly are not used in television.

Legislation clearly is desirable to establish the rights of television under the copyright statute. It is particularly desirable to establish that television use is not publication; or if it is, to permit copyrighting and the registering of copies of television programs, as distinct from scripts. The probabilities, but without certainty, are that television use, except where complete or substantial copying in facsimile occurs, will not be held to be publication. But the question persists whether or not, out of rational caution, it is advisable for television stations to insert the copyright notice on the screen in facsimile in the case of dramatic performances, or as to other programs using copyrighted or copyrightable material, until legislation or a definitive court decision is had. Although the publishing industry in the United States is prone to the use of futile notices (such as denials or limitations of the right of fair comment, or humorous denials in advance of privacy invasion), and although the television industry is so prodigal in facsimile notices or restraints upon the use of its broadcast programs, the use of copyright notices on copyrightable television material is studiously avoided.

Television stations probably do not use copyright notices because they fear such use may imply doubt as to whether or not television use is publication. Thus they create perplexing consequences. Worth-while doubts persist, however, as to the advisability of such hesitation.

195. ASPECTS OF COPYRIGHT NOTICES IN TELEVISION

The consequences will be grave indeed if the courts should subsequently hold that television is publication by reason of the steadily increasing use of facsimile printing therein. Many copyrights will be thrown into the public domain and destroyed.

The problem has three aspects:

1. Where literary material is used that has previously been copyrighted under the statute as a published work.

2. Where literary material is used that has been copyrighted under the statute as unpublished works (as a radio or television script).

3. Where material is used that is otherwise not published, and as to which protection is sought under a common-law copyright of unpublished works.

In the case of a published literary work, already registered under a statutory copyright as a published work, the entire work will be thrown into the public domain if television use is held to be publication and if no copyright notice is broadcast in facsimile by the television station. If the use is with the consent (as uniformly is the case as to copyrighted works) of the copyright proprietor, and if television use is held publication, the only defense open to the copyright proprietor who licensed the use of his copyrighted work in television will be that the failure to use a copyright notice was by a licensee, not by the copyright proprietor himself. That defense is fragile. If the court finds that the television use was a joint enterprise, or was by direction of the copyright proprietor, or involved direct consent not to use the copyright notice, the defense will probably fail. Knowledge by the copyright proprietor of the failure to use the copyright notice is dangerous. The risk involved is that of the copyright proprietor of the work, not of the television station. The failure to require the use of the copyright notice in facsimile thus may bring grief, as the loss of the copyright, to the copyright proprietor of a valuable work.

In the case of a work registered as an unpublished work, the use of a copyright notice is not required in television, if television use is deemed not publication.[10a] But if television use is publication, the work must thereupon be registered as a published work with the copyright office. And the consequences of failure so to do are the same, as to the copyright proprietor, as in the case of published works, just discussed.

Where reliance is made upon a common-law copyright, the same situation prevails. If television use is not publication, the common-law copyright is preserved.[10a] If television use is publication, the work must be registered and the copyright notice inserted. If television use is not publication, nevertheless the literary or musical work can be registered as an unpublished work.

The Copyright Statute did not contemplate television use. There is no specification therein as to depositing copies of a television program, or as to where the copyright notice should be inserted in television use. Sections 10, 19, 20, and 21 of the Copyright Statute, where the places of use of a copyright notice are specified in the Statute, all contain no helpful language on the point. There is no title page in a television program. But the customary printing in facsimile, at the beginning of television programs, of the title of a play or of a work used, makes reasonable the insertion of a facsimile copyright notice immediately following the title. The courts are quick to interpret the copyright act broadly as to uses not mentioned in the Copyright Statute.

An analogy arises as to the time of starting of the twenty-eight years of a statutory-copyright term, in the case of works copyrighted as unpublished works under the provisions of Section 12 of the Copyright Statute. Only in Section 24 of the Copyright Statute, which refers solely to published works, is the date of beginning of the twenty-eight years specified, and then only as to published works. Section 24 reads: "the copyright secured by this title shall endure for twenty-eight years from the date of first publication

* * * ." But a high court has interpreted the statute to mean that in the case of copyrights of unpublished works, registered under Section 12, the copyright term begins from the date of registration, although there is no such language in the Copyright Statute.[10]

The insertion of a copyright notice immediately after the title of a television production, in facsimile, would clearly conform with the Statute as to placing of the notice.

In the case of a televised work previously copyrighted under the Statute as a published work, deposit of a copy of the television program and application for registration as a published work would not be required, if television use is deemed publication. In the case of a work already copyrighted as an unpublished work, deposit of a copy and application for registration as a published work would be needed. The copy deposited could be a recording (as so commonly made and used) of a television program. This copy would be akin to the copy of a motion picture, now deposited with the Copyright Office, when motion pictures are copyrighted as required under the Copyright Statute's Sections 12 and 13.

Whether the Copyright Office would accept such a deposit of a recording of a television program is doubtful. An effort to require such deposit by court intervention would result in an adjudication on the point. Also it would result in a ruling as to whether television use is publication, as well as to whether copyright can be had of a television program as an unpublished or published work. Whatever the court ruling might be, the television industry and copyright proprietors whose works are used in television would thereby be adequately protected. As to common-law copyrights the same situation could arise. Can the common-law copyright in a television program be turned into a statutory copyright as a published, or as an otherwise unpublished work, by television use and by deposit of a recording?

Today the television industry relies too often on the belief that the original material it uses is protected under common-law copyrights. As a consequence, the television industry is denied the benefit of the ample statutory provisions as to recovery of damages and relief so copiously provided for in the Copyright Act in case of piracy. Also, in such reliance upon common-law copyrights, unless diversity of citizenship can be established, television stations must perhaps resort to several state-court suits for relief against infringers.

The procedural difficulties thereunder are considerable. Also, if television use be held to be publication, the common-law copyrights now relied on are all thereby destroyed.

More active efforts to obtain clarification of the rights of television as to copyright protection by court action or preferably by legislation, would be prudent. The fear of indicating a doubt that publication does not result from television use is imprudent.

196. FEDERAL LEGISLATION SUGGESTIONS

Since the rise of television, several lower courts have restrained the reception of television broadcasts of prize fights in halls or hotels where admission charges were imposed. But the decisions usually have been on preliminary applications. The opinions are not too authoritative.

Threat of litigation is not a satisfactory way of protecting a right. The public interest, as well as that of the television industry, calls for Congressional action. Television knows no state lines. Congress alone can fix the rights involved in so complete a form of interstate commerce through its control, under the United States Constitution, of interstate and foreign commerce.

So many valuable copyright properties are involved, and so many conflicting rights arise where restrictions upon television reception are imposed by notice, and so important has the television industry become overnight, that legislative intervention clearly is called for. To await a *general* copyright revision is wishful thinking; it is too remote; specific efforts to protect television are clearly needed.

Appendixes

Appendix A—Notes and Cases Cited

CHAPTER II

1. Restatement of Law by American Law Institute (a semiofficial organization), Torts, Sec. 867.
2. This phrase was first used by Cooley, one of the great legal writers on the law of personal and property injury, i.e. Torts.
3. Cason v. Baskin, 155 Fla. 198 (1944); 159 Fla. 31 (1947).
4. Smith v. Doss, 37 So. 2d (Ala.) 118 (1948).
5. Koussevitzky v. Allen, 188 Misc. (N.Y.) 479 (1947); affirmed 272 App. Div. (N.Y.) 759 (1947).
6. Harvard Law Review, Vol. IV, p. 193 (1890).
7. Prince Albert v. Strange, 2 Degex & Sm. 652 (1848).
8. Schuyler v. Curtis, 147 N.Y. 434 (1895).
9. Roberson v. Rochester Folding Box Co., 171 N.Y. 538 (1902).
10. New York Civil Rights Law, Secs. 50, 51, McKinney's Consolidated Laws of New York, Book 8.

CHAPTER III

1. Harvard Law Review, Vol. IV, p. 193 (1890).
2. Binns v. Vitagraph Co., 210 N.Y. 51 (1913) affirming 147 App. Div. 783 (1911).
3. Sidis v. New Yorker, 113 Fed. 2d 806 (1940).
4. Molony v. Boy Comics Pub. Inc., 98 N.Y. Supp. 2d 119 (App. Div. 1950).
5. Sutton v. Hearst Corp., 98 N.Y. Supp. 2d 233 (App. Div. 1950).
5a. Gautier v. Pro. Football, 304 N.Y. 354; lower court 99 N.Y. Supp. 812.
5b. Haelan Lab. v. Topps Chewing Gum, 202 F. 2d 866 at p. 868 (1953).
5c. Pallas v. Crowley, 334 Mich. 382 (1952); see also 322 Mich. 411 (1948).
5d. Eick v. Perk Dog Food Co., 347 Ill. Appeals 293 (1952).
5e. Donahue v. Warner Brothers, 272 P. 2d 177; 194 F. 2d 6 (1952).
5f. Gill v. Curtis Pub. Co., 239 P. 2d 630; in Dist. Court of Appeals, 231 P. 2d 565.
5g. Gill v. Hearst Pub. Co., 239 P. 2d 636 (1952); in Dist. Court of Appeals 231 P. 2d 570.
5h. 129 F. Supp. 817.
6. Melvin v. Reid, 112 Cal. App. 285 (1931): the court held privacy was included in a human-rights clause in the state constitution.
7. Bazemore v. Savannah Hosp., 171 Ga. 257 (1930).
8. Douglas v. Stokes, 149 Ky. 506 (1912).
9. Barber v. Time Inc., 348 Mo. 1199 (1942).
10. Mau v. Rio Grande Oil Co., 28 Fed. Supp. 845 (1939).
11. Metter v. L.A. Examiner, 35 Cal. App. 2d 304 (1939).
12. Peay v. Curtis Pub. Co., 78 Fed. Supp. 305 (1948).
13. O'Brien v. Pabst Sales Co., 124 Fed. 2d 167 (1942): the court also avoided deciding that privacy was a right recognized in Texas.

14. Damron v. Doubleday, Doran & Co., 133 Misc. (N.Y.) 302 (1928).
15. Swacker v. Wright, 154 Misc. (N.Y.) 822 (1935).
16. Eliot v. Jones, 66 Misc. (N.Y.) 95 (1910), affd. 140 App. Div. (N.Y.) 911 (1910).
17. Vassar College v. Loose-Wiles, 197 Fed. 982 (1912).
18. Blumenthal v. Picture Classics, 235 App. Div. (N.Y.) 570 (1932), affd. 261 N.Y. 504 (1933).
19. Sweenek v. Pathe News Inc., 16 Fed. Supp. 746 (1936).
20. Martin v. New Metropol. Fiction Inc., 237 App. Div. (N.Y.) 863 (1932), reversing 139 Misc. (N.Y.) 290 (1931).
21. Lahiri v. Daily Mirror, 162 Misc. (N.Y.) 776 (1937).
22. D'Altomante v. N.Y. Herald, 208 N.Y. 596 (1913).
23. Rose v. Daily Mirror, 284 N.Y. 335 (1940).
24. Kerby v. Hal Roach Studios Inc., 53 Cal. App. 207; 127 P. 2d 577 (1942) District Court of Appeals, 2d District.
25. Jeffries v. N.Y. Journal, 67 Misc. (N.Y.) 570 (1910).
26. Koussevitzky v. Allen, 188 Misc. (N.Y.) 479 (1947); affirmed 272 App. Div. (N.Y.) 759 (1947).
27. Hulton & Co. v. Jones (1909), 2 K.B. 44; affd. (1910) A.C. 20 (House of Lords).
28. Clare v. Farrell, 70 Fed. Supp. 276 (1947).
29. Restatement of Law, Torts, Sec. 564 (Chapter 24).
30. Youssoupoff v. Metro-Goldwyn-Mayer, 50 Times Law Reports 581 (1934).
31. Kelly v. Loew's Inc., 76 Fed. Supp. 473 (1948).

CHAPTER IV

1. Remington v. Bentley, 88 Fed. Supp. 166 (1949).
2. Hartman v. Winchell, 296 N.Y. 296 (1947).
3. Summit Hotel Co. v. National Broadcasting Co., 336 Pa. 182 (1939).
4. Youssoupoff v. Metro-Goldwyn-Mayer Pictures Ltd., 50 Times Law Reports 581 (1934).
5. Taylor v. Hearst, 107 Cal. 262 (1895).
6. Kennedy v. Washington Post Co., 55 App. D.C. 162 (1924).
7. Farley v. Evening Chronicle Pub. Co., 113 Mo. App. 216 (1905).
8. Upton v. Times Democrat Pub. Co., 104 Louisiana 141 (1900).

CHAPTER V

1. Sack v. New York Times, 270 App. Div. (N.Y.) 401 (1946).
2. Christie v. Robertson, 10 South Wales L. R. 157; approved De Savitsch v. Patterson 159 Fed. 2d 15 (1946).
2a. In Potts v. Dies, 132 F. 2d 734 (1942) the court held that calling an author who had defended Hitler a "Nazi Trojan Horse" was not a libel, saying:
    "Criticism of a published work usually implies criticism of its author or publisher. Though his private character is no more subject to attack than another's, the qualities which he has shown by what he has published are open to such analysis and comment as an honest and intelligent man might make.
    "Appellee's language did not exceed these limits."

3. Byszko v. N.Y. American, 228 App. Div. (N.Y.) 277 (1930).
4. Burton v. Crowell Publishing Co., 82 Fed. 2d 154 (1936).
5. Cooper v. Greeley—1 Denio N.Y. 347 (1845).
6. See Prosser, Torts, pp. 790, 797. For the New York narrow ruling that "the facts showing such damage must be fully and specifically set forth in the complaint, general allegations of damage are not sufficient" (p. 358) see O'Connell v. Press Publishing Co., 214 N.Y. 352 (1915).
7. Gross v. Cantor, 270 N.Y. 93 (1936).
8. Mencher v. Chesley, 297 N.Y. 94 (1947); Spanel v. Pegler, 166 Fed. 2d 298 (1948).
9. Garriga v. Richfield, 174 Misc. (N.Y.) 315 (1940).
10. Sack v. New York Times, 270 App. Div. (N.Y.) 401 (1946).
11. O'Donnell v. Philadelphia Record Co., 356 Pa. 307 (1947); Goodrich v. Reporter Publishing Co., 199 S.W. 2d 228 (1946).
12. Tidmore v. Mills, 32 So. 2d 769 (Ala.) (1947).
13. Sanctuary v. Thackrey, 72 N.Y. Supp. 2d 104 (1947).
14. The N.Y. decision is Sweeney v. Schenectady Union Publ. Co., 122 Fed. 2d 288 (1941). Affirmed 316 U.S. 642, 86 L. Ed. 1727 (1942) by an equally divided court.
15. The Tennessee and Ohio decisions are Sweeney v. Newspaper Printing Co. 147 S.W. 2d 406 (1941); Sweeney v. Beacon Journal, 66 Ohio App. 47; 138 Ohio State 330 (1941); Sweeney v. Patterson, 128 F. 2d 457 (1942, Ohio); the same result was reached in Pennsylvania in Sweeney v. Phil. Record, 126 F. 2d 53 (1942).
16. Spector v. News Syndicate Co., 280 N.Y. 346 (1939).
17. Martin v. Press Publ. Co., 93 App. Div. (N.Y.) 531 (1904).
18. Moffatt v. Cauldwell, 3 Hun. (N.Y.) 26 (1874).
19. Eckert v. Von Pelt, 69 Kan. 357 (1904).
20. Shelby v. Sun Publishing Co., 38 Hun. (N.Y.) 474; affd. 109 N.Y. 611 (1888).
21. Summit Hotel Co. v. National Broadcasting Co., 336 Pa. 182 (1939).
22. Snyder v. New York Press Co., 137 App. Div. (N.Y.) 291 (1910).
23. Parks v. Berry, 307 Ky. 21 (1948).
24. White v. Birmingham Post, 233 Ala. 547 (1937).
25. O'Connor v. Dallas Cotton Exchange, 153 S.W. 2d 266, Texas (1941).
26. Pullman Co. v. Local 2928, 152 Fed. 2d 493 (1945).
27. Kirkman v. Westchester Newspapers, 287 N.Y. 373 (1942).
28. Kingsley v. Herald and Globe Assn., 113 Vermont 272 (1943).
29. Rouadi v. New York Evening Journal, 255 App. Div. (N.Y.) 794 (1938).
30. Adle v. Herald Co., 36 N.Y.S. 2d 905 (1942).
31. Carroll v. Paramount Pictures, 3 F.R.D. 95 (1942).
32. Paris v. New York Times Co., 170 Misc. (N.Y.) 215 (1939); affd. 259 App. Div. 1067 (1940).
33. Gaffney v. Scott Publishing Co., 212 Pac. 2d 817 (1950).
34. Metropolis Co. v. Croasdell, 199 So. 568, Fla. (1941).
35. Rathkopf v. Walker, 190 Misc. (N.Y.) 168 (1947).
36. Ingalls v. Hastings & Sons, 304 Mass. 31 (1939).
37. Westropp v. E. W. Scripps Co., 148 O.S. 365 (1947).
38. Reed v. Patriot Co., 49 Dauph. 1. (Penn. Common Pleas, 1937).
38a. Bennett v. Commercial Advertising, 230 N.Y. 125, 127 (1920).

39. Hotz v. Alton Telegraph Printing Co., 324 Ill. App. 1 (1944).
40. Costello v. Suleski, 61 D. & C. (Pa.) 572 (1946).
41. Kelly v. Loew's Inc., 76 Fed. Supp. 473 (1948).
42. Wemple v. Delano, 187 Misc. (N.Y.) 710 (1946).
43. Thackrey v. Patterson, 157 Fed. 2d 614 (1946).
44. Pridonoff v. Balokovich, 215 Pac. 2d 929 (Cal. 1950).
44a. Cyran v. Finlay-Straus Inc., 303 N.Y. — N.Y. Law Journal, July 2, 1951.
45. Mell v. Edge, 68 Ga. App. 314 (1942).
46. Brewer v. Second Baptist Church of L.A., 32 Cal. 2d 791 (1948).
47. Cook v. Mirsky, 252 App. Div. (N.Y.) 496 (1937).
48. Sullivan v. Warner Bros. Theatres, 42 Cal. App. 2d 660 (1941).
49. Berg v. Printers' Ink Co., 54 Fed. Supp. 795 (1943).
50. De Seversky v. P. & S. Publishing Inc., 34 N.Y. Supp. 2d 284 (1942).
50a. Washington Times Co. v. Bonner, 86 F. 2d 836 (1936). The holding that
    fair comment is not privilege as to untruthful facts, and as to what
    constitutes libel, by Chief Judge Stephens, is an excellent, lucid summary
    of the law today. See also Washington Hotel Co. v. Riddle, 171 F. 2d
    732 (1947).
51. Campbell v. Cunningham Natural Gas Corp., 164 Misc. (N.Y.) 1 (1937).
52. Peabody v. Barham, 52 Cal. App. 2d 581 (1942).
53. Hall v. Binghamton Press Co., 263 App. Div. (N.Y.) 403 (1942).
54. Devany v. Shulman, 184 Misc. (N.Y.) 613 (1944).
55. Cabrey v. Cameron, 55 D. & C. (Pa.) 127 (1945).
56. National Variety Artists v. Mosconi, 169 Misc. (N.Y.) 982 (1939).
57. Cardiff v. Brooklyn Eagle, 190 Misc. (N.Y.) 730 (1947).
58. Tobin v. Boston Herald Traveller Corp., 324 Mass. 478 (1949).
59. Chase v. New Mexico Publ. Co., 53 N.M. 145 (1949).
60. Waldron v. Time Inc., 83 N.Y. Supp. 2d 826 (1948).
61. National Org. Masters, Mates, etc. v. Curtis Pub. Co., 81 N.Y.S. 2d 920
    (1948).
62. Weidberg v. La Guardia, 170 Misc. (N.Y.) 374 (1939).
63. Feinstein v. Kaye, 185 Misc. 185 (1945); affirmed 269 App. Div. (N.Y.)
    1044 (1945).
64. Restatement of the Law, Torts (Div. 5, Defamation, Sec. 582) (1938).
65. Prosser on Torts, p. 805.
65a. Stevenson v. News Syndicate Inc., 302 N.Y. 81 (1951).
66. Koussevitzky v. Allen, 188 Misc. (N.Y.) 479 (1947).
67. Prosser on Torts, p. 777.

CHAPTER VI

1. Chamberlain v. Feldman, 300 N.Y. 135 (1949). Some academic sources
   have criticized the Mark Twain ruling because of the public's right to
   have *all* discovered works and letters of long-dead authors made available. Suppose a poem or story of Poe's should be uncovered tomorrow?
   Yet we recognize the rights of literary executors to suppress defective
   works of great writers. The criticism seems academic since the heirs of
   great writers long dead usually sell for publication everything they discover, and the executors of recently dead authors can be trusted to be
   sensible.
2. Pushman v. New York Graphic Society, 287 N.Y. 302 (1942).

3. Donaldson v. Becket, 4 Burr. 2407 (1774).
4. Wheaton v. Peters, 33 U.S. 591, 8 L. Ed. 1055 (1834).
5. Falsom v. Marsh, 9 Fed. Cas. 342, Case No. 4901 (1841).
6. Rice v. Williams, 32 Fed. 437 (1887).
7. Copyright Statute, Section 8.
8. Falsom v. Marsh, 9 Fed. Cas. 342, Case No. 4901 (1841).
9. Knights of Ku Klux v. Intl. Magazine, 294 Fed. 661, 664 (1923); Grigsby v. Breckenridge, 65 Kentucky 480, 488; see also, Rights in Letters, 46 Yale Law Journal 493.
10. Baker v. Libbie, 210 Mass. 599, 607, Opinion by Chief Justice Rugg.
11. See 46 Yale Law Journal 493, where the cases are collected. Ryan's Estate, 115 Misc. (N.Y.) 472 (1921). Oddly, Justice Brandeis, in his famous article on privacy (see Sec. 4, supra), in using the common law right to prevent publication of a manuscript, as a basic Anglo-Saxon precedent for the right of privacy, did not note this inviolability of manuscripts and letters from publication even in satisfaction of the writer's debts. It is a far more cogent precedent for privacy.
12. Lumiere v. Pathe Exchange, 275 Fed. 428 (1921).
13. Lumiere v. Robertson-Cole Distributing Corp., 280 Fed. 550 (1922).
13a. As noted in footnote 3a to Chapter VIII, a copy of a photograph registered with the copyright office as an unpublished work probably need not bear a copyright notice, but no decisions are extant on the point and doubts can be raised. Usually a photograph or print, when copyrighted, is copyrighted as a published work and so bears a copyright notice. Thus if a photograph bears no copyright notice, only in rare cases need fear arise that there is a copyright proprietor other than the person selling, or permitting use, of the photograph. A confirmatory statement of the seller that no copyright is outstanding might be asked as a precaution.   .
13b. If there be no likelihood of a statutory copyright, no fear need arise, as to photographs published by sale, for the common-law copyright thereby is ended. Thus if there is no evidence of a statutory copyright, no copyright problem is involved.
13c. As to copyrights on photographs, the chances of a recorded assignment of the copyright are slight because only very valuable assignments are recorded.
14. Roberts v. Petrova, 126 Misc. (N.Y.) 86 (1925); see also language of Chief Justice Hughes, Ferris v. Frohman, 223 U.S. 424; 56 L. Ed. 492, at page 496 (1911).

CHAPTER VII

1. Wheaton v. Peters, 33 U.S. 591; 8 L. Ed. 1055 (1834).
1a. The Copyright Act and the Copyright Office Regulations do not so specify; but the Copyright Office so construes the statute as per a letter to the author.
2. United Thrift Plan v. N.T. Plan, 34 Fed. 300 (1888); Sieff v. Continental Auto, 39 Fed. Supp. 683 (1941).
3. Heim v. Universal Pictures Co., 154 Fed. 2d 480 (1946).
4. Marx v. U.S., 96 Fed. 2d 204 (1938). Tams Witmark v. New Opera Co. 298 N.Y. 163, 172 (1948). Here the Court's ruling is categorical.

4a. The opinion in DeSylva v. Ballentine (100 Law Ed., p. 869, decided June 11, 1956) is typical of the method of the courts in interpreting the Copyright Statute when obscurities in legislative drafting emerge. Then the Court's ruling professedly conforms to what the Court believes Congress intended—or, as in the instant case, should have intended. Dominant here was the Court's belief (accented by the fact that the widow was not the mother of the child involved) that social considerations required division of the author's renewal right between the author's widow and his children. To reach the result desired, the Court first had to hold that the statute was ambiguous because the word "or" did not mean "or" but meant "and". Next the Court had to refute common-sense conclusion as to Congressional intent revealed by changes in the language of the statute made by Congress in 1870 and again in 1909 when Congress changed the word "and" in the statute of 1871 to "or". The Court changed it back to "and".

5. Fisher v. Witmark, 318 U.S. 643, 87 L. Ed. 1055 (1942).

6. M. Witmark v. Fred Fisher, 125 Fed. 2d 949 (1942); Fox Films v. Knowles, 261 U.S. 326; 67 L. Ed. 680 (1922).

7. See M. Witmark & Sons v. Fred Fisher, opinion of Circuit Court of Appeals, 2d Circuit, 125 Fed. 2d 949 at p. 954 (1942).

CHAPTER VIII

1. Kraft v. Cohen, 44 U.S. Patent Quarterly 678 (1940); Copyright Decisions, Bulletin 23, p. 192.

2. National Comics v. Fawcett Inc., 93 Fed. Supp. 349 (1950); Goes Lithographing Co. v. Apt Lithographic Co., 14 Fed. Supp. 620 (1936).

3. National Comics v. Fawcett Inc., 191 Fed. 2d 594, 602 (1951), reversing 93 Fed. Supp. 349 (1950).

3a. No decisions have ruled that a copyright notice is *not* required on works "of which copies are not reproduced for sale" (Sec. 12, C.S.) when copyrighted solely under the provisions of Section 12.

In Patterson v. Century Productions, 93 F. 2d 489, 493 (1937), the court expressly avoided a ruling on the point. In American Tobacco Co. v. Werckmeister, 52 L. Ed. 208, at p. 215, under the earlier statute of 1901, the United States Supreme Court held, as to an unpublished painting involved, that the copyright notice need not appear on the original but that a notice on the copies used was adequate.

The Copyright Statute contains no provision requiring such notice in Section 12; the provision of Section 19, noting "specified" works, applies evidently only to such works when published.

Thus writings (scripts, plays, etc.) copyrighted under Section 12 as unpublished works, it would seem, do not require a copyright notice. As to works of art, photographs, motion pictures, etc., copyrighted as unpublished works but exhibited to the public, more doubt arises. Construction of the statute would indicate no copyright notice is required on these when unpublished.

But no harm can come from placing a copyright notice on copies thereof not published, but exhibited, or to which the public has access. Such cautionary procedure can be recommended. Motion-picture producers uniformly use the copyright notice on their "unpublished" prints of motion pictures.

4. Heim v. Universal Pictures Co., 154 Fed. 2d 480 (1946); see opinion of Chase, J., concurring in the result.
5. Heim v. Universal Pictures Co., 154 Fed. 2d 480 (1946); opinion of Chase, J.
6. Maddux v. Grey, 43 Fed. 2d 441 (1930).
7. Washington Publishing Co. v. Pearson, 83 L. Ed. 470 (1939).
8. Such is the inference from Sec. 16 C.S. reading in part "by any other process than those above specified in this section." Also note 17 U.S.C., C.S. 201.9, Regulations of Copyright Office.
9. Houghton Mifflin v. Stackpole, 104 Fed. 2d 306 (1939).
10. 63 U.S. Statutes 153.
11. U.S. Code Service, 1949, Vol. 1, p. 158.
12. U.S. Code Service, 1949, Vol. 2, p. 1321.
12a. There are no decisions, but it is unlikely that the term of the two copyrights can be extended beyond that of one ordinary copyright, i.e. twenty-eight years plus renewal.
13. Heim v. Universal Pictures Co., 154 Fed. 2d 480 (1946).
14. Copinger and Skone James, Law of Copyright, 8th ed., p. 271.
15. Italian Book Company v. Cardilli, 273 Fed. 619 (1918).

CHAPTER IX

1a. The courts reject this provision as a definition of publication. Patterson v. Century Prod., 93 F. 2d, 489, 492 (1937). Yet it is of significance in fact.
1. Atlantic Monthly Co. v. Post Pub. Co., 27 Fed. 2d 556 (1928).
2. Ferris v. Frohman, 223 U.S. 424, 56 L. Ed. 492 (1912).
3. McCarthy v. Fischer, 259 Fed. 364 (1919).
4. National Institute Inc. v. Nutt, 28 Fed. 2d 132 (1928).
5. McCarthy v. Fischer, 259 Fed. 364 (1919).
6. Palmer v. De Witt, 47 N.Y. 532 (1872).
7. American Tobacco Co. v. Werckmeister, 207 U.S. 284; 52 L. Ed. 208 (1907).
8. Werckmeister v. Springer, 63 Fed. 808 (1894).
9. Werckmeister v. Springer, 63 Fed. 808 (1894).
10. Carns v. Keefe Bros., 242 Fed. 745 (1917).
11. Wright v. Eisle, 86 App. Div. (N.Y.) 356 (1903). The English Copyright Act protects architects' plans far more extensively than does the U.S. Statute—even as to copying buildings. Many law articles have been written favoring wider protection for United States architects. But until our Copyright Statute is amended, only copying of copyrighted plans seems prohibited.
12. DeMille v. Casey, 121 Misc. (N.Y.) 78 (1923); Patterson v. Century Productions Inc., 93 Fed. 2d 489 (1937).
13. Universal Film Co. v. Copperman, 212 Fed. 301 (1914); affirmed 218 Fed. 577 (1914).
14. American Tobacco Co. v. Werckmeister, 207 U.S. 284; 52 L. Ed. 208 (1907).

15. Uproar v. National Broadcasting Co., 8 Fed. Supp. 358 (1934).
16. Shapiro Bernstein & Co. v. Miracle Recording Co., 91 Fed. Supp. 473 (1950).

CHAPTER X

1. Guthrie v. Curlett, 36 Fed. 2d 694 (1929).
2. Holmes v. Hurst, 174 U.S. 82; 43 L. Ed. 904, 906 (1898).
3. Bleistein v. Donaldson Lithograph Co., 188 U.S. 239; 47 L. Ed. 460 (1903).
4. Eichel v. Marcin, 241 Fed. 404 (1913).
5. Universal v. Harold Lloyd, 162 Fed. 2d 354, 360 (1947).
6. 35 U.S.C. Secs. 31, 73, 40; Eichel v. Marcin, 241 Fed. 404, 410 (1913).
7. Sheldon v. Metro-Goldwyn Pictures Corp., 81 Fed. 2d 49 (1936).
8. 35 U.S.C. Sec. 36.
9. Sheldon v. Metro-Goldwyn Pictures Corp., 7 Fed. Supp. 837, 843 (1934).
10. Bosselman v. Richardson, 174 Fed. 622 (1909).
11. Sheldon v. Metro-Goldwyn Pictures Corp., 81 Fed. 2d 49, 54 (1936).
12. Nichols v. Universal Pictures Corp., 34 Fed. 2d 145 (1929); affd. 45 Fed. 2d 119 (1930).
13. Underhill v. Belasco, 254 Fed. 838 (1918).
14. Gropper v. Warner Bros. Pictures Inc., 38 Fed. Supp. 329 (1941).
15. Echevarria v. Warner Bros. Pictures Inc. et al., 12 Fed. Supp. 632 (1935).
15a. In Golding v. RKO Pictures, 208 P. 2d 1 (1949), affirming 193 F. 2d 153 (1948), the Supreme Court of California sustained a holding of piracy for copying a stock murder plot. Though the language is broad, the court's construction indicated that treatment copying by the infringer was the basis of its affirmation of the jury's verdict.
16. Nichols v. Universal, 45 Fed. 2d 119 (1930).
17. Nichols v. Universal, 45 Fed. 2d 119 (1930).
18. MacDonald v. Du Maurier, 75 Fed. Supp. 655 (1948).
19. Sheldon v. Metro-Goldwyn, 81 Fed. 2d 49 (1936).
20. Sheldon v. Metro-Goldwyn Pictures Corp., 7 Fed. Supp. 837 (1934).
21. Sheldon v. Metro-Goldwyn, 81 Fed. 2d 49 (1936).

CHAPTER XI

1. Warner Bros. Pictures v. Majestic Pictures Corp., 70 Fed. 2d 310 (1934).
2. International News Service v. Associated Press, 248 U.S. 215; 63 L. Ed. 211 (1918).
3. Chicago Record v. Tribune, 275 Fed. 797 (1921).
4. International News Service v. Associated Press, 248 U.S. 215; 63 L. Ed. 211 (1918).
5. Broder et al. v. Zeno Mauvais Music Co., 88 Fed. 74 (1898).
6. Stone & McCarrick Inc. v. Dugan Piano Co., 220 Fed. 837 (1915).
7. Triangle Publications Inc. v. New England Newspaper Pub. Co., 46 Fed. Supp. 198 (1942).
8. Baker v. Selden, 101 U.S. 99; 25 L. Ed. 841 (1879).
9. Brief English Systems Inc. v. Owen, 48 Fed. 2d 555 (1931).
10. Downes v. Culbertson, 153 Misc. (N.Y.) 14, 22 (1934).
11. Chamberlin v. Uris Sales Corp., 56 Fed. Supp. 987 (1944); affd. 150 Fed. 2d 512 (1945).

12. Seltzer et al. v. Sunbrock et al., 22 Fed. Supp. 621 (1938); see also Seltzer v. Corem 107 Fed. 2d 75 (1939).

12a. Seltzer v. Flannagan, 99 N.Y. Supp. 2d 649 (1950).

13. Whist Club v. Foster, 42 Fed. 2d 782 (1929).

14. National Cloak & Suit Co. v. Kaufman, 189 Fed. 215 (1911).

15. Bleistein v. Donaldson Lithograph Co., 188 U.S. 239; 47 L. Ed. 460 (1903).

16. White v. Lombardy Dresses, 50 U.S. Patent Quarterly 564 (1941).

17. Bloom & Hamlin v. Nixon, 125 Fed. 977 (1903).

18. Fuller v. Bemis, 50 Fed. 926 (1892); cf. Savage v. Hoffman, 159 Fed. 584 (1908).

19. Daly v. Palmer, Fed. Cas. No. 3552 (1868).

20. Universal v. Harold Lloyd, 162 Fed. 2d 354 (1947).

21. Sheldon v. Metro-Goldwyn, 81 Fed. 2d 49 (1936).

22. 39 U.S.C.A. 371.

23. Banks v. Manchester, 23 Fed. 143 (1885); Callaghan v. Myers, 128 U.S. 617; 32 L. Ed. 547 (1888).

24. Sawyer v. Crowell, 46 Fed. Supp. 471 (1942).

CHAPTER XII

1. Chapter 32, Revised Statutes of Canada, 1877.

2. 1 & 2 Geo. 5, L. 46.

3. Frances Day & Co. v. Feldman & Co. 1914, 2 Chancery 728.

4. Canadian Copyright Act, Sec. 7 and 14.

5. Canadian Copyright Act, Sec. 19.

6. Canadian Copyright Act, Sec. 37–40.

7. Canadian Copyright Act, Sec. 22.

8. Ward v. De Combaite Masq., Cop. Cas. (1936) 78; see also Copinger and Skone James, Law of Copyright, 8th Edition, page 274.

9. See the report of Senate Committee on reporting the above amendment permitting importation of 1500 copies; U.S. Code Service 1949, Vol. 2, p. 1321.

CHAPTER XIII

1. Toksvig v. Bruce Publishing Co., 181 Fed. 2d 664 (1950).

2. Story v. Holcombe, 4 McLean 306 (U.S. Circuit Court, 1847).

3. G. Ricordi v. Mason, 201 Fed. 182 (1911); affd. 210 Fed. 277 (1913).

4. Daly v. Webster, 56 Fed. 483 (1892); Daly v. Palmer, Fed. case No. 3552; 6 Blatchford 256 (1862).

5. Kalem v. Harper Bros., 222 U.S. 55; 56 L. Ed. 92, 95 (1911).

6. M. Witmark & Sons v. Pastime Amusement Co., 298 Fed. 470 (1924).

7. M. Witmark & Sons v. Pastime Amusement Co., 298 Fed. 470 (1924).

8. Hill v. Whalen & Martell, 220 Fed. 359 (1914).

9. Fuller v. Bemis, 50 Fed. 926 (1892).

10. Kalem v. Harper Bros., 222 U.S. 55; 56 L. Ed. 92, 95 (1911).

11. Kreymborg v. Jimmie Durante & N.B.C., 21 U.S. Patent Quarterly 557 (1934); 22 Idem. 248.

12. Jennings v. Stephens, 154 L.T.R. 479 (1936).

13. See Copinger and Skone James, Copyright, 8th Ed. 1948, page 153.

14. M.G.M. v. Wyatt and Maryland Yacht Club, U.S. District Court, Copyright Decisions, Bulletin 21, p. 203 (1932).

15. Herbert v. Shanley Co., 242 U.S. 591; 61 L. Ed. 511 (1917).
16. M.G.M. v. Bijou Theatre, 50 Fed. 2d 908 (1931).
17. M.G.M. v. Bijou Theatre, 3 Fed. Supp. 66 (1933); 59 Fed. 2d 70 (1932).
18. M.G.M. v. Bijou Theatre, 3 Fed. Supp. 66 (1933).
19. Bobbs Merrill Co. v. Straus, 147 Fed. 15 (1906); 210 U.S. 339; 52 L. Ed. 1086 (1908).
20. Ginn v. Apollo, 215 Fed. 772 (1914).
21. Fawcett Publications v. Elliot, 46 Fed. Supp. 717 (1942).
22. Kipling v. G. P. Putnam's Sons, 120 Fed. 631 (1903).
23. Universal v. Copperman, 212 Fed. 301 (1914).
24. U.S. v. Paramount, 334 U.S. 131; 92 L. Ed. 1260 (1948).

CHAPTER XIV

1. M. Witmark & Sons v. Pastime Amusement Co. 298 Fed. 470, 474 (1924).
2. Regulations of the Copyright Office, Sec. 202.3, so provides: "Contributions to periodicals are also registered in Class B on Form B 5."
3. Kaplan v. Fox Film, 19 Fed. Supp. 780 (1937).
4. Cunningham v. Douglas, D.C. Mass. decided April 14, 1933, unreported and expressly not followed in Kaplan v. Fox Film, see Opinion in Kaplan v. Fox Film, 19 Fed. Supp. 780, at p. 782; also on appeal of the case on another point in 72 Fed. 2d 536, at p. 537 (1934).
5. Ring v. Spina, 148 Fed. 2d 647 (1945). The later decision on appeal to the Circuit Court of Appeals, decided January 9, 1951, does not modify the earlier holding of the same court in 148 Fed. 2d 647 upholding the preliminary injunction granted under the antitrust statute. The quotation in the text is from page 651 of 148 Fed. 2d.
5a. But a license, however drawn, will not endure into the renewal term, if the author be dead at the expiration of the first twenty-eight year term, and the renewal be taken out by his widow, children, etc.
6. Manners v. Morosco, 252 U.S. 317; 64 L. Ed. 590 (1920); Frohman v. Fitch, 164 App. Div. (N.Y.) 231 (1914).
7. Klein v. Beach, 232 Fed. 240 (1916).
8. Underhill v. Schenck, 283 N.Y. 7 (1924); Frohman v. Fitch, 164 App. Div. (N.Y.) 231 (1914).
9. Norman v. Century Athletic Club (Maryland Court of Appeals), 5 Pike & Fisher Radio Reg. 2057.
10. L. C. Page & Co. Inc. v. Fox Film Corp., 83 Fed. 2d 196 (1936), citation from p. 199.
11. Herne v. Liebler, 73 App. Div. (N.Y.) 194 (1902).

CHAPTER XV

1. British Copyright Act (1911), Sec. 2 (1) i.
2. Holt v. Liggett & Myers, 23 Fed. Supp. 302, p. 304 (1938).
3. Toksvig v. Bruce Pub. Co., 181 Fed. 2d 664, p. 666 (1950).
4. Millar v. Taylor, 4 Burr. 2303 (Kings Bench 1769).
5. Copyright Office Regulations, Sec. 201.2 (d) (1).
6. Copinger and Skone James, Law of Copyright, 8th Ed. p. 138.
7. College Entrance Book Co. v. Amsco Book Co., 33 Fed. Supp. 276 (1940).
8. Id., 119 Fed. 2d 874 (1941).
9. Hill v. Whalen & Martell Inc., 220 Fed. 359, p. 360 (1914).

10. Karll v. Curtis Pub. Co., 39 Fed. Supp. 836 (1941).
11. Broadway Music Corp. v. F.R. Pub. Corp., 31 Fed. Supp. 817 (1941).
12. Shapiro v. Collier, 26 U.S. Patent Quarterly 40 (1934).
13. N.Y. Tribune v. Otis, 39 Fed. Supp. 67 (1941).
14. Toksvig v. Bruce Pub. Co., 181 Fed. 2d 664 (1950).
15. Sayers v. Sigmund Spaeth, Copyright Decision, Bulletin 20, p. 625 (1932), N.Y. District Court, Southern District.
16. Henry Holt v. Liggett, 23 Fed. Supp. 302 (1938).
17. Farmer v. Elstner, 33 Fed. 494 (1888).
18. Macmillan Co. v. King, 223 Fed. 862 (1914).
19. Bloom v. Nixon, 125 Fed. 977 (1903); Savage v. Hoffmann, 159 Fed. 584 (1908).
20. Kipling v. G. P. Putnam's Sons, 120 Fed. 631 (1903).

CHAPTER XVI

1. Herbert v. Shanley, 242 U.S. 591; 61 L. Ed. 511, 514 (1917).
2. Alden-Rochelle Inc. v. ASCAP, 80 Fed. Supp. 888 (1948); 80 Fed. Supp. 900 (1948).
3. Maurel v. Smith, 220 Fed. 195 (1915).
4. Levy v. Rutley, 24 L.T. Rept. 621 (1871).
5. Edw. B. Marks Music v. Jerry Vogel, 42 Fed. Supp. 859, 864 (1942).
6. Edw. B. Marks Music v. Jerry Vogel, 42 Fed. Supp. 859, at p. 867 (1942).
7. Nillson v. Lawrence, 148 App. Div. (N.Y.) 678 (1912); Herbert v. Fields, 152 N.Y. Supp. 487 (1915); Klein v. Beach, 232 Fed. 240 (1916).
8. Vogel Music Co. v. Miller Music Inc., 272 App. Div. (N.Y.) 571 (1947).

CHAPTER XVII

1. Circus posters were held original enough for copyrighting by Justice Holmes in Bleistein v. Donaldson Lithograph Co., 188 U.S. 293; 47 L. Ed. 460 (1903); a plumber's pamphlet showing how to install plumbing in conformity with the local code was held copyrightable in Borthwick v. Stork-Davis Company 38 U.S. Patent Quarterly 327, Copyright Bulletin 22, p. 436 (1938).
1a. See Footnote 3a to Chapter VIII.
2. Jewelers' Circular Pub. Co. v. Keystone Pub. Co., 274 Fed. 932 (1921); West Pub. Co. v. Edward Thompson Co., 176 Fed. 833 (1910).
3. Callahan v. Meyers, 128 U.S. 617; 32 L. Ed. 547 (1888) where Justice Blatchford said (p. 561, L. Ed.), "one of the most significant evidences of infringement exists frequently * * * in the copying of errors * * *."
4. Perkins Marine Lamp & Hardware Co. v. Goodwin Stanley Co., 86 Fed. Supp. 630 (1949).
5. National Cloak & Suit Co. v. Kaufman, 189 Fed. 215 (1911).
6. Wireback v. Campbell, 261 Fed. 391 (1919).
7. Richardson v. Miller, 20 Fed. Cas. p. 722, Case No. 11791 (1877).
8. Pellegrini v. Allegrini, 2 Fed. 2d 610 (1924).
9. National Comics v. Fawcett Inc., 93 Fed. Supp. 344 (1950).

CHAPTER XVIII

1. Crimi v. Rutgers Presbyterian Church, 194 Misc. (N.Y.) 570 (1949).

2. Shostakovich v. Twentieth Century Fox, 80 N.Y. Supp. 2d 575 (1948); affd. 87 N.Y. Supp. 2d 430 (1949).
3. Dreiser v. Paramount, Supreme Court, Westchester County, 1928, Copyright Decisions, Bulletin, 22, p. 106.
4. Bret Harte v. De Witte, 1 Central Law Journal 360 (1874).
5. Clemens v. Belford Clark & Company, 14 Fed. 728 (1883).
6. Ellis v. Hurst, 70 Misc. (N.Y.) 122 (1910).
7. Curwood v. Affiliated Distributors Inc., 283 Fed. 219 (1922).
8. Vargas v. Esquire, 164 Fed. 2d 522 (1947).
9. William E. Clemens v. Press Publishing Co., 67 Misc. (N.Y.) 183 (1910).
10. De Bekker v. Stokes, 168 App. Div. (N.Y.) 452 (1915).
11. Drummond v. Altemus, 60 Fed. 338 (1894).
12. Eliot v. Jones, 66 Misc. (N.Y.) 95 (1910).
13. Jones v. American Law Book Co., 125 App. Div. (N.Y.) 519 (1908).

CHAPTER XIX

1. Rule 2 of the Supreme Court of the United States, approved March 4, 1909.
2. Dieckhaus v. 20th Century Fox Film, 54 Fed. Supp. 429 (1944); reversed 153 Fed. 2d 893 (1945).
3. MacDonald v. Daphne Du Maurier, 75 Fed. Supp. 655 (1946); also Id., 75 Fed. Supp. 653 (1946).
3a. Golding v. RKO Pictures, 208 P. 2d 1 (1949), has language suggesting the contrary, but the facts indicate treatment copying.
4. Edwards & Deutsch Lithographing Co. v. Boorman et al., 15 Fed. 2d 35, p. 37 (1926).
5. Carew v. R.K.O. Radio Pictures, 43 Fed. Supp. 199, p. 200 (1942).
6. Rosen v. Loew's Inc., 162 Fed. 2d 785 (1948).
7. Arnstein v. Porter, 154 Fed. 2d 464 (1946).
8. In Millstein v. Leland Hayward, 10 Fed. Rules Decisions 198 (1950) the district judge, when a plagiarism suit was brought against the producer of *State of the Union*, allowed summary judgment, saying summary judgment was designed specifically to put a quietus on that kind of claim (p. 200).
9. Decision of Supreme Court in Douglas v. Cunningham, Copyright Decisions, Bulletin 21, p. 179 (1935).
10. Jewell-LaSalle Realty Co. v. Buck, 283 U.S. 191, 75 L. Ed. 971 (1931); Id., 283 U.S. 202; 75 L. Ed. 978 (1931).
11. Sheldon v. M.G.M., 309 U.S. 390; 84 L. Ed. 825 (1940).
12. Carew v. Melrose Music Co., 92 Fed. Supp. 971 (1950).

CHAPTER XX

1. U.S.C.A. Title 15, Sections 1051–1127.
2. Affiliated Enterprises v. Rockola, 38 U.S. Patent Quarterly 35 (1937).
3. Warner Bros. Pictures v. Majestic Pictures Corp., 70 Fed. 2d 310 (1934).
4. Charles Chaplin v. Amador, 93 Cal. App. 358 (1928).
5. Paramore v. Mack Sennett, 9 Fed. 2d 66 (1925).
6. Hopkins Amusement Co. v. Frohman, 202 Ill. 541 (1903).
7. Social Register Assn. v. Howard, 60 Fed. 270 (1894).

8. Collier v. Jones, 120 N.Y. Supp. 991 (1910).
9. Patten v. Superior Talking Pictures Inc., 8 Fed. Supp. 196 (1934).
10. Pocket Books Inc. v. Meyers, 265 App. Div. (N.Y.) 17; reversed Id., 292 N.Y. 58 (1944); quotes from p. 63 of 292 N.Y.
11. Academy of Motion Picture Arts & Sciences v. Benson, 104 Pac. 2d 630 (1940).
12. Prouty v. N.B.C., 29 Trade Mark Reporter, 136; Copyright Decisions, Bulletin No. 22, p. 213 (1939).
13. Hemingway v. Film Alliance of the U.S., 46 U.S. Patent Quarterly 568; Copyright Decisions, Bulletin No. 23, p. 165 (1940).
14. Fisher v. Star Co., 231 N.Y. 414 (1921).
15. Navy Club of U.S.A. v. All-Navy Club of U.S.A., 85 Fed. Supp. 679 (1949).
16. Stone v. Marcus Loew Booking Agency, 63 N.Y. Supp. 2d 220 (1946).
17. Becker v. Loew's Inc., 133 Fed. 2d 889 (1943).
18. Tiffany & Co. v. Tiffany Productions, Inc., 147 Misc. 679 (N.Y.) (1932); affd. without opinion, Court of Appeals, 262 N.Y. 482 (1933).
19. Bulova Watch Co. v. Stolzberg; 69 Fed. Supp. 543 (1947).
20. Wall v. Rolls-Royce of America, 4 Fed. 2d 333 (1925).
21. Yale Electric Corporation v. Robertson, 26 Fed. 2d 972 (1928).
22. L. E. Waterman & Co. v. Gordon, 72 Fed. 2d 272 (1934).
23. Standard Brands Inc. v. Smidler, 151 Fed. 2d 34 (1945).
24. Armstrong Paint & Varnish Works v. Nu-Enamel Corp., 305 U.S. 315 (1938).
25. N.Y. World's Fair 1939 v. World's Fair News Inc., 46 U.S. Patent Quarterly 243 (1939).
26. Stork Restaurant Inc. v. Sahati, 166 Fed. 2d 348 (1948).
27. Oxford Book Co. v. College Entrance Book Co. Inc., 39 U.S. Patent Quarterly 7 (1938).
28. Fawcett Publications v. Elliott, 46 Fed. Supp. 717 (1942).
29. Atlas Mfg. Co. v. Street & Smith, 204 Fed. 398 (1913).
30. Dougherty's Sons Inc. v. Dougherty, 36 Fed. Supp. 149 (1940).
31. Gotham Music Service Inc. v. Denton & Haskins, 259 N.Y. 86 (1932).

CHAPTER XXI

1. International News Service v. Associated Press, 248 U.S. 215; 63 L. Ed. 211, p. 221 (1918).
2. See dissenting opinion of Judge Frank in Triangle Publications Inc. v. Rohrlich, 167 Fed. 2d 969 (1948).
3. Cheney Bros. v. Doris Silk Corp., 35 Fed. 2d 279, p. 280 (1929).
4. Erie v. Tompkins, 304 U.S. 64; 82 L. Ed. 1188 (1938).
5. Madison Square Garden Corp. v. Universal Pictures Co. Inc., 255 App. Div. (N.Y.) 459 (1938).
6. Triangle Publications Inc. v. Rohrlich, 167 Fed. 2d 969 (1948).
7. Vogue Co. v. Thompson Hudson Co., 300 Fed. 509 (1904).
8. Hanson v. Triangle Publications Inc., 163 Fed. 2d 74 (1947).
9. Fred Waring v. WDAS Broadcasting Station, 327 Pa. 433 (1937).
10. R.C.A. Manufacturing Co. v. Whiteman, 114 Fed. 2d 86 (1940).
11. Waring v. Dunlea, 26 Fed. Supp. 338 (1939).

12. Ray Noble v. 160 Commonwealth Avenue Inc., 19 Fed. Supp. 671 (1937).

12a. Trade-name protection of periodicals, magazines, and newspapers is subject to the same rules specified as to "goods" generally, under Section 1051, Title 15, U.S.C.A. (the Lanham Trade-Mark Act). New Metropolitan Fiction Co. v. Dell Publishing Co., 19 Fed. 2d 718 (1927). If a "coined", i.e. an arbitrary, fanciful name, be used, that name may be registered as a trade name. Since most periodicals use common names, or combinations thereof, trademark registration cannot be had and a secondary meaning must be shown to be attached, and relief sought under the theory of unfair competition.

13. Dale v. Ultem Publications Inc., Copyright Decisions, Copyright Office, Vol. 23, p. 108.

14. Warner Publications v. Popular Publications, 87 Fed. 2d 913 (1937).

15. McGraw-Hill v. American Aviation Associates Inc., 117 Fed. 2d 293 (1940).

16. Advance Music Co. v. American Tobacco Co., 296 N.Y. 79 (1946); Advance Music Co. v. American Tobacco Co., 268 App. Div. 707 (1945); Advance Music Co. v. American Tobacco Co., 183 Misc. 855 (1944); Remick Music Corporation v. American Tobacco Co., 57 Fed. Supp. 475 (1944).

17. Remick Music Corp. v. American Tobacco Co., 57 Fed. Supp. 475 (1944).

18. Marlin v. Shields, 171 N.Y. 384 (1902).

CHAPTER XXII

1. Helen Jenkins v. News Syndicate, 128 Misc. (N.Y.) 284 (1926).

2. Thompson v. Famous-Players Lasky Co., 3 Fed. 2d 707 (1925).

3. Ketcham v. New York World's Fair, 34 Fed. Supp. 657 (1940).

4. Schonwald v. Burkhart Mfg. Co., 356 Mo. 435 (1947).

5. Stanley v. C.B.S., 208 Pac. 2d 9 (1949).

6. Bowen v. Yankee Network, 46 Fed. Supp. 62 (1942).

7. Bristol v. The Equitable Life Assurance Society, 132 N.Y. 264 (1892).

8. Rodrigues v. Western Union Telegraph Co., 259 App. Div. (N.Y.) 224 (1941).

9. Williamson v. New York Central R.R. Co., 258 App. Div. (N.Y.) 226 (1939).

10. Singer v. Karron, 162 Misc. (N.Y.) 809 (1937).

11. Alberts v. Remington Rand, 175 Misc. (N.Y.) 486 (1940).

12. Lueddecke v. Chevrolet Motor Co., 70 Fed. 2d 345 (1934); see also Moore v. Ford Motor Co., 28 Fed. 2d 529 (1928).

13. Tutleman v. Stokowski, 44 U.S. Patent Quarterly 47 (1939); Copyright Decisions, Bulletin No. 23, p. 325.

CHAPTER XXIII

1. Cain v. Universal Pictures, 47 Fed. Supp. 1013 (1942).

2. Title 18, U.S.C.A. (1948), Chap. 71, Sections 1461 to 1464.

3. Title 18, U.S.C.A. (1948), Sec. 1461.

4. Title 18, U.S.C.A. (1948), Sec. 1462.

5. Title 18, U.S.C.A. (1948), Sec. 1463.

6. Title 18, U.S.C.A. (1948), Sec. 1464.

7. Title 19, U.S.C.A. (1948), Sec. 1305-A.

7a. Swearingen v. U.S., 161 U.S. 446; 40 L. Ed. 765 (1896).

8. Parmelee v. U.S., 113 Fed. 2d 729 (1940).

9. Regina v. Hicklin, L.R. 3 Q.B. 360 (1868).

10. Parmelee v. U.S., 113 Fed. 2d 729 (1940).

10a. U.S. v. Two Obscene Books, 99 Fed. Supp. 760 (D.C. Cal. 1951).

11. U.S. v. Levine, 83 Fed. 2d 156 (1936).

12. Parmelee v. U.S., 113 Fed. 2d 729 (1940).

13. U.S. v. One Book Entitled Ulysses, 72 Fed. 2d 705 (1934).

14. U.S. v. One Book Called Ulysses, 5 Fed. Supp. 182 (1933).

15. U.S. v. One Obscene Book Entitled "Married Love", 48 Fed. 2d 821 (1931).

16. U.S. v. Dennett, 39 Fed. 2d 564 (1930).

17. U.S. v. Rebhuhn, 109 Fed. 2d 512 (1940).

18. Roth v. Goldman, 172 Fed. 2d 788 (1949).

19. (1) 343 U.S. 495; (2) 343 U.S. 900; (3) 346 U.S. 587.

19a. In re Port Huron Broadcasting Co., 4 Pike & Fischer Radio Regulations 1 (1948).

19b. KFAB Broadcasting Co. v. Sorenson, 123 Neb. 348; appeal dismissed 290 U.S. 599, 78 L. Ed. 527 (1933), because a non-Federal question permitted sustaining the State Supreme Court. In Felix v. Westinghouse, 89 F. Supp. 740 (1950), the lower court held that a libelous statement by the manager of a candidate, uttered over the radio, could not be the basis of a suit against the broadcasting station in Pennsylvania because under the law of that state absolute liability is modified to require fault (see Sec. 22 supra) and the Federal Communications Statute had denied the station the right to censor. The Appellate Court reversed (186 F. 2d 1, 1950), holding that the Federal statute forbade censorship only as to political speeches by candidates, not by a manager of a candidate, as here was the case, and the station was at fault for not censoring the manager's speech.

20. N.Y. Penal Law, Sec. 1141, Subdivision 1 as amended, Laws, 1950, Chapter 624.

21. People v. Wendling, 258 N.Y. 451, p. 454 (1932); Penal Law (N.Y.) Section 1141, covers general literary works; Section 1140A thereof, here construed by the Court of Appeals, covers plays.

22. People v. Eastman, 188 N.Y. 478 (1907), construing Penal Law (N.Y.) Section 1141.

23. People v. Creative Age Press, 192 Misc. (N.Y.) 188 (1948).

24. People v. Vanguard Press, 192 Misc. (N.Y.) 127 (1947).

25. People v. Dial Press, 182 Misc. (N.Y.) 416 (1944).

26. Halsey v. N.Y. Society for Suppression of Vice, 234 N.Y. 1 (1922).

27. People v. Pesky, 230 App. Div. (N.Y.) 200 (1930).

28. People v. Friede, 133 Misc. (N.Y.) 611 (1929).

29. People v. Gotham Book Mart, 158 Misc. (N.Y.) 240 (1936).

30. People v. Brainard, 192 App. Div. (N.Y.) 816 (1920).

31. People v. Vanguard Press, 192 Misc. (N.Y.) 127 (1947).

32. Mutual Film Corp. v. Industrial Commission of Ohio, 236 U.S. 230; 59 L. Ed. 552 (1915).

33. Winters v. N.Y., 333 U.S. 507; 92 L. Ed. 840 (1947).
34. See dissenting opinion of Mr. Justice Frankfurter in Winters v. N.Y., 92 L. Ed. 840; 333 U.S. 507 (1947); 92 L. Ed. 840 at p. 853.
35. See People v. Doubleday & Co., 297 N.Y. 687 at p. 688 (1947).
36. People v. Doubleday & Co., 272 App. Div. 799 (1947).
37. People v. Doubleday & Co., 297 N.Y. 687 (1947).
38. Doubleday & Co. v. People of N.Y., 335 U.S. 848; 93 L. Ed. 398 (1948).
39. Near v. Minnesota, 283 U.S. 697; 75 L. Ed. 1357 (1931).

CHAPTER XXIV

1. Dieckhaus v. 20th Century Fox Film, 54 Fed. Supp. 429 (1944); reversed 153 Fed. 2d 893 (1945).
2. Fendler v. Morosco, 253 N.Y. 281 (1930).
3. Sherman Antitrust Statute, 15 U.S.C.A. Sec. 1 and 2; Ring v. Spina, 84 Fed. Supp. 403 (1945); affirmed, 148 Fed. 2d 647 (1945); see note 5 to Chapter XIV.
4. Bobbs Merrill v. Straus, 52 L. Ed. 1086.
5. Title 26, U.S.C.A., Sec. 210 as amended in 1950.
6. Goldsmith v. Commissioner, 143 Fed. 2d 466 (1944).
7. Sabatini v. Commissioner, 98 Fed. 2d 753 (1938).
8. Fox Film v. Doyal, 286 U.S. 123, 76 L. Ed. 1010 (1932).
9. Title 26, U.S.C.A., Sec. 107(b).

CHAPTER XXV

1. Title 18, U.S.C.A. Crimes & Criminal Procedure, Sec. 1464.
2. Title 47, U.S.C.A., Section 151.
3. Gautier v. Pro Football, 99 N.Y. Supp. 812, reversed App. Div. June 29, 1951, now on appeal to the Court of Appeals.
4. Rudolph Mayer Inc. v. Pathe News, 235 App. Div. (N.Y.) 774 (1932).
5. 20th Century Sporting Club Inc. v. Transradio Press Service, 165 Misc. 71 (1937).
6. National Exhibition Co. v. Teleflash Inc., 24 Fed. Supp. 488 (1936).
7. Pittsburgh Athletic Co. v. KQV Broadcasting Co. 24 Fed. Supp. 490 (1938). See also, Metropolitan Opera Co. v. Wagner-Nichols, 199 Misc. (N.Y.) 786, affirmed without opinion, Appellate Division, November 9, 1951, a discursive opinion enjoining the sale of unauthorized phonograph records made from recordings of broadcasts of Metropolitan performances. The result is in accord with the views in the text. But see Crown Pub. Inc. v. McKay, 107 N.Y.S. 2d 176 (1951) holding that the word "confidential" in the title of a book on baseball could not be enjoined as unfair competition by a publisher of "confidential" city-crime titles.
8. Penn. Sportservice v. Goldstein, D.C. W. D. Penn Copyright Decisions, Bulletin No. 23, p. 231 (1940).
9. Remington v. Bentley, 88 Fed. Supp. 166 (1949).
10. Marx v. United States, 96 Fed. 2d 204 (1938).
10a. See Footnote 3a to Chapter VIII.

Appendix B—The Copyright Statute

The Copyright Statute (Title 17 U.S.C.A.), before current amendments, is photographically reproduced as pages 323–342 of this book. Current amendments are also photographically reproduced on pages 343–348 as follows:

Copyright Law

OF THE UNITED STATES OF AMERICA

United States Code

Title 17—Copyrights[1]

CHAPTER 1—Registration of Copyrights

---

[1] Act of July 30, 1947 (61 Stat. 652). The enacting clause provides that Title 17 of the United States Code entitled "Copyrights" is codified and enacted into positive law and may be cited as "Title 17, U. S. C., § —". The Act of April 27, 1948 (62 Stat. 202) amended sections 211 and 215. The Act of June 25, 1948 (62 Stat. 869) repealed sections 101 (f), 102, 103, 110 and 111. The Act of June 3, 1949 (63 Stat. 153) amended sections 16, 22, 23 and 215.

§ 1. EXCLUSIVE RIGHTS AS TO COPYRIGHTED WORKS.—Any person entitled thereto, upon complying with the provisions of this title, shall have the exclusive right:

(a) To print, reprint, publish, copy, and vend the copyrighted work;

(b) To translate the copyrighted work into other languages or dialects, or make any other version thereof, if it be a literary work; to dramatize it if it be a nondramatic work; to convert it into a novel or other nondramatic work if it be a drama; to arrange or adapt it if it be a musical work; to complete, execute, and finish it if it be a model or design for a work of art;

AMENDED

(d) To perform or represent the copyrighted work publicly if it be a drama or, if it be a dramatic work and not reproduced in copies for sale, to vend any manuscript or any record whatsoever thereof; to make or to procure the making of any transcription or record thereof by or from which, in whole or in part, it may in any manner or by any method be exhibited, performed, represented, produced, or reproduced; and to exhibit, perform, represent, produce, or reproduce it in any manner or by any method whatsoever; and

(e) To perform the copyrighted work publicly for profit if it be a musical composition; and for the purpose of public performance for profit, and for the purposes set forth in subsection (a) hereof, to make any arrangement or setting of it or of the melody of it in any system of notation or any form of record in which the thought of an author may be recorded and from which it may be read or reproduced: *Provided*, That the provisions of this title, so far as they secure copyright controlling the parts of instruments serving to reproduce mechanically the musical work, shall include only compositions published and copyrighted after July 1, 1909, and shall not include the works of a foreign author or composer unless the foreign state or nation of which such author or composer is a citizen or subject grants, either by treaty, convention, agreement, or law, to citizens of the United States similar rights. And as a condition of extending the copyright control to such mechanical reproductions, that whenever the owner of a musical copyright has used or permitted or knowingly acquiesced in the use of the copyrighted work upon the parts of instruments serving to reproduce mechanically the musical work, any other person may make similar use-of the copyrighted work upon the payment to the copyright proprietor of a royalty of 2 cents on each such part manufactured, to be paid by the manufacturer thereof; and the copyright proprietor may require, and if so the manufacturer shall furnish, a report under oath on the 20th day of each month on the number of parts of instruments manufactured during the previous month serving to reproduce mechanically said musical work, and royalties shall be due on the parts manufactured during any month upon the 20th of the next succeeding month. The payment of the royalty provided for by this section shall free the articles or devices for which such royalty has been paid from further contribution to the copyright except in case of public performance for profit. It shall be the duty of the copyright owner, if he uses the musical composition himself for the manufacture of parts of instruments serving to reproduce mechanically the musical work, or licenses others to do so, to file notice thereof, accompanied by a recording fee, in the copyright office, and any failure to file such notice shall be a complete defense to any suit, action, or proceeding for any infringement of such copyright.

In case of failure of such manufacturer to pay to the copyright proprietor within thirty days after demand in writing the full sum of royalties due at said rate at the date of such demand, the court may award taxable costs to the plaintiff and a reasonable counsel fee, and the court may, in its discretion, enter judgment therein for any sum in addition over the amount found to be due as royalty in accordance with the terms of this title, not exceeding three times such amount.

The reproduction or rendition of a musical composition by or upon coin-operated machines shall not be deemed a public performance for profit unless a fee is charged for admission to the place where such reproduction or rendition occurs.

§ 2. RIGHTS OF AUTHOR OR PROPRIETOR OF UNPUBLISHED WORK.— Nothing in this title shall be construed to annul or limit the right of the author or proprietor of an unpublished work, at common law or in equity, to prevent the copying, publication, or use of such unpublished work without his consent, and to obtain damages therefor.

§ 3. PROTECTION OF COMPONENT PARTS OF WORK COPYRIGHTED; COMPOSITE WORKS OR PERIODICALS.—The copyright provided by this tile [2] shall protect all the copyrightable component parts of the work copyrighted, and all matter therein in which copyright is already subsisting, but without extending the duration or scope of such copyright. The copyright upon composite works or periodicals shall give to the proprietor thereof all the rights in respect thereto which he would have if each part were individually copyrighted under this title.

§ 4. ALL WRITINGS OF AUTHOR INCLUDED.—The works for which copyright may be secured under this title shall include all the writings of an author.

§ 5. CLASSIFICATION OF WORKS FOR REGISTRATION.—The application for registration shall specify to which of the following classes the work in which copyright is claimed belongs:

(a) Books, including composite and cyclopedic works, directories, gazetteers, and other compilations.

(b) Periodicals, including newspapers.

(c) Lectures, sermons, addresses (prepared for oral delivery).

(d) Dramatic or dramatico-musical compositions.

(e) Musical compositions.

(f) Maps.

(g) Works of art; models or designs for works of art.

(h) Reproductions of a work of art.

(i) Drawings or plastic works of a scientific or technical character.

(j) Photographs.

(k) Prints and pictorial illustrations including prints or labels used for articles of merchandise.

(l) Motion-picture photoplays.

(m) Motion pictures other than photoplays.

The above specifications shall not be held to limit the subject matter of copyright as defined in section 4 of this title, nor shall any error in classification invalidate or impair the copyright protection secured under this title.

§ 6. REGISTRATION OF PRINTS AND LABELS.—Commencing July 1, 1940, the Register of Copyrights is charged with the registration of claims to copyright properly presented, in all prints and labels published in connection with the sale or advertisement of articles of merchandise, including all claims to copyright in prints and labels pending in the Patent Office and uncleared at the close of business June 30, 1940. There shall be paid for registering a claim of copyright in any such print or label not a trade-mark $6, which sum shall cover the expense of furnishing a certificate of such registration, under the seal of the Copyright Office, to the claimant of copyright.

---

[2] So in original. Probably should read "title".

§ 7. COPYRIGHT ON COMPILATIONS OF WORKS IN PUBLIC DOMAIN OR OF COPYRIGHTED WORKS; SUBSISTING COPYRIGHTS NOT AFFECTED.— Compilations or abridgments, adaptations, arrangements, dramatizations, translations, or other versions of works in the public domain or of copyrighted works when produced with the consent of the proprietor of the copyright in such works, or works republished with new matter, shall be regarded as new works subject to copyright under the provisions of this title; but the publication of any such new works shall not affect the force or validity of any subsisting copyright upon the matter employed or any part thereof, or be construed to imply an exclusive right to such use of the original works, or to secure or extend copyright in such original works.

§ 8. COPYRIGHT NOT TO SUBSIST IN WORKS IN PUBLIC DOMAIN, OR PUBLISHED PRIOR TO JULY 1, 1909, AND NOT ALREADY COPYRIGHTED, OR GOVERNMENT PUBLICATIONS; PUBLICATION BY GOVERNMENT OF COPYRIGHTED MATERIAL.— No copyright shall subsist in the original text of any work which is in the public domain, or in any work which was published in this country or any foreign country prior to July 1, 1909, and has not been already copyrighted in the United States, or in any publication of the United States Government, or any reprint, in whole or in part, thereof: *Provided*, That copyright may be secured by the Postmaster General on behalf of the United States in the whole or any part of the publications authorized by section 1 of the Act of June ³ 27, 1938 (39 U. S. C. 371).

The publication or republication by the Government, either separately or in a public document, of any material in which copyright is subsisting shall not be taken to cause any abridgment or annulment of the copyright or to authorize any use or appropriation of such copyright material without the consent of the copyright proprietor.

§ 9. AUTHORS OR PROPRIETORS, ENTITLED; ALIENS.— The author or

AMENDED

§ 10. PUBLICATION OF WORK WITH NOTICE.— Any person entitled thereto by this title may secure copyright for his work by publication thereof with the notice of copyright required by this title; and such notice shall be affixed to each copy thereof published or offered for sale in the United States by authority of the copyright proprietor, except in the case of books seeking ad interim protection under section § 2 of this title.

§ 11. REGISTRATION OF CLAIM AND ISSUANCE OF CERTIFICATE.— Such person may obtain registration of his claim to copyright by complying with the provisions of this title, including the deposit of copies, and upon such compliance the Register of Copyrights shall issue to him the certificates provided for in section 209 of this title.

§ 12. Works Not Reproduced for Sale.—Copyright may also be had of the works of an author, of which copies are not reproduced for sale, by the deposit, with claim of copyright, of one complete copy of such work if it be a lecture or similar production or a dramatic, musical, or dramatico-musical composition; of a title and description, with one print taken from each scene or act, if the work be a motion-picture photoplay; of a photographic print if the work be a photograph; of a title and description, with not less than two prints taken from different sections of a complete motion picture, if the work be a motion picture other than a photoplay; or of a photograph or other identifying reproduction thereof, if it be a work of art or a plastic work or drawing. But the privilege of registration of copyright secured hereunder shall not exempt the copyright proprietor from the deposit of copies, under sections 13 and 14 of this title, where the work is later reproduced in copies for sale.

§ 13. Deposit of Copies After Publication; Action or Proceeding for Infringement.

AMENDED

§ 14. Same; Failure to Deposit; Demand; Penalty.—Should the copies called for by section 13 of this title not be promptly deposited as provided in this title, the Register of Copyrights may at any time after the publication of the work, upon actual notice, require the proprietor of the copyright to deposit them, and after the said demand shall have been made, in default of the deposit of copies of the work within three months from any part of the United States, except an outlying territorial possession of the United States, or within six months from any outlying territorial possession of the United States, or from any foreign country, the proprietor of the copyright shall be liable to a fine of $100 and to pay to the Library of Congress twice the amount of the retail price of the best edition of the work, and the copyright shall become void.

§ 15. SAME; POSTMASTER'S RECEIPT; TRANSMISSION BY MAIL WITHOUT COST.—The postmaster to whom are delivered the articles deposited as provided in sections 12 and 13 of this title shall, if requested, give a receipt therefor and shall mail them to their destination without cost to the copyright claimant.

§ 16. MECHANICAL WORK TO BE DONE IN UNITED STATES.

AMENDED

§ 17. AFFIDAVIT TO ACCOMPANY COPIES.—In the case of the book the copies so deposited shall be accompanied by an affidavit under the official seal of any officer authorized to administer oaths within the United States, duly made by the person claiming copyright or by his duly authorized agent or representative residing in the United States, or by the printer who has printed the book, setting forth that the copies deposited have been printed from type set within the limits of the United States or from plates made within the limits of the United States from type set therein; or, if the text be produced by lithographic process, or photoengraving process, that such process was wholly performed within the limits of the United States and that the printing of the text and binding of the said book have also been performed within the limits of the United States. Such affidavit shall state also the place where and the establishment or establishments in which such type was set or plates were made or lithographic process, or photoengraving process or printing and binding were performed and the date of the completion of the printing of the book or the date of publication.

§ 18. MAKING FALSE AFFIDAVIT.—Any person who, for the purpose of obtaining registration of a claim to copyright, shall knowingly make a false affidavit as to his having complied with the above conditions shall be deemed guilty of a misdemeanor, and upon conviction thereof shall be punished by a fine of not more than $1,000, and all of his rights and privileges under said copyright shall thereafter be forfeited.

§ 19. NOTICE; FORM.

AMENDED

[AMENDED]

§ 20. SAME; PLACE OF APPLICATION OF; ONE NOTICE IN EACH VOLUME OR NUMBER OF NEWSPAPER OR PERIODICAL.—The notice of copyright shall be applied, in the case of a book or other printed publication, upon its title page or the page immediately following, or if a periodical either upon the title page or upon the first page of text of each separate number or under the title heading, or if a musical work either upon its title page or the first page of music. One notice of copyright in each volume or in each number of a newspaper or periodical published shall suffice.

§ 21. SAME; EFFECT OF ACCIDENTAL OMISSION FROM COPY OR COPIES.—Where the copyright proprietor has sought to comply with the provisions of this title with respect to notice, the omission by accident or mistake of the prescribed notice from a particular copy or copies shall not invalidate the copyright or prevent recovery for infringement against any person who, after actual notice of the copyright, begins an undertaking to infringe it, but shall prevent the recovery of damages against an innocent infringer who has been misled by the omission of the notice; and in a suit for infringement no permanent injunction shall be had unless the copyright proprietor shall reimburse to the innocent infringer his reasonable outlay innocently incurred if the court, in its discretion, shall so direct.

§ 22. AD INTERIM PROTECTION OF BOOK OR PERIODICAL PUBLISHED ABROAD.[5]—In the case of a book or periodical first published abroad in the English language, the deposit in the Copyright Office, not later than six months after its publication abroad, of one complete copy of the foreign edition, with a request for the reservation of the copyright and a statement of the name and nationality of the author and of the copyright proprietor and of the date of publication of the said book or periodical, shall secure to the author or proprietor an ad interim copyright therein, which shall have all the force and effect given to copyright by this title, and shall endure until the expiration of five years after the date of first publication abroad.

§ 23. SAME; EXTENSION TO FULL TERM.[5]—Whenever within the period of such ad interim protection an authorized edition of such books or periodicals shall be published within the United States, in accordance with the manufacturing provisions specified in section 16 of this title, and whenever the provisions of this title as to deposit of copies, registration, filing of affidavits, and the printing of the copyright notice shall have been duly complied with, the copyright shall be extended to endure in such book or periodical for the term provided in this title.

---

[5] Sections 22 and 23 as amended by the Act of June 3, 1949 (63 Stat. 153).

§ 24. DURATION; RENEWAL AND EXTENSION.—The copyright secured by this title shall endure for twenty-eight years from the date of first publication, whether the copyrighted work bears the author's true name or is published anonymously or under an assumed name: *Provided*, That in the case of any posthumous work or of any periodical, cyclopedic, or other composite work upon which the copyright was originally secured by the proprietor thereof, or of any work copyrighted by a corporate body (otherwise than as assignee or licensee of the individual author) or by an employer for whom such work is made for hire, the proprietor of such copyright shall be entitled to a renewal and extension of the copyright in such work for the further term of twenty-eight years when application for such renewal and extension shall have been made to the copyright office and duly registered therein within one year prior to the expiration of the original term of copyright: *And provided further*, That in the case of any other copyrighted work, including a contribution by an individual author to a periodical or to a cyclopedic or other composite work, the author of such work, if still living, or the widow, widower, or children of the author, if the author be not living, or if such author, widow, widower, or children, be not living, then the author's executors, or in the absence of a will, his next of kin shall be entitled to a renewal and. extension of the copyright in such work for a further term of twenty-eight years when application for such renewal and extension shall have been made to the copyright office and duly registered therein within one year prior to the expiration of the original term of copyright: *And provided further*, That in default of the registration of such application for renewal and extension, the copyright in any work shall determine at the expiration of twenty-eight years from first publication.

§ 25. RENEWAL OF COPYRIGHTS REGISTERED IN PATENT OFFICE UNDER REPEALED LAW.—Subsisting copyrights originally registered in the Patent Office prior to July 1, 1940, under section 3 of the act of June 18, 1874, shall be subject to renewal in behalf of the proprietor upon application made to the Register of Copyrights within one year prior to the expiration of the original term of twenty-eight years.

§ 26. TERMS DEFINED.—In the interpretation and construction of this title "the date of publication" shall in the case of a work of which copies are reproduced for sale or distribution be held to be the earliest date when copies of the first authorized edition were placed on sale, sold, or publicly distributed by the proprietor of the copyright or under his authority, and the word "author" shall include an employer in the case of works made for hire.

§ 27. COPYRIGHT DISTINCT FROM PROPERTY IN OBJECT COPYRIGHTED; EFFECT OF SALE OF OBJECT, AND OF ASSIGNMENT OF COPYRIGHT.—The copyright is distinct from the property in the material object copyrighted, and the sale or conveyance, by gift or otherwise, of the material object shall not of itself constitute a transfer of the copyright, nor shall the assignment of the copyright constitute a transfer of the title to the material object; but nothing in this title shall be deemed to forbid, prevent, or restrict the transfer of any copy of a copyrighted work the possession of which has been lawfully obtained.

§ 28. ASSIGNMENTS AND BEQUESTS.—Copyright secured under this title or previous copyright laws of the United States may be assigned, granted, or mortgaged by an instrument in writing signed by the proprietor of the copyright, or may be bequeathed by will.

§ 29. SAME; EXECUTED IN FOREIGN COUNTRY; ACKNOWLEDGMENT AND CERTIFICATE.—Every assignment of copyright executed in a foreign country shall be acknowledged by the assignor before a consular officer or secretary of legation of the United States authorized by law to administer oaths or perform notarial acts. The certificate of such acknowledgment under the hand and official seal of such consular officer or secretary of legation shall be prima facie evidence of the execution of the instrument.

§ 30. SAME; RECORD.—Every assignment of copyright shall be recorded in the copyright office within three calendar months after its execution in the United States or within six calendar months after its execution without the limits of the United States, in default of which it shall be void as against any subsequent purchaser or mortgagee for a valuable consideration, without notice, whose assignment has been duly recorded.

§ 31. SAME; CERTIFICATE OF RECORD.—The Register of Copyrights shall, upon payment of the prescribed fee, record such assignment, and shall return it to the sender with a certificate of record attached under seal of the copyright office, and upon the payment of the fee prescribed by this title he shall furnish to any person requesting the same a certified copy thereof under the said seal.

§ 32. SAME; USE OF NAME OF ASSIGNEE IN NOTICE.—When an assignment of the copyright in a specified book or other work has been recorded the assignee may substitute his name for that of the assignor in the statutory notice of copyright prescribed by this title.

CHAPTER 2—Infringement Proceedings

§ 101. Infringement:
>   (a) Injunction.
>   (b) Damages and profits; amounts; other remedies.
>   (c) Impounding during action.
>   (d) Destruction of infringing copies and plates.
>   (e) Royalties for use of mechanical reproduction of musical works.
>   (f) Rules of procedure. [*REPEALED*]

§ 102. Jurisdiction of courts in enforcing remedies. [*REPEALED*]

§ 103. Joinder of proceedings for different remedies. [*REPEALED*]

§ 104. Willful infringement for profit.

§ 105. Fraudulent notice of copyright, or removal or alteration of notice.

§ 106. Importation of article bearing false notice or piratical copies of copyrighted work.

§ 107. Importation, during existence of copyright, of piratical copies, or of copies not produced in accordance with section 16 of this title.

§ 108. Forfeiture and destruction of articles prohibited importation.

§ 109. Importation of prohibited articles; regulations; proof of deposit of copies by complainants.

§ 110. Jurisdiction of actions under laws. [*REPEALED*]

§ 111. District in which actions may be brought. [*REPEALED*]

§ 112. Injunctions; service and enforcement.

§ 113. Transmission of certified copies of papers for enforcement of injunction by other court.

§ 114. Review of orders, judgments, or decrees.

§ 115. Limitation of criminal proceedings.

§ 116. Costs; attorney's fees.

§ 101. INFRINGEMENT.—If any person shall infringe the copyright in any work protected under the copyright laws of the United States such person shall be liable:

(a) INJUNCTION.—To an injunction restraining such infringement;

(b) DAMAGES AND PROFITS; AMOUNT; OTHER REMEDIES.—To pay to the copyright proprietor such damages as the copyright proprietor may have suffered due to the infringement, as well as all the profits which the infringer shall have made from such infringement, and in proving profits the plaintiff shall be required to prove sales only, and the defendant shall be required to prove every element of cost which he claims, or in lieu of actual damages and profits, such damages as to the court shall appear to be just, and in assessing such damages the court may, in its discretion, allow the amounts as hereinafter stated, but in case of a newspaper reproduction of a copyrighted photograph, such damages shall not exceed the sum of $200 nor be less than the sum of $50, and in the case of the infringement of an undramatized or nondramatic work by means of motion pictures, where the infringer shall show that he was not aware that he was infringing, and that such infringement could not have been reasonably foreseen, such damages shall not exceed the sum of $100; and in the case of an infringement of a copyrighted dramatic or dramatico-musical work by a maker of motion pictures and his agencies for distribution thereof to exhibitors, where such infringer shows that he was not aware that he was infringing a copyrighted work, and that such infringements could not reasonably have been foreseen, the entire sum of such damages recoverable by the copyright proprietor from such infringing maker and his agencies for the distribution to exhibitors of such infringing motion picture shall not exceed the sum of $5,000 nor be less than $250, and such damages shall in no other case exceed the sum of $5,000 nor be less than the sum of $250, and shall not be regarded as a penalty. But the foregoing exceptions shall not deprive the copyright proprietor of any other remedy given him under this law, nor shall the limitation as to the amount of recovery apply to infringements occurring after the actual notice to a defendant, either by service of process in a suit or other written notice served upon him.

First. In the case of a painting, statue, or sculpture, $10 for every infringing copy made or sold by or found in the possession of the infringer or his agents or employees;

Second. In the case of any work enumerated in section 5 of this title, except a painting, statue, or sculpture, $1 for every infringing copy made or sold by or found in the possession of the infringer or his agents or employees;

Third. In the case of a lecture, sermon, or address, $50 for every infringing delivery;

Fourth. In the case of a dramatic or dramatico-musical or a choral or orchestral composition, $100 for the first and $50 for every subsequent infringing performance; in the case of other musical compositions $10 for every infringing performance;

(c) IMPOUNDING DURING ACTION.—To deliver up on oath, to be impounded during the pendency of the action, upon such terms and conditions as the court may prescribe, all articles alleged to infringe a copyright;

(d) DESTRUCTION OF INFRINGING COPIES AND PLATES.—To deliver up on oath for destruction all the infringing copies or devices, as well as all plates, molds, matrices, or other means for making such infringing copies as the court may order.

(e) ROYALTIES FOR USE OF MECHANICAL REPRODUCTION OF MUSICAL WORKS.—Whenever the owner of a musical copyright has used or permitted the use of the copyrighted work upon the parts of musical instruments serving to reproduce mechanically the musical work, then in case of infringement of such copyright by the unauthorized manufacture, use, or sale of interchangeable parts, such as disks, rolls, bands, or cylinders for use in mechanical music-producing machines adapted to reproduce the copyrighted music, no criminal action shall be brought, but in a civil action an injunction may be granted upon such terms as the court may impose, and the plaintiff shall be entitled to recover in lieu of profits and damages a royalty as provided in section 1, subsection (e), of this title: *Provided also,* That whenever any person, in the absence of a license agreement, intends to use a copyrighted musical composition upon the parts of instruments serving to reproduce mechanically the musical work, relying upon the compulsory license provision of this title, he shall serve notice of such intention, by registered mail, upon the copyright proprietor at his last address disclosed by the records of the copyright office, sending to the copyright office a duplicate of such notice; and in case of his failure so to do the court may, in its discretion, in addition to sums hereinabove mentioned, award the complainant a further sum, not to exceed three times the amount provided by section 1, subsection (e), of this title, by way of damages, and not as a penalty, and also a temporary injunction until the full award is paid.

(f) RULES OF PROCEDURE.—[*Repealed*] [6]

§ 102. JURISDICTION OF COURTS IN ENFORCING REMEDIES.—[*Repealed*] [6]

§ 103. JOINDER OF PROCEEDINGS FOR DIFFERENT REMEDIES.—[*Repealed*] [6]

§ 104. WILLFUL INFRINGEMENT FOR PROFIT.—Any person who willfully and for profit shall infringe any copyright secured by this title, or who shall knowingly and willfully aid or abet such infringement, shall be deemed guilty of a misdemeanor, and upon conviction thereof shall be punished by imprisonment for not exceeding one year or by a fine of not less than $100 nor more than $1,000, or both, in the discretion of the court: *Provided, however*, That nothing in this title shall be so construed as to prevent the performance of religious or secular works such as oratorios, cantatas, masses, or octavo choruses by public schools, church choirs, or vocal societies, rented, borrowed, or obtained from some public library, public school, church choir, school choir, or vocal society, provided the performance is given for charitable or educational purposes and not for profit.

§ 105. FRAUDULENT NOTICE OF COPYRIGHT, OR REMOVAL OR ALTERATION OF NOTICE.—Any person who, with fraudulent intent, shall insert or impress any notice of copyright required by this title, or words of the same purport, in or upon any uncopyrighted article, or with fraudulent intent shall remove or alter the copyright notice upon any article duly copyrighted shall be guilty of a misdemeanor, punishable by a fine of not less than $100 and not more than $1,000. Any person who shall knowingly issue or sell any article bearing a notice of United States copyright which has not been copyrighted in this country, or who shall knowingly import any article bearing such notice or words of the same purport, which has not been copyrighted in this country, shall be liable to a fine of $100.

§ 106. IMPORTATION OF ARTICLE BEARING FALSE NOTICE OR PIRATICAL COPIES OF COPYRIGHTED WORK.—The importation into the United States of any article bearing a false notice of copyright when there is no existing copyright thereon in the United States, or any piratical copies of any work copyrighted in the United States, is prohibited.

---

[6] Sections 101 (f), 102 and 103 were repealed by the Act of June 25, 1948 (62 Stat. 869). However, see sections 1338 and 2072 of Title 28, United States Code, and the Federal Rules of Civil Procedure.

§ 107. IMPORTATION, DURING EXISTENCE OF COPYRIGHT, OF PIRATICAL COPIES, OR OF COPIES NOT PRODUCED IN ACCORDANCE WITH SECTION 16 OF THIS TITLE.—During the existence of the American copyright in any book the importation into the United States of any piratical copies thereof or of any copies thereof (although authorized by the author or proprietor) which have not been produced in accordance with the manufacturing provisions specified in section 16 of this title, or any plates of the same not made from type set within the limits of the United States, or any copies thereof produced by lithographic or photoengraving process not performed within the limits of the United States, in accordance with the provisions of section 16 of this title, is prohibited: *Provided, however,* That, except as regards piratical copies, such prohibition shall not apply:

(a) To works in raised characters for the use of the blind.

(b) To a foreign newspaper or magazine, although containing matter copyrighted in the United States printed or reprinted by authority of the copyright proprietor, unless such newspaper or magazine contains also copyright matter printed or reprinted without such authorization.

(c) To the authorized edition of a book in a foreign language or languages of which only a translation into English has been copyrighted in this country.

(d) To any book published abroad with the authorization of the author or copyright proprietor when imported under the circumstances stated in one of the four subdivisions following, that is to say:

First. When imported, not more than one copy at one time, for individual use and not for sale; but such privilege of importation shall not extend to a foreign reprint of a book by an American author copyrighted in the United States.

Second. When imported by the authority or for the use of the United States.

Third. When imported, for use and not for sale, not more than one copy of any such book in any one invoice, in good faith by or for any society or institution incorporated for educational, literary, philosophical, scientific, or religious purposes, or for the encouragement of the fine arts, or for any college, academy, school, or seminary of learning, or for any State, school, college, university, or free public library in the United States.

Fourth. When such books form parts of libraries or collections purchased en bloc for the use of societies, institutions, or libraries designated in the foregoing paragraph, or form parts of the libraries or personal baggage belonging to persons or families arriving from foreign countries and are not intended for sale: *Provided,* That copies imported as above may not lawfully be used in any way to violate the rights of the proprietor of the American copyright or annul or limit the copyright protection secured by this title, and such **unlawful** use shall be deemed an infringement of copyright.

§ 108. FORFEITURE AND DESTRUCTION OF ARTICLES PROHIBITED IMPORTATION.—Any and all articles prohibited importation by this title which are brought into the United States from any foreign country (except in the mails) shall be seized and forfeited by like proceedings as those provided by law for the seizure and condemnation of property imported into the United States in violation of the customs revenue laws. Such articles when forfeited shall be destroyed in such manner as the Secretary of the Treasury or the court, as the case may be, shall direct: *Provided, however,* That all copies of authorized editions of copyright books imported in the mails or otherwise in violation of the provisions of this title may be exported and returned to the country of export whenever it is shown to the satisfaction of the Secretary of the Treasury, in a written application, that such importation does not involve willful negligence or fraud.

§ 109. IMPORTATION OF PROHIBITED ARTICLES; REGULATIONS; PROOF OF DEPOSIT OF COPIES BY COMPLAINANTS.—The Secretary of the Treasury and the Postmaster General are hereby empowered and required to make and enforce individually or jointly such rules and regulations as shall prevent the importation into the United States of articles prohibited importation by this title, and may require, as conditions precedent to exclusion of any work in which copyright is claimed, the copyright proprietor or any person claiming actual or potential injury by reason of actual or contemplated importations of copies of such work to file with the Post Office Department or the Treasury Department a certificate of the Register of Copyrights that the provisions of section 13 of this title have been fully complied with, and to give notice of such compliance to postmasters or to customs officers at the ports of entry in the United States in such form and accompanied by such exhibits as may be deemed necessary for the practical and efficient administration and enforcement of the provisions of sections 106 and 107 of this title.

§ 110. JURISDICTION OF ACTIONS UNDER LAWS.—[*Repealed*] ⁷

§ 111. DISTRICT IN WHICH ACTIONS MAY BE BROUGHT.—[*Repealed*] ⁷

§ 112. INJUNCTIONS; SERVICE AND ENFORCEMENT.—Any such court or judge thereof shall have power, upon complaint filed by any party aggrieved, to grant injunctions to prevent and restrain the violation of any right secured by this title, according to the course and principles of courts of equity, on such terms as said court or judge may deem reasonable. Any injunction that may be granted restraining and enjoining the doing of anything forbidden by this title may be served on

---

⁷ Sections 110 and 111 were repealed by the Act of June 25, 1948 (62 Stat. 869). However, see sections 1338 and 1400 of Title 28, United States Code.

the parties against whom such injunction may be granted anywhere in the United States, and shall be operative throughout the United States and be enforceable by proceedings in contempt or otherwise by any other court or judge possessing jurisdiction of the defendants.

§ 113. Transmission of Certified Copies of Papers for Enforcement of Injunction by Other Court.—The clerk of the court, or judge granting the injunction, shall, when required so to do by the court hearing the application to enforce said injunction, transmit without delay to said court a certified copy of all the papers in said cause that are on file in his office.

§ 114. Review of Orders, Judgments, or Decrees.—The orders, judgments, or decrees of any court mentioned in section 110 of this title arising under the copyright laws of the United States may be reviewed on appeal in the manner and to the extent now provided by law for the review of cases determined in said courts, respectively.

§ 115. Limitations of Criminal Proceedings.—No criminal proceeding shall be maintained under the provisions of this title unless the same is commenced within three years after the cause of action arose.

§ 116. Costs; Attorney's Fees.—In all actions, suits, or proceedings under this title, except when brought by or against the United States or any officer thereof, full costs shall be allowed, and the court may award to the prevailing party a reasonable attorney's fee as part of the costs.

Chapter 3—Copyright Office

§ 201. Copyright Office; Preservation of Records.—All records and other things relating to copyrights required by law to be preserved shall be kept and preserved in the copyright office, Library of Congress, District of Columbia, and shall be under the control of the register of copyrights, who shall, under the direction and supervision of the Librarian of Congress, perform all the duties relating to the registration of copyrights.

§ 202. REGISTER, ASSISTANT REGISTER, AND SUBORDINATES.—There shall be appointed by the Librarian of Congress a Register of Copyrights, and one Assistant Register of Copyrights, who shall have authority during the absence of the Register of Copyrights to attach the copyright office seal to all papers issued from the said office and to sign such certificates and other papers as may be necessary. There shall also be appointed by the Librarian such subordinate assistants to the register as may from time to time be authorized by law.

§ 203. SAME; DEPOSIT OF MONEYS RECEIVED; REPORTS.—The Register of Copyrights shall make daily deposits in some bank in the District of Columbia, designated for this purpose by the Secretary of the Treasury as a national depository, of all moneys received to be applied as copyright fees, and shall make weekly deposits with the Secretary of the Treasury, in such manner as the latter shall direct, of all copyright fees actually applied under the provisions of this title, and annual deposits of sums received which it has not been possible to apply as copyright fees or to return to the remitters, and shall also make monthly reports to the Secretary of the Treasury and to the Librarian of Congress of the applied copyright fees for each calendar month, together with a statement of all remittances received, trust funds on hand, moneys refunded, and unapplied balances.

§ 204. SAME; BOND.—The Register of Copyrights shall give bond to the United States in the sum of $20,000, in form to be approved by the General Counsel for the Department of the Treasury and with sureties satisfactory to the Secretary of the Treasury, for the faithful discharge of his duties.

§ 205. SAME; ANNUAL REPORT.—The Register of Copyrights shall make an annual report to the Librarian of Congress, to be printed in the annual report on the Library of Congress, of all copyright business for the previous fiscal year, including the number and kind of works which have been deposited in the copyright office during the fiscal year, under the provisions of this title.

§ 206. SEAL OF COPYRIGHT OFFICE.—The seal used in the copyright office on July 1, 1909, shall be the seal of the copyright office, and by it all papers issued from the copyright office requiring authentication shall be authenticated.

§ 207. RULES FOR REGISTRATION OF CLAIMS.[8]—Subject to the approval of the Librarian of Congress, the Register of Copyrights shall be authorized to make rules and regulations for the registration of claims to copyright as provided by this title.

[8] Published in Title 37 of the Code of Federal Regulations and the Federal Register.

§ 208. Record Books in Copyright Office.—The Register of Copyrights shall provide and keep such record books in the copyright office as are required to carry out the provisions of this title, and whenever deposit has been made in the copyright office of a copy of any work under the provisions of this title he shall make entry thereof.

§ 209. Certificate of Registration; Effect as Evidence; Receipt for Copies Deposited.—In the case of each entry the person recorded as the claimant of the copyright shall be entitled to a certificate of registration under seal of the copyright office, to contain the name and address of said claimant, the name of the country of which the author of the work is a citizen or subject, and when an alien author domiciled in the United States at the time of said registration, then a statement of that fact, including his place of domicile, the name of the author (when the records of the copyright office shall show the same), the title of the work which is registered for which copyright is claimed, the date of the deposit of the copies of such work, the date of publication if the work has been reproduced in copies for sale, or publicly distributed, and such marks as to class designation and entry number as shall fully identify the entry. In the case of a book, the certificate shall also state the receipt of the affidavit, as provided by section 17 of this title, and the date of the completion of the printing, or the date of the publication of the book, as stated in the said affidavit. The Register of Copyrights shall prepare a printed form for the said certificate, to be filled out in each case as above provided for in the case of all registrations made after July 1, 1909, and in the case of all previous registrations so far as the copyright office record books shall show such facts, which certificate, sealed with the seal of the copyright office, shall, upon payment of the prescribed fee, be given to any person making application for the same. Said certificate shall be admitted in any court as prima facie evidence of the facts stated therein. In addition to such certificate the register of copyrights shall furnish, upon request, without additional fee, a receipt for the copies of the work deposited to complete the registration.

§ 210. Catalog of Copyright Entries; Effect as Evidence.—The Register of Copyrights shall fully index all copyright registrations and assignments and shall print at periodic intervals a catalog of the titles of articles deposited and registered for copyright, together with suitable indexes, and at stated intervals shall print complete and indexed catalog for each class of copyright entries, and may thereupon, if expedient, destroy the original manuscript catalog cards containing the titles included in such printed volumes and representing the entries made during such intervals. The current catalog of copyright entries and the index volumes herein provided for shall be admitted in any court as prima facie evidence of the facts stated therein as regards any copyright registration.

§ 211. SAME; DISTRIBUTION AND SALE; DISPOSAL OF PROCEEDS.[a]— The said printed current catalogs as they are issued shall be promptly distributed by the Superintendent of Documents to the collectors of customs of the United States and to the postmasters of all exchange offices of receipt of foreign mails, in accordance with revised list of such collectors of customs and postmasters prepared by the Secretary of the Treasury and the Postmaster General, and they shall also be furnished in whole or in part to all parties desiring them at a price to be determined by the Register of Copyrights for each part of the catalog not exceeding $25 for the complete yearly catalog of copyright entries. The consolidated catalogs and indexes shall also be supplied to all persons ordering them at such prices as may be fixed by the Register of Copyrights, and all subscriptions for the catalogs shall be received by the Superintendent of Documents, who shall forward the said publications; and the moneys thus received shall be paid into the Treasury of the United States and accounted for under such laws and Treasury regulations as shall be in force at the time.

§ 212. RECORDS AND WORKS DEPOSITED IN COPYRIGHT OFFICE OPEN TO PUBLIC INSPECTION; TAKING COPIES OF ENTRIES.—The record books of the copyright office, together with the indexes to such record books, and all works deposited and retained in the copyright office, shall be open to public inspection; and copies may be taken of the copyright entries actually made in such record books, subject to such safeguards and regulations as shall be prescribed by the Register of Copyrights and approved by the Librarian of Congress.

§ 213. DISPOSITION OF ARTICLES DEPOSITED IN OFFICE.—Of the articles deposited in the copyright office under the provisions of the copyright laws of the United States, the Librarian of Congress shall determine what books and other articles shall be transferred to the permanent collections of the Library of Congress, including the law library, and what other books or articles shall be placed in the reserve collections of the Library of Congress for sale or exchange, or be transferred to other governmental libraries in the District of Columbia for use therein.

§ 214. DESTRUCTION OF ARTICLES DEPOSITED IN OFFICE REMAINING UNDISPOSED OF; REMOVAL OF BY AUTHOR OR PROPRIETOR; MANUSCRIPTS OF UNPUBLISHED WORKS.—Of any articles undisposed of as above provided, together with all titles and correspondence relating thereto, the Librarian of Congress and the Register of Copyrights jointly shall, at suitable intervals, determine what of these received during any period of years it is desirable or useful to preserve in the permanent files of the copyright office, and, after due notice as hereinafter provided, may within their discretion cause the remaining articles and other things

---

[a] Section 211 as amended by the Act of April 27, 1948 (62 Stat. 202).

to be destroyed: *Provided*, That there shall be printed in the Catalog of Copyright Entries from February to November, inclusive, a statement of the years of receipt of such articles and a notice to permit any author, copyright proprietor, or other lawful claimant to claim and remove before the expiration of the month of December of that year anything found which relates to any of his productions deposited or registered for copyright within the period of years stated, not reserved or disposed of as provided for in this title. No manuscript of an unpublished work shall be destroyed during its term of copyright without specific notice to the copyright proprietor of record, permitting him to claim and remove it.

§ 215. Fees.[10]—The Register of Copyrights shall receive, and the persons to whom the services designated are rendered shall pay, the following fees:

For the registration of a claim to copyright in any work, except a print or label used for articles of merchandise, $4; for the registration of a claim to copyright in a print or label used for articles of merchandise, $6; which fees shall include a certificate of registration under seal for each work registered: *Provided*, That only one registration fee shall be required in the case of several volumes of the same book published and deposited at the same time: *And provided further*, That with respect to works of foreign origin, in lieu of payment of the copyright fee of $4 together with one copy of the work and application, the foreign author or proprietor may at any time within six months from the date of first publication abroad deposit in the Copyright Office an application for registration and two copies of the work which shall be accompanied by a catalog card in form and content satisfactory to the Register of Copyrights.

For recording the renewal of copyright and issuance of certificate therefor, $2.

For every additional certificate of registration, $1.

For certifying a copy of an application for registration of copyright, and for all other certifications, $2.

For recording every assignment, agreement, power of attorney, or other paper not exceeding six pages, $3; for each additional page or less, 50 cents; for each title over one in the paper recorded, 50 cents additional.

For recording a notice of use, $2, for each notice of not more than five titles; and 50 cents for each additional title.

For any requested search of Copyright Office records, .or works deposited, or services rendered in connection therewith, $3 for each hour of time consumed.

§ 216. ADDED BY AMENDMENT

---

[10] Section 215 as amended by the Act of April 27, 1948 (62 Stat. 202) and the Act of June 3, 1949 (63 Stat. 153).

Public Law 575—82d Congress
Chapter 923—2d Session
H. R. 3589
AN ACT

All 66 Stat. 752.

To amend title 17 of the United States Code entitled "Copyrights" with respect to recording and performing rights in literary works.

Be it enacted by the Senate and House of Representatives of the United States of America in Congress assembled, That subsection (c) of section 1 of title 17, United States Code, is amended to read as follows:

Title 17, U. S. Code, amendment. 61 Stat. 653. Literary works.

"(c) To deliver, authorize the delivery of, read, or present the copyrighted work in public for profit if it be a lecture, sermon, address or similar production, or other nondramatic literary work; to make or procure the making of any transcription or record thereof by or from which, in whole or in part, it may in any manner or by any method be exhibited, delivered, presented, produced, or reproduced; and to play or perform it in public for profit, and to exhibit, represent, produce, or reproduce it in any manner or by any method whatsoever. The damages for the infringement by broadcast of any work referred to in this subsection shall not exceed the sum of $100 where the infringing broadcaster shows that he was not aware that he was infringing and that such infringement could not have been reasonably foreseen; and".

Recording and performing rights.

SEC. 2. This Act shall take effect on the 1st day of January 1953. .

Effective date.

Approved July 17, 1952.

Public Law 743 - 83d Congress
Chapter 1161 - 2d Session
H. R. 6616

AN ACT

To amend title 17. United States Code, entitled "Copyrights".

Be it enacted by the Senate and House of Representatives of the United States of America in Congress assembled, That section 9 of title 17, United States Code, is amended to read as follows: Copyrights. 61 Stat. 655.

"§ 9. Authors or proprietors, entitled: aliens

"The author or proprietor of any work made the subject of copyright by this title, or his executors, administrators, or assigns, shall have copyright for such work under the conditions and for the terms specified in this title: *Provided, however,* That the copyright secured by this title shall extend to the work of an author or proprietor who is a citizen or subject of a foreign state or nation only under the conditions described in subsections (a), (b), or (c) below: Works of aliens.

"(a) When an alien author or proprietor shall be domiciled within the United States at the time of the first publication of his work; or

"(b) When the foreign state or nation of which such author or proprietor is a citizen or subject grants, either by treaty, convention, agreement, or law, to citizens of the United States the benefit of copyright on substantially the same basis as to its own citizens, or copyright protection, substantially equal to the protection secured to such foreign author under this title or by treaty; or when such foreign state or nation is a party to an international agreement which provides for reciprocity in the granting of copyright, by the terms of which agreement the United States may, at its pleasure, become a party thereto.

"The existence of the reciprocal conditions aforesaid shall be determined by the President of the United States, by proclamation made from time to time, as the purposes of this title may require: *Provided,* That whenever the President shall find that the authors, copyright owners, or proprietors of works first produced or published abroad and subject to copyright or to renewal of copyright under the laws of the United States, including works subject to ad interim copyright, are or may have been temporarily unable to comply with the conditions and formalities prescribed with respect to such works by the copyright laws of the United States, because of the disruption or suspension of facilities essential for such compliance, he may by proclamation grant such extension of time as he may deem appropriate for the fulfillment of such conditions or formalities by authors, copyright owners, or proprietors who are citizens of the United States or who are nationals of countries which accord substantially equal treatment in this respect to authors, copyright owners, or proprietors who are citizens of the United States: *Provided further,* That no liability shall attach under this title for lawful uses made or acts done prior to the effective date of such proclamation in connection with such works, or in respect to the continuance for one year subsequent to such date of any business undertaking or enterprise lawfully undertaken prior to such date involving expenditure or contractual obligation in connection with the exploitation, production, reproduction, circulation, or performance of any such work. 68 Stat. 1030. 68 Stat. 1031.

"The President may at any time terminate any proclamation authorized herein or any part thereof or suspend or extend its operation for such period or periods of time as in his judgment the interests of the United States may require.

"(c) When the Universal Copyright Convention, signed at Geneva on September 6, 1952, shall be in force between the United States of America and the foreign state or nation of which such author is a citizen or subject, or in which the work was first published. Any work Universal Copyright Convention.

to which copyright is extended pursuant to this subsection shall be exempt from the following provisions of this title: (1) The requirement in section 1 (e) that a foreign state or nation must grant to United States citizens mechanical reproduction rights similar to those specified therein; (2) the obligatory deposit requirements of the first sentence of section 13; (3) the provisions of sections 14, 16, 17, and 18; (4) the import prohibitions of section 107, to the extent that they are related to the manufacturing requirements of section 16; and (5) the requirements of sections 19 and 20: *Provided, however,* That such exemptions shall apply only if from the time of first publication all the copies of the work published with the authority of the author or other copyright proprietor shall bear the symbol © accompanied by the name of the copyright proprietor and the year of first publication placed in such manner and location as to give reasonable notice of claim of copyright.

"Upon the coming into force of the Universal Copyright Convention in a foreign state or nation as hereinbefore provided, every book or periodical of a citizen or subject thereof in which ad interim copyright was subsisting on the effective date of said coming into force shall have copyright for twenty-eight years from the date of first publication abroad without the necessity of complying with the further formalities specified in section 23 of this title.

"The provisions of this subsection shall not be extended to works of an author who is a citizen of, or domiciled in the United States of America regardless of place of first publication, or to works first published in the United States."

SEC. 2. Section 16 of title 17, United States Code, is amended to read as follows:

"§ 16. Mechanical work to be done in United States

"Of the printed book or periodical specified in section 5, subsections (a) and (b), of this title, except the original text of a book or periodical of foreign origin in a language or languages other than English, the text of all copies accorded protection under this title, except as below provided, shall be printed from type set within the limits of the United States, either by hand or by the aid of any kind of typesetting machine, or from plates made within the limits of the United States from type set therein, or, if the text be produced by lithographic process, or photoengraving process, then by a process wholly performed within the limits of the United States, and the printing of the text and binding of the said book shall be performed within the limits of the United States; which requirements shall extend also to the illustrations within a book consisting of printed text and illustrations produced by lithographic process, or photoengraving process, and also to separate lithographs or photoengravings, except where in either case the subjects represented are located in a foreign country and illustrate a scientific work or reproduce a work of art: *Provided, however,* That said requirements shall not apply to works in raised characters for the use of the blind, or to books or periodicals of foreign origin in a language or languages other than English, or to works printed or produced in the United States by any other process than those above specified in this section, or to copies of books or periodicals, first published abroad in the English language, imported into the United States within five years after first publication in a foreign state or nation up to the number of fifteen hundred copies of each such book or periodical if said copies shall contain notice of copyright in accordance with sections 10, 19, and 20 of this title and if ad interim copyright in said work shall have been obtained pursuant to section 22 of this title prior to the importation into the United

61 Stat. 653.

61 Stat. 656.
61 Stat. 657,
658, 663, infra.
61 Stat. 658;
post, p. 1032.

63 Stat. 154.

61 Stat. 657,

Printing in
U. S.
61 Stat. 654.
68 Stat. 1031.
68 Stat. 1032.

61 Stat. 656,
658; infra.
63 Stat. 154.

'All 68 Stat. 1032.

States of any copy except those permitted by the provisions of section 107 of this title: *Provided further*, That the provisions of this section 61 Stat. 663. shall not affect the right of importation under the provisions of section 107 of this title."

SEC. 3. Section 19 of title 17, United States Code, is amended to 61 Stat. 658. read as follows:

"§ 19. Notice; form

Notice of copyright.

"The notice of copyright required by section 10 of this title shall consist either of the word 'Copyright', the abbreviation 'Copr.', or 61 Stat. 656. the symbol ©, accompanied by the name of the copyright proprietor, and if the work be a printed literary, musical, or dramatic work, the notice shall include also the year in which the copyright was secured by publication. In the case, however, of copies of works specified in subsections (f) to (k), inclusive, of section 5 of this title, the notice 61 Stat. 654. may consist of the letter C enclosed within a circle, thus ©, accompanied by the initials, monogram, mark, or symbol of the copyright proprietor: *Provided*, That on some accessible portion of such copies or of the margin, back, permanent base, or pedestal, or of the substance on which such copies shall be mounted, his name shall appear. But in the case of works in which copyright was subsisting on July 1, 1909, the notice of copyright may be either in one of the forms prescribed herein or may consist of the following words: 'Entered according to Act of Congress, in the year   , by A. B., in the office of the Librarian of Congress, at Washington, D. C.,' or, at his option, the word 'Copyright', together with the year the copyright was entered and the name of the party by whom it was taken out; thus, 'Copyright, 19—, by A. B.'"

SEC. 4. This Act shall take effect upon the coming into force of the Effective date. Universal Copyright Convention in the United States of America.

Approved August 31, 1954.

Effective Date of P.L. 743 and of the Universal Copyright Convention—September 16, 1955.

Public Law 452 - 84th Congress
Chapter 109 - 2d Session
H. R. 5876

AN ACT

To amend the copyright law to permit, in certain classes of works, the deposit of photographs or other identifying reproductions in lieu of copies of published works.

Be it enacted by the Senate and House of Representatives of the United States of America in Congress assembled, That section 13 of title 17, United States Code, is amended to read as follows:

Copyrights. 61 Stat. 656.

"§ 13. Deposit of copies after publication; action or proceeding for infringement

"After copyright has been secured by publication of the work with the notice of copyright as provided in section 10 of this title, there shall be promptly deposited in the Copyright Office or in the mail addressed to the Register of Copyrights, Washington, District of Columbia, two complete copies of the best edition thereof then published, or if the work is by an author who is a citizen or subject of a foreign state or nation and has been published in a foreign country, one complete copy of the best edition then published in such foreign country, which copies or copy, if the work be a book or periodical, shall have been produced in accordance with the manufacturing provisions specified in section 16 of this title; or if such work be a *61 Stat. 657.* contribution to a periodical, for which contribution special registration is requested, one copy of the issue or issues containing such contribution; or if the work belongs to a class specified in subsections (g), (h), (i) or (k) of section 5 of this title, and if the Register of Copy- *61 Stat. 654.* rights determines that it is impracticable to deposit copies because of their size, weight, fragility, or monetary value he may permit the deposit of photographs or other identifying reproductions in lieu of *70 Stat. 63.* copies of the work as published under such rules and regulations as *70 Stat. 64.* he may prescribe with the approval of the Librarian of Congress; or if the work is not reproduced in copies for sale there shall be deposited the copy, print, photograph, or other identifying reproduction provided by section 12 of this title, such copies or copy, print, *61 Stat. 656.* photograph, or other reproduction to be accompanied in each case by a claim of copyright. No action or proceeding shall be maintained for infringement of copyright in any work until the provisions of this title with respect to the deposit of copies and registration of such work shall have been complied with."

Approved March 29, 1956.

Public Law 331 - 83d Congress
Chapter 137 - 2d Session
H. R. 2747

AN ACT

To amend title 17 of the United States Code entitled "Copyrights" with respect
to the day for taking action when the last day for taking such action falls on
Saturday, Sunday, or a holiday.

*Be it enacted by the Senate and House of Representatives of the
United States of America in Congress assembled,* That title 17, United   Copyright
States Code, is hereby amended by adding at the end thereof a new   Office.
section 216 to read as follows:
"§ 216. When the day for taking action falls on Saturday, Sunday, or a   68 Stat. 52.
        holiday.   68 Stat. 53.

"When the last day for making any deposit or application, or for
paying any fee, or for delivering any other material to the Copyright
Office falls on Saturday, Sunday, or a holiday within the District of
Columbia, such action may be taken on the next succeeding business
day."

SEC. 2. The table of contents of chapter 3 of title 17 of the United   61 Stat. 665.
States Code is amended by adding at the end thereof "216.   When the
day for taking action falls on Saturday, Sunday, or a holiday."

Approved April 13, 1954.

Index

349